THE ULTIMATE EXPERIENCE
The Many Paths to GOD

BOOKS ONE, TWO, & THREE, REVISITED

Verling CHAKO Priest, Ph.D.

Order this book online at www.trafford.com
or email orders@trafford.com

Most Trafford titles are also available at major online book retailers.

Printed in the United States of America.

ISBN: 978-1-4269-7664-3 (sc)
ISBN: 978-1-4269-7665-0 (e)

Library of Congress Control Number: 2011912378

Trafford rev. 07/18/2011

www.trafford.com

North America & international
toll-free: 1 888 232 4444 (USA & Canada)
phone: 250 383 6864 ♦ fax: 812 355 4082

COPYRIGHT BOOK ONE

The cover design is by Microsoft Word and the Author.

TITLE PAGE for THREE BOOKS

THE ULTIMATE EXPERIENCE
The Many Paths to God

Books ONE, TWO, & THREE, REVISITED

Presenters: God, Sananda, Maitreya, Jesus, Lady Nada, Mary Magdalene, Mother Mary, Djwhal Khul, Sanat Kumara, AA Metatron, Confucius, and Kuthumi.

Verling CHAKO Priest, Ph.D.

BOOK LIST

By **Verling CHAKO Priest, Ph.D.**

The Ultimate Experience: the Many Paths to God series:

BOOKS 1, 2, & 3 REVISITED (2011)
REALITIES of the CRUCIFIXION (2006)
ISBN # 1-4251-0716-8
MESSAGES from the HEAVENLY HOSTS (2007)
ISBN # 1-4251-2550-6
YOUR SPACE BROTHERS and SISTERS GREET YOU! (2008)
ISBN # 978-1-4251-6302-0
TEACHINGS of the MASTERS of LIGHT (2008)
ISBN # 978-1-4251-8573-2

PAULUS of TARSUS (2010)
ISBN # 978-1-4269-2529-0
THE GODDESS RETURNS to EARTH (2010)
ISBN # 978-1-4269-3563-3
ISBN # 978-1-4269-3564-0 (e-book)
JESUS: MY BELOVED CONNECTION TO HUMANITY AND THE SEA (Publication Pending 2011)

Available at Trafford: 1-888-232-4444
Or Amazon.com
www.godumentary.com/chako.htm

EXPLANATION TO READERS

After I finished writing and **self-**distributing the first three books, I decided **not** to take the next step in contracting with a self-publishing company in order to let it handle the mailings just yet. I was well into writing my fourth book, *Realities of the Crucifixion*, and I did not want to put my focus on another project that would be quite time-consuming.

However, now **is** the time, as my guidance is suggesting. I decided to put all three of my **first** books into one—hence I "married" them in the following pages. However, in order to keep the integrity of **each** of the three books as being separate entities, I treated them as such. You will find each segment has a *Front Cover, Copyright, Dedication, Preface, Acknowledgments, Introduction, Closing Statements,* and an *Epilogue*. I deleted *About the Author* on the first two books but kept it in for the last book. The *Table of Contents* was a little trickier, for it is a different insert program not only to identify the material but also to paginate the pages. I decided to delete that old Table of Contents program and just type the titles of the messages, then create a grand *Table of Contents* for the **whole** book.

I hope this explanation will clarify how this book is set-up, for my editor, Heather Clarke, was confused at first. I thought if **she** was confused, imagine how the Readers are trying to cope! Read on, and I hope you enjoy my efforts of bringing these **three books presented as one** to you.

Blessings, Chako

THE ULTIMATE EXPERIENCE SYNOPSIS ONE

The words of wisdom in this BOOK ONE, which were received from Lords Jesus, Sananda, Djwhal Khul, Maitreya, and Lady Mary Magdalene, with a statement and blessing from God, will intrigue and enlighten Readers. Jesus narrates much of this book, providing personal history to some of the stories in the Bible. Jesus speaks of his birth, and that his father acted as midwife. He narrates of his time on the cross, and why his shroud was left in the tomb upon his ascension.

Djwhal Khul tells of his life as a young Tibetan who heard God's voice telling him to seek his teacher at the Temple. He speaks about the significance of Rays, Initiations, and Truth for the soul. He gives the Reader a peek into the future of Heaven on Earth.

Mary Magdalene tells her poignant story of Jesus, their love, and marriage. She points out how *crucifixion* has become a metaphor for describing events in people's lives.

Maitreya states how important it is for people and countries to share. He speaks of *restitution* in its higher interpretation, as *bringing into balance* a particular dynamic. *Hear, oh America, for when God calls upon us to make restitution, the veils will be ripped from the deep-seated lies that permeate this ruling government (2004).*

Jesus states that the purpose of this book is to help Readers take off their rose-colored glasses. Religions need modernization. Spiritual leaders keep trying to put ***ancient wordage into modern ears***. The rhetoric has become too mechanical; *religions and spiritual practices have become a habit, addictive, and devoid of profound experiences with God.*

The **twenty-two** mini-lectures will provide insight and teachings for humanity on a vast array of subjects: Desire, Marriage and Divorce, Compassion, Abused and Abuser, Restoring Your Faith, Tsunamis, and much more. The Reader will be enhanced by the knowledge and depth of wisdom from this book. It is mind provoking in nature—a book that is to awaken you and provide much fertile ground for your seeds for change.

Read on, dear hearts . . .

PREFACE #1

I was meditating one afternoon in August 2002, when I felt this soft caress of my cheek. My body started shaking and tingling as this higher vibration moved closer to me. I have been a student of metaphysics for over thirty-five years and have taught consciousness-raising classes to beginning students. Therefore, I knew an entity was making contact. I mentally said to it, *Who are you, Lord* (giving him his respectful recognition just in case he really was a Lord)? He replied *it does not matter*. Oh, but it mattered to me! I persevered.

Are you Jesus? I queried hopefully. *He is an* ***aspect*** *of me,* replied the Being. *Bingo,* I thought, for I then knew it had to be Lord Sananda, Christ's ascended Light Body. I was not that personally familiar with the Ascended Masters at that time. Therefore, I was not quite sure what an *aspect* meant either. Was this really an Ascended Master coming to make contact with **me**?

I phoned Jane Elizabeth, a well-known astrologer in Arizona, and told her about my experience. She replied with a giggle, *Yep, that's how they talk*! The Master Jesus had guided Jane Elizabeth throughout most of her life and career. Therefore, I trusted her discernment.

This was the beginning of many hours of mental communication with a few of the masters. They have never come and stroked my cheek again, but they do come into my heart. I feel tearful and feel their love at that moment on an emotional level. In fact, I use this criterion as validation of their presence. I may hear them mentally first, but unless I feel them in my heart, I do not communicate with them.

During several meditations, there would be discussions about a book I had agreed to write before I was born. The book's purpose was to dispel some of the myths that had developed, mainly through misinterpretations by the scribes of the Bible. Not only had myths developed, but also facts had been purposely deleted by the churches for control of the people.

One day when I had decided firmly to state my intent on starting the book, I mentally heard, *I AM Jesus. Pick up your pen, dear one.* I became just a tad flustered, for I had not expected to start immediately after my declaration of intent. I was not sure whether he just wanted me to write in my journal or to take dictation on a tablet for the book. He of course read my mental queries and repeated again, *Pick up your pen, dear one. Now write what you hear me say. Keep your mind as clear as you can and do not anticipate my words. I shall start slowly.* With those few short sentences, our book was launched. He dictated for almost an hour while I wrote rapidly covering four pages.

Writing for about an hour in the morning and again in the afternoon set the pace for most of the following days. Frequently, I ran what I called *My Doubting-Thomas Mode*, but I received encouragement from my electronic mail pen pal, Sally LeSar, whose own channeled book, *Treasures from the Universe . . .*, had just come out. Jesus spoke telepathically to me, *Do not even for a minute think you are not worthy of our attention and thoughts . . . your book will come to fruition. It surely will*! At another time I asked, *Why me*? The answer was, *Why not*? I could think of no reply.

One time when I had pulled back from the book because of my inner struggles over it, Jesus said, when I finally had resumed writing, *dear one, do not fuss so over your lessons*! I must admit that simple statement went right to the core of my uncertainties. It brought a smile to my lips and helped me stay more focused.

I am not a student of the Bible. Any Biblical story I know is as a layperson. My references are from the *King James Version, Royal Publisher, Inc., 1971,* and *Reader's Digest Family Guide to the Bible, a Concordance, and Reference Companion to the King James Version, 1984.*

This first book has been a labor of love. I feel so blessed to have been a part of this unfolding endeavor. I have enclosed a section called *Dreams and Journal Notations* in the Appendix of the book. These show the evolutionary process of this book, which I feel may enhance your discernment of the following material. Allow your heart to open to receive what may be new and controversial information for you that could spark your seeds for change. The choice is always yours.

Blessings, CHAKO

(Revision May 2011)

Readers, I am well aware that some of the material you will read may differ in content here and there from the rest of the series: Books 4-7. I have struggled with this fact until Jesus/Jeshua stated to me, *now I know you already have had questions as to whether you ought to let the channeling stand as is, or to even delete parts of it. Keep in mind that the dynamics may be in different dimensions—some of it took place, or none of it did. We gave you the books at a certain time in your growth for you! Many reading these books are still not ready to learn about different realities—how an act could happen in one dimension and not in another. So let the books stand on their own merit. This is a huge project for you with many woman-hours involved. You are being guided and you have listened well. I AM Jeshua.*

Dear friends, please do not inundate me with queries as to "why this is said differently than in another book." Believe me, I am well aware of that. That is one of the reasons it has taken me so long to offer these three books. Keep an open mind; check to see what belief systems you carry that you can now let go. We are going in and out of so many dimensions now that most of us cannot even fathom the changes that are taking place within our systems!

DEDICATION

To the two Janes in my life:

Janedare Humphrys Winston, Ed.D.
And
Jane Sayers Masowdi

What fun and adventures we shared.

I know you are experiencing the Ultimate Adventure now.

ACKNOWLEDGMENTS

My first acknowledgment must be to God and the Ascended Masters: Jesus, Sananda, Maitreya, and Djwhal Khul, who are my Teachers. They have provided the context of our book with not only their personal stories, but also their wisdom on many issues that face humanity today. I thank them and feel blessed to have them in my life. I thank Lady Mary Magdalene for her poignant story of that painful event in her life of long ago.

I give loving thanks with a great appreciation to my oldest daughter, Susan Verling Miller O'Brien, for all the book formatting that she did. No matter how many corrections were made, she cheerfully accepted the changes and diligently sat at her laptop computer hour after hour. We spent many hours in discussion as to the placement of chapters and in editing the content. The Masters gave us free rein and much latitude in what I call our *grunt* work. Susan was invaluable indeed in this project. Thank you, dear heart! (Readers, keep in mind that this was my **first** endeavor in channeling a book!)

People who channel telepathically know they must strive to keep their energies as clear and pure as possible when channeling in order to keep from contaminating the data that is being transmitted. One's little ego, or an implant—a *wanna-be*—or just entities one has around one can "muddy the waters" if allowed. Therefore, I decided to speak with Lord Jesus through someone other than myself after the Lords had declared our book finished, and after God had transmitted His blessing. It was my way of validating my work. I asked the Master through whom did he wish to communicate. He suggested my email pal, Sally LeSar of Indianapolis, IN, for he had dictated many of the pages of her book, *Treasures from the Universe* . . . She also strives for purity in her channeling. We decided to have the telephone consultation on New Year's Day. What a propitious time to start the New Year—over an hour's time speaking with Lord Jesus. How cool was that!

There were a few adjustments in some of the wordage, but then the Master pronounced the book *perfect*. He told me, through Sally, to have faith in what was given to me, that *it is Truth and the Light of God*. Therefore, dear Sally, your channeling validated my work, my first effort to bring into physical reality one of the books I had agreed to write before I was born. Please accept my deepest appreciation for the many encouraging emails, channeling expertise, and for your friendship.

At this time, I still had no editor. Heather Clarke showed up out of the blue for BOOK TWO and has been with me ever since. I will speak more of her in the next book. However, since she is my official editor of all my books, she now has edited BOOK ONE at long last (smile). Thank you, heart of my heart!

TABLE OF CONTENTS

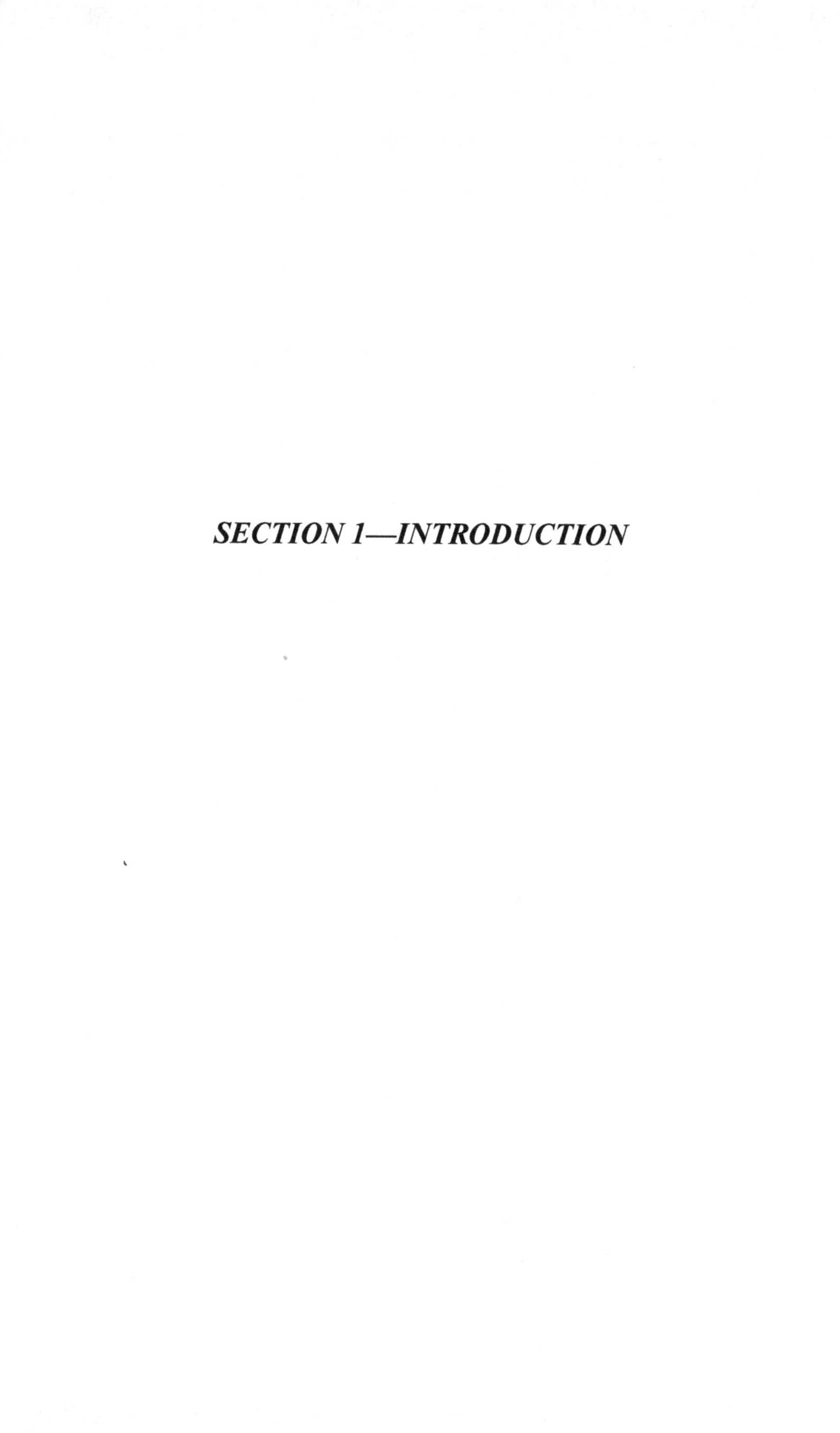

SECTION 1—INTRODUCTION

ADMISSIONS—Jesus

I AM Jesus, the Christ. I come to you, dear Readers, in order to impart to you reading material by which you can run your life, reading matter you can discuss with one another, reading matter that will perk up your brain cells, and reading matter to tweak your curiosity, your thirst to know more.

It is hoped that from this book, change will occur. Alternatively, let us say that the seeds of change will be planted. At least the author can no longer be beheaded or burned at the stake for being a witch. However, she can be ridiculed for allowing us to speak mentally to her and to write our words and thoughts down and send them out to the world. Everyone who will be involved in birthing this book is volunteering service and accepting assignments with joy and anticipation. I have stated to the author, *humanity has not experienced the joy that abounds when one is doing service for God*. It too is the Ultimate Experience.

Great souls of Light will be imputing their wisdom and adventures in the following pages. Keep an open heart, dear Reader—open to the possibilities, the boundless possibilities that will be presented here for your enjoyment and learning—as a great adventure is born for everyone.

In my journey while in embodiment for a greater understanding of Heaven on Earth and my search for wisdom, I often spoke to the Father concerning free will. Our discussions always ended with, *it is the person's ultimate choice to come back Home to Me, the Father*. It was still my choice whether to turn my will over to God or not, even while on the cross in a half-unconscious state. I could have used my will to summon the legion of angels I could see as plainly as I saw the distant crowd. I could have chosen to say, *I'm out of here*! I would have liked nothing better than to end it all—to save myself. That was a human reaction, but in my heart, I knew I **must** see it to the finish or it would all be for naught. I prayed to God and talked to my Teacher constantly until that moment when I knew it was finished, and that I had won.

In my lifetime as Jesus, I was often quoted as saying *I AM the way*. That is an incorrect interpretation. In other words, your inner heart, that deep God-cell that each person has, the I AM Presence of you, is the way back to God. There is a God-cell in the heart, but the soul also carries this Cell of God. Remember, both particles of God are present—body and soul. Therefore, I AM **is** the way—**you**, not me!

Everyone needs to understand *going Home*; the Ultimate Experience of being reunited with God at last is a personal choice that has to come from the individual. Each person makes this choice for him/herself. No one can do it for you. However, there is always a great deal of help just waiting for the person asking. If one truly expresses, *I want or wish to have help in returning to God*, then the person will receive this help in abundance.

In times gone by, the many sages and prophets who walked the Earth were never alone. They had over a hundred Beings surrounding them, sometimes even a thousand, or a legion, if one counted the angels. For man/woman to believe that the way to God is impossible, that the way to God is through the churches or a priest is erroneous thought. The way to God is through your own **I AM THE WAY Presence**—the inner way. In addition, your help comes from the Ascended Ones, Angels, and Spiritual Teachers that surround you. You are never alone!

Humanity has an erroneous perception of the journey back Home—to God. Humanity seems to believe that their particular religion is the only way. Some of humanity war and teach hatred to their children. Consequently, there are generations believing that their way is the only way. Everyone else is either sinful, devil-possessed or infidels. None of that is truth. The only truth is that all spiritual love leads to God. All religions lead to God.

Some people will be making their passage into the other side simply because they no longer wish to struggle on the Earth plane. Many have finished their assignment. Many have decided they will take a break and come back again at another time. There are those who have chosen to stay through old age when one can reap one's wisdom the most. It is the age of fifty onward when older people reap this harvest. How wise they have become. One often hears Humanity exclaim that if only they were as wise in their twenties, thirties, and forties as they are now at fifty. However, sadly, it is in the senior years that the body starts to break down from the ravages of undesirable living. How many people smoked most of their life, drank too much alcohol, or exercised by sitting on the couch crossing and uncrossing their legs while reaching for fatty snacks? This type of living has taken its toll. The body loses its youth. The brain cells start dying off and do not rejuvenate. The arteries clog. As the whole system starts to break down, the person becomes so preoccupied with his/her physical ailments that there is little incentive to teach one's wisdom to others or even to be the living example. Grandchildren, in their innocent perception, know grandpa or grandma drinks and smokes too much; grandchildren are quick to perceive and often intuitively know the truth of things before the adult does.

Therefore, dear Reader, many souls decide it is time to go Home, for life becomes too much of a struggle. They carry their wisdom Home with them if their death is a clean and conscious one, meaning the releasing of all resentments, all grievances, all victimizations, all greed, all hatred, all feelings of unworthiness, and all areas of negative thought-forms. If they can leave their bodies in God's Grace, they really can die whenever they wish to. However, if they die in order to escape what they perceive as a *rotten life*, they will come back and find that those lessons repeat themselves. One does not grow by escaping, ever.

When people learn to respect each other's cultural beliefs with no judgment, when they learn to respect their neighbor's ideas and beliefs, it does not mean they have to adhere to them nor does it mean they must agree with them. It just means they are to respect another's right to free will and different beliefs. When people can let others have their beliefs and not feel they have to kill those who do not believe as they do, when people can be nonjudgmental, then people become more like God. That is a way to God and Home.

Sometimes the help is unconscious. The soul has asked for the help and the masters do help. The person may not always realize what is taking place behind the scenes, however. We of the Spiritual Hierarchy, and there are many of us, are drawn into service when we hear a soul's plea. No one can do this alone, for we are one, interconnected. Why would one think when one does anything of such magnitude and importance that you would do it alone? It is impossible. Therefore, souls only need to ask once, just once, and they are surrounded with God's Messengers.

In my Biblical days, when I walked your Earth, I was constantly in contact with our Father. He was my constant companion. He was my refuge. At the same time, I had my Master Teacher, Lord Maitreya, who was the Christ at that time. He was the voice in my ear. It was his instructions I chose to obey. It was he who literally entered my body at the time John the Baptist baptized me. It is written this was when the Holy Spirit descended upon me. That is somewhat erroneous, for the Holy Spirit of God had never departed from me! However, the Holy Spirit freshly anointed me at that time. When Lord Maitreya entered me, the Holy Spirit entered again also. It is called an *anointing*. Christians seek the anointing, always wanting more; it becomes a constant ebb and flow. Therefore, since it was a part of me from the very beginning, I knew little difference. The impact was my beloved Teacher, Lord Maitreya, the true World Teacher, who entered, embodied me and subsequently taught the disciples and helped people heal themselves.

What I wish to convey at this moment is that I was human flesh and blood. I had my uncertainties just as my brothers had. I knew I would suffer. I knew I would be beaten and spat on. I kept the focus of my Father in front of me, but the encouraging words of Lord Maitreya were what kept me balanced, and going forward. You see, I knew what I had come to Earth to do. God showed me what the Plan was. I saw the cross I was nailed to. I saw the struggle to carry it with much of the crowd crying out for my blood. I was shown who would betray me, who would be my judge and condemn me. I met with all the souls involved in this once-in-a-lifetime drama before I was born. No one, least of all God, ordered me to take on this grand adventure.

I sat for many hours in the Halls of Wisdom viewing the whole scenario. At first, I was aghast at the level of difficulty of this task, for it had so many facets to it, from changing the genetics of humankind, to delivering humankind from its bondage to the body. I was to show them the way Home. My crucifixion was to end once and for all man's ignorance of the one God, for many still lived in their lower energy centers of survival, lust, power, and disrespect for women—many who were wiser than the men they serviced in all ways. I was shown my whole life, my travels, my trials and tribulations. I viewed these scenes in living color with sound and smell. I was so prepared that I was able to keep most of the veils from dropping and knew without doubt what my next adventure would be while in embodiment.

People seeing me hanging limply on the cross with blood streaming down my face into my eyes, from the thorns that stuck into my head and brow, did not realize that this was a winning situation. I must admit the spear thrust into my side was a bit of a jolt, but blessedly my body was in an altered state where I no longer felt much pain. Much has been written on my cross experience. However, dear Readers, I wish to tell you **I was not dead,** but in a deep altered state, similar to yogis in India who can walk on nails and/or stop their heartbeat. That kind of deep, altered consciousness can simulate death. I was placed in the tomb, washed, wrapped in cloth, and left for dead.

This may be difficult for people to understand, but I was translated (the molecular structure is changed and the person's body can be in different dimensions instantly, back and forth), and **ascended with my body leaving the shroud behind. The shroud became a reminder to people that ascension had actually occurred**. If the shroud had disappeared with my body, people would be left without evidence that I indeed had been there. People would have invented stories to explain the fact there was no body present. They would soon forget that such a miracle had actually happened. I was to be an example of Heaven on Earth. Therefore, when I returned, my form had changed and I remained on Earth, privately taught, and traveled until my seventy-ninth year when I again made my transition.

I am aware that many Christians will take offense at this story. It is human nature to want to believe a fairy tale. Humanity does not want to change ideas two thousand plus years later. Well, the purpose of this book is to help people start making that transition from the past. People buy jewelry crosses of me hanging emaciated from the cross. The Catholic churches have me hanging on the cross. I am hoping that the cross can once again be a symbol of Heaven on Earth—a cross where the arms are equal in length and are encircled by a circle, the circle of this planet and its oneness. What a beautiful piece of jewelry that would make—just the symbol of this most sacred cross without the death of a person who no longer wishes humankind to picture him in their minds attached to its arms.

As people throughout the world thought of me as their Savior, a role I gladly took on, I started feeling how the energies were changing, as one group would claim me while another would disclaim me. I understood the war that was brewing in my name. I understood the level of consciousness that people were in, but it had me feeling sad, for while Christianity grew, the hatred of me grew also. What was supposed to bring people back to God as peoples united was causing great rifts. The churches, the kings, and their crusades all distorted the messages of the scriptures. Where was the love that had been taught when so many of the Crusaders were pillaging and raping as they swept throughout the countryside? The churches of the Spanish Inquisition were in a category of their own where they judged, played God, and condemned many innocent people who were tortured and martyred. Most of the Saints won their sainthood because they were martyred while refusing to deny God.

In my lifetime as Jesus, much has been written about my ability to change water into wine at a wedding. Well, dear Readers, that wedding was my own. **I married the love of my life, my twin flame that at that time was in the form of Mary Magdalene.** I knew her the moment I saw her. Remember, I knew the characters of our play. She too knew me as one she would love, but the veils had fallen more on her so she did not know she was for me. She just knew when she saw me that she loved me.

How my heart glowed with love when I saw her. I saw only her beauteous light and recognized her immediately. She had played the role assigned to her, and I had played mine. Moreover, we met repeatedly and we married and had children. My family was joyous for my mother did know that Mary Magdalene was special and sent by God. Many came to our wedding. We did run out of wine, and I did perform that miracle after first asking the Father for His permission as I had indeed turned my will over to Him. I performed the miracle to emphasize that God gave humankind the miracle of *love*. How *love* changes people. My Mary and I loved each other beyond any measure. I performed that water-to-wine miracle to show the world that our love could overcome all adversities. Water was changed to wine. Our love changed humanity, for we were changing the molecular structure for future bodies. The Bible has portrayed my Mary as a harlot. That is a gross misinterpretation. However, I will let Mary tell her own story in this book, for she was not the sinner as she was portrayed to be. That is all I will say for now.

My childhood was one of plenty. My mother doted on me. One of my favorite meals was warm bread with vegetables and lamb stew. It was filling and tasty, for my mother used savory herbs. It was a natural fare in that era. I was particularly fond of it, as I felt full afterwards. Remember, dear Readers, I was a typical boy and had a robust appetite. Every mother who has sons will know what I mean, for boys can have a bottomless stomach. Young lads were not taught to do dishes and clean up after a meal, for there was a boundary drawn between a woman's work and a man's. I am afraid this started at a young age, for even though I would pick up my bowl to help, I was shooed away. I was not permitted to do what was thought of as women's work.

When I was in my late teens, I knew I would be having problems with people taking me seriously. Remember, Readers, I stated I did not have many of the veils in place. In fact, very few veils shielded me from my purpose. As a teen, I already knew I had to get started on this monumental task of bringing a new consciousness to humanity. I decided to start with the temple. The Bible writes that I separated for a while from my family, and indeed the Bible is correct in that. Nevertheless, I was a teenager, and considered an adult in the Jewish tradition. Therefore, once I had come into adulthood according to this tradition, I became quite zealous in my actions and beliefs. ***Matthew 21:12*** *And Jesus went into the temple of God, and cast out all them that sold and bought in the temple, and overthrew the tables of the moneychangers, and the seats of them that sold doves.* I did turn over the moneychangers' benches and tables; but I was not very compassionate to the fact that these people were simply doing what they had always done. This boy-adult came along with a bit of I-know-the-way arrogance mixed with his anger. I was always quick to flare, but I also was quick to forgive. Once I had let out that steam and stated my reasons for doing so, I was more affable.

In every soul's development, there are many lessons and many trials and tribulations. This is the honing, the refining process to perfection. This is what drives the soul to re-unite with the

Father-Mother God. When a soul first incarnates, it is veiled and becomes caught up in the web of life's problems, its choices, its desires, its humilities, its wealth, and its feelings of might or unworthiness. It goes through the gambit of learning. The free will that God gave the soul is the driving force while the soul is embodied. Soon after many incarnations, the soul realizes the lift-up of its consciousness, and the yearning to be closer to God becomes its driving force. Many eons of time ago, man/woman was occupied only with survival. It was survival of the body. In many instances, the soul became so caught in the snare of the body's survival that the life ended far too early, and the soul had to re-evaluate the progress or non-progress of that lifetime. The process was slow and tedious.

Meanwhile in the higher dimensions (those particular levels of energy that blend back and forth, with each holding a different dynamic of being from the lowest, in survival, to the highest, spiritual), the soul was being shown an easier, more productive way to be while in the body. The soul was taught to focus on God while in the body—develop the chakras, keep one's attention on its higher centers. Souls would incarnate into undeveloped bodies, undeveloped in the sense that they were spiritually unaware.

People would join nunneries. Alternatively, men would become monks associated with a particular religious order. Some would become hermits and go off to a cave in order to try to become closer to God. Some succeeded. Some did not. I would say the majority did not, simply because the consciousness of the body itself could not tolerate the isolation. Many became mentally imbalanced with what psychologists today would name as schizophrenia, or bi-polar disorders. The body would die and now the soul would have to have a lifetime where mental illness would be part of the equation. Once a soul had created that condition in a body, the soul would have to return and attempt to restore balance to that kind of body so that the voices it heard were not a mental disorder, but truly Messengers of God. The trail back to God seemed more difficult than had been planned, for the soul only has the reality of the body once it is in it. Therefore, dear Reader, do not become complacent in your spiritual practice of prayer and meditation, for this **is** the way back to God.

My Christian teachings were carried on great winds of adversity. Each generation would carry the polluted teachings in even more distorted ways. In modern times one need only look at the whole Middle East to see how the Palestinians, who think only Allah is God and hatred is the way, to the Jewish sector that still clings to the old order of even sacrificing animals in God's name. That is no longer the way of it. All of those laws of the past had a purpose of which cleanliness played a big part. For example, the practice of the Orthodox Jew where certain utensils are only for milk products and can never intermingle with utensils for animals is all of the past. A great revision needs to take place, a modernization of all religions, for the Fundamentalists in any of the religions need to loosen up a little. The priests, rabbis, and ministers are so concerned about losing control of their people that they end up possessing their followers. Before the Earth can be a peaceful paradise, the heavy control of all religions needs to lessen. The great religious leaders need to take only the pure teachings out of the various creeds. Religions need to be rewritten. Well, shocked Readers, this is exactly what will happen in years to come.

As the planet moves into the higher dimensions, it will encounter more of the cosmos. The Beings from the stars and outer space are many times closer to God than religious people on Earth are. In the galaxies, the Oneness of God becomes the religion. In fact, many star systems would not have a word for religion in their language, for they would speak of Unity and God. Earth-people would need to put the Oneness of God into a religious setting in order to relate to it. There is nothing wrong in having religions as part of a particular culture. However, religions must be changed—go through a metamorphosis—and soon.

My Spiritual Brothers and I are on the planet to make some of these changes to religions. Christianity will have a major overhaul. I will start it at the Vatican where I already have two of my disciples in place, John and Peter. When the present pope makes his transition, the new pope will be one of my disciples. Some people have heard this possibility already and think I will be the next pope. In that way, I truly would sit on a throne with the gold hat. However, I say to you it will not be I, Jesus, on that Vatican throne, but one of my disciples. I will not tell you which one, but suffice to know he is truly beloved.

Many years ago I was worshipped as a Son of God—the Messiah. However, I say to you, dear Readers, I was not the Messiah at that time. When I come again to humankind, when I once again appear on the Mount, it will be as the Messiah, but not only of the Jews. I am sad to say that it will be years yet before man's consciousness is such that I am able to fulfill Scripture, even though Christians fervently wish it to be.

We of the Spiritual Hierarchy feel that in a few years your planet Earth will be able to have raised its vibratory rate to an even higher level. It is moving higher each day. Every day that peace is in the hearts of men and women, fewer wars are fought, and people walk in God's Grace brings the vibrations of planet Earth higher. You are in the fourth dimension now. Earth is striving for the fifth dimension already. Many people of the higher frequency are already vibrating in the fifth dimension and are reaching toward the sixth. It is not beyond one's ability this lifetime to do so.

I AM known throughout history as the Great Physician, while in actuality your Higher Self does the healings. I was merely your catalyst to what you yourself had desired. If you desired life, I helped you. If you chose death, I helped you make that passage. You see, I merely helped what your intention had already implied. When one refers to the Great Physician, that person is really referring to God—the Ultimate Physician, the Ultimate Experience—the path back to God. You know God heals, but the Higher Self, that Divine part of you needs to agree for the healing to take place. In that sense, the Higher Self is the healer. Your mighty I AM works in conjunction with God.

When God created such a diversity of peoples, He did give them their free will, but He also gave them their cultures, their colors, their behaviors—for each culture behaves differently. A case in point is the Aborigines of Australia. This glorious race of indigenous peoples is so close to Mother Earth that they act Earth-like. They have rituals tuned to the Earth and Nature. The Aborigines worship their gods of the Earth in a very Earth-loving way.

Therefore, dear Reader, I have given you a taste of what will be portrayed in this book, *The Ultimate Experience*. It will be a book whose purpose is to shatter many of the myths that surround me and to bring new ideas to people; to shed light on misinterpretations from the Bible, and hopefully to spark a light for change in the many religions. There always needs to be growth and change. The religions are badly in need of this. One of my missions is to bring that change to Christianity for sure. In other religions, the leaders are not quite ready to let go of their control of the people.

I want to reiterate to you, dear Readers, that while there are many inaccuracies in the Bible, there is also much Truth. Two thousand plus years later, this Truth still stands up to the marches of time. The Truths are vast in number and I wish to name a few of them for you. While this book's purpose, as I have stated, is to dispel the many myths concerning my life and others involved with me, the Truths warrant their own place in history.

Think what it would have been like in your world if there were no Ten Commandants. Your lives would have no firm basis on which to establish your morals. **The Truths in the Bible far outweigh the fallacies**. I really want you to understand this. You have a saying: *don't throw out the baby with the bath water.* I could not have said it more succinctly myself.

Therefore, please keep this foremost in your minds. I am not negating the whole Bible! It is too valuable a tool and will be for centuries to come. You see much of the Truth in your Bible is from God. The scribes may not always have transcribed the events or sayings exactly to the letter, but there is enough Truth left for the energy to be intact. It is that point I wish you to carry away after reading this book. **Do not negate the whole Bible**. It is written Truth, which will live on until God removes His Energy from it.

There is healing energy in the Bible. If one's belief was such and faith was strong enough, one could hold the Bible in one hand, the left hand, and put the right hand on the area one wished to be healed and it would happen. It could be an instant healing or a progressive one. Nevertheless, the healing energy is still in that Bible waiting to be tapped. In addition, it makes no difference if it is the King James Version or one of the other publications. The energy is still the same.

Many times people have heard that the energy of a Master permeates a book. This is Truth. The Bible is an astounding example.

The Ultimate Experience . . . book will not have an impact as direct as the Bible, but **effect** it surely will have, for words are energy. The effect you experience will directly correlate to your level of awareness. Interesting thought, is it not?

SECTION 2—PERSONAL JOURNEYS

EXODUS—Jesus

I AM Jesus. We come now to the days of Moses. I will not expand on the Biblical story of finding Moses in the bulrushes, as that is quite true and he was watched over closely by his sister Miriam. I wish to comment more on the flight from Egypt. It was not just one glorious exodus, but there were actually several over a span of a few years. Pharaoh allowed many of the Israelites to leave. They would go to various relatives in other locations. However, when Moses left, he took the majority of the Israelites, the last to be released with him. Even then, some of the people just decided to stay in Egypt—usually the more elderly who could not make the long journey.

The Biblical rendition of Pharaoh chasing the Israelites is partly true. Remember he was Moses' brother whom he did love. Pharaoh was not chasing the Israelites, but he accompanied the people. ***Exodus 13:17-18*** *And it came to pass, when Pharaoh had let the people go, that God led them not through the way of the land of the Philistines, although that was near; for God said, Lest peradventure the people repent when they see war, and they return to Egypt.(17) But God led the people about, through the Red sea: and the children of Israel went up harnessed out of Egypt.(18)* The parting of the water was indeed the force of God, but by His Angel, Micah, who was under the tutelage of AA Michael. Moses wielded the rod, which became a symbolic gesture of God's power.

Exodus 14:21-22 *And Moses stretched out his hand over the sea; and the LORD caused the sea to go back by the strongest wind all that night, and made the sea dry land, and the waters were divided.(21) And the children of Israel went into the midst of the sea upon the dry ground; and the waters were a wall unto them on their right, and on their left.(22)* It was not as simple as different movie versions have portrayed, for the bottom was not totally dry and solid, although it was quite firm in certain areas, just like a beach is when the tidewaters are out. People were obliged to step over or around all manner of fish and did make it across without loss of life in spite of the enormous difficulties. The Egyptians did not try to follow for they knew what was happening, and God kept the waters pulled back until all were safely across.

They were safely across, not as in safe from Pharaoh, but safe in that no one drowned, for there were mighty forces holding the waters back; hence, the rush to get through. It was an awesome experience. After they had reached dry land, camp was made for all were tired and the animals needed calming down. Henceforth, Moses and the Israelites camped and regrouped.

The Bible has the Israelites wandering in the desert for forty years. That is quite accurate, for the energy and consciousness of the people had to be raised. Readers who know the chakra system will know the people of that era were pretty much in their lower chakras or, in other words, the lower centers of energy. The first chakra is survival energy, and the second is life/death and sexual energy. The third is the integrator of the energies of all the chakras, the power center. The people in the desert had to raise their consciousness up to the third center in order to integrate these energies.

You see, dear Readers, the land of milk and honey, the land promised to the Israelites, is the planet's heart center. Consciousness must be integrated at the third before one's consciousness is ready to be in the heart energies. God wished His people to be at that heart level before entering into the Promised Land. How was God going to accomplish this? Wander the desert for years and years. This allowed many of the older generation to die off and allowed the new consciousness of the children to be the dominating energy, instead of the bondage-energy mentality. Remember what I have said about evolution being a slow process. It took many years before people were ready to release the slavery programming.

I now wish to address Moses' nomadic life while in the desert. Your movie versions are quite accurate, maybe made his life more dramatic than it was. Put yourself in his sandals. Being a nomad for forty years while waiting for others to catch up to your level of understanding of God was tedious and he was impatient at times. He kept himself busy attending to the people, but there was not much to stimulate one's mind. I guess one could say that *being a leader of many peoples in the desert for forty years is not a very stimulating or glamorous job*! Of course, he spent much time communing with God; but Moses was in a human body and at times felt impatience and frustration with it all. He would ask God if we could not hurry the process along a little. He would always answer that the people are not ready. In his heart, he knew that. However, his humanness grumbled at the **testing of patience, and his anger surfaced**.

The case in point obviously is the Biblical story of creating the golden calf, an idol to worship instead of God. ***Exodus 32:7-8 And*** *the LORD said unto Moses, Go, get thee down; for thy people, which thou broughtest out of the land of Egypt, have corrupted themselves. (7) They have turned aside quickly out of the way which I commanded them; they have made them a molten calf, and have worshipped it, and have sacrificed there unto, and said, these be thy gods, O Israel, which have brought thee up out of the land of Egypt.(8)*

Many people have wondered at the story of Moses' anger when he broke the tablets. ***Exodus 31:18*** *And he gave unto Moses, when he had made an end of communing with him upon Mount Sinai, two tables of testimony, tablets of stone, written with the finger of God.* Moses was so filled with God's Grace and Light as he carried those exquisite tablets of the Commandments down from the mountain and then to be confronted with the golden calf, he just instinctively became enraged. Here he held a beautiful creation in his arms. He was full of hope and joy for the people. When he saw the calf made of anything of gold that the people had given, his human ego took over. He knew the people were not ready to cross over the Jordan River to their inheritance. The disappointment overrode common sense, for it meant he too had to drift and roam for years more. The grief was almost more than he could bear. For those of you Readers who know grief, anger is a large component of the grieving process. What the Bible does not tell you is that Moses spent many a night in his tent in prayer asking for God's forgiveness interspersed with many a tear of frustration. He ran the whole gambit of emotions for he was human, you see.

The years passed by without any particular incidents. All were well fed by the manna that rained down each morning, like dew drops that would solidify somewhat. It carried all they needed in proteins, vitamins, and minerals. It was God's food. What could one add? His food was perfect. Illnesses consequently did not occur. Their bodies were kept quite healthy. The people had their sheep and therefore wool that the women spun into threads and wove into garments. Leather came from the animals also. It was stretched out, dried and made into sandals or carrying bags. Life went on as only a nomadic life does. The people would find places that had water. They were led hither and yon. Therefore, the years passed. (*The manna came from the space ships that were following the group all that time.*)

The Biblical rendition of finally being led to the Jordan River where the people would make their crossing is as accurate as any oral history can be. (*Joshua/Jesus led them.*) Moses stood and then sat on a rock cropping near the Jordan. Each member of a certain tribe passed by him where he blessed them as each made his or her passage into the Promised Land. A part of Moses was relieved it was finished, while another part of him was deeply grieved that God was not allowing him to lead the people to their sacred land. (*This author was a 9-year-old boy who made the crossing and then died a short time later—the soul's mission completed.*)

There has been a great deal of speculation on the reasons God did not allow Moses to cross over the river. People theorized it was a punishment from God for his breaking the Tablets. However, I say to you, dear Readers, Our Father is not One of punishing people for their humanness. Moses was not allowed to go for his destiny was to die in the desert in order to bring closure to the Exodus. (*However, God had given Moses full knowledge of the whys and wherefores of this journey. As the people's faith wavered, so did Moses.' He had yet to master his emotions. It was after his faith wavered* ***when*** *he had full knowledge as to the purpose of the game plan that God did not allow him to cross over with Joshua.)* Remember, that whole area was the life-death energy and as the people raised their consciousness, they moved to the third center, the integrator.

While Moses had long ago risen up the chakras to the crown, the energy cycle of the Exodus had to be brought to closure. It was the ending of the cycle. Moses was born in Egypt; led the people out of **slavery** and brought them to their new land—the heart center. His death therefore would be closing that chapter of the Israelites—birth, bondage, the journey out and then death. He was symbolic of humankind's journey to this day—birth, journey through life, and then death to be reborn! When the people crossed the Jordan, they ended cycle with that whole Exodus story and were reborn into the heart center energy. It was a transformation from chrysalis to butterfly. The people were no longer caterpillars, but butterflies of beautiful colors and freedom. (*Moses then had another lifetime to practice faith.)*

The Moses story is a touching story for it has the fairy tale within it: A baby is found and taken into a palace to live as a prince. He then hears he is of poor birth but profound spirit of which he is not aware. He then goes back to his people to learn about his origins. He becomes their spiritual prince, leads them out of poverty and bondage, and shows them a land of milk and honey and freedom. There were princes, pharaohs, and a peasant who became Light in his own right. The fairy tale was reality within a spiritual journey. (*Lord Kuthumi and Jesus blended their energies as Moses in that lifetime, for when souls have an assignment as huge as that one was, they always combine forces with other Beings of Light and come as One.*)

We now travel through history and visit my life as **the boy, Jesus**. I wish to convey to you, dear Readers, I was not always focused on my spiritual tasks. I enjoyed my boyhood. I felt special, but not knowing why, for we were all God's children. I just knew I was loved by my family but not always understood. Much has been written about my years leading to the cross, but little has been written about my boyhood years. That was because there were no scribes making note of my words and actions. Only my mother and father knew I had been chosen by God. However even they did not know about the cross. I knew, but it is similar to today's youths being told they would die at thirty-three of a drive-by shooting. The fact does not seem very pertinent, as it is so distant in the future. I, therefore, just did not dwell upon the facts of my future cross experience.

I loved working with my father. He was a fine carpenter and would be considered now an artisan in fine woodworking. Keep in mind all woodworking was done by hand. We did not have the miter-cutting machines and the electric sander as woodworkers have now. I relished the smell of lumber, the feel of the wood in my hands and enjoyed the beauty of the grains that was teased out by much sanding. I also enjoyed the birds that would come, chirp, and sing to me as I worked. I always talked to them also.

Therefore, dear Reader, life was not in the fast lane in those long ago times. We seemed to appreciate the simpler, quieter ways of living without radios and television. Little did we know the changes that would ensue by the act of crucifixion years later!

MARY'S STORY—Mary Magdalene

I AM Mary Magdalene. I am Jesus' twin flame. I was his wife in your Biblical days. I was raised in what would be called a normal fashion. I was not particularly a pretty girl, and somewhat awkward in all that I did. One could say I had more of a pixie look than a woman-of-the-world look. At that time, I did not know of my destiny. I was a plain child of an older sister who was quite beautiful. I stayed in the background so that she could shine. I felt that I would not have a very exciting life.

Much has been written about my being a woman of ill repute. That is so incorrect. I was shy and not worldly. When a man smiled at me, I could detect his intentions. I instinctively knew if it was a kindly smile, or one of flirtation, or one of lust. You see, I was quite child-like in build. Some men found this quite alluring and were more forward than they ought to have been. It was always the older men. The younger men thought I was too much like a young sister to be teased or ignored. The older men, not all of them, but one in particular, made inappropriate advances. When I pushed him away in repulse, he became enraged and even more lustful. I was on the verge of being raped when the commotion caused others to come running to see what was going on.

In order to cover his embarrassment in front of his friends he started defaming my reputation to the actual point of trying to stone me. Some others joined in, as their own sins made them feel guilty. It was at this time my Lord came. He knew who I was, but I only knew that someone had come to my rescue. By this time, I was in tears. I had been pushed into the dirt and was dirty and terribly afraid. My Lord looked at me with so much love for he recognized who I was. When I saw his love, my heart burst open with love for him and I forgot my fear.

The Bible's version where my Lord wrote in the dust to the men is true. He did not say to **me** to go and sin no more for he knew I had **not** sinned. Ever! I was too young and not worldly enough. From that moment on, we were together as much as was appropriate for a young woman and a Rabbi to be. The Bible portrays this incident as a major part of my life while in actuality, it was not, for I knew I was innocent. It was ugly while it lasted, but the Father was watching closely so that it would not get out of hand.

The actual lesson was for the men and not me! Those words . . . *go and sin no more*, were to the men! You see, Readers, again this story has been written and rewritten throughout the ages. The scribes, who were men, only saw the play from a man's point of view. If a man heard Jesus, say . . . go*, and sin no more*, it would have to be to the woman trying to escape. Right? Wrong! It was not a large crowd—just a few. Nevertheless, the whole scenario was to teach men. I was the injured party—the woman the scribes could not believe was innocent. ***John 8:4, 7, 10-11*** *They say unto him, Master, this woman was taken in adultery, in the very act. (4) So when they continued asking him, he lifted up himself, and said unto them, He that is without sin among you, let him first cast a stone at her. (7) When Jesus had lifted up himself, and saw none but the woman, he said unto her, Woman, where are thine accusers? Hath no man condemned thee? (10) She said, No man, Lord. And Jesus said unto her, neither do I condemn thee; go, and sin no more. (11)*

I have carried this injustice for over two thousand years. It is time to move on and see it for what it was—a man's lust, ignorance, and blame, in order to save his own reputation. My Lord truly was a Savior—my flesh and blood Savior. I gave him my heart that blessed day for it brought us together forever.

INDIA—Jesus

I AM Jesus. I come once again to give you, dear Readers, an opportunity to learn something new of me. You have read throughout the millenniums that I had traveled a great deal before my journey took me to the cross. However, you may not know that I traveled even more **after** my cross experience! After I had ascended and returned in a somewhat changed form, I instructed my disciples how to teach and carry on without my physical presence. Then I took my wife, Mary Magdalene, and my baby daughter, Sarah, and we made a long arduous journey to India.

Since everyone thought me dead, unmarried, and certainly without children, it was easy to maintain a disguise of sorts. Mary, as my wife, was three months pregnant when I went to the cross. After my translation, we remained quietly in the background until after Sarah's birth. We thought that a good time to travel, as the wee babe would be well fed with her mother's milk. Only our Light could give us away, if people were evolved enough to notice it. Several of the yogis in India did note the Light, but one of the highly evolved usually does not speak of each other's Light. One follows a certain protocol. Therefore, when the yogis saw our Light, nothing was said; but we could feel an aura of greater respect for us grow.

As you know, it is a long trek to India. We joined a caravan and when it tarried in different countries, so did we. It was not my first trip, so I had an idea of the journey and length of time. In modern times, one could say the trip was similar to the English safaris. The tents were put up each evening, rugs were laid out, and the many candles lit up the tents in quite an opulent way. The food was simple fare of typical flat bread and goat or lamb stew, which was a favorite of mine. There were dried vegetables, herbs, and fruits. We did not suffer at all. In fact, our journey was not a lesson of trials and tribulations. We had nothing to prove. We were a young married couple with a precious baby girl, and we all basked in our love for each other. It was a true honeymoon, for it was the first time we were on our own. We could socialize or not as we wished. We had a curtained-off section in one of the tents. It was a loving and adventurous time for us.

Our long journey gave us many chances to know different peoples and sects. We did not stay within the Jewish sectors but branched out in order to learn as much as we could of the different cultures. We did observe the Hebrew Sabbath but also incorporated the new spirit of Christianity. People were eager to learn about Christianity so we were able to teach by conversation and example of *loving thy neighbor.* People had heard about the crucifixion and they were eager for political news. Remember in those far off days, news was carried by word of mouth and of course, not all was repeated accurately. I taught about *love*, and Mary taught the women that they were equal to men. Women were not second-class citizens. All were equal in God's eyes. This information was not always received well by the men as you can well imagine, as we ventured further into those Far Eastern lands with their different cultures. We flourished in those exotic lands. Foods were different, the vegetation different. The flowers were extraordinarily beautiful.

Little Sarah, as she grew older, was a born linguist and knew several languages and dialects she had picked up from her many friends. She was a likable child and looked very much like her mother, small-boned. She had a sweet smile and would climb onto my lap and just nestle in while we conversed. Not much is known to humanity of our Sarah. Suffice to tell you that she grew to be a lovely, strong-willed, caring adult with a fine mind. She married young while she was in a far-away country. Her genetics were programmed well by carrying both Mary's genetic makeup and mine.

We arrived in India tanned, well, and in good spirits. Sarah would have been about six months old, for our journey covered several months. During the caravan journey, I had many opportunities to talk with visiting parties. Of course, I only conversed with the men. I had a watchful ear as to our guidance. I knew that God would provide for us, but it was up to me to listen to Him and to know when a certain message that I had heard in the caravan was meant for my family and me. Therefore, when I heard of a particular village that was in the higher elevations without the density of extreme poverty, I knew that was where we were supposed to journey and settle.

When the caravan started splitting up with some going on to cities and others to smaller sectors, I knew which group to go with. There were Inns and, although crude compared to modern times, the amenities were adequate. The rooms were clean and opened to the crisp air with shutters to close at nightfall. We kept being led further. Every time I thought this village was meant for us, I would get the guidance to keep traveling after a short rest. By now, we had switched from camels to donkeys. People mostly walked and the newer mothers rode the donkeys. I was not comfortable riding a donkey, as my legs were quite long and those saddles did not come with comfortable stirrups. My feet would mostly drag in the dust unless I raised my knees up and that got tiresome. It was just easier for me to walk. I provided Mary with many a giggle as she watched me attempt to adapt to those creatures.

We soon found our new village. There were many flowers and trees around it. We found lodging at a reasonably priced Inn where the food was abundant and quite good. I always looked for cleanliness. People could be quite poor, but if there was water, they needed to have washed themselves and their garments. Mary gathered with the women at the well. Most the women had servants to carry the water jugs; but I would cause quite a stir, as I would come and help Mary carry the water jugs back to our quarters. I felt she had her hands full carrying our six month old. How could Mary be expected to handle the water too? It was a simple task for me and that spoke to the women present that men needed to help the women in some of these labors. There need not be a demarcation between man's works versus a woman's domain. While I had an impact, I doubt if there was a change in this regard because of it.

I knew that change of any kind, physical or spiritual, could be slow in coming. Therefore, I taught by example. At the same time, I would give them a sentence or two that they could carry away with them. One of those sentences that I used many times was, *when you perceive that a hurtful word or action has been done to you or another; just know that you do not need to retaliate.* I would go on to explain that God has also perceived the same dynamic to which you have reacted. Your task is to stay in your heart and let God give back to the sender what the person has created by that particular action. I did reiterate that neither he nor she need do anything in way of retaliation. Let God take care of it. Even in these modern times, people either do not know or forget this plain fact. You need do nothing!

God is the Ultimate Teacher. Allow Him to do the teaching. It is only natural that the hurt person wants or may even demand instant retaliation, but dear Readers, this is not God's way. His timing is different from yours. This lesson is one I would teach repeatedly: *let God handle this in His infinite way with infinite wisdom and all knowing*. People were slower to grasp this meaning in those ancient days. It is hoped that in these modern times people will practice this in their lives. However, with the rising incidents of road-rage, one can discern that the lesson of letting *God do the doing* has not been fully learned.

I often observed men verbally putting women down. There was no equality. When a man was courting a young woman, he was quite solicitous, but after the marriage he would fall back on his programming that he had observed when growing up. Women were treated as servants. They did most of the labor in the home while the men gathered and discussed the latest spiritual phrase they felt needed redefining; or they talked about neighboring areas and gossiped about the women. Oh yes, men also gossip.

Whenever I would join a group to sit and socialize, the conversation invariably would center on a particular woman under discussion. She usually was one of disputed reputation. I would attempt to steer the conversation away from the judgments and toward equality of women. My Mary and I would have long discussions on this and I gained the woman's perspective from her. I would offer observations to the men such as, *why is it that a woman cannot do anything except what is considered woman's work*? *Why can she not be a carpenter or a scribe? Why can she not pray in the presence of men? Who set those rules*? *How did they come about*? Heated debates ensued over these questions. Teaching *equality of women* to men definitely was a losing argument in those days, but I planted the seed, the questions for change.

In the years to come, our sojourn in India ended. I was guided to seek a new country, a new culture. I chose to go to Europe. By now, our family had grown. We had three more children, our boisterous sons. Sarah was now in her early teens. I needed to move our family, for Sarah's destiny was not in India, but in France, and it was up to me to get her there safely. This departure took over a year in planning, farewell parties, and saying goodbyes. We loved India. The Far Eastern Indian people are beautiful in all ways, and it was with great sadness we bid our farewells.

YOUNG TIBETAN—Djwhal Khul

I AM Djwhal Khul, Lord of the Second Ray. I come to impart to you dear Readers my experience of the Ultimate Experience back to God.

When I was just a young Tibetan lad of sixteen or so years, I was in the mountains one day and I kept hearing a voice. I would look around and there was no one there. I was just a goat herder, a lonely goat herder. I listened and heard only the bells tinkling as my goats grazed. As I settled down again I would hear this voice. I was a volatile young lad, so I yelled, *who are you? Why do you hide yourself*? With that, the voice said to me, *Djwhal, I am your God*. Of course that meant to me it must be Lord Buddha. I listened intently and still nothing more was said. Therefore, I again settled down to try to figure out these strange circumstances. For the third time I heard, *Djwhal, I am your God*. By this time, I was getting rather agitated. Picture a young lad who was not worldly and knew only goat herding. I just sat, stood, sat, stood, and sat. The final time the voice spoke to me that day left me speechless. The voice told me how my life would unfold from now on; how I was to study under a great master monk in the temple, and how I would become a great scholar and would be able to visit different worlds while still being in this one. I was told to go to this temple for my Teacher was awaiting me.

I called the goats in and trudged back to my village. I told no one, thinking if this truly is my Teacher he will welcome me, and if he is not I will be sent home quickly enough. I splashed some water on my face and hands, patted some of the dust off my clothes, and presented myself at the temple.

I immediately was led to a dim room lit only by candles, for there was no electricity in the village in those early days of the 1800's. I stood in the center of this room, since no one had offered for me to sit and there were only some cushions in a corner. I did not know at the time that my Teacher was already in the room observing me. He had the ability to be in another dimension that my physical sight could not see.

While I stood somewhat nervously, from behind me I heard, *ahem*. I turned around with a start and there stood my Teacher in his yellow robes. He had a twinkle in his eye, but the countenance of his mouth was stern. He said to me, *well what brings **you** to the temple*? How could I tell this stranger that I had heard a voice while on the mountain that called Himself God and that I was supposed to come; therefore I pretended I did not know why. *I do not know*, I mumbled somewhat truthfully. I really did not know why I was there. With that honest reply, the Teacher broke into a grin and asked me, *did a voice tell you to come*? I replied that indeed, I did hear a voice say that He was God and I was to come to the temple in order to be with my Teacher, but I did not understand any of it.

So began my years of training in every aspect that my Teacher could teach me. Surprisingly, I was like a sponge and soaked up everything I was taught. I was so eager to know and to learn. Those years were the happiest of that lifetime. Consequently, dear Reader, from very humble beginnings, I learned my lessons well enough, was devoted to God so that I ascended and became the Master that some of you have heard of and many who have not.

I am best known for my work in helping great souls write their books, mainly Madam Blavatsky and Alice Bailey. Those souls opened their hearts and channels to me, and we wrote much about the spiritual mysteries and of course information on the Rays and Initiations. **I was best known as the Tibetan**, during which time I overshadowed Alice Bailey and dictated her many books.

The title of this book, *The Ultimate Experience* . . . , was formulated by a group effort of Jesus, the author in Spirit, and others, for they wished information to reach ever outward that could help lead people Home to God once again. It is through the inner plane, through meditation and the gateway of the heart that one can travel back to God. You see, dear Readers, each one's path is trod differently. Since each soul is unique, would not one's path be unique also? **My purpose in writing this chapter is to list some of the ways people can use to return to God**. In my case, it was in having a Teacher, a physical Teacher who not only taught, say *manifestation*, but also then would demonstrate it right before my eyes. Therefore, having a physical, wise teacher who teaches about the spiritual realms, ascended masters and the different galaxies is one way.

The Spiritual Hierarchy of Lords Jesus, Sananda, Maitreya, Hilarion and Serapis Bey became as familiar to me as if they were flesh and blood. I knew each one well, and it was with such joy after I had ascended to be able to greet them in their dimension. Oh yes, Reader, I still felt in awe of them for I was so new to this special group of Ascended Ones. While I knew they were old beyond measure, I was not prepared for their youthful and startlingly handsome looks when they chose to appear in form.

I opted not to transform my features; so anyone who has a picture of me will see that I do look much the same as I did when I last walked the Earth. I soon discovered that even though my Teacher had taught me well of spiritual matters, there were gaps in my education, and I spent many of your Earth-time hours learning more, so much more about my new Home, the many miraculous possibilities that I never knew had existed.

One of the miraculous abilities that fascinated me was to be able to see all thought forms in living color and sound. It was similar to viewing an ever-ongoing motion picture show. When I would view one of my students, for by this time I had several, I could plainly read his thoughts in living form. It quickly gave me the student's level of awareness and literally gave me what he was thinking. Now bear in mind that when a Master agrees to teach a soul, a chela we would say, that student is already advanced compared to where humanity is now operating. If the student were feeling anger over unresolved issues, we Masters would not only see all his dark, red energies, but the thoughts that went with them. I found this fascinating and brought to mind the various times I would react in anger while in my Earth-life. Although that was long in the past, I was new enough to this world of the Masters to remember my lack of control with a feeling of sadness. However, I also realized I was then in a human body, and I did have those emotions to control.

My life as a young boy and then as an adult was one of learning. Being out with the goats put me in an introspective position, for one has no one to talk to but a favorite goat or two. I talked to my goats and I talked to nothing in particular. If I saw a bird I would talk to it as it flew by; but mainly I talked to myself. I knew when I was being lazy or productive in my thoughts. I could just daydream or I could really ponder a particular issue.

One of my thoughts would inevitably be *where was I going in this life? Was this all there was—to be a goat herder for my entire life? What was I to do*? As I mused and speculated, I would slip into an altered state not consciously known to me. I would see visions of myself as an adult. I noted I was tall, that I was not particularly handsome. I seemed to be surrounded by books, and this puzzled me for there were few books in my village. Only the wealthier would own a book. Moreover, when I say, *wealthy,* I mean the person owned many goats, for that is how we measured wealth. We did not wear fine jewelry, but beads of glass that were crudely strung together by today's standard. Life was simple in the village. Therefore, I was puzzled as to all the books I would see in my visions, for that is what the pictures were called, my Teacher told me. I grew up in my Teacher's Ashram. The books in there were actually stacks of parchments that were rolled, for there were no bookbinders in those days in our village. Therefore, **Teachers are one of the ways back to God.**

Another way is for one to isolate oneself from the outside world and spend one's time in deep meditation and prayer. This is a most difficult path to maintain in my opinion, for it means ignoring the needs of the body. I view this way, this path, as one of sacrifice, for you see it does not have a balance to it. God's plan is for Heaven to be blended on Earth—as *above, so below*. Nevertheless, when one refuses to walk out among the people, to hold jobs, to serve in some way, **this particular path becomes more self-serving versus being a service to others**. Although there are those who have reached God on this path, it is no longer looked upon as a particularly productive path.

Another path and the one now viewed as the more desirable way to God is through service of some kind. When I refer to service, that is really quite broad in its meaning. Most people think of service as being a doctor or teacher, psychologist, social worker, body-worker, or skilled laborer. Nevertheless, there can be people who are just friendly Light Bearers. They spread their Light through friendly greetings, a handshake, a hug, car-pooling, or coaching. Anything that has a person doing something on a positive level for others is in service. The typist for this book is in service. Attending groups for meditation is being in service, for the energy that is generated goes out to humanity and the Earth. That is service. The facilitator for groups, the self-help groups are all in service. Ministers, rabbis, priests are doing an obvious service, for they keep reinforcing the Oneness of all. Service and its many facets most definitely are paths toward God.

We in the higher dimensions jump at the chance to serve repeatedly. As one advances on the path to enlightenment and God, the desire to serve in all ways becomes a way of life for us. You see our hearts are so full of love that we seek ways that we can serve people, to help them feel this love as our love surrounds them.

Every master who contracts with a student infuses that student with his Light and Love. At every opportunity that arises, the student receives more of that Light and Love. This increases the strength of the heart chakra, the depth of it and raises the Light-quotient therein. Readers, you have all heard that wise adage, *Love makes the world go around*. Well, Love indeed makes the physical world go around more lovingly while it lessens judgments at the same time.

You may recall that in the early beginnings of the planet, people were so occupied with survival that they did not know true, pure *love*. They only knew those more base emotions of lust, anger, and greed. It was a time of the survival of the fittest. Those who were weaker fell by the wayside, either by the wild animals or by their neighbor's ax. People took what they wanted and coveted. There was little *love* felt or shown. Probably, the closest women of that era came to experiencing real *love* was during the rearing of their babies and small children.

Men expressed their feeling either in lust for all things or in pride—pride in a kill, pride in a strong son and lust for young girls—many times their own daughters. *Love* as a pure emotion actually had to be taught. This is what that Great Soul Jesus taught—*Love thy neighbor . . .* Even thousands of years ago, Love did not have the purest of energy. While many men of God did walk the Earth before Jesus' time—Buddha, Krishna, Confucius, Abraham—most of their followers were not enlightened and did not have the same ideals of Light and Love in their hearts. Those men of God taught their followers the lessons of *love* and *obedience* to the one God. They were the forerunners of today's spirituality. Humanity needed centuries of hearing the teachings before it could move forward and practice these teachings with joy versus habitual machinations.

During my years of study, I would ponder where these teachings were leading me. By this time, I was not so naïve and was fast coming into my twenty-first year. I loved the routine that had been set. I lived at the temple and arose early for meditation and prayer. We were served a simple breakfast of hot cereal—you would call it a *porridge,* for it was not very thick but drinkable. Most of us chelas would simply pick our bowls up and noisily drink our breakfast. We also had tea heavily enriched with butter. Breads of any kind were served at the midday meal. After our breakfast, there was a short period when we could wash and attend to personal needs. Soon the call would go forth and we all would hurry to our classrooms for instruction. The classes were small and we had our own rooms. The Teachers taught much the same thing, but as the students advanced, they would be sent to Teachers who recognized that that student was ready for spiritual advancement. This could mean the student was being taught *teleportation*, for example, for this is required knowledge at the higher initiations.

The day came when I was told I was to join fellow students in the outside world. There was great excitement as my family made new traveling clothes for me. It is difficult for Westerners to understand how great an honor it is for parents when their son is accepted into the temple. They know they are turning their guardianship over to the lamas then and that their son is being given a great honor. There is much excitement as the temple astrologer casts the chela's horoscope in order to see when the auspicious moment will be for the adult-child to leave the temple and to venture out into the world.

The closest to venturing into the outside world from my village was to travel many days into distant India. Many of us traveled that route and followed those who had done it many times before. We had to carry our provisions with us. Water was not much of a problem as there was always snow on the ground at those higher elevations. The snow could just simply be scooped up and melted by campfires. Our food stayed pretty much as though it were in your modern day refrigerators. We packed a great deal of butter in parchment paper and then cloth. These were put into small baskets and draped over the donkeys or horses. With the cold, frosty air, butter was kept at a spreadable consistency versus in a melted state. We brought cheese and bread and of course tea. Our fare was simple but adequate, for the cheese was pure and had a high protein count. While the butter was fat, our bodies required that fat because of the high altitude. Our bodies' metabolism burned the calories quickly and the fat gave us insulation from the severe cold.

The young men and I were excited, for this was indeed a high adventure, many of us never having left our village before. The Tibetan people in the early decades were not a worldly people. However, one could say they were a people who were more advanced spiritually over the Westerners. In the outside world, money and position were coveted, while in Tibet, nothing was coveted. People were just as happy with glass beads and butter tea, versus diamonds and champagne of the outside world. A fermented drink can be made from the grains that were grown for bread, but the ones who made this Tibetan beer were rare. We were taught in the Temple that alcohol of any kind was not a desirable path to God. The euphoria was short-lived and not Nirvana in its truest sense as we of the modern world now know.

My years of Temple teachings ended as I passed into my twenty-first year. I was being honed more deeply for I had yet to experience life in the outside world. We students were taken to an ashram in India. My Teachers now were of the higher dimensions, the spiritual world. These masters would appear suddenly before us while in our meditations. We would be alerted by a bright, soft light. We would often hear celestial music—the music of the angels singing God's praises. The years passed, and we were taught many esoteric mysteries. While we were being taught, we too were earning our initiations. I was told I was to bring many of these spiritual mysteries to the outside world through the writing of books, many books. I was shown how to overlay a candidate, one who was able to channel at a deep level. Now I was able to move around quite easily in the other dimensions. I found a worthy candidate for this work of channeling a book in Madame Blavatsky. While tiny in stature, she had such a clear and pure channel that I was able to impart great writings to her telepathically. One of the more known is *The Secret Doctrine.* Another great channel was Alice Bailey. I brought forth much of the information from the Secret Doctrine and simplified it more, for it was too academic for the average reader. With my dictations to Alice Bailey, I used simpler forms of the same information as in *The Secret Doctrine* because I wanted it to reach an even broader population of readers.

You see, dear Readers; much of the esoteric writing was too complex and too complicated in thought—even too wordy. Now I am aware the Work needs even further simplification. It is a difficult process for me, for I tend to write too much in the scientific mode and not enough in general terms. With this chapter in this book, I am toning down the rhetoric and stating the facts in a less scholarly way. This can be rather frustrating for both the person channeling and me. We strive for a higher scholarly presentation, and at the same time, we write in simple terms in order to attract more of humanity.

This book's title, *The Ultimate Experience . . . ,* conveys there is a climax, if you will, that precedes all other experiences relating to God. Imagine, Reader, being deep in your meditation, prayers, and adoration of the Father, when you feel yourself literally lifted off your cushions, hover for a second, and all of a sudden just shoot off. I did not take my body with me, for the flesh had slumped into the cushions when I changed consciousness. I had a feeling of joy and bliss and wanted it to last forever. I lost track of time but have since come to realize it was not of a long duration. I was traveling at a tremendous speed but at the same time felt almost stationary. My only comparison as to how fast I was going was to notice occasionally another form also prone. I would pass it by. The color was what I can only describe as a soft black with tiny flashes of light dotted here and there.

I did not realize at the time that I was traveling through a tunnel but have come to know that that was the case. I saw in the distance a soft glow of light, and as I traveled closer to it, it enlarged. All the while, the music was getting louder and the euphoric bliss more pronounced. I had no thoughts of fear. I did not even remember I had left my body. I was completely in the NOW consciousness where only the present action is noted. Then I arrived, set upright by unseen hands, and gently propelled forward. By then, I was completely engulfed in this white Light. I felt so much love in me and around me. I just knew then that I was *love*. All of my thoughts and feelings, for I still could feel things, were of *Love*.

You must remember, dear Reader, that everything being in the NOW means all is happening simultaneously. I felt, I saw, I thought, I heard, all at the same time. I felt euphoric and in total bliss. I saw angels surrounding this Light that I was barely able to look through. I thought, for I was wondering at my experience; I heard the angels' voices singing God's praises. In addition, I heard God's voice, the same one I had heard on that Tibetan mountain in my youth. The Father was all-loving, and I felt I could do no wrong in His eyes. He told me how pleased He was to have me Home again. He told me how pleased He was in my many endeavors and in me during my Earth lives. We talked and shared for just a few minutes of Earth-time, but it seemed a long time of a loving communication in that Heavenly place. That, dear ones, is *The Ultimate Experience,* that actual experience of being in that highest dimension and standing in the Presence of God. Once a soul has experienced that presence, it wishes to stay in that *love* forever.

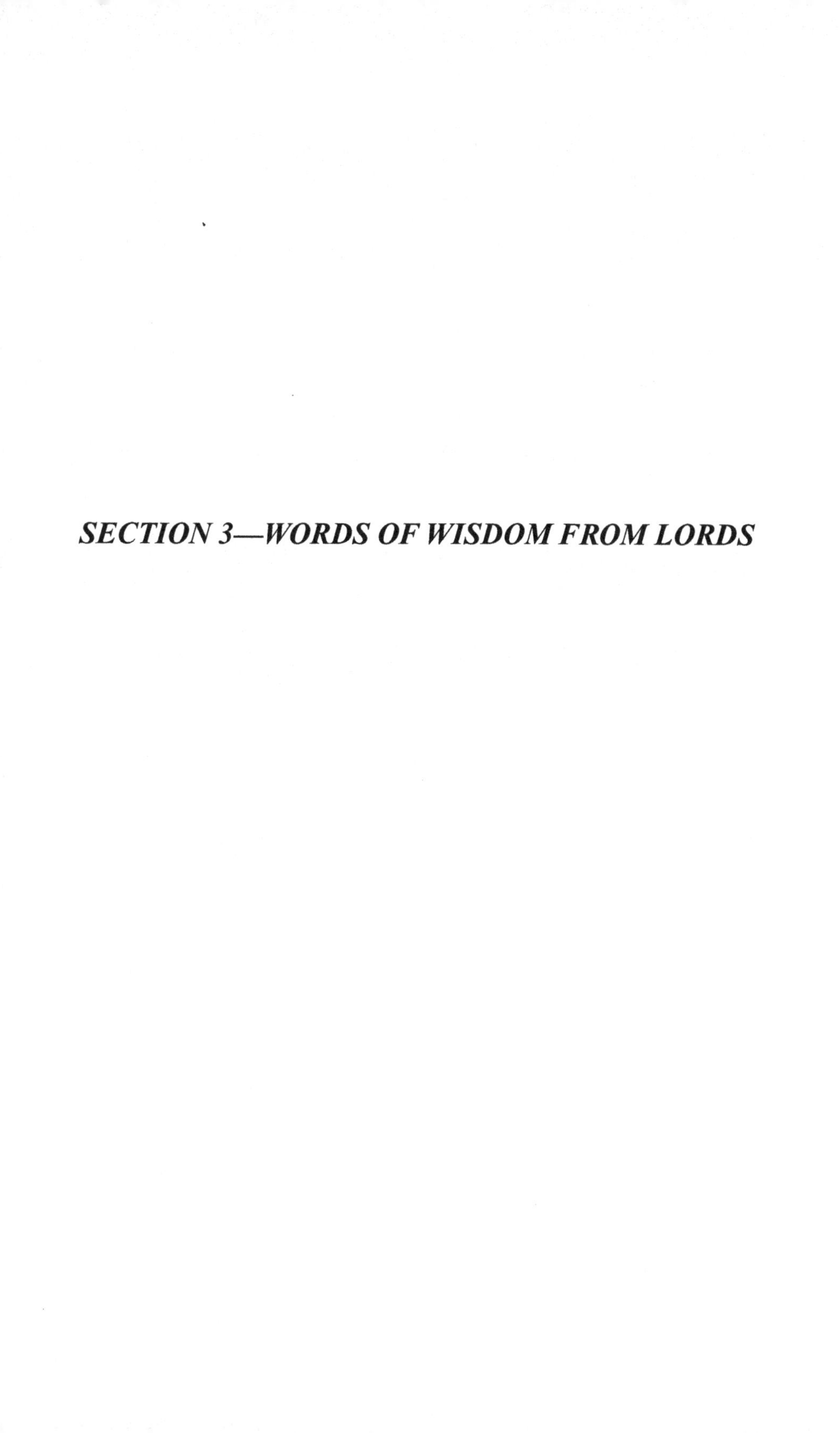

SECTION 3—WORDS OF WISDOM FROM LORDS

ADDRESSING MYTHS—Jesus

I AM Jesus. In the eons of time since the Bible was first transcribed, there were the scribes who wrote down from memory what the rabbis and various prophets and Teachers were saying. If the scribe fully understood the material, he would transcribe the words of these great sages accurately. If he did not understand the meaning, he would substitute his own interpretations. **The Biblical material many times was contaminated by the scribe's own projections.**

Throughout the years, as various religious leaders read the Christian Bible and found material with which they did not agree for fear of giving the people too much control, the fathers of the church would just leave certain passages out. **As each church unit did its own interpretation, sacred information was lost. The Vatican has much of these original writings**. It has passages I even wrote, in my handwriting, on reincarnation. I was telling people how they are born repeatedly in order to perfect their soul's evolutionary process. The church fathers of those ancient times did not understand Earth was a school for the soul. This schoolhouse was created so that souls could expand their knowledge, turn it into wisdom, and proceed up Jacob's ladder that he had seen in a dream. ***Genesis 28:12*** *And he dreamed, and behold the ladder set up on the Earth, and the top of it reached to heaven; and behold the angels of God ascending and descending on it.* This ladder symbolically has come down through the ages, for the fathers had not grasped its full significance. They did not know that Jacob's ladder was telling of the process of initiation and every rung of that ladder was an initiation level. In order to climb up onto the next rung, the aspirant or initiate had to pass various tests that could only be performed on Earth. Hence, the soul needed to come back repeatedly, reincarnate, in order to perfect itself. The angels ascending and descending the ladder were symbolic of souls on the evolutionary path.

Many Fundamentalists have an erroneous view of reincarnation. It became muddied, this concept of rebirth, when people started mixing religious ideas from other religions. The Far Eastern religions have a concept where one is born repeatedly because of karma, usually bad karma—but in actuality karma can be positive also. It is just another term for perfecting the soul. Many souls in their Earth-lives have much to learn. If they do not understand their lessons, or shirk them in some way, they will have another Earth life—many of them. Souls were advancing up that ladder and taking initiations, not because of karmic belief necessarily, but because the initiations to which they were aspiring demanded a certain level of expertise in learning to control first their physical body, then their emotional body and after that the mental body. There could be much karma involved in that process, if one wishes to use that philosophy, for the souls were attempting the long climb back to God.

Therefore, in the process of transcribing what the great sages had said, the scribes would use their own interpretations. Many times in the Jewish religion, great debates would arise over what was meant, for Hebrew is multifaceted and the scribe could not obliterate one letter or it would change the meaning of the whole word. The fallacies in the Christian Bible run deep. It will take centuries before people of different levels of understanding will all agree on a particular concept. In the writing of this book, I, Jesus, will be addressing some of the misinterpretations. It is time, dear Readers, to let go of some of those ancient ideas, misquotations, and practices. It is time to bring religion into the 21st century. However, I am in full realization that this can be a most controversial and, in many cases, unpopular decision on my part.

During my lifetime as Jesus, I had full consciousness of my task. I knew my mission. Now as I perceive the distortions of not only the scribes but also of the modern-day interpretations, I am proceeding to break up the energies that have held me on the cross and held humankind in a different kind of bondage. I knew the time had come where humanity had raised its consciousness enough that it might let other ideas in. This time it is not bondage of the physical body as religious teachers expound, but the bondage of erroneous belief systems. It is time to break up that dynamic. I am therefore going to start with different passages of the Bible that were wrongly interpreted. I will be addressing the New Testament for now, for the Old Testament is so full of symbols, it would take a monumental endeavor to address all of those interpretations.

Matthew 1:2 *Abraham begat Isaac; and Isaac begat Jacob; and Jacob begat Judas and his brethren.* In this passage, the first passage of the New Testament, there are errors, for not all the offspring of Abraham were noted. The scribes portray only Isaac. Abraham was old and had had several children, as did Isaac. However, the scribes only noted the children who would fit the Biblical oral history. Keep in mind that Matthew was telling his story which had been interpreted by many. When the scribes were writing, they drew upon the Old Testament, which was mainly oral in its tradition, and then a scribe wrote that down. These renditions from the different scribes are suspect. Common sense is also in order. If a modern reader took nothing away from my words except the concept that no one had just one child in that era, for the men would have had several wives in order to bring forth children who carried on their bloodline, that reader would be well on the way to breaking a myth.

Matthew 24:15-16 *When ye therefore shall see the abomination of desolation, spoken of by Daniel the prophet, stand in the holy place.(15) Then let them which be in Judea flee into the mountains. (16)* In these passages are the warnings of great catastrophes to come that have been prophesized by Daniel and for those in Judea to flee. All of this was attributed to my sayings. Every time I referred to great strife for the soul, the scribes interpreted it in a physical way happening to the body. The scribes wrote only at their level of understanding and took everything I was purported to have said in the physical and did not know I was speaking spiritually many times. People were warned to live a righteous life. They were not raising their awareness. I told them to stay in that holy place which was in their hearts. I told them that their way of life was an abomination and that it held dire consequences if they did not heed these warnings and followed a false god.

The Reader needs to keep in mind that it is close to impossible to quote someone directly unless a person knew shorthand or had a tape recorder. Why would a scribe get my words accurately? He would not. Therefore, what I am speaking about now is to cause a crack in that person's belief system while reading this. The Bible is full of beautiful and somewhat accurate renditions, but the direct quotes attributed to me and others just are not accurate. Now that I have laid that corner stone, I wish to start addressing the erroneous misconceptions about the story of my life.

I was born in Bethlehem. My mother was a virgin for she was very young and not worldly. However, it was **after** she had married my father that she became pregnant with me. The angel Gabriel did come. ***Luke 1:30-31*** *And the angel said unto her, fear not Mary: for thou has found favour, with God (30) and, behold, thou shalt conceive in thy womb, and bring forth a son, and shalt call his name JESUS. (31)* Nevertheless, he did not implant the seed. My father, Joseph did, in that beautiful act that married couples do to consummate their union. The angel appeared to both of them to tell them Joseph had implanted the God-seed successfully. My mother and father had been shown before they were born that they would be bringing me into the world. In order to ensure that the veils lifted enough so my parents would know their responsibility, the angel was sent. Joseph knew Mary was a virgin. All men know this physiological fact when they first are intimate with a woman. However, Readers, why it is called the *Immaculate Conception* is because both Mary and Joseph were able to hold the higher consciousness and vibrations. In order for me to be conceived, their energies and thoughts had to be immaculate. If they had dropped their energies to lust, the conception would not have taken place, for I could not enter through that kind of negative second chakra energy and still proclaim to the world I was their savior and would die for their sins. How could I if the energy I came through was not of the purest kind? I realize this last fact is quite startling to people. Nevertheless, it certainly is a myth that my whole life has been based on. Since I am breaking up the myths, I must start at the very beginning, my own foundation!

Matthew 2:11 *And when they were come into the house they saw the young child with Mary his mother and fell down and worshipped him . . .* Most of what has been written concerning my birth has been embellished. I know humanity would like to see me in a manger in the barn, but, dear Readers, I was in a small room at the back of the Inn near the stables. My parents had a servant's room. It was there that I was born. We were close to the stables, but not in them. That was an embellished story, also. I know the Christmas celebration of me lying in a manger is a touching story, but dear ones, it simply is not true. Those kinds of myths are endearing, so they are perpetuated and built upon to make the story even more charming. Believe me when I say people seeing my mother holding me while lying on a crude single bed is quite charming in itself. I did have a rudimentary cradle that was in the Inn. My cradle was more like a drawer on little rockers—sort of in between a cradle and a drawer. One of the servant girls brought it in. The labor was not long, nor short. We were flesh and blood. We were human in every way and therefore had similar experiences most people do. My father, Joseph, was naturally nervous and caring. **There was no mid-wife**. My father and mother went through this by themselves although a kindly servant girl helped by bringing some tea and bread. However, my Father also helped. He comforted my mother and he cradled my head as I was born.

These are facts. You see men in that era were not supposed to touch women's blood. How silly. What was he supposed to do with his young wife—not help catch and clean me? Of course he did. He was as much a part of my birth as my Divine Mother was. The servant girl was younger than my mother was and did not have the consciousness to know she was witnessing God's miracle. She had seen her own mother give birth. She was just matter-of-fact about it all. That was all there was.

My father was experienced with farm animals and knew about births. Moreover, as an aside, there were no lambs involved. The lambs are symbolic of the people—my people. There were also many unseen angels, God and Masters helping on the spiritual plane, overseeing my birth, giving us all encouragement and infusing us with God's Love and Energies. I was born in the energy essence of prayer, you see, and the prayers came from my Light ship.

Astrologically the planets were aligned for a propitious happening. However, the Light everyone saw was really my Light ship hovering over the inn. The Light ship was brought into the third dimension in order to provide emotional support for my parents. They could look at the Light and know God and the Light Bodies of the Ascended Ones were close. People are apt to forget our spiritual history covers millions of years. That era of Biblical history is just a few years compared to what has gone before. **The light seen in the sky was from my own space ship made of Light and formed by pure thought**. I understand that this will be too incredulous for many of the readers. They will wish to negate this information. Nonetheless, if Heaven is going to be on Earth, it is time, way past time, for the truth of our Space Brothers to come out. They indeed are here. In addition, they were then and have been for millions of years. You see this was not the first time I was to walk on the Earth. After my many Earth lives, I would return to the higher dimensions, confer with the Father, and return to my Light ship where many of my Soul Group also were. We would do our spiritual work and get ready for our next lives. **My ship was called the *Bethlehem Star* at that time and it watched over me for the rest of that life.** It was depicted as a star that miraculously moved across the sky. ***Matthew 2:7, 9, 10*** *Then Herod, when he had privily called the wise men, enquired of them diligently what time the star appeared.(7) When they had heard the king, they departed; and, lo, the star, which they saw in the East, went before them, till it came and stood over where the young child was.(9) When they saw the star, they rejoiced with exceeding great joy.(10)* Space ships were not in the people's consciousness. There was no vocabulary for space ships. People saw a bright light and thought it was a moving star. It was that simple.

Matthew 2:13-14 *. . . behold, the angel of the Lord appeared to Joseph in a dream, saying, arise, and take the young child and his mother and flee to Egypt, and be thou there until I bring the word; for Herod will seek the young child to destroy him.(13) When he arose, he took the young child and his mother by night, and departed into Egypt.(14)* The story of King Herod wanting to kill the first-born babies is accurate. My father was told in a dream to go to Egypt. This we did and escaped the slaughter. Our little family was a typical one. My father excelled in carpentry as is written. He was always able to find work and provide for my mother and me.

I had an inquisitive mind as most toddlers do. I was into everything and knew no fear. My mother watched over me in a loving and caring manner. However she also did not let me be disrespectful when I was trying out my negative two's as the saying goes. I remember my childhood even to this day. I do remember telling my mother that I did not like snakes, for there were always snakes on the land. Children were watched over closely because of this threat. In those days there was not anti-venom. Snakebite was very serious. Young children did die from those deadly bites given when children were tempted to pick one up. I was instructed by my ever-watchful mother never to go near one.

The years of development went by. It soon became safe enough for us to return home to Capernaum and a grand reunion with all the families and extended families. I grew to what the Jewish faith considers manhood at the age of twelve—what would be considered puberty now and not the time for a child-adult to make many decisions for himself. However, in those ancient times, humanity matured faster and had more responsibility. The local Rabbis at the Synagogue gave my schooling to me.

My intuition was highly developed, as was my intellect, so that many times I knew what they were going to ask me and what answers they expected. I rarely gave them the answers they were expecting but would expound on the answers way beyond what the average boy ought to be saying. I did not do it to puff myself up, but the information would roll off my tongue, for my brain was like a spigot. I would start answering a question and the information just flowed forth much to the chagrin of some of my teachers, since I would be telling them the teachings they had pondered over. Needless to say, I was not always looked upon in a fond manner because some of the rabbis were quite put out that I seemed to know more than they did, although I never said that I did.

There has been controversy about my names. The Bible calls me *Jesus*. I say to you that I was always called *Ye-shu-a,* (with the accent in the middle) in Hebrew. However, since I preferred speaking Aramaic, for that was the language of the common people, my name would be *Jeshua*. The "Y" was changed to a "J" with the accent at the beginning. Centuries later, the name Jesus evolved and it carried as much of my energy as do the names, Jeshua and Yeshua. It does not matter. My mother called me Yeshua. My Mary called me Jeshua. All my names were tenderly said by my family. Most of humanity calls me Jesus. I answer to all of my names.

(Now Jesus prefers to be called ***Jeshua****. Spelling it with a* ***Y*** *still carries a Hebrew vibration of 2000+ years ago. However, he has found that many people do not know who Jeshua is so that he will call himself Jesus if the situation warrants it. 2011)*

HUMANS and BEASTS—Jesus

I AM Jesus. In the beginning of humanity, while the wild beasts roamed the Earth, little was thought of God. The Light Beings had become solidified, having taken bodies that were solid. In fact, the mating with animals was the game of souls then. Your myths of centaurs and flying creatures are true. That was truly abomination in God's Eyes, for He watched the downfall of the humans with their Light diminishing.

When humans had sunk to such a low, **God knew a higher truth must be instilled in souls**, so that they no longer would make that choice to mate with animals, that animal mating would no longer be tolerated. The molecular structure was changed on both sides, animal and man. Animals could not conceive with a human's seed and vice versa. It may seem strange for most people that the desire to mate with an animal could even happen. It was even stranger that those animals would be drawn to mate with a female human. Nevertheless, this did happen many thousands of years ago. Animals were being animals, but then so were humans. They were in their most basic emotions, one of lust and strong sexual urges. The Father saw what was happening and knew how entrapped the souls had become. If they were ever to find a path Home, He must step in.

God then had a dilemma on His hands: how to kill off the half-animal, half-human creatures and yet keep the beautiful planet. He decided on a great flood. It was not the flood told in the Noah story; it was a great flood even before that. God had His elementals create great storms that literally dumped water from those clouds and rained almost non-stop. Most of the human-beast creatures were killed before their allotted time, as were the beasts themselves. This cleansing period did not last for just a few days. The rain was heavy, almost continuous for several months. There would be a short respite and then the rains would come again. While intermittent, the water eventually covered a great portion of the Earth. The portions that did not flood were those areas already iced and frozen over.

God then made changes in the bodies that souls would be incarnating. Never again could the human and animal energies come together and create forms that were mythical in nature, but solid in reality. Reader, keep in mind that evolution is not instantaneous. It is a long process covering thousands of years. Conversely, even with the flood, there were bodies that would still genetically hold this crossbreeding. The scientists on both Lemuria and Atlantis had established what we would term *hospitals* today. In those ancient times, the buildings where people could have their tails removed and so forth were more like laboratories. The healers were able to remove tails, repair webbed hands and toes, and hoofed feet. Even to this day, there is a bleed-through of these conditions.

People of today who are born with such defects must not condemn themselves. These bodies carry those genetics and it is a brave soul indeed who says, *I will take on that body so as to help clear that genetic line.* Conversely, some of the people **had played** the beast-human mating game. Souls were always seeking knowledge and wisdom. However, once they had ended the game, they had to clean up that karma that had occurred during their learning lifetime. The body elementals needed to evolve also; but it takes a formed body in order to do this. This dynamic is similar to alcoholism. There is lifetime after lifetime of alcoholism. It is now genetic. It takes lifetime after lifetime of sobriety to change those genetics. The same principle applies to the creature-bodies. Those body elementals needed a brave soul to allow them to form the mythical-like, deformed body in order to change those genetics. Of course, not all birth deformities are the result of creature mating. There are different reasons for those birth defects that doctors have defined well.

You see, dear Readers, there is a belief that God gave free will to humankind and never monitored it again—just let it go. That is incorrect. God definitely watches what humans are doing with their gift. If they use it to kill each other, He lets them, for death is not the end-all to Him. The people may think so, but God knows that people will just return to spirit form where the Lords of Karma will counsel them. However, when people used His free will gift to mate with beasts, He knew He must step in and make some adjustments, or He just may not see those particles of Himself ever again. Hence, from that time onward, souls' Truth level was intensified.

INITIATIONS—Djwhal Khul

I AM Djwhal Khul. I now wish to continue where I was speaking of the spiritual aspects of the Rays. Let us begin.

As one proceeds up Jacob's ladder—the initiation process—the initiations become more difficult as they become more centered on the cosmic versus the Earth plane. In the Alice Bailey book, *Initiation Human and Solar,* I wrote a book for those people either just beginning the Probationary Path, or for those still earning the first three to four initiations. The next book, *Rays and Initiations*, is for the more advanced soul. There are definitive explanations given of the initiations one through seven, but less of eight and nine.

However, the eighth and ninth initiations remain somewhat of a mystery for most people. You see, dear Readers, when one's consciousness is not in tune with those higher vibrations, it is close to impossible to make sense of any of it. Of course, one can stretch to try to understand, but it is similar to attempting calculus before one has learned algebra. It simply is not feasible. It is just common sense.

Since there are more people of the higher initiatory state on the planet than ever before, I have decided to distill some of the information—tease some of it out and put it in a way the initiate of say a three or four level can understand. First off, let me reiterate that the initiatory process is a way Home and therefore, each attainment at each level from the third to the ninth is an *Ultimate Experience* for the initiate. I highly recommend the two books I have mentioned for the serious student of esoteric studies. Since the books speak so fully of those initiations of one through the seventh, I wish to concentrate more on the eighth. I touched on some of this in the books mentioned above, but I am now attempting to bring an abstract teaching into the physical plane. That is not an easy task.

The eighth initiation is so cosmic it barely pertains to this world. I am addressing it now for there are perhaps only two dozen Beings on the planet at this time that have attained this level of consciousness. It is a study of the cosmos in its purest sense, for one literally is speaking of the Solar Logos level. Once a person has attained the sixth and especially the seventh initiation, that person is no longer tied to Earth by karma. The wheel of birth-death-rebirth has been broken. A person of those higher levels returns to Earth only for service to God. The person always has a discussion with the Father so that mutual agreements as to what needs to be done to further the Father's Plan can be made. Now that is for the sixth and seventh initiation.

Multiply that dynamic several times and you may have a slight sense of what is involved with the eighth initiation. At that stage of one's development, the person is under the control of the monad. The soul becomes similar to what the personality is to a body. The soul comes under the dominion of the monad. The monad and God meet under conditions that allow it the greatest intimacy with God that the average person cannot even fathom. The monad knows the Plan to its very core. The monad is such a part of God, the Oneness and unity, that the monad experiences no separation whatsoever. It is part of the cells of God. The monad influences the energies of souls of the lower initiatory status just by its Light presence. Its wisdom is vast. There is a huge expansion of the energies.

When an initiate of the eighth and higher levels creates a body, it will do so only for the reason of being of service while on the planet. Remember that it no longer is held by planetary lives. In this modern age, people have a more advanced level of awareness than they did fifty years ago when I wrote about the initiations. Therefore, with the rise in consciousness, people are seeking more knowledge about the initiations, what each one means and where is the individual's status in that process. Bear in mind, Reader, that these higher initiations of the fifth upward are still quite rare. The eighth and ninth are out of most people's reach in this lifetime. I will not go into comparison, but many of us Masters did not take those higher initiations until **after** we ascended and remained in our Light Body. However, there are those courageous souls who have come onto the planet at a very high degree—sixth and seventh—and have gone on to earn the eighth while still in embodiment.

What this means to the Reader is that once the soul has the **choice** to be born again or not, the task set before that soul becomes more and more difficult. The soul will purposely take on much of, say, the family karma of the past in order to help clear that line of severe illnesses, for example. Most high initiates at the seventh and eighth degree level have taken on very difficult lives. Remember, Reader, in my previous books on initiation, I have told you the difficulty at the fourth initiation, a life of trials and tribulations. So much so, it is called the *crucifixion*. Now multiply that at least by two or three times and one may have some idea of what the level of difficulty is for someone at, say, the seventh initiation.

One of the problems that these high initiates frequently encounter is there is such a lack of information for the more-evolved soul. The person seeks to find the higher knowledge in religions and in attending different groups. Eventually, the soul realizes that it is usually only by developing the ability to hear the Masters mentally that he or she will be able to learn higher knowledge and attain more wisdom. The goal is to bring Heaven to Earth—as above so below.

People of the eighth degree of initiation do not feel much different while in body from those of the lower levels of attainment. They have a great sense of dedication toward any task they take on. They will persevere and rarely give up. I say *rarely* for it would be more from a health issue or some such circumstance that could cause the initiate to put a project on hold. It is common for the higher initiates to accomplish more in their later years, their senior years. The years leading up to that time would be devoted to life and its problems and the embracing again of all the previous initiations from other lifetimes.

You see, Reader, there is never a complete cessation of any of the initiations. If one earned initiation 2 in a previous lifetime, the next lifetime will be about embracing all that entails not only the second initiation but also the first as well. This must be done and integrated before proceeding to the third. Now take an initiate at the seventh level. In times past such a person would be finished with Earth-lives, as I have said. However, with the planet reaching for her own higher dimensions, high degree initiates are incarnating more and giving of themselves in service to help Earth achieve her goals.

Therefore, do you not see how a soul at the seventh degree must excel and keep forging ahead in order to touch again and integrate **all** seven of those previous initiations? Usually, it will take a high initiate most of a lifetime problem solving many tasks before it is **allowed** to move forward and earn the eighth initiation, for each level must be integrated before proceeding forward. After that, there are sublevels that the soul earns before reaching the ninth. Therefore, we say a soul is an 8.2 or an 8.3, meaning it has earned the eighth initiation and has completed two or three of the sublevels. The sublevels can be subtle. Consequently, one is not always aware that another step up Jacob's ladder has occurred.

Since these higher initiations address the cosmic realms, they are quite abstract in nature. When I say that an eighth degree initiate on a soul level is in the energy center of the planetary Logos, this concept is out of the reality of most people. Suffice to say, one really does not need to know all that is happening in the monad's domain, for the person is being guided now by his/her *I AM Presence.*

COMPASSION—Jesus

I AM Jesus. There have been times throughout history where *compassion* was sadly lacking in the hearts of humankind. Many people of that era had little heart energy of pure love, therefore, little compassion. I would define *compassion* as the pure energy that emanates from pure *love*. It is the ability to empathize with someone you, Reader, may not agree with. It means you can allow the person to have whatever belief system he or she wishes; but you acknowledge also the fact that the person may be in some emotional place that is quite painful. This need not necessarily be from a death in the family. It could be because the person is unemployed or is homeless. These are painful conditions for the human Being. It requires consciousness on your part to be compassionate and not judgmental.

In the past eras, most people did not have the ability to be compassionate, for they did not love in the purest sense. You see, Reader, *compassion*, *empathy*, and you can add *caring* to this mix, are all part of the equation of *love*. There has been much written about *love* and *hate* being of the same coin. This is not true; but *compassion*, *empathy,* and *caring* are all faces of *love*. I would say in your present history, in your everyday lives, *compassion* is one of the least understood and most undervalued commodities in your lives. Without this feeling, one cannot be spiritually complete.

Our Spiritual Worlds are engulfed in this energy. It is a state of Being. It is so much a part of us that it takes no effort or thought on our part to be compassionate. Most people have illusions about the Spiritual Worlds—the Heavens. People are apt to think we are without any problems whatsoever. Dear Readers, problem solving is growth. We in our world are ever striving for higher initiations and growth. We take on assignments that would amaze most of you if you but knew the complexities involved. We watch the struggle of our Brothers and Sisters as they solve these complex problems. Moreover, solve them they do. However, on Earth, the struggle and perseverance to achieve a particular result can be overwhelming to the average person. We stand ever ready to help when we are asked. Compassion just pours forth from us, for we have all been in identical situations. We do not judge our fellow Brothers and Sisters. We simply pour our love and compassion out to them.

Therefore, Readers, *compassion* is a facet of *love* that must be awakened. People wonder why the lessons are so difficult at times on schoolhouse Earth. It is quite simple. **Souls ask for these lessons**. I hope you take this into your hearts and consciousness.

People ask the Father to take away a particular hardship. One could say that the soul is having a difficult lesson, for again, you, Reader, are getting the lesson you have asked for and have created. However, God does hear your prayers. Always! He then uses His discernment to ascertain whether the soul has truly learned the lesson it has asked for or not. If the soul has learned it quickly, the hardship is lifted, and the person finds his/her life's problem being resolved.

Have you noticed an increase in identity theft lately? Is it not amazing that the soul has created this particular lesson where one's whole identity can be stolen? The heartache that is involved as people see the invasion of their personal history and the disappearance of their financial assets is horrendous. Do you not see how that dynamic of *compassion* for one's relative or friend can develop? There is an interesting fact that when one sees a person suffer from some adversity, one may start to worry that the same thing could happen to him/her. *Compassion* starts to awaken in people. It is a domino effect, which tends to fan out to those identity-robbed people. Identity theft is a profound experience and more and more souls are opting to experience this phenomenon.

There is a grave situation that also needs addressing. It has to do with the soul's inability to release the body even when it no longer has one. Take this scenario. A person has lived a full and productive life. He or she, we will say "he," has been so busy throughout his life that he has tended not to do his personal homework. He had children; however, he had become estranged from some of them for various reasons. He had a good mind and was well educated. He owned a house to which he was much attached. He studied spiritual works and learned modalities that he used in association with many people. As he turned to his inner work, he developed his energy centers and could read other people's energies and auras. He had been married several times. He ended cycle with them through divorce and continued his life. He, himself, was in therapy, always seeking to know the *why* of things. He was familiar with some of the Masters and had read many new age books.

As he grew older and was into his sunset years, he did not resolve many family issues that had come up. Instead, he drifted from some of his children, as well as relatives. He knew he ought to make an effort to reconcile with his children; but he kept putting it off. Eventually his body started dying, for it was his time to leave the Earth plane. It is not important to know from what at this time. What is important is that he kept justifying why he did not contact relatives in order to take care of his unfinished business. He just kept putting it off and not putting too much effort into the thought his guides were bringing to his attention. He kept thinking he would have more time before he died, as he procrastinated day after day.

Well, dear Readers, he died with a great deal of unfinished business. However, the fact he had not brought resolution to his affairs affected him in such a profound way. I will say this very clearly. **He died and did not know he was dead!** He stayed in his house, a little confused, but for him he thought his life continued. He was cremated and still he did not believe he was dead. There was a beautiful memorial for him two weeks later where many friends of his past and relatives paid eulogies to him. However, he was living an illusion to the grossest degree. He had many Beings around him that allowed him his illusion. Readers, please bear in mind how serious this is. I am telling you a true story that is repeated many times around the world.

How sad it indeed is when a soul cannot detach and make that journey back to God. He will eventually awaken to the fact he has died, but what I am stressing is the importance of being able to release—to release your children and all of your belongings. You have heard so often that you cannot take it with you. Now add another dimension to that and know you cannot leave your world unless you are detached from it! You must let go of the material life and turn to your spiritual life—*the inner life.*

The purpose of this true story I have been telling you is to bring awareness to people, to break up another myth that one goes straight to Heaven after one dies. That happens when the soul is not veiled in illusion, attachment, and possession. I strongly urge you to give this little story some great thought. If you are estranged from your children, relatives, friends, business associates, now is the time to reach out with forgiveness in your heart. Remember *forgiveness* is a two-way street. You must have forgiveness in your heart for yourself, before you can forgive others. The soul in my example came to realize eventually that he had indeed died. With that acceptance and with great caring from all the Beings around him, he did make the successful transition.

I have put this story of not realizing you are dead purposely in this chapter on COMPASSION. It takes a great deal of compassion in order to forgive. If you hear of a soul that has not been released from its life and still thinks it is alive, even after being cremated, send *love*, and feel great compassion for that soul. People who are therapists and mental health workers often hear stories from people in grief. They tell of a dead spouse, perhaps, who is still much present. The spouse might even be seen. These souls have not been able to make the proper exit. They either have left their affairs in a mess or were attached to someone or something. Be aware of this phenomenon, dear ones. So many people are not being told the truth from their spiritual advisors. It does no service to the bereaved to tell them the deceased is already with Jesus. Unless they have detached themselves in the true sense, I have not seen them! One can be a Born-again Christian, but if he or she cannot release possessions, that transition can be a long and arduous one. You must do your part in your death. No one can do it for you.

Heed this myth, that all deaths are great releases for the soul, who can rush right Home after death. The soul has a great deal of work to do. Dying **is** work; the letting go and forgiveness need to be addressed. Also, please note I am not implying that all deaths are *failures*. Most are quite beautiful. However, toss out that myth about all deaths are a perfect release for the soul. They are not always. The soul must have enough awareness in order to detach and come Home. Only then is it the *Ultimate Experience.* Hold compassion in your hearts for the soul who is oblivious of having died and still clings to Earth's hEarth and home.

DESIRES—Jesus

I AM Jesus. Readers, have you ever given thought as to **what creates a desire?** There are many kinds of *desires*. The obvious ones are wealth, employment, good health, friends, lovers, and family. Nevertheless, what actually creates a *desire*?

As the soul evolves, it must learn certain lessons. One of those lessons is how to control one's desires, for there are varying degrees of a desire. Some people desire little out of life, while others wish for all that Heaven allows. **Desires are a manifestation of the soul's thoughts and actions.** If the soul desires a house, the soul will create a job that will create the money to buy the house. You take action on what you think you want. Desires can escalate one's ambitions, one's perseverance, to bring the desired object into fruition. Therefore, to backtrack, the soul thinks about something. It decides it wants this, needs that, or covets this. The energy of repetitious thought creates a thought-form. Now a living energy is formed. It carries such a form of thought that a person who can read energies will be able to see this form in the shape of a house for example. The thought-form increases in size as one puts more and more thought into it. However, this does **not create** a desire.

Would it surprise you, Reader, to know that much of what you desire was already given to you before you were born? Everything you have won in a lottery, everything of substance like a house and car are given you before you were a day old. **You** brought in what you would desire. Therefore, what actually creates a desire is your **memory** of what you had already received in those dimensions before you were born. Now, in the physical, it is up to the soul to make the desired object manifest. For example, you, as a soul, talk over your next life with your Teachers and conclude as to what you are to have. There are even movie monitors that show you what you are to manifest on Earth. The rest is up to you. **The desire stems from the memory of what has already been given you.** As you mature in your Earth-life you have chosen, you awaken the memory by seeing people around you having a car, house, family and so forth.

This sparks the memory in you that allows your desire to come forth in a concrete form.

However, many times obstacles are put in the way of a person's attempting to make the desired object manifest. This is where growth will either hinder you or advance you. How you create your desire is all-important. I am sure you have heard that it is not the object you attained, but **how** you obtained it. The process of obtaining the desired object is wherein the learning lies.

Humanity does not have a full grasp of how to manifest a *desire*. The danger arises when the person starts to covet an object versus wanting something he can manifest through perseverance and many times hard work on its own. When someone covets an object, the person is not willing to work for it. In other words, why do you think so many cars are stolen? For a thief, it is easier to steal one, more thrilling, than to work long hours and buy one. Humanity many times would prefer everything given to it free and without any struggle on its part. However, where is the growth potential in that? Moreover, when he changes the dynamic and covets the object, he has polluted the energies and the object does not manifest in a clean way. The person finds himself in jail instead.

As the awareness of people raises, you will see, Readers, the desires of people will increase. You have been told by Evangelists many times that one's abundance is guaranteed in Heaven. One just has to sow a seed in order to reap that Harvest. Well, there certainly is Truth in that concept. However, I would add another element to that. When a person truly desires something, the person must not only realize he or she already has the object waiting to manifest, but the person needs to make some effort toward obtaining that object over and above sowing a monetary seed. One must walk toward that desire. If one desires a house, one has to awaken the memory of the house the person can obtain. Hence, one must walk towards that house by looking at houses, pricing houses, and finding in what neighborhood one wants that house to be. In addition, one must *work* towards it.

To reiterate, one makes manifest by **doing**. The desire is created by the **memory** of what already has been given before birth. Once the memory has been activated, one must start the manifesting process by actually doing something that eventually will bring the desired object into fruition. This does not mean by theft, for if one chooses that way to create what one needs or wants, one is bringing forth an entirely different form of manifestation. Theft is a unique dynamic in itself. Since souls strive for experience and wisdom in every facet of Earth-life, there are times when a soul will choose a lifetime as a thief. Remember that saying, *Rich man, poor man, beggar man, **thief*** . . . souls do take on all of those roles in order to gain growth and wisdom. However, I am not referring to that particular life's dynamic. I am referring to when a soul steps off the path of goodness and tries to obtain something it has not earned. Stealing a house is a little harder to do, but it can be done by stealing a person's inheritance or cheating someone just because the person is naïve about legal matters.

Therefore, while a desire to make something manifest seems easy enough, it is **how** it is manifested that provides the soul not only the object, but also the karmic lesson that goes with it. I urge you **not** to covet another's material objects. You have your own gifts just waiting for you to remember. Writing this book is, as the saying goes, *walking the talk.* The author knew she would some day write a book. The memory was activated. The desired object is being made manifest now. The only way for a desired book to be made manifest is to write one! You see, readers, it is in the **doing** that brings all your desire to fruition.

JOY versus PLEASURE—Maitreya

I AM Maitreya. I am known as your World Teacher and Christ. I have come today in order to tell you about Earth's joy for a soul, versus pleasures created by ego.

On Earth there is so much that can bring pleasure to the personality and body. However, have you ever noticed, Readers, what was pleasure a short time ago either has now dissipated or no longer delights you? In that category fall most relationships whether they are in the category of friends, lovers, marriage, and or business partners. Something has happened to cause a ripple of discontent in that relationship.

On the other hand, if the effect one experiences is one of joy, the effect does not dissipate, but merely ripens. In days of lore, most of humanity sought survival and, if pleasure was possible, so much the better. However, pleasure for a Victorian orphan or street urchin was hard to come by, let alone to find joy. Pleasure was finding food in another's garbage. Pleasure was being warm in winter. The souls that chose those lives to experience often died early. The suffering was too intense. They came into the urchin's body, experienced the extreme poverty, and most often, lack of joy of any kind. Those lives terminated early on purpose. The soul had *gotten the picture*, as the saying goes. Therefore, the souls terminated at the first opportunity.

You see, Readers, there are usually several *windows of opportunity* in order for a soul to have the choice to go through the window and make that transition from death of the body or not. Now one would expect there to be great joy for the soul for having had the courage to ask for an experience of a poverty-type of lifetime. Nevertheless, it may not surprise you to know that not all souls experience joy then. Many souls find that when they have their life's review, there is still unfinished business, even for that urchin's lifetime. Hence, the soul requests to come back and experience another facet of that game plan. Therefore, where there ought to be joy in what was accomplished, the soul is not joyful, but more determined than ever to try again—to have another lifetime with similar circumstances.

Pleasure is a dynamic of the personality, the little ego. The person is frequently seeking what will bring it pleasure. It is an **external** dynamic, for it must feed the me, me, and me of the ego. Most people are able to name what brings them the fleeting *pleasure*: entertainment of some kind, usually movies. Alternatively, pleasure can be found watching Broadway shows or sports of all kinds. Racecar events bring pleasure to many people who take their pleasure in tragic car crashes. They may feel terrible for the persons involved, but for these spectators, there is a thrill watching cars careen off walls with other cars jamming into them.

Many people seek pleasure in the gaming houses where there are cities that cater to that degree of pleasure; Las Vegas and Atlantic City come to mind. There are people who seek pleasure in shopping, buying what they do not need, but wanting merely to experience the few moments of fleeting pleasures, as in buying another pair of designer shoes. I believe the term that is used is, *Must-haves*. That dress is a *must-have*. They walk out a while later with more charges on their plastic cards and with less in their pockets. Was the fleeting pleasure worth it when reality strikes with the large credit card bill they now are facing? I am sure you, Readers, can name even more pleasures than I have stated.

Now in the same vein, let us discuss *joy*. **Joy is a soul dynamic and therefore internal.** It is always with you and is not fleeting. You may experience facets of joy, bits and pieces, but it stays with you. Take watching a sunset or sunrise. Seeing the magnificent shades of colors disappear one evening and appear the next morning (if the clouds have not hidden the sun) brings great joy to the soul. It stirs the memory of the magnificence of the energies one sees in the Heavens.

One may make the argument that joy does not always seem permanent. However, one remembers that joyful feeling that incorporates peace and reverence when watching the sunset or sunrise. The joy a mother experiences when she first sees and holds her newborn baby is a permanent memory that is elicited every time she sees another's baby. Can you, Reader, feel that pleasure you felt over your new pair of shoes? Yes, there is a memory. However, can you recapture the feeling of it—the pleasure? No, you cannot. You can fantasize the pleasure; but it is an illusion. Joy on the other hand comes forward in memory and you again recall the beauty of the moment in all of its nuances.

Therefore, dear Readers, ask the question of whether you are seeking *Pleasure* or manifesting *Joy*. Let this questioning strengthen not only your discernment, but also your resolve. Resolve to bring joy into your life and not always bring just pleasure. **Joy is a component of the soul**. Each time you acknowledge joy, you are acknowledging soul. This exercise helps bring you closer to you in the body. Differentiate between *Joy* and *Pleasure*. You are then well on your way of walking your path.

MARRIAGE and DIVORCE—Jesus

I AM Jesus. It is often preached and implied that divorce and second marriages are disfavored in the Eyes of God. Readers, as time marches on, so must the teachings evolve. In the past, people were told they had to marry their brother's wife if he had died. There were genealogical reasons for this and for staying married. It was to keep the bloodline intact and pure as much as possible. Eventually, people branched out further and married cousins, which perpetuated not only the strengths of the family tree, but also the weaknesses.

Every body-structure that is created carries a genetic weakness. It is just the way of things. Therefore, people soon came to realize a particular family stock generated the same illnesses repeatedly, throughout the ages. Eventually, suitors did branch out and marry into different bloodlines. They also divorced.

The point of telling you this is to bring to your attention that a marriage is **not** always expected to be forever! I know this statement will be very unpopular with Evangelists, for they frown upon *divorce.* However, if one puts this in the perspective of a soul's evolution, the dynamics of one-marriage changes. What Evangelists teach is that two people marry *'til death do us part.* Maybe that is indeed true for that couple (*but it does not **have** to be so).*

However, for another couple, they are to marry and have children, bring in the souls for which they contracted, and then divorce. It is called, *Ending Cycle*. Souls come together on the Earth plane according to a carefully laid out game plan with the soul who has agreed to this play before he or she is born. There is a contract even, although it is not always completely binding.

If souls have had many lifetimes together working out various lessons in developing a relationship, and they have learned all they need to have learned, they are encouraged then to say *Goodbye.* Now even in the ending of cycles there are lessons. Many people decide to end cycle by death. In the next lifetime, they will contract with a new partner. Other souls ask for the lesson, which involves *divorce.* What an emotional rollercoaster that lesson can be!

Do you see, Readers, where divorces can elicit many kinds of emotional reactions and thus learning lessons? One of the partners may have more awareness. Therefore, he or she understands the spiritual dynamic of *ending cycle*. The other spouse, perhaps now the ex-spouse, is full of outrage that this could be happening to him or her. Divorce is a severe lesson to learn, but one the soul chooses in order to gain wisdom on this complex dynamic.

Now here is a thought. Do you not think if a game plan was adopted by two souls for their reincarnations that they would not have another game plan that is to follow after the first one was completed? Do you not think that after divorce the two people could go their separate paths? Do you not think that eventually one or both of the former spouses would find the next soul they had contracted with, fall in love, and marry again? Some souls contract for two or more marriages. However, there can be multiple marriages, which were not contracted. The souls were to meet in this lifetime and then end cycle—end the relationship **before** a marriage takes place and not keep marrying every karmic tie.

The Mormon religion contracts marriage for life. I am not going to call them *wrong*. That is just one of numerous game plans the soul can choose for a lifetime. However, neither is to say a Born-again Christian wrong for divorcing a spouse. Those souls have learned their lessons, are following their game plan, and are ready to move on. God gives everyone free will, as you know. He does not judge them for exercising that will, nor would He judge them for divorcing. How God experiences life is through you. You experience divorce and so does He, for you and He are One.

What is hurtful is when the less aware person makes a judgment on a divorced person. Religious leaders are in error when well-meaning souls place guilt on one another for not remaining married. The divorced person not only has the emotional vicissitudes associated with divorce but must now withstand the worst of misplaced recriminations from relatives and spiritual counselors.

Relationships are complex. Some are meant to be experienced for a whole lifetime. Other relationships are meant to close. New relationships are to be developed. People who expound on one particular concept, without memory of the spiritual world and its varied contracts and experiences offered to the souls, are walking a narrow path indeed. There are very few *constants* in life. One marriage with no divorce certainly is **not** a constant. It can be a beautiful choice if that is the souls' contract. However, please do not judge those who do divorce and remarry. They too are following their path and honoring their agreements.

God does bless a marriage. However, He also blesses the soul who keeps growing, experiencing all facets of life, and is courageous enough to divorce his/her partner in order to keep evolving, if that was the pre-life agreement. Therefore, dear Readers, do not feel guilty over a divorce if you feel it is the correct choice. Even if the opposing spouse has an affair and you feel you must take action, if you know in your heart that this is correct, let the marriage go. Allow yourself the grieving process, which certainly must include a thorough soul searching of the part you played. How could you have reacted in a more correct way perhaps? Always ask yourself for the correct way to proceed. Ask for your inner I AM guidance. Seek professional help from a therapist. The reason for all of this introspection is so that you may understand fully your actions in the play. In order to remarry and have a new relationship at a higher level, one must address the previous circumstances that led to the divorce. If you allow your awareness to open fully and embrace the fact that your first marriage was a contract that had a termination date on it, you may find you are able to move through your lesson with fewer traumas more quickly. The choice is always yours.

God will bless your second marriage as He did the first one. Keep in mind He does not judge you. If you feel guilt from your decisions to divorce and later re-marry, it is **you** judging you. Let that all go before you start the next phase of your lesson and activate another contract with your new partner. It is called *evolution of the soul.*

(Many times a person does not do his/her inner work and then draws to him/her an exact replica of the spouse that was left behind. One sees this played out repeatedly in alcoholic and in other abusive relationships. 2011)

TRANSITIONS—Jesus

I AM Jesus. I come to speak on that great journey, *death.* Throughout the ages, the death experience has been discussed. There have been séances in order to contact the dead. There have been philosophical debates about the death of the body and the hereafter for the soul. Death is a transition from one dimension to the next for the soul. If one takes an Earth-life, the body must die in order to end cycle with that lifetime and its lessons.

Always keep in mind, Readers, that death in itself is not some horrible fate. It is as natural a process as birth is. In fact, the soul finds it much easier to die and leave the body than to be born into one. Imagine how traumatic a birth can be for the soul. It is leaving a Heavenly place and taking on what could be a long, arduous, and most likely a painful life. The soul has been well instructed by its Teachers, guides, and angels. There even are farewell parties of sorts, where the soul is wished well and experiences much love before it departs.

Imagine the impact upon the soul when it is born and remembers little of its Heaven and has chosen parents for various reasons who do not particularly love the child. *What a difference a day makes*, I believe is one of your songs. The soul then completes its lessons and now it is time for the body's death and the soul's return Home. There is a long process in the release of the body and detachment of all of its energy cords. The soul sees the Light, goes through what you perceive to be the tunnel, and is met by loved ones. That is a good case scenario and one that really is more the norm these days.

Conversely, there is the soul that has come to its time of transition. However, while it may slip out of the body easily enough, the transition was so quick that the soul literally does not know it has died. Such was the case in point in the Compassion chapter. There are various reasons why a soul does not know it has died. One of the most common is if there is an accident of some kind. (**Keep in mind there are truly no accidents. All is planned**.) The body's silver cord to the Oversoul has been severed. In such cases, the soul goes merrily on its way, not realizing an automobile has run over its body while out jogging.

In cases of these kinds of sudden "accidental" deaths, help for the soul is immediate. The guardian angel, guides and Teachers are there stabilizing the astral body and helping it through the tunnel where it will receive healing help. You might be wondering what happens during vicious deaths—murders for example. Again, the soul has set this in motion, but that kind of death of the body presents a different set of circumstances for the soul. Many times in "accidental" or vicious deaths of the body, the soul is ejected from the body before the actual act has happened. The soul's Teacher has helped release the soul, pulled it out so to speak, the instant before the "accident" or vicious death has occurred.

Readers, keep in mind that, as varied as there are deaths, so the soul's experience of the release is just as varied. Remember my saying that you need help in going Home. With all of the ways to die and to make one's transition to the Heavenlies, is it any wonder that indeed you do need help? In addition, while one's spirit-guides wish to help, they are not always allowed to. Ah, yes, free will. Would it surprise you to know that even in death you have free will? In the example in the Compassion chapter, it is **because** of free will that the loving Beings watching over the soul that still thinks it is alive could do little but watch. It is the soul's task using its free will to recognize that he is in a different dimension and he has indeed died.

Therefore, what I am imparting to you is that one's free will also will determine one's death and transition. Dead or alive—only the soul can answer that question. He has only to question this fact and then one's guides can step in to help him or her to move on.

(Many times Earth's benevolent Space Brothers and Sisters whisk the soul out and up when the pending death is violent. Case in point was the series of violent storms in Tornado Alley this spring of 2011. Many of those souls were brought aboard one of the ships.

As we approach closer to 2012 and the Ascension, the Teachers are instructing us that a body no longer has to die. ***We can ascend with our bodies, breaking that karmic wheel of birth and re-birth****. 2011)*

EQUALITY—Jesus

I AM Jesus. In the past, humanity worshipped many different religions. There were the Eastern traditions, Islam for one. The Jews had their Hebrew writings; American Indians of ancient times worshipped the One Spirit and their power animals. Over two thousand years ago, I, known as Jesus throughout history, formed what was called *Christianity*. Of course the name was a play on words—the word *Christ*. I had come to Earth for several reasons, but one of prime importance was to bring humanity the concept of *brotherly love*. Dear Readers, if you could but picture how humankind was so limited in their thinking way back then!

The majority of people all over the world paid little attention to connecting with their soul, let alone with God. If people were of the groups I have already mentioned, they followed the dictates of their spiritual leaders. However, cheating and lying were rampant. People's consciousness just could not rise above their bodily needs and wants. There was such a class distinction in all the religions that people were not given an incentive to raise themselves to a higher stratum.

In the new religion of long ago, I taught of *love* and *equality of people*, no matter what sex they were, or in what trade they were. One of the reasons I chose my disciples as I did was to show people that fishermen were as equal as the educated and privileged Judas was. Of course, they did not know they were chosen before their births. There was jealousy and a shuffling to try to become the one chosen by me as my confidant. I played no favorites. All were equal in my heart. However, there were times I chose the disciples for different tasks, as one could be more suited for various reasons over another.

I taught them by example. My Mary played a larger part in educating the Twelve than history portrays her. I allowed her to be as much a part of our gatherings as was possible. I use the term *allowed* to illustrate the choice was hers to be equal. When you *allow* someone to do something, it means you have given your permission for something to take place.

In those Biblical times, women would be waiting on the men. They would not be sitting at the men's table. History has portrayed just the twelve at the Last Supper. My Mary, as well as my mother, sat at our table. They were my anchors. They carried such Light that they sustained me and brought a balance to the table.

Christianity, unfortunately, has not carried that lesson I provided—the equality of women—by having them at the Last Supper. In the Catholic religion in particular, I still see inequality. The men are a group in themselves with a priest hearing nuns' confessions and *prescribing* what to do, how many prayers to say and when to say them. Sadly, the concept of Christianity having equality for all seems to be lacking.

As the new Christian religion grew and developed, the spiritual leaders or priests became more power hungry. They liked having control over the people. They liked the extraordinary wealth they accrued. They liked sipping their wine out of the gold goblets. There has been so much written about finding the chalice, and that the original is buried safely away. That is total fabrication. There is no cup. However, the myth creates a lovely fairy tale as people search everywhere for it. Nevertheless, interestingly enough, what would they do if they found it? Fight over it, murder over it, hoard it, or sell it for billions of dollars? There seems to be a character flaw in many people. ***They covet the unattainable.*** In addition, if by any remote chance they do obtain their object, it brings out the worst in them. Greed and hoarding seem to lurk in their shadows.

Therefore, dear Readers, use the **symbol** of the Holy Grail. Let it represent the seeking of your soul. Let it represent the attainment of your Oneness with God, for many do not know they are already One with Him. Let the Holy Cup represent drinking in Life. Keep your cup half-full, never half-empty. As I sipped the wine representing my blood, I had an inner vision of blood running down the hillside. As it passed over the barren land, flowers sprang forth and I knew that the spilling of my blood would also bring life in the form of a new religion; one that forgave people for their sins and shortcomings; one that taught equality for all. As I looked upon my beloved family that last night, I knew it was finished. I had accomplished what I had come to Earth to do.

I will leave you now, Readers, to ponder this. While Christianity has had many growing pains, it has provided *a path* to God. It has given *hope* to people. It has given examples how to teach *loving thy neighbor*. As with any new teachings, it was truly a gift for humanity. It was given in its purity from God. With the foibles of humankind, much of Christianity has lost its purity. It has decayed. In the next century or so, you will find Christianity will undergo a complete metamorphosis. All great philosophies need such a change in order to die out, or to re-establish a more pure teaching.

RAYS and TRUTH—Djwhal Khul

I AM Djwhal Khul. I greet you, Readers, once more. I last left you with a description of my ascension, my *Ultimate Experience* that indeed led me right to God. I am now going to address some areas of great importance. People of the New Age have read about the various Rays and their significance. They may refresh their memories in my writings in the Alice Bailey book, *Rays and Initiations.* I wish now to impart further information about the energy of rays.

The soul during its evolution will take on the different ray energies to experience the particular dynamic of that energy essence. As the body, mental body, and personality develop, each of those parts also has a dominant ray. Think of it as holding different positions on a chessboard. One move you are a knight, a queen, and a king and so forth. Each lifetime you had the ray that you chose to experience and would influence you physically, mentally, personality wise and spiritually. What is little known is that as the soul and its body aspects take on these energies, the **rays' influences propel the soul upward in development.** If one did not have these rays to influence them, there would be stagnation. The flowing energies of the rays keep the soul and its body aspects moving.

How often has one seen a person not moving forward much during his life cycle? There is such stagnation, for the energies of the rays are no longer flowing. The person has taken a downward spiral. Keep in mind that the rays are dualistic in nature. They hold the glorious positive pole as well as the lowest end of that energy dynamic. If one is familiar with the ray, one can spot what aspect of a person is off-kilter. I cannot emphasize enough how important these rays are.

The world is moving into the fifth dimension. The ray influence will be even more pronounced. The aspects of the soul and body will change rays repeatedly, before settling on the dominant three. When a person's monad and soul settle on a particular ray, it conveys that there have been eons of time and many lifetimes of learning before choosing the ray that will be dominant and will blend the most with whom that person truly is.

The more evolved the soul is, the more pure the energies, which enables the soul to move into the domain of pure *light, truth* and *love*. If a soul has not developed these attributes, the soul cannot advance. It is so important for people to realize that not only *love*, but also *truth* becomes one of the main ingredients for returning Home to the Father. There are many paths to God, but one of the highest other than *love* is the level of *truth* that a soul holds.

When a person is in the physical, one is taught not to tell a lie, but we are speaking way beyond that. Most people know that there are many ways to be untruthful—not to admit one does not agree at a board meeting is an example. The person just goes along with what someone else has said. Once you do not express your opinion, you too are part of the lie. Silence is one of the biggest lie-makers that exists. As with most of the dynamics on Earth, there are poles of duality. Silence can be positive when one is not being a constant chatterbox or has nothing constructive to say. However, silence, when a lie has been put out there in the work force, is acquiescence—and can be entrapping.

Throughout a soul's development, it evolves and becomes less dense because it has worked through that evolution of lies. In the spiritual realm, a lie clouds the energies of the soul. As it makes its progress forward, however, its energy lightens and becomes more fluid, more etheric, like a rainbow. The soul is so full of Light and so pure and free of lie-energy, that it becomes more diaphanous. The more evolved the soul becomes, the less it can be seen in the lower dimensions of the spiritual world. Is not that a revelation? The higher-evolved souls are so full of *truth* that their Light becomes brilliant. There is no form. In the highest dimensions, one only can see the Eyes. Therefore, obtaining the purity of energies **is** one of the paths to God. Just because someone has died and is in the astral planes, it does not necessarily mean that soul can perceive the higher souls. It sees only at its own level or lower, never higher, unless the great masters choose to step down their energies and show them. The higher always can see the lower. It cannot be in reverse—not the lower seeing the higher—only if the masters wish to be seen.

I have told you that the Rays are a pathway to God, and that *truth* is yet another one. *Love* also is a pathway to God. Keep in mind about duality. Love has many faces that humankind has put on it.

We say that *love* is a constant. Humankind has distorted its purity in jealous love, lustful love, possessive love, cheating love, cruel love, and revengeful love. People have put these distorted faces onto love. However, *love* in its purest sense is God. Since God is not all of those negative connotations, *love* cannot be them either. Humankind has taken the pure energy of *love*, defiled *love*, and made *love* lesser. Dear, Readers, always keep in mind that whatever you call *love* with a negative connotation, it is **you** caught up in the lower emotions. It is not *love*, for it is not God. It is that simple.

ABUSED and ABUSER—Jesus

I AM Jesus. The abused child is never a subject people like to address. However, with the rising incidents of sexual abuse, pornography, and child neglect, it is time to bring these abominations more into the people's awareness. Television news reports those of the grossest incidents of deliberate starvation, severe isolation, with children locked in closets and children sexually exploited on the Internet. However, more subtle abuse does not make the news. These abuses are usually perpetrated by family members. I do not need to give you examples. You know who you are, whether the abused or the abuser.

This is not a pleasant topic, but it is one of which we in the Spiritual Realms are very much aware. Readers, these dynamics of abuse are also part of your life's lesson, the play to which you have agreed before you were born. I know this can be hurtful for many of you Readers, especially those who have been abused. I can only repeat this is **your** play. You wrote the script.

However, did the contract state to what extreme the abuse was to be? It did not. The soul may have agreed to the isolation, starving even, but it did not agree to the severity or duration of the sexual abuse. The perpetrator was to maintain some restraint. The game was not to kill the person—not this game anyway. The person was not agreeing to murder. Nevertheless, when infants are abused far beyond what their bodies can tolerate and then die from the consequences, a game has gotten out of hand.

People, I know this is a most difficult lesson and if you are hearing it for the first time, this concept of a pre-birth agreement becomes overwhelming. Allow me to bring some sanity to such a suggestion. Keep in mind, rarely with any circumstance that occurs is it the first lifetime to do so. Souls play out a whole spectrum of activities concerning one dynamic. Say this dynamic is sexual abuse. Now go back several lifetimes that could encompass hundreds of years. Take one of those ancient lifetimes and know that you may have been the perpetrator, the *pedophile*. What do you think will be your role in this new play if you were the pedophile of ancient times? Sadly to say, it will be to be the child being abused by a pedophile playing the same game you played in varying degrees hundreds of years ago.

You may be wondering at such a phenomenon. It is an agreement you have made for retribution or karmic debt. I am sure you have heard of *Cause* and *Effect* for what you have caused to happen, at some time you must be the effect of the happenstance. You see, dear Reader, even though souls ask for these learning lessons, the severity is up to the souls, the participants. The person's free will causes the severity. Incest really is in the same category as murder, to my mind. Sexual abuse can be so damaging to a personality that that person may never come out of it in a whole way. Many times the abused person will wish he or she were dead. In most cases the person rarely is whole, and there can be much fragmentation of the personality resulting in what psychology specifies as *Multiple Personalities—Multiples.* Such is the risk when a soul takes on sexual abuse as a lesson in order to advance the soul in wisdom.

Therefore, dear Readers, know that these kinds of lessons are not condoned by God. However, He does allow them in order for the soul to address his/her karmic piece and to gain wisdom. Remember that this is schoolhouse-Earth and the lessons are not always of a desirable nature. Just keep in mind, an extreme case of child abuse was the perpetrator's free will that carried the act to the extreme, even if the abused had agreed to the play. There are correct ways to carry out an agreement for a karmic debt or lesson. However to lock a child in a closet or small room with no food or water and let the child lie in excrement for long periods is beyond what was contracted. The perpetrator(s) has stepped over the line into evil. People in these kinds of categories will no longer be allowed to play out those evil games. Whether they will be able to have a life on Earth again is doubtful. Since the Earth is evolving, these lower types of games will no longer be tolerated on the planet.

HOPE—Jesus

I AM Jesus. Dear Readers, as I come to you this glorious sunny day in Arizona, there are people in other parts of America who have awakened to a typical winter day. It is gloomy, overcast, and cold, and there could be ice and snow on the ground. People look out the window and may growl aloud, especially if they are elderly and their joints are aching in protest to the cold air that seeps in through the window sashes. Some may think, *I can hardly wait until spring, so I can feel warm again and see flowers, and green leaves, instead of the dead leaves on the trees.* When people express a desire for better conditions in their environment, they are using the energy of *hope.*

There is that term—*hope springs eternal.* In addition, indeed it does for those who will reach out for it. We have spoken about the gifts from God. *Hope* is another one. It is an actual band of energy into which one must tap. You must go to it. *Hope* does not come to you unless you instigate the feeling for it. All people deserve to receive *hope*. There are aspects in the nature of *hope*, such as a *knowing* that there will be a *change* of some kind; knowing the change will be of a *positive* kind; knowing that *hope* will bring *joy*; knowing that our *prayer* for something *has been heard* and *will be answered.* These are all aspects of *hope.*

God created this beautiful energy for His people. He knew there would be difficult tasks to perform on Earth. There needed to be an energy that people could tap into that would help them persevere and finish their particular endeavors. He knew as the people experienced the many illnesses they would encounter, they needed an energy that would help in their healing process. Many times unaware physicians give out their diagnoses without providing an element of *hope*. The patient hears only the worse and gives up on his/her healing process. As soon as the person believes there is no *hope,* the life ends.

Readers, be aware when a person dies, or some like the term, *makes a transition,* some even say *graduates*— whatever their special term is for the death of the body and continuation of the soul—there is *hope* in abundance for the soul. There is *hope* that the soul has an unencumbered death or crossing, that the busyness is truly finished, whether a sudden death or not. There is always the *hope* that the soul of that person will go into the arms of its loved ones and will be with God or whatever the person's religious belief is. *Hope* is also a part of dying, you see, for there are many facets or layers in that energy band.

Sometimes patients create a learning lesson for themselves where they must tap into *hope* and bring it into their life to help sustain them through a difficult time. People who have experienced a death of a child or spouse suffer greatly. They lose *hope* that there will be a positive change for their future. After their period of mourning, people will have new babies, or marriages, or will be led to give more of their time to others. Keep in mind that humanity will have its lessons and will follow its game plans. However, it is through *hope* that many of their trials and tribulations can be made more bearable.

Hope is also an energy that is closely related to *love*. Where there is a great deal of *love* in the heart, there is usually *hope*. *Hope* also parallels *courage*, for many times courageous people carry much *hope*. They have an innate knowing that the outcome will be positive.

Hope **is** eternal. It comes from God. Your *hope-quotient* will depend on how much love you carry in your body. A pessimistic person does not carry as much of the *hope* energy as an optimistic person. It is a matter of ratio actually—the amount of *love* and *hope* ratio. Therefore, Readers of my heart, increase your *hope quotient*. Walk with not only *love* in your heart but an abundance of *hope*.

HAVE YOU SAID YOUR PRAYERS TODAY?—Jesus

I AM Jesus. In years past, people were taught to pray by priests, rabbis, and later on, pastors. However, in modern times, humanity has learned that they really do not need anyone teaching them how to pray. What is *prayer*? It is communing with God. It is that simple. How that is accomplished is by simply talking to Him. One can be doing household chores. Men or women in the business world can just mentally ask for His help on a particular problem. Construction workers can talk to Him as they walk high in the air on the steel beams for a building or bridge. Humanity seems to hold on to the misguided idea that one needs to be in a church or temple in order to pray and have God listen.

Dear ones, prayers are heard instantly, even if you are in a bathroom showering. It makes no difference where you are. Prayer is meant to be a continuous dialogue with your Heavenly Father. It is a dialogue, a rambling on freely, of your troubles, **or**, your delights, your struggles, and your gains. Prayer is meant to be a constant flow between Heaven and Earth. Clergy have made prayer so mysterious with certain steps to take before He will hear you. Dear ones, God hears all. He just may choose not to reply, especially if you are in a negative energy, being the victim, being in greed, vindictive and so forth.

In your sports activities, both sides pray to win. It is a locker-room ritual. Nevertheless, dear ones, do you not think that God leaves it up to your free will as to who will win? Let the teams with the least mistakes win, or the athletic team that excels, say, in passing the ball. Humanity does not realize that sport teams have their karma also. If there has been foul play and unnecessary roughness, that team will bear the consequences during another game. Sports are a wonderful venue for you for *trust, patience,* and *faith.* A whole team in football may have a test in *trust* for the quarterback to lead them to victory. In baseball, the whole team may have to have a test in *faith* that the pitcher will pitch a winning game.

Golf provides another example. Here there are not teams, but an individual hoping to win. The golfer has to have *patience* while he waits for others to tee off. He or she must *trust* that he/she will hit the ball as close to the hole as possible. The person must have *faith* and *self-worth* in his/her abilities. Many times a particular sports star will rise to fame quickly. However, after a time, he may see his game start to slide downwards. The person's swing in golf can be off in some way. The person starts changing golf clubs; maybe a newer iron will work better. This has then become a lesson for the player in *sportsmanship*. How many times have we seen players on the green slam down their club and stalk away? They display their anger at themselves. It bubbles over and out with an angry show of sportsmanship. One can see the level of maturity and ego that is on display for all to view.

Many times the athlete will say little prayers to him/herself just before competing. Ice skaters who jump and twirl, landing on a slim blade, defying gravity it seems, say little prayers to themselves throughout their jumps. *God, let me not screw up in front of all those people*! So many little prayers, but is this really praying or expressing *hope*? As I have stated in the *HOPE* chapter, *hope* is a gift from God. It is an energy we need to tap into every day of our lives.

I had stated to the Author that our book was finished; but as I watched how football teams were playing in order to see who was going to go to the Super Bowl, and heard all the variations of prayers, I wished to bring to your attention, Readers, that prayer has many facets. Any prayer that comes from the heart without the negative emotions and does not have victimization connected to it will be answered. However, the answer may not be what **you** think you prayed for.

If your prayer is to *cream* the other team, then, *no,* God will not answer that kind of prayer. However, if the whole team plays in sportsmanlike manner, without kicking and punching after the play has ended, then your prayer is acknowledged. There are so many reasons why a prayer is not answered as you would wish. There is always the karmic reason. Alternatively, it is simply the other person or team's chance to shine—to win.

Therefore, dear Readers, pray from your heart. Talk to your Angels that surround you. Ask for their protection. Tell the Father your dreams and aspirations. Cry out your fears. Above all else, be honest in your emotions and during your prayers, if at no other time.

The Father answers only *truth*. Ask of Him what you wish, no matter how outrageous it may seem, then walk your talk, be honorable, have self-worth. There is nothing that keeps you from having your prayers answered, but you!

GIFTS from GOD—Jesus

I AM Jesus. I wish to tell you this beautiful Thanksgiving morning about the gifts that God has given you and humanity, if you would but claim them. The most talked-about gift is the one of *free will.* Most of you, Readers, have heard of this gift. However, there are other gifts, which perhaps you do not realize are gifts, which come from God.

Look at your rainbows. See the beautiful colors that blend into each other yet are distinct in their own right. The colors are showing you the colors of your Rays as well as the colors of your energy centers, the chakras. The colors are also in your energy field, the aura. The field expands and contracts. By looking at a rainbow, you are reminded each time of what **you** look like in your perfection. What a glorious sight you are when you gather in a spiritual group and display these colors.

Another gift that God has given you is *love*. When He created you, you were from His energy. If you wish to put this in physical terms, you were cut from the same bolt of cloth. Since God is *love*, you also are *love*. Each time a mother gives birth to a baby, she is giving that soul a **gift** of a body to cherish while on the planet. In the same vein, when God birthed you, and since He is *love*, that too was a gift to you.

Women who bear babies are exhibiting a gift from God. For a woman's body to hold the seed and form a child and carry it internally, is she not receiving this gift and giving it to the outside world for all to see? God has given women an exquisite gift to be able to bring forth a completed form. This is not to say that those women who cannot conceive or who miscarry do not have the gift. There are many complex reasons for this medically, or there could be karmic reasons. There can be many lessons involved that explain these reasons.

You also have the gift of *discernment.* This is being able to analyze and discern the truth of things. One uses discernment to evaluate one's journey through life. If one uses discernment in place of judgment, the person is not accruing karma, for one is evaluating different facets of a person, place, or thing, which allow one to make decisions based on wisdom versus ego. People need to use this gift more often instead of dashing right into a situation that the ego demands.

Another gift is one of *joy*. I spoke previously in the chapter Joy versus Pleasure. ***Joy* is an innate gift that the soul carries within its makeup.**

Have you, Reader, ever thought about where your passion comes from? *Passion* is another gift the soul carries. Passion elicits excitement, drive, tenacity, perseverance, and joy. Artists experience a passion for their work. There could be no better example than Michelangelo's work displayed in the Sistine Chapel of the Vatican. Many athletes have a passion about their particular sport. They excel in it and most play cleanly and with honor. Therefore, *passion* is certainly a gift.

God has given many gifts to the peoples of Earth. Many of the gifts people take for granted. They are so used to them; they either have not given them much thought, or just do not think of them as a gift. I refer here to the ability of people to dream. Psychologists explain dreams as coming from the subconscious and that is true. However, the whole concept of a *dream* from the subconscious is a gift that God has bestowed. It is a way that He has given people so they may process the happenings in their lives. It helps balance out the body. Those people who have the ability to analyze their dreams have an easier time throughout their lives. Life makes more sense to them. They are less confused, for they recognize the reasons for their circumstance. They recognize when their body is off balance. They learn their individual dream symbols and know what they mean. They can perceive the meaning of the colors they see. All of this is helpful for the individual. It is God's gift to be able to dream, analyze, and incorporate this in daily life.

Another gift God has given humanity is *freedom.* When one views the whole planet, people who exercise this gift of *freedom* are in the minority. Of course, *freedom* is predicated on the country in which you live. Souls that incarnate into China for example, find that *freedom* is sadly lacking. Remember that souls choose where they will incarnate either to learn the lessons available in a particular country, or to bring about change. China is moving more toward *freedom* and some day this great country will be a democracy. However, beware, for even great democratic countries can lose their *freedom*. This is God's gift to humanity. It is man's will and love of power that erodes the freedom that is the people's God-given right—His Gift.

How about *justice*? Have you thought about *justice* being a gift from God? It most assuredly is. Many times people seek *justice* in the courts. Sadly, they do not always receive *justice*, but instead, the results of unqualified jurors passing out a recommendation from their subjective and projected ideas of *justice*. The Judges also are biased many times. True *justice*, this gift from God, needs souls of the higher initiations to mete out sentences. To have a system where one is judged by one's peers is an altruistic theory, but not that practical. Notices are sent out to report for jury duty. The lawyers interview them and the jurors are selected. Will the accused receive true *justice*? Not in God's eyes most likely. People are apt to believe if the jury is comprised of the more educated; the jury will do a better job. This is not necessarily so. Some of the less educated could be more spiritually evolved, and I do not mean in the religious sense. I mean some jurors are further up Jacob's ladder than others are. Bringing in a verdict of *guilty* or *not guilty* requires a higher consciousness, which is not always present in a jury. I am not going to go into a long discussion whether there ought to be a death penalty or not. This is such a loaded topic. Some people need to be put to death, especially those who commit multiple murders, for they are truly evil and need to be taken off the planet.

However, there are times when *life in prison* can be a more just sentence simply because it provides the perpetrator years and years for self-evaluation. He or she is surrounded by like-minded felons, dozens of examples, usually many justifying their misdeeds. These puppets-of-evil many times come to know God for the first time in their lives. People have a tendency to snicker at the felon for having *gotten religion*. However, God uses these prisons to help make a change for the better in such individuals. If you can view it from this perspective, you can discern how *justice* was indeed done by the sentence of *life in prison* versus death. To humanity, *death* is the worse punishment. People view *justice* as revenge of some kind, whereas the gift of *justice* could be a long prison sentence with time to reflect and to repent.

GIVING and RECEIVING—Jesus, Sananda, Maitreya

We are Jesus, Sananda, and Maitreya. Good morning, blessed Readers. We are going to discuss what it means to *give* as well as to *receive*.

Let us start with *giving*. Oh, Readers, if you only would stop and think before you give to someone. Are you giving out of duty or are you giving from your heart? So many people feel compelled to give to someone for it is a duty to be carried out. How many of you give gifts at birthdays, Christmas, and celebrations because it is expected of you?

As you approach your holiday season, many people over-give or under-give. Rarely is there moderation. People are apt to overspend during holidays. They use their credit cards and rack up tremendous bills. They then spend most of the next year paying off their cards, getting them ready so they can repeat the process over again as the holidays arrive once more.

Humanity has a problem finding the middle road in most endeavors, which includes the *art of giving*. In your pioneer days when life was simpler, rarely were gifts bought. The gifts would consist of woodcarvings, simple homemade instruments, rag dolls and of course gifts of food. Women would share their pickles and jams with great pride and delight in the present they were giving someone.

What are missing for many in the **recipe of *giving* are heart, common sense, generosity, and caring.** One may query how one can give and be generous and still be moderate? It is very simple. When you give from the heart, the gift is always generous. For example, most of you have heard that story where a young woman sold her hair in order to buy her husband a gift only to find he had sold his prized watch in order to buy his cherished wife a decorative comb for her hair. In that example the two people had little money, but sold items in order to give the gift that would please the other the most—gifts from the heart.

Frequently, people with a great deal of money gift their children with cars, jewelry, and designer clothes. Several years ago, people gave gifts of expensive fur coats, but that type of gift has gone out of favor because of the many animals that were slaughtered in order to have these fine furs. However, what happens when the wealthy have everything they desire? This dynamic creates a subtle change. The people no longer appreciate what they have. They lose common sense. Instead of six pairs of shoes or less, one hears of the wealthy owning two hundred pairs of shoes. One pair for their two hundred outfits most likely.

We are not saying people are wrong for having a vast shoe and clothes wardrobe, but only if they truly wear and use these items with appreciation. It is doubtful anyone with such vastness of apparel truly is satisfied. Some of the items may be gifts from others, but in reality, the person has gifted herself. This brings us back to the topic of giving. One needs to give to oneself. However, again there needs to be common sense and not the energy of hoarding. There certainly is generosity in her gifts to herself, but it is generosity to the extreme.

There are people who give and give and give to others. They usually are people who have difficulty in *receiving*. You often can recognize these people for they have difficulty in receiving compliments. Where a simple *thank you* would do, they tend to brush away compliments. They may make a little joke that puts them down in some way—demeans them. One would think that *receiving* would be a simple thing to do. However, we observe that it is quite difficult for most people. This is a learned response for there is a difference between *receiving and taking*.

On a soul level, you already know how to do this. However, when you are in a body, the little ego can be such a strong influence that it rules the personality. How often are you in a room where there can be one person who comes in and he is loud, boisterous and centering the attention on himself. It is his ego demanding to be recognized. He is taking from the energy in that room. Other people may arrive quietly and warmly greet people. They are not taking and are comfortable as to who they are.

To take is the negative aspect of to *receive*. To give out of duty, or to give too effusively, or too stringently are the negative aspects of *to give*. Moderation—a balance—is required in your lives. Giving and receiving are a large part of your life's play. Monitor yourself.

Question what your motives for giving are. Graciously *receive* your compliments. Keep in mind, you will frequently be tested on your lessons of which right *giving* and *receiving* are major components. If you are unable to receive life's gifts, how much more difficult it could be to accept the many gifts from God! Ponder this.

CHARITY—Jesus

I AM Jesus. This chapter will be on *charity* and it is not by accident that it follows the previous lesson on Giving and Receiving. Let us suppose you, Reader, receive a great deal of money *unexpectantly.* Most people's thoughts range from *I wonder what the taxes will be. I can buy a new car! I will give to charity.* This last statement becomes a major decision of importance for it involves to whom you give and how much.

If people would just ask for guidance on this—go to their I AM Presence and then ***wait*** for guidance. So many people rapidly write the donation checks just to get them out of the way—to free themselves up so they may take that cruise, buy that car, jewelry, or pay those bills. First, let me underline for you that your money comes from God, *if* you received the money in the correct way.

In a previous chapter on *Desire*, we told you your abundance was already ascertained before you were born. At the same time, you made agreements as to what major charity to give to! It may surprise some of you to learn even charities have karma—especially those of long standing. I am **not** going to name specific ones and their specific karmas. That is for you to ascertain. However, be aware that the large charities are either cleaning up past karma, or are accruing new karma. It is just the way of it. Therefore, I will address certain issues and leave the ascertaining as to which ones I am referring to, for your discernment.

A large charity could be one that is first on the scene after a natural disaster. It has a budget of millions of dollars. Your homework would be to learn how much of those monies go to the people to help them and how much go into staff salaries; what percentage of your money is actually given to the people in the disaster zone? You might be surprised to learn it is less than 50%. This is where your discernment, free will, and choices come into play. Some people will say that less than 50% is fine with them. They can still take their donation off their taxes.

There are charity organizations that are spiritually oriented. However, they are so righteous that they will turn down gifts, huge gifts of money if the money comes from a lottery-win, perhaps. Readers, the people who win huge amounts in the lottery are usually being given a gift by God! He has answered their prayer. The winner wishes to give to a charity a large amount of his winnings. The organization does not accept it for the CEO would not accept lottery monies. In his narrow belief system, he could not see this was God's way of gifting the organization for its goodness. By not being able to receive from God, this organization now will have negative karma and will go through much testing and possibly a decline.

There are always periods of ups and downs for charitable organizations, usually stemming from their karmic debt. There are various Evangelical ministries throughout America. Some have a vast following with partners who give monthly. Some are so huge in the services that they provide—Crusades, products to purchase, and 24-hour prayer availability—that it can be difficult to monitor all of the various departments.

In the money-counting room of these large ministries, there can be so much money laying around that a quarter here, a dollar there is pilfered, for the volunteers are not always as honest as they proclaim themselves to be. Finally, the thefts are discovered, but not discovered before hundreds of dollars have disappeared over time. This happens all over the world. It does not make the pastor and his organization less, for their good works far outshine the pilfering. Unfortunately, not all people are pure enough to resist money temptations.

Another aspect of *charity* is giving to friends and family in need of something they are not able to spend money on for themselves. It could be college tuition, a needed item for the home, appliances or carpeting. It can be dentistry or anything that makes the recipients happier and brings joy to their lives.

People are apt to think *charity* is only giving to the poor. There are many aspects to *charity*. It is charitable to give to a wealthy neighbor. Volunteer work is being charitable. Moreover, certainly giving to relatives and friends is a charitable act of kindness and caring. Eliminate the connotation of charity as being for the poor. *Charity* is for everyone. Even the wealthy have need of charity at times in the context of a caring act. It goes back to that question, *what do you give to someone who has everything*? It is not another expensive item that is not really needed, but something that shows you care. I will let you decide your gift.

Therefore, dear Readers, practice discernment in your money gifts to charities, especially if God has graced you with a large sum of money. Ask for guidance. Maybe you are to give only a small portion to an organization, while a larger portion is for relatives, as well as for yourself. Be conservative. If you have received a large sum, divide what you will immediately give and what you will give the following year. In addition, *always* give to yourself in some way that brings you great joy. Remember when you are giving monies back to God, **you** are part of the equation as to whom to give to. It is called *receiving*.

(*Money and all of its aspects are tests for the soul. One lifetime you may be wealthy; another lifetime you may struggle with poverty. The soul is learning "there is no lack in my Father's House," versus poverty consciousness. 2011)*

SHARE—Jesus, Sananda, Maitreya

We are Jesus, Sananda, and Maitreya, coming as a blend of energies to speak with you through this book. In days of yore, not all was peace and quiet. There were many struggles for power going on. People always had to try to maintain balance in their lives. So much of humanity has belief systems that proclaim incorrect ideas. In each generation, there is always strife. Ages ago in history, humanity faced many difficult lessons. There was pestilence; there was famine; there was plague; there were class distinctions—the rich against the poor.

The rich struggled to maintain their wealth. Men's clothes for the upper classes were very ornate, so the cost for clothes was staggering. Men also wore as many jewels as their fingers could hold. The stones were not of a dainty size either. Therefore, the wealthy spent a great deal of money on the material side of living—**on themselves**.

The poor on the other hand spent what money they had on food. They would scrounge the refuse from the wealthy kitchens. They would cluster around the garbage bins of restaurants. Many a waiter earned extra money by selling the scraps off people's plates to the poor waiting outside the door. Those were the historical times of about the 1200's. This would happen in the large cities mostly. The point we are conveying to you is that these *rich man—poor man* games have not changed all that much. There are still the Haves and the Have-nots.

You see, Readers, **the world, and its difficulties stem from the consciousness of the people.** There has not been a Utopia in the history of this planet. Christians would like to believe that the Garden of Eden was perfect, where in actuality it was short-lived. Even that story has not been depicted truthfully in its entirety. Just keep in mind there is much symbolism in the Bible, and therefore, Adam and Eve while real, were symbolic of mini-nations.

There is a Tree of Knowledge and it still stands, but most people do not know where it is. That Tree also is symbolic of people's consciousness. There are branches, twigs, and leaves. Each portrays a level of a person's awareness. In fact, the Jews use this Tree as the basis for their teachings, except they refer to it as the Tree of Life. Therefore, down throughout history there have been people who only hold a leaf or twig of wisdom in their consciousness. Others hold branches and boughs. Always keep in mind that almost any teaching, whether mythical or real, has a symbolic foundation. Moreover, that foundation is usually spiritual. It is through different translations, oral history, as it passes from one person to another, one person's awareness to another's, one person's culture to another's, that the distortions of the Truth become manifest.

Humanity has been in survival for so long, it is not apt to be in a hurry to share. Remember your history—the potato famine in Ireland. Can you imagine what it must have been like to scrounge for one potato in order to feed six people? Families shared within families but were unable to share with their neighbors. The reality was that even if people from their hearts wanted to share; common sense proclaimed it was nonsensical to try to feed twelve people on one potato.

Any soul who takes embodiment at that particular period in history had agreed to a part in the play of famine or pestilence and so forth. Nevertheless, at the same time there is an opportunity for any advanced soul to make a change. Maybe the change will come through an agricultural or medical discovery of some kind, or through the discovery of electricity. Each generation brings a rise in awareness, a discovery that will better humankind.

Nevertheless, as the consciousness of humanity broadened, the *sharing* did not necessarily keep up. Here in America, the wealthiest nation in the world, the sharing of its abundance is not at a positive level. There is so much suffering in the world, all having to do with one's wealth. No longer in America is a family happy in owning a farm and attending to its animals and harvesting its plantings. Along with the invention of radio and television, and we must add motion pictures also, along with these wonderful inventions came lack of happiness, let alone, joy. Remember, we spoke about joy being of the soul. Well, dear Readers, the more people embraced the new inventions, the more they tended to forget their soul. They lost the connection to that which they really are—*love*.

Now humanity chased the money trail in whatever way it could. In countries where drug plants were easy to grow and were the acceptable crop by corrupted governments, the spiritual lives of people also became polluted. If a country were primarily Catholic, people would go through the motions of going to Mass and having the many corrupt priests bless their evil endeavors. We say *evil,* for money was coveted in any way that it could be obtained. Drugs became the ideal answer, which led to evil addictions to the drugs to the point people would murder in order to keep control of their cartels. Hence, the new inventions not only brought entertainment, but much dissatisfaction with the average person's way of life.

There is nothing wrong in striving to better one's life. However, as we have said in the *DESIRE* chapter, it is how one walks toward *abundance* that matters. Certainly killing others for one's harvest is not the way. Down through history the struggle has always been there. Readers, do you not realize that it is your game plans and your free will choices while in embodiment that perpetuate the struggle for prosperity? Not everyone is supposed to be wealthy beyond reason. It brings to mind the disproportion of young athletes' outrageous contracts. These young people do not have the wisdom yet to handle such huge monies. Their egos will not let them act in rational ways. Frequently, television will show some of the angry antics that erupt during a sports game. The crowd fans the fuel by words of abuse and deeds. From our points of view, the whole scene is ego-fed and immature. We are making a discernment of the actions and evaluating the situations. **We believe the disproportionate amount of money is the root of the disrespect of others either on the playing field or court or in the stands.**

There are athletes who give to charities, visit hospitals, and start a foundation in order to share their wealth. They are to be commended. However, oh, so much more could be done. People have heard perhaps that God's Plan is to have Heaven on Earth. However much needs to be done with countries' **sharing** more of their wealth with the countries that need lifting up. Some years from now, there will be a more moderate, a more level playing field for the many souls that wait in line, so to speak—waiting to come to Earth and help her evolve.

Humankind needs to evolve also. Raise your awareness. Watch your little egos, the little self, in order to allow your soul to connect with you on a deeper level. In God's World, there is unending abundance. Do you want a piece of that action? Modify your behavior. Earn your advancement and the abundance that comes with it. Then **share** your harvest with love, caring, and compassion. Share from your heart, never from duty.

ASCENSION—Jesus

I AM Jesus. In the past twenty or so years there has been much written and discussed on the topic of *Ascension*. This topic holds not only fascination for people but affords great debates just by means of this concept being so mysterious. People who have a religious background view ascension as that act that Elijah did, disappearing in a flaming chariot. ***2 Kings, 2:11*** *And it came to pass, as they still went on, and talked, that behold, there appeared a chariot of fire, and horses of fire, and parted them both asunder; and E-li'jah went up by a whirlwind into heaven.* People without religious teachings are just plain puzzled about this whole dynamic.

When a body dies, two avenues of departure are open for the soul: take one's body with one or leave the body to either be cremated or laid to rest in a casket in the ground. For humanity, either one is a scary thought. In fact, most people avoid thinking about it as much as possible. It is usually the very ill or elderly who addresses his or her death. Remember, Readers, the soul does **not** die but just ascends in one form or another.

Let us now address *ascension* in the broadest sense. Every soul throughout its lifetime is ascending at every moment of everyday. Bear in mind not to be ascending would be stagnation—a no-growth. Of course, that does happen, but I am speaking of a positive process in general terms. As a soul evolves, no matter what it is doing of a positive nature now, it is ascending.

Religions, in the last twenty plus years, are emphasizing ascension for the evolved soul. They proselytize that people will be lifted up in some kind of mass departure—the *Rapture*. I say to you, Readers, any type of Rapture is in the far distant future and I mean distant. There have been books written about benevolent space ships evacuating people by the thousands. That is always a possibility, but it is for emergencies, such as massive nuclear wars, where people need to leave in a hurry or risk being annihilated. Twenty or more years ago, such a nuclear war was a possibility, but this has dimmed over the years. Your Space Brothers of the *benevolent* kind will not allow those wars to happen, according to the Will of God. He has stepped in, in order to save the planet from complete destruction. Therefore, the Rapture, the lifting off much of humanity by spacecraft flown by the peace-loving Galactic Masters, is not a viable option at this time. Please separate *Rapture* from *ascension*.

If a person is so filled with God's Light, the body will lift off like a speeding bullet. There will be fire because of the release of the atomic structure and friction. The soul, of course, is involved at the time of the body's death but for the soul, it is a metamorphosis. The astral body disintegrates as the human body also disintegrates. Picture the rocket ships that explode upwards at lift off and then release another aspect that is propelled forward.

When one has ascension, as Elijah did, there needs to be the destruction of the Earth body in order to release the astral body. As the astral body travels at terrific speeds, it too disintegrates and the soul is free of any encumbrance. Now one can proclaim to be in one's Light body and take on any form one wishes. People have associated *ascension* with some religious concept simply because the Bible speaks of it. The fact is that ascension **is** a spiritual journey to God. If one never heard of the Bible and was full of Light, the person could ascend in that fiery Elohim act.

Ascension was a hot topic twenty plus years ago to prepare people for the fourth dimension in order to help the planet evolve. If souls became eager to take ascension, they would have to strive harder to meet the standards—mainly to be full of God's Love and Light. The more the souls were practicing *peace* and *love*, the higher their vibrations would rise, which in turn would promote evolution for the planet. There have been people ascending but only through soul evolution and not in fiery waves of burning bodies. Many Readers will notice the mounting excitement over ascension has gradually dissipated. People have become more balanced over the concept of ascension. They realize it is a mental state of evolution. The actual Elijah phenomenon is still rare, if at all.

Readers, do keep striving for ascension, however, for it means the evolution of the soul. It means climbing Jacob's ladder ever higher. Always bear in mind what you see around you on Earth is illusion. It is not real in the sense that the higher dimensions are real. Everything there is seen, never hidden. There is not lying or cheating. There is *kindness, caring, love, compassion*, and *Light*. There is no *duality*. Ascension **is** the *Ultimate Experience,* the path to God.

(*Many people believe in the Rapture and in May 2011, there were groups of people who gave away all of their possessions for their leader had prophesized that at a certain hour that night the Rapture would happen. This was the second time that the leader had led them down a false path.)*

AFTERMATH of the TSUNAMIS—Jesus and the Spiritual Hierarchy

I AM Jesus. We are the Spiritual Hierarchy. So many people are calling upon my name for rescue of their broken hearts and mending for the many departed souls. I thought by giving you another talk, even though you will not read this until spring of **2005**, the destruction and heartache, bewilderment, and grief will not be overcome easily, or brought to resolution anytime soon.

Dear ones, in the past centuries, your Earth has tilted its tectonic plates repeatedly. This creates undulations on the top layers of Earth and a resettling at the lower levels. It is Mother Earth having a bit of a shake of her *skin*. Of course what follows is devastation and many times great loss of life.

In the chapter on Transitions, I told you how healing angels were immediately present helping the soul who has had a sudden death. The same dynamic is happening with the aftermath of the tsunamis. The Father has dispatched legions of angels to help the souls that have crossed over into what you perceive as death, while in actuality the soul still lives. There are healing edifices on the other side. These are huge buildings for healing techniques that are unique in their practices. Healing is manifested using sound, music, colors, and above all, loving Beings ministering to the souls.

As each soul is guided to these edifices, it is assigned healers who counsel and heal the soul. Its memory of its soul group is re-activated and the soul soon joins its own group. Some souls take longer to heal than others. They rest, sleep, and are given much tender, loving care. There are giant movie monitors and the soul is shown how it died and the impact of its departure on the family. It is given its life review, in living color and sound. This is all part of the healing process. It is shown how it had chosen to experience that particular kind of death, not only to gain wisdom for itself, but also to provide the lessons its Earth family had asked for.

It is difficult for people to accept the fact they choose the way they will die. All of your relatives are part of the players in your death-play. One might argue where does free will come in. Maybe the soul has changed its mind and does not wish to die in a tsunami. In one of those miracles one hears reported, a person is found on a high tree limb. The person had climbed the tree in order to escape. Others took flight to the higher floors in hotels. Others took to boats and were able to ride the waves. However, the escape was manipulated, the free will and the strong survival urge of the body kept the person from dying. Those people on the beaches who were swept away went to their deaths as planned.

It is most difficult for people to grasp the dynamic of choosing one's own death, when the death is such a tragic, unexpected transition. One seems to understand a death better if one went through chemotherapy and still died. People say, *it was meant to be.* Well, my dear children, this tsunami was tragic if one puts it in those terms. It is tragic to see the devastation, the grief people express, the bewilderment, and the wonderment of what to do next. How will one cope? How will one heal emotionally from such a horrendous loss? It is so difficult for humanity to grasp that this or that lesson is what they on a soul level had requested. It is never easy.

If one is not to play the victim to these horrendous Earth changes, changes that affect so many thousands of people, having awareness that souls choose their lives, the relatives, the dynamic of that life **and** the death will bring understanding. However, since we are talking about a grief process, having awareness will not lessen the pain of the loss—the sorrow involved. When one is not playing the victim to its circumstances, the mental body is clearer. The person can control his emotions, solve problems, and help others.

In most families, there is a dominant figurehead. It is not necessarily the father or mother. It could be one of the children, or an aunt. It will be a person who carries more awareness—the soul is more evolved. This person is capable of making decisions of rallying the family into a cohesive group. On the other hand, if the person is now single, the person attracts others to him/her and helps in the emotional healing process of another family.

Humanity as of now is being inundated with the graphic television pictures of the tsunami disaster. This will continue for the greater part of next year. I am stating this just before New Year's Day of 2005. Remember what I told you about c*ompassion* and how a disaster will awaken *compassion* in you. People are giving money.

America is sharing. Lord Maitreya has long been an advocate for *sharing*. America can now do her part.

This disaster of the tsunami has taken the Iraqi war practically off the television screens. The tsunami lights up the probability this very same scenario **will** happen on the West Coast of America. The disaster will happen—but when is anyone's guess. Mother Earth will stretch and turn again, just as she has in the past. America's West Coast is very vulnerable to being the next calamity. Is she ready to cope with a disaster of such magnitude? An Earthquake of 9.0 is certainly stupendous. One of 10.0 would be off the charts! It could change the topography of the whole coast. Picture the tsunamis from that one! Are the states able to withstand such a calamity financially? Are the insurance companies able to pay out the millions in claims? I think not.

People, the New Agers have known about the dangers of Earth changes for the West and East Coasts for years. It has almost gotten to the point of crying *wolf* too many times. People have become complacent and have bought and built beautiful homes overlooking the oceans. **Beware** Beloveds! This tsunami disaster in the Indian Ocean areas is a wake-up call. Hear it!

The Father and all of the Spiritual Hierarchy, and that includes the Archangels and our Space Brothers of the benevolent kind, are helping as much as we possibly can, always in the boundaries of your free will. We hear your cries of anguish and pleas for help. You are not alone. Each one of you in that disaster is watched over in a tremendous way. Know in your hearts we are with you. If you pray to Buddha, we are with you. If you pray to your Earth gods, or to Jesus, or to Krishna, we are with you. Remember that anger can be a part of grief. Be honest in your emotions. Be in your heart. Share your wealth whether it is food, water, or compassion for others. You are all God's children. He is watching over you, even though you may not realize it.

We will close now. We are with you and surround you with our love. **We are the Spiritual Hierarchy.**

(*Our benevolent Space Team was very busy lifting souls out of their bodies as the tsunami struck. There was almost a repeat in action when Japan was struck by a devastating Earthquake and subsequent tsunami this year, 2011)*

RESTITUTION—Maitreya

I AM Maitreya, The World Teacher. Readers, as our book draws to a close, I am drawn to say a few more words in the mini-lecture series. I shall title this one *Restitution*. What I mean by that is there are times when a soul seeks *restitution*. It is allowing a higher part of itself or another to commit a service of some kind. People often seek restitution to settle a particular life problem. I am using this term *restitution* in a broad sense to incorporate the Higher Spiritual World.

We in the Spiritual Hierarchy many times seek *restitution*. It is bringing to rest certain problems, to fix a situation, to solve a puzzle, to bring to fruition a certain dynamic. Humanity uses restitution when wanting to pay back to someone. A person has done something in either a negative or a positive way. This has caused the recipient pain or joy. The recipient now wants restitution—to take revenge, or to reward. Therefore, the energy of *restitution* carries a duality of negativity in the lower frequencies. On the other hand, it carries a pleasing, giving nature in the higher frequencies.

When is using this dynamic of *restitution* appropriate on a positive side or damaging on a negative side? The term *to get even* needs little explanation. A person does something that creates a negative response from someone. The *victim* (there are no victims) seeks restitution—revenge. Alternatively, suppose an act has been committed that brings great joy and happiness to another. The recipient wants to reciprocate, to reimburse in some way. This is called *restitution*.

Raise the bar of your awareness now and picture how this dynamic or concept of *restitution* plays out in the Heavenlies—our Spiritual World. We in these higher dimensions have the ability to travel great distances, faster than the speed of Light. In our many travels to different worlds and star systems, we may find inadequacies, either in planetary life or in the varied cultures. (Earth is **not** the only populated world.) There are High Councils of which we may be a part. After hearing the problems, conditions, and inadequacies, and after discussion, we come to the agreement where the act of *restitution* will take place. If the certain dynamic under advisement has brought an imbalance to that world, we will suggest ways to help make restitution in order to regain balance and equilibrium for that world.

Humanity in this planet is quite out of balance. There is too much greed, not enough sharing, not enough thoughts of peace, and not enough consciousness. That is quite a heavy load to bring back into balance—to make restitution. Therefore, *restitution is really a dynamic of balancing* versus getting even or paying back a karmic debt, as in *to make restitution*. The higher thought is truly *how to bring balance.*

We of the Spiritual Hierarchy are called everywhere by other worlds and the Father to help bring balance. The Universes are one of order. There may be chaos at times, but that does then bring order. It is the restitution process, combined with *love*, *caring*, and *compassion,* that helps bring balance to the chaos. Whenever a world is as out of balance as Earth is, with its mini-wars, its misguided decisions for power and greed, it creates chaos from those imbalances.

As of now, America is becoming more and more chaotic in its imbalances in almost every facet of its existence, from social, economical, and religiosity. It is time for a spiritual awakening in order to bring in *restitution*. It will not be done with its present government, which is under the **illusion** it was chosen by God, simply because the incumbent is a Christian (*George W. Bush*).

This present government is walking in delusion, ego-born of power and greed. There will be a period of restitution. There has to be, for chaos and ruin loom on the horizon. The loss of *freedom* is insidiously inching further into people's lives. Where and how does one stop the creeping destruction of all that was good with America? Her great name is being sullied as her liberties are eroded and her reputation tarnished throughout the world. Hear, oh America, for when God calls upon us to make restitution, the veils will be ripped from the deep-seated lies that permeate the ruling government.

There will come a period in people's lives when they must confront where they have given over their sovereignty to this ruling government, where even the Supreme Court is but a hand-shake away from becoming puppets, cloaked in reams of legalese which no one can decipher. There will come a time when restitution will take place—the Fall of the Roman Empire all over again? *RESTITUTION*! It is a two way street toward *justice*. It is a rebalancing after chaos. It is a cleansing from on High—God's Methodology in action!

RESTORING YOUR FAITH—Jesus

I AM Jesus. I wish to bring to your attention, Readers, that we of the Spiritual Hierarchy are quite aware that humanity has started losing faith in its religions. Catholics have left the church in droves, due to the sexual abuse scandals coming out of the closets of the many ill-serving priests. These are little men who profess loving me, but then entice young boys into dark secrets. It is so sad to observe this. It is the right hand giving in communion and the left hand promiscuously taking away the innocence of these young children.

As the scandals and lawsuits continue—and they are still surfacing—as the scandals escalate, it is a period of uncovering the many years of perversion perpetrated by the priests. The nuns also are not free from the scandals, for there has been many a nun acting promiscuously with young girls. Therefore, you have these sins becoming known. People of good hearts and values have become disillusioned and tend to blanket all priests and nuns with hidden agendas.

Christians become disenchanted with pastors preaching the same rhetoric repeatedly and yet there is in-fighting at the board meetings. There is jealousy. There is stealing in the counting-rooms. There are distorted Teachings as to what I have said. It seems as if people become more complacent in their spiritual practice after a period of time. They tend to make worshipping a **habit**, instead of experiencing true feelings of love for God. Therefore, as with all habits, one's spiritual life becomes ritualistic and even addictive, but rarely profound. I would say that the act of worship is so polluted by people's **wants** versus needs that little of the prayers are being answered by the Father. He **does hear all** your prayers but is quite particular on what He chooses to answer! This may surprise you, but it is so.

There are other religions, but since Christianity stems from my Teachings, I will address mostly this religion. I pose a question to you, Readers: *Why do Protestants think they must* ***save*** *Catholics and Jews*? We in the higher dimensions view this as nonsensical. No one can save another's soul! Only the person whose soul is housed in his/her body can save one's own soul, if you must use that term. What does saving a soul mean? What if I said, *no soul needs to be saved?* What if I told you that saving anyone is a misnomer? In addition, yes, I know I used that term two thousand plus years ago, but People, languages change. The interpretations change. To *save* is not even written in many languages. People do not know what that means!

I did say *salvation*. Dictionaries say that means *to save*. However, I would like to impose another interpretation. What would happen if you substituted the word *love* for *salvation*? Can you not see how *love* is the answer—the cue? To love in the highest, purest sense is all one needs to do. Please think of every thought being energy. I have said this in other books, Sally LeSar's book, *Treasures from the Universe . . . ,* for one. If you can think in terms that thoughts are energy, then how wonderful it could be to think and use *love* in various situations. How about loving a person, instead of trying to save a person because of different belief systems? Do you not see how the energy of *love* could make a change in that person you are attempting to save?

However, you may make the argument that people who have not heard of Jesus need to know me in order to obtain entrance into God's Kingdom. Again, that is an incorrect interpretation. I walked the Earth in many lifetimes **before** my Jesus-life. I started some of those religions that many people embrace today. People are Buddhists or follow Krishna's Teachings. Well I did not say *save* in those times, but I did teach about walking the correct path and to love all.

Remember, Readers, that saying, *different strokes for different folks*. There needed to be different thoughts arranged in that particular language so that that particular culture could respond. Why do you think those religions have been sustained throughout the ages? It is because they address the same principles I taught in Christianity and fulfilled a need for people. Therefore, release yourself from thinking you **have** to save anyone! Even if a felon at the bottom of the barrel professed that he believed in me and I died on the cross, which I did not, even if this felon embraced me, that **does not save** him! What *saves* him is to walk the path of *love. Go and sin no more,* spoken to **men** in those Biblical days (John 8:11).

The reality of *salvation* is one of *hope.* A felon must bring *love and hope into his life,* and then walk his talk. Do not steal and kill. Walk in the new way of *love thy neighbor*. That is what brings *salvation,* if you persist in using that term. It is **you,** changing your morals, your attitudes, your habits, addictions, and belief systems. No one can do this for you. Now if an Evangelist proclaims you are *saved*, **if** you agree to the spiritual terms he is giving you—that I died on the cross, which I did not—if these concepts, that by accepting me your sins are absolved, if these concepts help release those old belief systems, so much the better. However, dear Readers, I am not the only way. **Christianity is not the only way!** I AM a Wayshower. I show you **a** way. It is up to you to walk it, not make it a habit. Not to forget the Teachings while in the back rooms of your churches. If I AM the Way in your mind, you must walk and talk *love*, my friends. You must show by example.

I have always preferred teaching by example, rather than by tired rhetoric that has only been memorized, and becomes too mechanical. In the Bible, there are so many phrases—*The Word* it is called. People memorize these catch phrases and use them instead of their own thoughts! Making a habit of saying scripture repeatedly does not impress anyone. Alternatively, it does not give someone the incentive to change. It just brings to mind the nasty little catchword of a *Bible Banger*. For some Evangelists, this unfortunately is what they are. For others, they use The Word to fill their hearts, to deepen their faith. It does no good to shout it at others and then walk off the platform. Some of those Evangelists get so full of fire and brimstone, so filled with their own ego-need to make a lot of noise, that one sitting in the congregation is either fired up and with him/her or the fire is squelched—put off by the theatrics. They up and leave.

Other pastors have grand diagrams and mini stage sets that depict different Biblical scenes. Of course, the Babe in the Manger is a touching scene, but a tad unauthentic. There also are many scenes of Solomon's Temple and how the rabbi had a rope tied around his ankle so that he could be pulled out of the Holy of Holies if he dared in his arrogance to touch the Untouchable and drop dead. All of these dramatics are appealing to some people. Many pastors think they must entertain as well as teach. They must provide a visual effect that would entertain the congregation in order to keep them from falling asleep, for sometimes a sermon drones on and on.

People of my heart, there are so many ramifications that stem from all of these Teachings; the various sins are played up. Social issues are discussed. Priests, pastors, rabbis have extended their roles to be not only saviors, exorcists, or mental health practitioners, that their simple task of helping people find *love* and *faith* in their hearts becomes lost. **Religions have become too elaborate in their presentations**. The cathedrals and churches are outrageously ornate. For what reason are they ornate? What does creating a place of worship have to do with wealthy trappings? If one sat under a tree and was filled with *love* and *light* and spoke gently to passersby who tarried a while, that miniscule space would be filled with the Holy Spirit Presence, far more than in huge opulent churches.

As the centuries advanced, and as people raised their awareness and broadened their horizons, so did the wants of the clergy. Their church must be more ornate than the one down the street. Nowadays, it is not down a street, but what freeway interchange would be the most accessible toward building a place of worship, for a **huge** parking lot is necessary to go with the **huge** building for the **huge** expectant crowds near a **huge** freeway. Do you see, Readers, how ridiculous getting religion and being *saved* has become?

When pastors and congregations opt for opulence versus substance, one can see how the Teachings have become contaminated. One could say it is worshipping the Golden Calf (Exodus 32:8) all over again. Humankind enjoys sitting on plush seats. Pastors revel in looking out at vast audiences in their vast churches and cathedrals. Many times, they are counting in their minds the amount of money that will be brought in during the offerings that day or evening. Balance, people. There must always be balance. The balance has been tipped toward *greed*.

Now in defense of some of the Evangelists, I will say some are still sincere in their hearts, still give good examples on how one can approach life. However, I am sorry to say those pastors with great heart and truths are becoming too sparse in the arena of giving out The Word. I have decided that changes must be made. You may not agree with me, but that is always your choice, for I am going to make a very controversial statement: **"Go back to basics!"** The "saving industry" has become too out of touch with my Teachings and my purpose for coming to Earth.

Humanity is not all of the Christian Faith. Christians ought not to influence governments in order to create an environment where everyone must think as they do. How could they when America is such a melting pot of diverse cultures? Each culture is entitled to its unique belief systems, as long as the cultures respect each other and Mother Earth. People of different cultures can indeed pray to an unseen God. They can choose not to pray. They can tenderly nurture the environment, the trees for example. Instead, certain cultures are destroying the forests to make way for housing developments or shopping malls. So much damage seems to come before birth of a new living area is created. As many people know, the forests play a large part in the eco-systems, cleansing the air and providing needed oxygen to the hemispheres.

If only people would make social changes at the same time they advance in consciousness. So many prisons have overcrowded conditions. Felons are let off from their sentences early for there is no room for them as new inmates take up residence. Where has the balance gone? Where is there balance in eco-systems, in crowded prisons, in crowed slum areas? Young people leave the farms for the cities. Farms are sold for big money in order to make way for huge developments of some kind. Such imbalances are in almost every facet of life. Do you not see that when there are social imbalances that there would be imbalances in religions also?

So many pastors expound on *receiving a word*, a message from God or me. Many times, they have and many times, they have not. Their little ego-selves have given them a message. Spiritualists of old held séances and many spirits spoke forth. Were they truly the departed? They were not. They were spirits taking on the role of Aunt Ethel, but were not necessarily **the** Aunt Ethel. Entities such as I will not step down our frequencies to such a low level. The energy is too solid and there is little Truth flowing, especially if the Spiritualist is not of the advanced kind and does not carry purity in his/her aura. Remember, an element of energy is what we are really discussing.

How many of you Readers have driven by seedy strip-malls and have seen the signs that a fortuneteller will display? No one of advanced energies and consciousness would advertise in that way. There would be no need to. I have seen and heard people who have gone to a psychic-parlor. Much money has been negotiated just so the innocent searcher can hear of his/her loved one. Dear ones, keep your checkbook in your pocket or purse. You will be deceived severely. Christians preach that any type of astrology or spiritual readings by a psychic is a sin. Again, this is a distorted truth.

The Essenes had used astrology extensively in order to know the propitious time to conceive or plant a crop. The planets do affect us. They do have an influence on us. Our birth signs do give us certain characteristics. Charts can be helpful in looking at the compatibility in relationships. They provide us an avenue for understanding our spouse and children. It may surprise you to know that our children many times cause friction in relationships simply because of their birth sign. That was the game plan. This was the lesson you asked for. However, by knowing some of the influences and characteristics of different signs, you are more able, more prepared to be tolerant. Not every sign will be compatible with another.

Psychics have gotten a bad rap in my opinion from the Christian Community. People are ostracized if they seek a psychic for help in understanding something in their life. The term *psychic* has so many connotations. A true definition by some would be, *a psychic is a seeker of truth*. Someone else would think of a psychic as a legitimate *seer*. Others might think a psychic is a *fortuneteller*. There are elements of truth in all of the descriptions. It is a question of *semantics*. Pastors warn people to stay away from astrologers and the psychics of the world. Again, keep in mind that was **then**, for people needed to obtain their own answers and were too easily led astray. In fact they still need to go to their I AM Presence for their answers. That is the ideal.

Conversely, many times pastors tell television audiences they have *received a word of knowledge*. Alternatively, Evangelists will say that there is a man or woman wearing something red and that God is healing the body. For those of you who understand the chakra systems and how energies and altered states work, one **could** say that the pastor is a *psychic*. Now I know this will freak some of you out, but that is exactly what is happening. He or she is using all the centers in an altered state (*prayer*), just as a psychic does when giving a reading. If a psychic said he/she was receiving a word of knowledge, most likely the person is. However, the word of knowledge may not be from God necessarily. It depends on how advanced his/her developmental powers are. The person could be receiving the knowledge from the Readee's own soul and/or Master guide. If a person is at an even higher level of development, the person could receive information from me or other Masters and Archangels. Humanity needs to let go of its phobias against astrologers and psychics. Any highly developed Being is psychic. All highly spiritual people are psychic. Conversely, not all psychics are highly spiritual, although they may profess to be.

Therefore, *semantics* plays such a major role in interpreting the Bible and understanding other religions. However, with the Fundamentalist, and there are Fundamentalists in all religions—some call them *Orthodox*, again semantics—there are just so many of these intertwined meanings. What I hope I have conveyed to you is for you to let go of the strict way of interpreting scripture in any of the religions. Moreover, that definitely includes Hebrew.

There is nothing wrong in practicing one's faith, but currently religions have become too restrictive. Why not enjoy the beautiful triangles of sacred geometry in the Star of David? People are strangling themselves in trying rigidly to adhere to their particular religion or spiritual practice. Why do you think there is such a tremendous surge in what is called *New Age Thought*? People needed new thoughts and teachings. They wanted something else that their particular religion was not providing them. They needed to feel that deep spiritual connection with God again and with the many Ascended Ones—the Masters about whom one could only fantasize in a religion.

This is a hands-on generation. They want something they can see and feel. Look at the revival of the great religious epics in your movies, for example, *The Passion of the Christ*. Unfortunately, so much of the film is spent on the gory details. The Channel, although she bought a video copy of the movie, has yet to watch it. I hear her thoughts of how she does not think she could bear to watch my suffering. I do not blame her. Even **I** would not want to watch my being nailed to that cross. You see, I still retain full recall and vivid memory of all my past lives. I came to Earth, knowing I would suffer;

but I do wish people would keep me off the cross and concentrate on my Teachings of *love*. That is what is so sadly missing in the world today.

I wish to comment now on those great Crusades that people attend in arenas throughout the world. At first, a Crusade was called a *Revival*. Maybe a hundred people or so attended. It was held in a tent. Soon a tent was not large enough, so larger facilities had to be contracted for. Nowadays, any area, the sports arenas or outdoor acreages, is used. These Crusades no longer play to a few hundred, but thousands. In Africa and India, Crusades are being held where millions are attending.

These great Crusaders are going to where God and I are leading them. The pastors who are holding these Crusades are honorable men and indeed are obeying God, although I do not necessarily like that word *obey*. When one has God in his/her heart, it does not feel like obeying a command. It is more on the level of eagerness, eager to fulfill the wish of the Father, the Parent. When *love* is the motivating factor, how blessed is the giving of oneself! Each of these great Evangelists, the ones who have agreed to travel to distant lands, these great men are walking their talk. They are human in that they have their uncertainties, such as even I had in my Biblical days.

Every great man/woman has an ego to bring under control. It becomes his/her task to recognize the ego, to know that it will attempt to pump you up to be more pompous, more than you are. Each person is learning these kinds of lessons or one would not be on the planet. Maybe one's lesson is how to speak to millions—how to stand before millions and be bombarded with the energies swirling around you. However, the person, if his/her faith is strong and has vast wisdom, will innately know there is a protective shield that we put around him/her. We need to keep the pastor's energies as pure as possible in order that he/she can do what the work demands. Moreover, there are very strong women Evangelists that magnetize huge crowds of people to them. Therefore, I do recognize them also.

Now, why am I making a point of addressing these huge Crusades? In the Biblical times as I walked the Earth, I was bringing in the new religion of Christianity. I told the disciples to go out and preach the gospel throughout the world. ***Matthew 24:14*** *And this gospel of the* *kingdom shall be preached in all the world for a witness unto all nations; and then shall the end come.* Remember the energies of the planet, as well as the peoples, were not that aware. I wanted the Teachings to reach those unaware people, to love thy neighbor, to cease so much fighting. It was for those times in history. Now in this 21st century, people are more aware, and yet there are pockets of peoples all over the world who do not have the awareness of *love* in its purest sense. They love in their own ways, but many times, it is greed and coveting what they do not have. They have no one to teach them how to raise themselves up in order to raise their awareness.

While the Crusades contain drama and entertainment for some, the Crusades also provide an arena for brotherly love to manifest. For the first time, people of different faiths are joined in sharing and fellowship. The beautiful spiritual music offers them joy and touches many people. As the pastors read some of the passages and offer the *altar call* to come and be saved, that is the standard way to get people to respond—to spark a change. Moreover, yes, it is semantics again. As I have said, people cannot be saved by another. However, in their professing a desire to be saved, do you not see how their free will choice may activate changes in them for the better? Thousands and now millions respond to that ceremony. It is just a ceremony, but for the people involved and especially if the Holy Spirit does visit them and they find themselves falling under the Spirit, this is many times a life-changing, dynamic event.

Most people who have made a choice for some particular change in their life can become overzealous, fanatical, or become Fundamental. However, the dynamic of change is what is occurring—whatever it takes to get people out of their complacency, their addictions, and their unproductiveness. As millions make a change, they are raising their awareness and their energy frequencies. Spiritually, they are making a positive effort for change. Thoughts and actions change and become cleaner. The people refrain from using negative and degrading verbiage in an attempt to give more of themselves, to be more in service to God. All of this then influences the . How can it not?

The Earth can raise her vibration then because the people have raised theirs. Do you see, Readers, how Crusades become a glorious, methodological service for the Father's Plan? The many pastors, those of high morals, ideals, and love for humankind, are instruments of God. They are the doers whose soul purpose is to raise people's consciousness so the planet can move into the fourth and then into the fifth dimensions. These pastors know their purpose and are doing a magnificent job. Most pastors are Fundamentalists, but they do no harm. They may be over zealous, but they fire people up because of their own fire.

I have talked of many facets of religions that need to change. Even the great pastors need to think in terms of semantics, that there could be a possibility not everything they read in the Bible is total truth. It is impossible for it to be. The pastors themselves in their deep meditation and prayer time need to ask me some of those questions New Agers accept. Did I die on the cross? Did I marry? Whom did I marry? Was Mary Magdalene really a sinner? Who all was sitting at the table for the Last Supper? How old was I when I died? These many questions the New Agers address eagerly. The Fundamentalists think of those kinds of questions as blasphemy. It frightens them, for then they would have to change some of their belief systems they have expounded upon and from which they built their lives. It is a scary thought for them. Therefore, they put blinders on and keep putting out the same Biblical stories and rhetoric that are suspect in their truth.

Therefore, the task before us all, if we are going to move Christianity into the 21st century, is to cease the relentless rhetoric, the constant quoting of scripture. It does little to inspire people. Pastors who build their sermons from a particular passage—take out a theme—are using their own fine minds. They are grounding the theoretical teachings, making them real to people. Today's generation does not speak, let alone think in Biblical terms. It is too esoteric and not of their everyday world as they understand it to be. You have noticed perhaps, Readers, how I have taken several modern phrases and woven them among my words. It is getting back to basics.

You know when I was teaching my disciples, they did not know what I was talking about half the time. That is why I had to make up little stories and parables, to put the teachings in a way that would make sense for them. I was talking to good-hearted, simple men—men who had their humanness and their ego-drives. To take twelve of them and turn them into teachers was really a daunting task. I just kept hammering away at a certain concept using any method, story, or example I could. You note I just said *hammering*, a modern-time word, but quite graphic. I chose terms that were for **that** Biblical era. The scribes then attempted years later to make heads or tails of what I was saying.

After years passed, my disciples tried writing what I was saying. Well, if they had difficulty then when I was with them, how much harder it was to grasp my meaning when I no longer taught them! They were to go out on their own and teach people. Simple fishermen were now supposed to be great Teachers. Well, they **were** on a Spirit level, but not their physical selves. When the Holy Spirit came upon them, they were given gifts of communication; however, they were not necessarily given complete memory of what I said. No one could.

Take one of our brilliant minds of today and ask him/her to quote verbatim from his special schoolteacher. He may remember some phrases, but to quote exactly what the teacher had said during a lecture is impossible, unless the person has photographic memory, which is quite rare. Therefore, dear Readers, please let go of having to quote every scripture, memorizing each word, and deciphering its meaning. It is a futile exercise in my opinion and loaded with people's projections of what they perceived that I said. Know that *truth* is many times not a constant. There is fluidity and change to it. When it becomes such a solid fact, it no longer is truth. Truth carries a great deal of change.

One of the examples I could give you is that when a body dies, it goes into decay. Not much is left and even less is left if the body is cremated. However, the truth is this dead body still has life in its ashes. It is called *fertilizer* if it is an animal. If a human, the body is referred to as ashes, which must go back to the land as in, *ashes to ashes, dust to dust*. There is much life in those ashes. If scientists knew how to read those ashes well, they would see the DNA cells in a dormant state. Nevertheless, there is life in that dust and its properties can bring life to plants. It helps them grow strong. The point I am making is the way *truth* has different aspects to it. There are changes in *truth* because of different circumstances surrounding it.

Dear Readers, keep progressing. Do not embrace a concept, no matter where it originates, and strangle it. Allow changes to occur.

Christianity needs to change. Fundamentalists need to become more flexible, to see other points of view, or if they cannot see it, to allow others their belief systems. If God created one religion, how could he not have varied religions for His varied cultures? The way Christianity has progressed down throughout the ages, it has picked up many negative aspects to it: burning at the stake to try and drive a sacred belief out of a person; sitting in judgment of people and throwing them in prison if they did not think like you. It served only to drive people underground, to sneak, and to lie. The growth of Christianity held horrid birth pains. There is much karma attached to that religion. Remember my telling you organizations have karma? Well, so do religions. All have their negative as well as positive karmas. What is happening to Christianity through the rigid beliefs of the Fundamentalists is compounding the negative karma. Remember the Cause and Effect rule. That comes from God.

The problem as we in the spiritual planes see it is that people in their narrow viewpoints become so righteous in a negative way. If a neighbor does not believe as they do, that neighbor is condemned, no matter what the religion is. Where to begin? Well, it begins with you. After you read this chapter, take a few deep breaths and read it again, and again, and again. Let go of your stereotypical belief systems. Let go of having to save your neighbor. The only constant you need is *love*. Love your neighbor and be the Wayshower. You will do more in helping your neighbor's growth in awareness than you can ever imagine. **We** cannot do this, bringing people to God. Only you in love and consciousness can help move people forward. Remember we all have a purpose. Ours is to give you needed information. Yours is to receive it and change.

(*Actually, Jesus had 24 Disciples—12 men and 12 women with Mary Magdalene being one and His adopted cousin-sister, Mariam, being another. Jesus tells us also that only approximately 500 people ever listened to him. 2011)*

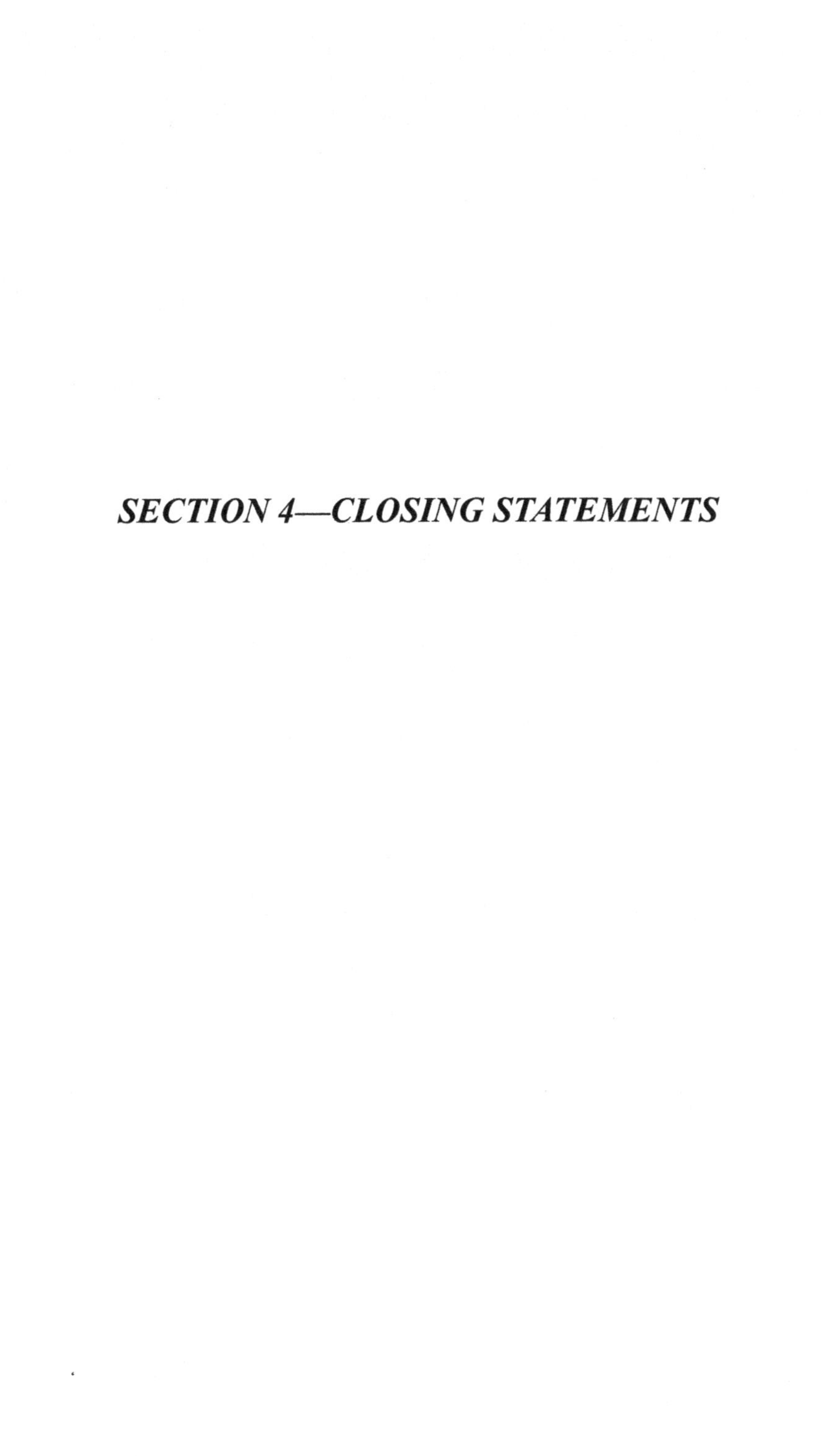

SECTION 4—CLOSING STATEMENTS

CLOSING STATEMENT from JESUS

I AM Jesus. My Spiritual Colleagues and I have given you much information. It is our hope that you will receive this without judgment, either of the Author, Us, or more importantly yourself. People forget sometimes that they are judging themselves when they make a derogatory statement about others and themselves. Do not judge. Love yourself. Love others.

In creating this work, I have purposely taken off the rose-colored glasses for you. I wish for you to come to another point of view. Humanity loves *sameness*. It is so slow to change. If someone says some object is *blue,* humanity will see it forever as the color blue, while the color may have faded over time and is no longer its original color. Yet people do not notice this. Many of the Teachings in the Bible need different interpretations. They need updating, new energy brought to them. How one does this is to realize the time and place in history.

Realize the cultural differences. Realize the modern nomenclature. Realize that modern pastors are still attempting to decipher age-old wordage. **Realize they are trying to bring ancient wordage to modern ears**. Realize this generation has a very different language. There were not the Internet, computers, automobiles, and huge places of worship, not counting Solomon's Temple, in that era.

If you carry away one concept from this book, make it be that **Spirituality is a pathway to God that needs modernization!** The old ways carry much wisdom, but only if there is flexibility. Most people do not know what true *spirituality* is. In its purest form, it is a direct path to God. It is a simple path to believe in, but most intricate to trod upon, for we are speaking of energy. Everything is energy. *Spirituality* is a practice that incorporates all the vast energies that have been made available by God. It is *Light* and *sound*. It is *color*, *music*, energy bands of *truth*, *caring*, *hope*, and above all, *love*. Spirituality is a knowing—knowing how to manipulate energies, to be able to move in, around, and through them. It is being able to travel to the planets and star systems into, through, and beyond vast Universes. That is all part of *spirituality*. To try to confine one's belief system to a few passages in one Bible is such a narrow viewpoint. There is so much more to God's World and much to explore.

I bless you, Readers. I remain forever your Friend, who loves each of you, as you walk your path that is unique to you. No one can tell you how to walk it—no priests, pastors, nor rabbis. Not even me. I can only show you a way. Allow me into your hearts. I have never left you. Many, many paths lead to God. Which one will **you** take?

CLOSING STATEMENT from DJWHAL KHUL

I AM Djwhal Khul. I will now help bring this book to a close by my closing remarks. First, I wish to thank the Author for her telepathic diligence and perseverance in mentally bringing in the material for this book. It has been my deep pleasure to be a part of this work.

In decades past, when I walked your Earth in a physical body, I always had my head in the clouds, so to speak. I was filled with love and the desire to actually see and commune with God and the exalted Spiritual Masters. I spent many hours in meditation making contact with many of them. Now that I am in that higher dimension that I was dreaming about and anticipating, I realize I had missed some vital opportunities. I did not take the time *to smell the roses*, as you Readers might say. I did not fully appreciate what living on Earth was all about. What a great privilege it is to have a body given to you, to care and nurture it to maturity. I realize I was more interested in the Spiritual World than the beautiful Earth upon which I was privileged to walk.

Now I have seen both ends of the spectrum. I see the advantages of having a body, to be able to walk among the people and greet them and feel their emotions, as well as experience mine. Being in the etheric dimensions, I can still walk among you, and I have many times, but it is somewhat frustrating, for most cannot hear me, let alone see me. I wish it both ways—for us to see and hear each other.

It is a glorious future that looms on the horizon, for Heaven on Earth is coming closer in reality. There will be no veils. You will see me as well as I see you! You will talk to me, as well as I will speak with you. You will hear me easily, as I will hear you. That will be a glorious time. As the Earth raises her vibrations and ascends fully into the fourth and fifth dimensions, this two-way communication will manifest. While we of the Spiritual Hierarchy will come and go, disappear and reappear instantly, this action will be so normal; people will not think anything of it. In fact, some of humanity also will have the same ability. We can appear in Etheric Light-bodies or take a more solid form and appear as humans. Whatever the situation calls for, we will do. However, it will be a normal circumstance, so not much attention will be drawn to us. The reaction will apt to be one of, *oh, there goes Jesus. He was just here; you can catch him tomorrow.* The present concept of separation between you and us will be no more. We never have been separate, but since the majority cannot see or hear us, there is that myth that we do not exist. Well, the evidence is in this book! We are here.

Therefore, dear Readers, know in your hearts that the time is coming when you will see us, finally. There just has to be some more adjusting and growth of humanity's consciousness, the raising of frequencies for both you and Earth, and then it will happen. There will be no more veils and fewer mysteries about us and more *peace, love*, and *unity*. I bless all of you and I bless this Author and our book. It has been an honor for me to be part of this endeavor.

CLOSING STATEMENT from MARY MAGDALENE

I AM Mary Magdalene. Good morning to all the Readers of this most auspicious book. We know that much of the material may be startling to you. That is why we gave you just a few simple pages of text and then spoke of other issues like *hope* and *compassion*. In days of lore, life seemed difficult for us. We had many conflicts with the Romans on how to live our lives. We wanted to be left alone to pray to God, but they were so afraid of losing power that they kept watchful eyes on any of our activities. It culminated in those terrible crucifixions. What an agonizing death for felons in those days. The Romans bandied about this punishment like the English and Europeans did for stealing a loaf of bread long ago. Those poor beggars were thrown into prison to die, while in other ancient times, the punishment was crucifixion.

You see, I did not know my Lord Jesus, the keeper of my heart, was **not** going to die. Put yourself a moment in my place. We were married. I was pregnant with our daughter. Not only did I have the emotions acting up from the hormones, but also here my husband, whom I cherished, was going to be crucified! Picture those ugly, large, homespun nails going through your hands and feet! Even now, I at times cannot bear to remember the agony of all that. I saw him suffering. I saw his blood dripping down. I thought I would faint from the agony of watching it all.

Why am I telling you this all over again? To keep you awakened. To help you raise **your** awareness. To help you lift your veils. Readers, when tragic events take place in history, they can be used as metaphors in modern-day living. One can use *crucifixion* to illustrate one's feeling of a certain happening in your life—the pain of it, the humiliation of it, and the degradation of it. How it can kill you **if** you let it.

Humanity does use this word to illustrate the various emotions I have mentioned. However, dear Readers, know also that in your lives today, when your *freedom* is being eroded, when *equality* is not practiced, when there are edicts that do not allow *Christmas songs* in schools, when *prayer* is not allowed in schools, when the

Ten Commandments are not allowed to be written on government property, something has gone terribly wrong. Your balance in life, being able to have your freedoms in all things, is badly eroding. Is this not a crucifixion in itself? Are these not nails being driven into your symbolic bodies? They very definitely are. Your emotional and mental bodies are experiencing elements of crucifixion.

Therefore, as this book ends, I leave you with the prayer that humanity will not allow itself to be crucified. Whenever you make decisions of great importance, such as with the election of a government, be discerning. Ask yourself; *am I being crucified, even strangled, because of all the newly formed agencies that are invading my liberties*? Delve deeply within yourself, your I AM Presence, for your answers. You will know the answer. Ask what you need to do for you, always in a peaceful, loving way and never with violence and loss of life.

I bring you glad tidings of joy and my love for all of you.

CLOSING STATEMENT from GOD

I AM your God, your Father. My dear daughter, I come to tell you I AM most pleased. Dear child, I note your dedication, your perseverance for the task. My Son and I have chosen well for this task. Your daughter, Susan, also is to be highly commended. You make an outstanding team of mother and daughter.

In the days to come, I will be watching over you even more so, for these holidays seem to carry much stress for not only you two, but for humanity. I perceive the frenzied pace to make preparations and to buy specific gifts for all on one's list. What a joy it is to observe this. However, as you know, it is also disturbing to see the darker side of humanity—mainly *greed, hoarding, the intent to kill or maim* in the wars and outside of war. My children are still learning their lessons. *The lessons are of living in peace, sharing one's abundance with others, loving one's neighbor, and allowing others their different beliefs.* Many lessons are still to be learned before *peace* can reign.

I send the world My Energies of *love, peace, hope, and compassion.* It breaks My Heart to observe so much despair, when in actuality there ought to be none! My Kingdom is open for all to enter. He or she does **not have** to be Muslim, Jewish, Buddhist, or Christian. You are **all** My children in your beautiful shades of colors, with your unique looks, actions, and cultures. What a glorious melting pot you are, My children.

In this book, My Sons and Daughter have spoken of some of their personal histories. However, they have only touched upon a speck of those ancient past lives. The Lord known as *Djwhal Khul,* with his brilliant mind, is a profound walking encyclopedia, as you might say—vast knowledge of the Cosmos. There is so much more he could have said. My Daughter known as *Mary Magdalene* also has a vast range of experience and wisdom. She has given you Readers a wee nibble of her many adventures. Happily, the one she does speak of had a wonderful ending for they **did** go off to other countries and had a glorious life. You know much of My Son Jesus, known in other Universes and Star Systems by a myriad of other names. All are revered, and greatly respected and admired. Readers, you have been privileged to receive their messages. They took great pleasure in giving them to Chako, but I do wish to emphasize it was not just a casual happenstance. You have received the Energies of Living Gods in their own right. This fact is not to be taken lightly.

In all probability, there will be several more books, all of which I will bless as I have blessed this one. Enjoy your reading adventure, dear children. I carry each one of you in My Heart, for I have been with you and you with Me forever.

I AM your Father, who is not on high and inaccessible, but in your hearts and throughout this beautiful planet, Earth. Part of My Plan is for Heaven to be on Earth—that there is such a blending that there is no more separation.

I bid you *good day* and give all of you My Eternal Blessings!

EPILOGUE #1

Once the holidays had ended, I concentrated on preparing this manuscript for publication. Even though the editing was rough at best, I was told by the publisher I had chosen to send it in anyway. She preferred reading what the Masters had said with little editing. I took her at her word and mailed in the manuscript in mid-January 2005.

I am quite naïve about the publishing world and did not realize I would not hear from the publisher. In the meantime, I again read the book from cover to cover, correcting any typos and changing some of the punctuation. I therefore decided I would continue getting the book ready to distribute. The one fact I know is I was **not** to keep the masters' wisdom to myself. It does not make any difference in what form this work is presented. The fact you readers are holding these pages and absorbing the information is all that matters.

The number **three** plays a definitive part in my life. I completed this first book in **three** months—September 25, 2004—December 25, 2004. The second one is almost completed. By the time it is completed, it will have been **three** months—mid-January 2005—mid-April 2005. I am to write **three** books in this series. That is my pre-birth agreement. The number **three** is a completion number in physical reality. As I look back on my life, I can see how that number came up for me repeatedly. Moreover, by the way, I have **three** daughters!

(In fact, I ended up writing 6 more books in this series.)

APPENDIX—DREAMS AND PERSONAL JOURNAL NOTATIONS

As I persevered in writing this BOOK ONE, I received encouragement through my dreams and Jesus' personal comments, which I wrote in my journal.

The following are some of the dreams and journal writings I would like to share. I have not written the dreams out in their entirety, but only the parts I felt were pertinent to my book-writing process.

A personal interpretation and **not** a full analysis will follow each dream segment.

Date October 14, 2004

Dream

I am thumbing through a book. On that last page is a check-off list, and all the sentences had a check mark in front of them. I see the date, April 4.

Interpretation

This dream segment speaks for itself. I make the assumption the year is 2005 and that our book will be distributed in one form or another.

Date October 18, 2004

Journal

Jesus gave me the title of our book: *The Ultimate Experience: The Many Paths to God.* He gave me the specifics for the book, including what the cover might look like.

Dream

I am sitting next to a man. He has two large flat glass baking dishes on his knees. They are filled with bite-sized roast chicken morsels. He tells me they are excellent chicken livers and offered me one. I take it and pronounce it, *Good*. It is pure white meat.

Interpretation

The man is Jesus. He is feeding me excellent pieces of information, which I say is *good*. The 'chicken livers' is in reference to the fact Jewish women often cook chicken livers. This was a code for me to know it was Jesus, for he was a Jew.

Date October 25, 2004
Dream
I am telling a man we need some new towels. The old towels are getting faded and frayed. I open a closet and there are sets of towels in a rich forest green. The towels are all stacked according to their sizes. The closet is beautifully organized. I exclaim, *oh, those green towels will do.*
Interpretation
The closet represents where our book still is. It has not been distributed yet. The positioning of the towels represents the chapters being organized. The forest green color was rich information to replace the old myths, perhaps.

Date October 26, 2004
Journal
I AM Jesus. I wish to tell you a story, dear one. It is a story of courage and perseverance. It was many lifetimes ago. Before I was Jesus, you and I were brother and sister. I was older, but you were wiser. We enhanced each other. One day when we children were in our adolescence, and we had finished our midday meal, we decided we would venture forth and go beyond where we knew we ought not to go. Not only could we become lost, but also there were many poisonous snakes out.
However, as little bodies do, we did not listen to our elders, but ran and played hither and yon, turning in different directions and losing all sense of where our camp was. Eventually, we tired and became hungry and decided we had better head back to camp. Well, it soon became obvious we did not know in which direction camp lay. We became anxious. I wanted to go one way; you, my baby sister, wanted to go another. We eventually tried both ways. Neither was right.
Finally, as the stars started appearing, we snuggled down on the ground, hoping our parents would search for us. We were afraid and tearful and oh, so regretful. We found strength in the closeness of each other. We knew we could perish if we separated. Your trust in me as your older brother held me in my courage and strength. You trusted me so much that I would take care of you that it strengthened me in that resolve not to let anything harm you.

Eventually, we heard voices and saw the torch lights of our parents and others searching for us. We gladly yelled our position, and we were soon reunited with our family. You see dear one, your trust and faith in your big brother made **me** stronger. We had each other and our love gave us courage to persevere and not panic.
The moral of this little story of so many thousand of years ago, before anyone had heard of Moses, let alone Jesus, shows how *love, courage, and perseverance* overcome obstacles. As you struggle at times with birthing this book, trust your Elder Brother to take care of you to help you with this process.

Date October 26, 2004
Dream
I find a pair of light-blue suede sandals in a closet. My name is printed on the toe area, *Verling Priest*. I know that the sandals are meant for me. I put them on and they fit perfectly. The scene changes and I am sitting with two men. One is a doctor with caring energy and calls me *Sweetheart*. The other man is a tradesman. I am wearing my blue suede sandals. The doctor poses a question to me, *whom would you thank for your sandals, the doctor who prescribed them, or the tradesman who made them? I reply, the tradesman, for it is his skill that has made the sandals.* The doctor seemed pleased with my answer.
Interpretation
In my channeling for the chapter Exodus, Jesus is describing Moses' journey and asked the Reader to put him/herself in his *sandals*. Therefore, I know that the dream refers to this book, and the doctor was Jesus. While he is giving me much of the material for the book, the tradesman (Chako) is doing the actual work. I ought to be giving myself some thanks also. My soul is on the second Ray, which is blue, hence, the *blue* sandals. In addition, they were in the closet, until I put them on, "walking the talk," writing the words that were being given to me for this book.

Date November 8, 2004
Dream
Someone shows me the color of paint that is being applied to the walls of my room and closet. The color is a soft shade of green.
Interpretation
The closet is the dream symbol of where my book resides since it is not yet finished. A soft shade of green depicts new growth. My book may be growing not only in pages, but as soon as I could let go of some of my uncertainties, there was a subtle change in the energy for the book. On November 13, 2004, Jesus gave dictation for the chapter DESIRES.

Date November 12, 2004
Dream
I am lying in bed with my eyes closed. There is a coverlet of many colors on the bed. There is a man sitting in a chair next to the bed. He is telling me something. I do not open my eyes until he has finished talking to me. I then look straight at him.
Interpretation
A bed is my dream-code for a particular dynamic I am doing. There is that saying, *you have made your bed, now lie in it*. Therefore, the dream shows me in bed in whatever situation I have created. In this case, it is the writing of my book. The man is Jesus teaching me. The coverlet is symbolic of the *coat-of-many-colors*, which Jesus wore in his lifetime as Joseph of Egypt. The coverlet-coat blankets my bed. There is something I am not seeing to which I have closed my eyes. I only opened them when he had finished teaching. Perhaps the dream is showing me that I have opened my eyes now. I cannot recall what he was saying to me, unfortunately.

Date November 16, 2004
Journal
I AM Jesus. Dear one, I wish to address the progress of our book and the direction it is taking. As you have noticed, I have begun a series of mini-lectures on areas of concern for modern humanity. You will not find in the Bible references to *desire* stemming from memory, or *road-rages*, or *identity theft* and so forth. Therefore, beloved, you will receive several more mini-lectures that speak to **this** generation.

I do suggest the placing of these chapters be interspersed among the personal material of me.

Date November 30, 2004
Journal
We are the Lords, Jesus, Sananda, and Maitreya. Good morning, dear one. A beautiful day for Arizona compared to many parts of your country. We come today as three in order to tell you our book is almost at the completion stage. We will finish the chapter *CHARITY* and then one or two more. We will dictate then the closing chapter. This book will not be large in length, but quite large in content. We do not see it exploding on the market ***yet.*** However, it will sell by word of mouth. We will guide you as to whom to give the book and as to what publisher. The end is in sight.

Date December 5, 2004
Dream
My daughter, Susan, and I are in a large building full of people milling around. There is a man with us. We decide to go outside and take a walk. As we approach the front door I exclaim, o*h, someone left the door wide open*! The three of us go through the door to the outside. It is a beautiful sunny day. The walkway is pink. It leads to the left and to the right. We decide going left would only take us back to where we had been. We go right. The walkway is smooth, clean and with no debris on it or around it. It seems to lead us through budding rose gardens and as far as one can see the path has no vicissitudes, but gentle curves.
Interpretation
In February 2004 after attending a Benny Hinn Crusade in Phoenix, I received this telepathic communication. *It is time to put on your mantle of purple majesty and walk with purpose and love for humanity. Your life is about to make an extraordinary change, a right turn which will bring you to me forever.* Seven months later, September 25, he told me to pick up my pen and write. I feel the dream showed me I had made a right turn in writing this book and was walking the path that stretched smoothly and cleanly before me. In addition, Susan had taken that right turn with me. I believe the man in the dream was Lord Jesus and he was right at our heels. He

had left the door wide open for us to walk through. We went through it with no hesitation at all.

Date December 15, 2004
Journal
Jesus comments to me, Let us discuss our book. It is brief, exactly what it is supposed to be. You see, if it is kept short, people are more apt to read it from cover to cover. Some people, like your Susan, will like the Teachings (mini-lectures) best. Others will like only the more personal pages. This book will not please all. It is their level of evolvement. However, it is what it is supposed to be. Your next book could be longer or not. There is always leeway.

Date December 22, 2004
Journal
I AM Jesus. I wish to comment on our ship, the *Bethlehem Star* that Ashtar (Commander of the Galactic Fleet of Spaceships) spoke of this morning (channeled by Ziranna in the Wednesday group I attend). The ship is indeed circling the planet sending good tidings to Earth. As people think of that long ago Biblical era, they will receive the energy put out by our ship—one of *love, peace,* and *good will* to all.
With the casualties of war, many families will be heart-broken during Christmas. Send them *love* and *Light*. Those souls are now in our care. We will heal their bodies. For those souls, even though it was their game plan, they may find they really are not ready to let go. Therefore, the healing angels will help them and their families. War is always a tragic experience, whether for the dead or those alive. We will be with them on **both** sides of the veil.

Date December 23, 2004
Journal
I AM Jesus . . . . . would you like to go to your tablet. I have Someone who wishes to make a few comments. I have mentioned previously that I had a surprise for you. I will step back now. My surprise turned out to be **God** mentally speaking with me. His comments bring to a close this, as well as the section on Closing Statements. What an honor!

Date December 25, 2004
Journal
It is interesting to note that the Lord Jesus instructed me to pick up my pen and write his dictation on September 25, 2004. Three months later, the book is finished. Now all that remains is the grunt work, pulling all the pieces together, editing, distributing, and so forth. It has not totally sunk in that we wrote a book in three months! I can feel already the second book just waiting to manifest.
He came to me mentally on Christmas morning with this message: Dear one, again thank you for your lovely energies, being so dedicated, and with such a willingness to be of service. We are all so thankful you are so dedicated and that you persevered, even with your uncertainties. However, look how far you have come, our sister! I will close now with a blessing upon you on this . . . Holiest of Days. My love surrounds and keeps you, beloved; **I AM Jesus, your Lord, Teacher, and Friend. Adieu.**

Readers, this concludes the Dream and Personal Journal Notation segment. I hope you found this section insightful—a glimpse into the birthing process of our first book. Until we meet again in BOOK TWO
Blessings, CHAKO

NOTATIONS

FRONT COVER TEXT BOOK TWO

THE ULTIMATE EXPERIENCE
The Many Paths to GOD

BOOK TWO

Verling CHAKO Priest, PhD

COPYRIGHT BOOK TWO

THE ULTIMATE EXPERIENCE SYNOPSIS TWO

Those Readers who are familiar with the format used in BOOK ONE, will feel like they have greeted an old friend when they peruse this BOOK TWO. However, this book does not address myths about the Master Jesus, as much as it speaks about *beginnings.* In each of the twenty-three mini-lectures, the Reader is invited to discern the *beginning,* which is the underlying teaching. We are not always aware of *beginnings* in our life.

The Lords showcase their humor in their choice of chapter titles. The Master Jesus' title for the chapter from BOOK ONE, *Have You Said Your Prayers Today,* is a good example. One would expect the topic to be in religious terms. However, the narrative centers more on sports—how teams and players pray to win.

The Lord Jesus describes again some of his experiences while on the cross. He spoke of this on Good Friday and titled the chapter, *Jesus Speaks. I did not let fear enter in or touch me in any way.*

Lords Jesus, Maitreya, and Sananda spoke on Easter and titled their talk, *Easter Thoughts. Hence, dear ones, the words Resurrection and Ascension can be used interchangeably. We are ascending every minute—raising consciousness. We are being resurrected in those moments. We are being reborn into a different consciousness.*

Lord Sananda narrates many of the chapters, each one of which leads the Reader to read the next one and then the next, always discovering a new perspective. In the chapter, *Death of a Great Saint,* he pays tribute to Pope John Paul II. *We pay homage to this Saint who fulfilled his purpose, served the Father all of his life, and died with dignity and in God's Grace . . . We salute you great Saint.*

AUTHOR'S HEADS UP #2

I deleted the previous material in this section for it was pretty much a repeat of BOOK ONE. You can scroll back up to that PREFACE if you wish to tweak your memory on how this journey of book writing began.

You have noticed and will notice that whenever there is additional material or tidbits of information I think you Readers might enjoy, I have added that here and there in italics for your edification.

I do not have an Appendix section with this second book, telling of my dreams and Journal notations. I had gotten feedback from my daughters and they did not think the dreams enhanced the book experience, so I dropped that.

My books seemed to be manifesting so rapidly back then that I gave up the idea of seeking a publisher and just took my material to Office Max, printed out the orders, and had the books spiral-bound. That worked to a point, say for a couple of years. When BOOK FOUR came forth, I knew I had to make other arrangements. That is when I found Trafford, a self-publishing company, and have been using them ever since.

It also was the time I let it be known that the first three books had not been published, per se, for fans of my books kept trying to find them on the Internet. Therefore, the first three books would not be available, and they had no ISBN number at that time.

However, here they are at last. And you are reading BOOK TWO now. I do hope your long wait was worth it for you!

Blessings, Chako (6-01-11)

SPECIAL STATEMENT #2

To my three beautiful daughters,

Susan, Sandra, and Sara.

What a joy it is to watch each of

you grow, touch your Truth,

moreover, fulfill your purpose!

THANK YOUS #2

My first acknowledgment once again must be to God and the Ascended Masters: Sananda, Maitreya, Jesus, and Djwhal Khul who are my Teachers. They have provided the context of our book with not only their personal stories, but also their wisdom on many issues that face humanity today. I thank them and feel blessed to have them in my life.

I give loving thanks with a great appreciation to my oldest daughter, Susan Verling Miller O'Brien, for all of her computer skills. No matter how many *boo-boos* I made, she cheerfully made the 45—minute drive to my house and spent many an hour correcting my errors and instructing me on how to frame Book TWO, as well as Book THREE. Susan was invaluable indeed in this endeavor. She is also the one who implemented the design for the covers using Microsoft Word. The little curly cues going up the side of the page, symbolically speaking, really do look like they could be the various paths people take to God. Thank you, dear heart!

People who work telepathically know they must strive to keep their energies as clear and pure as possible when channeling in order to keep from contaminating the data that is being transmitted. One's little ego, or an implant—a *wanna-be*—or just entities one has around one can 'muddy the waters,' if allowed. Therefore, I wished to speak with Lord Jesus through someone other than myself, after the Lords had declared our first book as finished. It is my way of validating my work. I asked the Master through whom He wished to communicate. He suggested my e-mail pal, Sally LeSar of Indianapolis, IN, for He had dictated many of the pages of her book, *Treasures from the Universe* . . . She also strives for purity in her channeling. He pronounced the first book *perfect*. Now here I am asking the Masters again, through Sally, if Book TWO is to their satisfaction. May I send it out to be copyrighted? My answer lay in the fact that they have started Book THREE already. Oh, joy! Therefore, dear Sally, thank you for your support and friendship. I am still *receiving* their Teachings and it is wonderful.

I attend a Metaphysical Spiritual Group facilitated by Mary Helen Wichmann. She has been so supportive of my work with the Masters. Thank you so much, Mary Helen. Your encouraging remarks meant a great deal to me. I presented BOOK ONE recently to that group. The work was enthusiastically received, and many of the participants seemed eagerly awaiting the distribution of this second book. I thank you and feel much joy, as I am sure the Masters do also.

I had requested help in the form of a proofreader for this book, for my eyes and brain simply do not agree on what I am seeing. My prayer was answered in the form of Heather Clarke, a professional proofreader, who recently joined our Wednesday group. What an angel they have sent me in Heather. Is it not amazing? I put out there that I need help and a few weeks later there she is! Thank you, Heather, and thank you Masters!

(Heather Clarke is the founder of the Arizona Enlightenment Center. She has been invaluable in becoming a resource person for those in the Valley who seek venues for their teachings and products. From the get-go she became my editor and has become a dear friend.)

SECTION 5—LEAD-IN #2

THE BEGINNING—Maitreya, Sananda, Jesus

I AM Maitreya. In this BOOK TWO, there will be several more of the masters who will speak, not just Jesus. Therefore, we decided I would give the Introduction chapter this time. You may find all kinds of implications in your mind, as you wonder what **he** will speak of with that kind of title. It carries a connotation of a start of some kind. It can be the start of a book, but since this is BOOK TWO, logic would proclaim that that is not quite right.

Another speculation could be that I will speak of *In the beginning . . . ,* like the Bible starts out. That too is a possibility but will not be in this situation. I hope I have kept you in suspense somewhat. By now, you ought really to be questioning, *what **is** he talking about*? As Jesus has said, we are purposely entitling the chapters so there is an element of surprise about the content. I will not tease you further. This title, ***The Beginning*****, simply means this BOOK TWO will have many subjects of which you will just get a nibble.** It will give you many and varied subjects for speculation and musings. **Each little lecture will be a *beginning* of a topic** that can be carried forth by you in discussions with others, or in those quiet moments when you start contemplating something.

In this BOOK TWO, you will be introduced to different concepts—a different take on a particular idea or belief system. It is hoped that by the end of each chapter, you will have a new perspective, and I hope it will spark a change in you. We have stated often, not only in BOOK ONE, but in different channelings too numerous to be specific, that humanity is slow to change. People tend to grab a particular concept that touches them in some way. They embrace the idea and make it evermore their Truth. This is how people learn and grow. However, as the person matures, it also becomes an opportunity for one to let go of a certain way of looking at a particular dynamic.

In your pioneer days, people had belief systems about cleanliness. There was the Saturday night bath for the family, so all would be clean for church the next day. Nowadays one has a shower or a tub to step into at anytime one wishes. That would have been a new concept for that generation. People had simpler lives then, so their belief systems were also simpler. Go even further back in time when men of science proclaimed the Earth was flat. It took a brave soul to venture forth in a boat for months at a time. Now travel back further than that to Biblical times. Imagine what it must have been like living as an Egyptian and actually believing that their pharaoh was a god. If one put that into the context of hero worship, one can look at the youth of this modern day and see in what direction their idolatry and beliefs lie. Music is a good example. There are youths who are drawn to the heavy metal and the antics of the longhaired musicians undulating to their own beat. Therefore, each generation builds its own energy band.

In America, some of the energy correlates with designer clothes. The name seems to mean everything. If the garment does not have a name brand, even a fake one, the article of clothing is passed up in disdain. There are your youths who attempt to make a statement. They go against the norm. They have differently dyed hair and different hairstyles. The more out of the norm, shown by all the face piercing and body piercing, the more they try to outdo one another. These young people try so hard to be unaccepted by society and are only accepted by the people of their own out-of-the-norm energy groups.

Readers, each society has a *beginning* of some dynamic. From where did those exceedingly different modes of dress, hairstyles, and body-piercing come? What **was** that *beginning* that swept the nation and then the world? What was the belief system of those individuals that said, *ah, now I have found my niche*? Would it astound you to know that this type of outside-the-norm mode of being came from other star systems? Does it surprise you to know that many of the *beginnings* that seem to appear on Earth actually had their beginnings from outer space? There are societies throughout the Universe that dress as these youths do; wear their hair as they do and use metal for body decoration.

In our Heavenly sphere, the women are statuesque with beautiful, long hair and have large, intensive eyes of blue, violet, green, or brown. You see they are a representation of the Divine—the perfect female body. Men also are statuesque, muscular, and may wear flowing robes, or garments of natural materials. Many wear what you call *jewels*, but their stones are for a purpose. Each stone carries a certain vibration that the wearer is attuned to. While the stone ornaments are quite beautiful on arms, waistbands, around the neck and on the forehead, these large stones emanate a particular vibration—a pulsation. When one of the Earth sees a great master wearing a huge aquamarine on his belt, it can be an awe-inspiring experience, especially if one comes close enough to feel the pulsating energies.

Beginnings—everything has a beginning. In this BOOK TWO, we will speak about the beginning of different concepts. The various masters who will speak have prepared a particular story that will tell of such beginnings. We do enjoy giving forth sacred information to humanity. It is gratifying to us. It also becomes a barometer for us, for it tells us how well some new concept is being received.

Therefore, dear Readers, it is our hope for you that each page you turn will hold an interest for you. Just as in your music, some will be drawn to one presentation versus another. That is our purpose—how we have formulated BOOK TWO. Of course, not all information will resonate with everyone. Speaking on a variety of subjects, using titles that will tease your curiosity, we hope there will be chapters that will teach you, will be informative for you, will spark a new belief in you, will facilitate letting go of an outdated belief system, and above all else bring joy to your hearts.

Therefore, I will step back now, for another soul will continue this theme and introduction. I bless you, Readers. Enjoy!

I AM Sananda. In the beginning of each of your journeys, Readers, there was always a plan. You may not have known the plan, but your soul did. While you on a personality level jostled in your mind something you might do, your soul was waiting patiently and maybe not so patiently, for you to take that first step, that beginning step that would walk you toward, into, and through an achievement in your life. For the younger crowd, they could be hesitating to take that step toward college. For another, the person may be gathering courage to leave an employment and to start a new job, either working for someone else, or starting his/her own business.

Each time there is a transition in your life, it marks the beginning of something. As you all must know by now, all *beginnings* are not necessarily fruitful and successful. However, you must also realize by now that there are no accidents. Each occurrence in your life was meant to happen. People might say, *well, that is pre-ordained then*! However, I say to you, your free will does indeed influence your choices around a certain endeavor; but, dear Readers, did you know that perhaps you had different *beginnings from which to* choose?

You can visualize this by thinking in terms of walking a path. You come to an intersection. There are several highways leading hither and yon, crisscrossing each other. There are no printed signposts. It is you standing alone attempting to make the correct choice as to which freeway or roadway upon which to step. Now when I said, *alone*, I meant you **think** you are alone, but you have a whole troop of Beings with you. You have your angels, master guide, as well as other guides, all giving out signals in order to help you make the most productive choice. However, as it is with the way human Beings think in their 4D world, they are apt many times to take a path that is exceedingly difficult and not always needed for that situation.

I am sure you have heard about people who seem to make a problem more difficult than it needs to be. However, the fact that they did not choose the easier lesson does not necessarily make them wrong. They just learned a lesson of a different kind. It may have involved *patience* or *faith* in them. If they are more spiritual, one could say that they also learned to *trust* in their God, that He heard their prayers.

Let us go back to the intersection where a person is at a crossroads of some endeavor. It truly is a *beginning* for that person. The little known fact is that **all** of those roads would have eventually led to where he/she wanted to go! To give you an example, take a person who has graduated from high school and has started college. The person was struggling with the classes. During that time, the person met his/her spouse. One dropped out, the other graduated, and then they married and had a wonderful and exciting life.

Was the person wrong for quitting college and marrying? No. The person merely took another road, a path, and at the end of that path, it led that person to the same product. The person went back to school after an absence of thirty plus years and resumed what had been planned by the soul at the very beginning anyway. One could say there were two *beginnings* for that person. With both ways, many lessons were learned, and there was tremendous growth for the soul.

Therefore, dear Readers, do not become confused when you first start to walk your path—beginning something new. Know in your heart that you will not choose a **wrong** path, just one that will offer you a different journey, a different perspective than you had previously planned. Whatever way your soul was leading you to the beginning of something, it was your choice—free will—that gave you the impetus to venture forward. Think of it this way. You made a movement of some kind. You made a change. It makes no difference as to the direction, even if the choice would be viewed by some as less than positive. You went for the glass that was half-empty versus half-full. However, you still moved! You still learned, so that maybe the next time you will reach for the glass that is half-full. You will choose positively versus negatively. While you may have learned a great deal, you may also have saved yourself some heartache if you had chosen differently.

Therefore, dear Readers, know that *beginnings* are just that. They are a step in some direction. You will go wherever you put your symbolic feet. However, you may also change direction, unless you had trod on wet cement and are forever more stuck in a habitual pattern with no change in sight. Even that situation stems from your choices.

Thus, lift your feet high. Dare to step forth on dry land, so that you may turn around whenever you wish and take a new direction—start a new beginning toward something. ***Beginnings* are just that—a new step that will take you in a new direction**. Give some thought to your *beginnings.* The ideal would be to contemplate with God and commune with your mighty I AM Presence. It might stimulate and awaken you and let you know you **have** your answers and direction deep within your heart.

I AM Jesus. Both Maitreya and Sananda spoke of different aspects of this chapter, *The Beginning*. I will now end this section with my rendition.

Readers, you have been given a taste of how to view a *beginning* in your life. Most of humanity does not think about the many facets of the word *beginning.* It has a varied dynamic of past, present, and future. I will speak about changes that occur when one is beginning something in his/her life.

So often people pay little attention to the many paths they trod. If they are at the work place and someone expresses the desire to go to a particular out-of-town seminar, some will decide quickly they will attend. Others will pass up the opportunity. Sananda told you that it really was your choice. A choice that had you on a certain path and eventually you would end up at the end-point where Spirit had guided you toward at the beginning. However, look at the changes that occurred while on that path. Once you take those steps toward something, **all** of your life will change. The changes can be subtle or very noticeable.

Some people do not realize the influence their journey has had on them. Take the person at the work place, the one who decided to go to the seminar. We will make our example a woman. She arranged for her travel, got her wardrobe together, for clothes are important to most women, and arrived tired at her seminar, but with great anticipation. She met different people. It was nice being away from work for a while. However, she found the seminar did not fulfill all of her expectations. She was somewhat disappointed but changed her attitude from her expectation of learning a new skill to *this was a nice little vacation.*

She arrives safely home again feeling refreshed. When people asked her how the seminar was, she replied it was interesting in spots, but she really did not learn anything new. However, it was great getting away. *Oh, you ought to have seen how beautiful some of the women looked—so well groomed and trim. I felt kind of like a country field mouse paying a visit to my city folks*, she remarked. She then declined dessert at lunch, stating she was too full. Little by little, she starts changing her eating habits. She finds that she has no desire for her former diet. She starts making subtle changes for a trim, healthier body without noticing the change she is making in her choices.

Change, people, can be subtle and over time, or it can be immediate. Perhaps her colleague at her work place was greatly impacted at the seminar. She learned a new skill and became eager to incorporate it at her workplace. What do you, Reader, think had happened? It is obvious to us that her soul had been able to connect more with its body and was then able to initiate the changes. **Whenever change is to take place on a positive nature, the soul will be involved**. If the soul is not involved, then it is the body ego doing its thing, usually in excess. The addictions and the habits just become more reinforced.

Keep in mind that all *beginnings* are a change in something. There are many facets involved. Will one facet be a change for the better? There can be a change from negative choices just as much as from positive choices. Your positive change will stem from whether your soul has been able to make a deep enough connection to its body in order to instigate such a change. If you are not that connected to your body, you could still have some change; but it will not be for which you have hoped.

Therefore, dear Readers, as you read this book, know that each chapter is **formulated** to spark some movement in you, to help facilitate a change, hopefully a positive one. When the author asked me about BOOK TWO that she felt was sitting on top of her head, I told her BOOK TWO was still being formulated. This is what we were doing. All the Presenters in this book gathered, and we discussed what we would bring to these pages and what was needed to fulfill the book's purpose.

The first book was to break up some myths, to spark seeds of change in you. As you read the chapters, you were infused by the energies still in our words. For some, the change(s) is subtle. For others, it will be the light bulb effect—the great *Ah-ha*! Therefore, dear Readers, as you read the ensuing pages, even though the material may seem delicately simple with the style of writing easy to understand, know that the energies of us several Masters are in each word. Remember again that all is energy. Therefore, there is energy in each word, even in the tiny ***a***. As such, you will be impacted in some unsuspected way. All books that are channeled from the Masters act in a similar way. Please awake to this fact. Maybe just those statements could be news to you. Enjoy your readings. Enjoy the changes you have chosen to make by taking that step to buy these books, and there will be others. Most likely, you have no idea what this *beginning* holds for you. It could prove to be worth your while. It was your soul reaching for this book in anticipation of *The Beginning* of a new change within you!

SECTION 6—THE MASTERS' STORIES OF BEGINNINGS

AN OLD MONK'S TALE—Maitreya

I AM Maitreya. Many eons ago there was a monk in an old abbey who loved God above all else. However, try as he would, he could never hear God's voice. The monk prayed repeatedly, asking the Lord to speak aloud so he could hear his voice. He never shared this passionate want with the others in the abbey. The monks were supposed to pray with humility and repeatedly asking to hear God's voice would seem too arrogant a request. Therefore, the old monk did not tell his fellow brothers.

One day when he laid himself down to rest after a strenuous day of working in the fields, he felt himself rise above his body. He felt strange but was so tired he really could not help himself. He floated up higher and higher. Now he was able to see a figure lying on the bed. The figure seemed very old and looked as if he were sleeping. He himself was starting to move up through the ceiling of his little cell-like room. He thought the experience to be most unusual. He had not heard of his fellow monks ever having told of such tales. He soon found he had somehow gone through the ceiling and was now outdoors.

Once outside, he realized he could see things he had never seen while inside the abbey. He noticed Beings walking about who were very tall. He thought they must be angels. He tried calling to them to ask about this strange happening, but they seemed not to take any notice of him. He also saw that all the vegetation had a light about it. Trees were lit up. He could see their sap of life flowing up the trunks and out the branches. He saw flowers whose colors were more brilliant than he had ever imagined. He still met no one who paid any attention to him, but he enjoyed just the sensation of floating with the sun shining brilliantly down upon him.

After a while, he noticed that he was descending and before he knew it, he was back into his cell-room and was being pulled into the prone figure on the narrow cot. He realized it was his body. His body then seemed to stir and awake as if he had been in a dream. He stretched his arms and legs, sat up, and got off his bed. *I seem to be in one piece*, he thought. However, he now noticed he could see light around the frame of his cot, his washstand, and the cross on the wall. He wondered if he ought to tell his superior, but decided not to in case it all was an old man's imagination.

The next day this same experience happened to him again, and it continued happening day after day. As this wondrous adventure continued, he noticed he was able to see light around his brother monks. In fact, they were a kaleidoscope of colors with circles of light of different colors going from their feet to the tops of their heads. He also noticed that not everyone had the same shape to their circles, nor were the colors the same. Some of his brothers had circles that were asymmetrical, some circles were bigger than others were, and some were not in an even row. He also noticed that those brothers who had taken a vow of silence had the most active circles from dull to brilliant in color.

Again, the monk did not share these observations with others. He began to notice that each day he floated out of his body (for now he realized this is what he was doing), each time he would then acquire some extraordinary skill. He could see clearly the lights of energy all around animate as well as inanimate objects. He noticed his hearing had improved to the point it quite astounded him. He heard voices not only from across the table, but down the long table. However, what astounded him the most was that he could hear what his brothers were thinking! At first he thought that he had heard their actual conversation, before he came to realize that some of the monks who had sworn to be silent were quite chatterboxes, even though he could not observe their lips moving, nor did they make eye contact with anyone as if they were engaged in a conversation. However, he could hear everything people were thinking. He also noticed he was able to listen or not, as he chose.

As the days and weeks progressed, his gifts increased and expanded. Still he told no one. Subsequently, imagine his astonishment to hear a voice of someone calling his name, when he knew there was no one else but him in his little room. He thought perhaps it was someone outside his door, but when he opened the door, there was no one there in the dark hallway. He thought that maybe someone was outside his window. He climbed upon a stool to look out the small aperture that served as his window. There was no one there either. He therefore threw himself more fervently into his prayers, asking to hear God's voice and to tell him the secrets of the Universe.

Again, this new happenstance of hearing someone call his name happened repeatedly. One day he strongly thought he had heard music. He was quite wondrous about this, for music was only provided at the masses—never outside of a certain mass and certainly not when he was hearing it now. Again, he kept this latest development to himself and prayed even more fervently. Now he was asking God to heal him, for he feared he was losing his mind. He now not only saw the lights around everything, but he also heard thoughts, music, and now the animals were talking to him, as were the trees. The birds would fly by and chirp and he could understand them. This occurrence and expansion of his gifts continued for many a month.

He was still floating out of his body when he had laid his weary body down. Now the tall people outside seemed to notice him. They started nodding and smiling to him. Still none of them spoke, nor could he hear their thoughts. He had come to accept all of these strange occurrences with himself.

One day after he had had his usual experience of floating out of his body and then returning, he felt a different sensation. His body was quivering with goose bumps. He felt a kind of electrical impulse flow through him. He did not understand what was occurring and the sensation was so strong, he was a bit shaken and a bit frightened. He fell on his knees and started praying, for he thought that perhaps this feeling was a negative happenstance. He prayed as fervently as his limited prayer ability allowed. He kept repeatedly asking God for guidance as to what was happening to him. He accepted the fact by now that he had experienced strange movements with his body, but nothing like this had ever happened to him before.

As he knelt, he felt as though his heart might burst with his love for God. He felt tears flow hotly down his cheeks. He was now sobbing with such strong emotion, he felt he may be having some kind of a breakdown. He noticed he was firmly on his knees, even though he could see the lights around his bed and furniture. He was stationary, not floating as he had done in the past. Now he was hearing the most glorious music he had ever heard. He knew he had never heard this from the abbey choir. At the same time, he started hearing his name being called. All the sensations, thoughts, and emotions he had experienced in the past several months intensified.

He prayed and prayed trying to calm himself while noticing how intense it all was—the profound experience. He knelt for what seemed a very long time. He heard his name called repeatedly. The voice strengthened and seemed to fill the room. He would sob often. *Oh God, let this all subside. I fear I am losing my mind*! With that, a Light filled his room. It was so bright that he could see nothing else. It permeated everything in his room until the furniture was no longer distinguishable—only the Light was present. While he was marveling at this, he again heard his name called, but this time he heard the added words, *I have come!* The monk felt very small and with deep humility he asked, *who are you Lord?* The voice replied, *I AM your God. You have called for Me repeatedly. I answered you many times, but you did not know me. I have shown you My Light so that you will never again doubt that I had not heard you or that I am not approachable. Do you not know my Light flows through you constantly? Our connection is unbreakable. I created you and blew breath into you. Trust that this is so and keep your faith that it will be forever.*

With those sweet words, the Light gradually dissipated. The bodily sensations also slowly stopped. Now the monk felt euphoric. He had been touched by God and was in a state of bliss. He remained in his room, missing his supper and evening prayers. Still he stayed on his knees. Gradually, he became more aware of his surroundings and could feel the pain in his knees, after being in such a position for so many hours. He slowly rose to his feet and felt as if he had come out of a deep dream. He looked around him and all seemed to be in its natural state, except for himself.

The old monk now knew that he had been touched by God. He felt as if he were floating again, but he noted that he was not. All his senses were acutely aware, having been heightened by his encounter with God's Light and Energy. Consequently, the old monk lived out his remaining years in great peace and love for his fellow brothers. His humility never faltered, and he was greatly respected for his wisdom and gentle manner.

Dear Readers, many of you may have had similar past lives. I can say that most everyone has, for it is the evolution of your soul. In olden times, it was an opportunity for souls to ask for such a life. It would hone the soul and teach it how to be humble and not arrogant; how to live with few materialistic attachments, if any; but mainly it was a way of closing off the outside world so one could concentrate on touching God.

Some souls had several lifetimes living these austere lives, but rich in spiritual attainment. Nowadays one is not so apt to cloister oneself in an abbey, for there are other opportunities for the soul to touch God while being of service to Him in the outside world. We of course are speaking of different *beginnings* that a soul can choose. Remember, they are but different paths to God. All will lead you Home if that is your desire.

THE FARMER'S DREAM—Sananda

I AM Sananda. I am going to give you Readers a little story that happened many centuries ago to an old farmer. He loved his farm, his animals, and his vegetable garden. However, one day he felt ill and when he tried to arise that morning, he found that he could not. A doctor was sent for and after he had come, made his diagnosis, and then left, the old farmer just laid in bed stunned. The doctor had told him that he had suffered a massive stroke during his sleep.

Now this was centuries ago so that there were no rehabilitation facilities where one could go for physical therapy. His wife and children helped him the best they knew how, but it was more in keeping his body fed and cleansed than anything else. There certainly was no manual manipulation of his muscles.

One day, after the farmer had been fed and bathed and left alone for a while, he heard his name called. He turned toward the voice and saw a young man standing by his bed. The man just smiled and wished the farmer good health and then walked out of the room. When the farmer's wife entered their bedroom to ask if he wanted anything, he told his wife about the man and asked her when he had arrived and who was he? The wife exclaimed that no one had come to the house, let alone entered their bedroom. She certainly would have noticed that! She left the room in kind of a fluster, for she thought the stroke had affected her husband's mind, as well as his limbs.

The next day at approximately the same time, the young stranger appeared again. This time he had a small box under his arm, which he proceeded to open. He took out a small vial and asked the farmer to put out his tongue. The stranger put two drops of liquid on the farmer's tongue. The stranger at the same time uttered some words in a language that the farmer had never heard before. After the stranger had left, promising to return the next day, the farmer tried to repeat the words that were said but could not quite get them right, for the words were odd to his ears.

This wonderment continued for several days. His wife never was in the room and never saw the stranger. Meanwhile the farmer noticed he was gradually able to move his limbs a little. He could not direct them yet; but when he wanted to move them, he could, ever so slightly. This too continued for many days.

After this daily occurrence went on for quite a few weeks, the wife decided she would remain in the room no matter what she needed to do around the house. She got her knitting, sat stoically in the rocker, and waited. Sure enough, the young man walked through the doorway with the small box, took out the vial, and put two drops on the farmer's tongue. Neither of the men spoke to the woman sitting in her rocker knitting. Nor did she seem to notice what was happening on the other side of the bed. After the stranger left, the farmer asked his wife what she thought of the young man. The wife snapped that she was tired of playing this game. *What young man, you crazy old farmer,* and she stormed out of the room.

Now the farmer was in a deep quandary as to what was happening. Was he really going crazy? Had he imagined all of this? The stranger appeared at the same time every morning. Had he imagined that also, and the two drops on his tongue? He could still feel the sensation of coolness from the drops on his tongue. There did not seem to be any particular explanation, except the farmer knew the stranger was real. However, the next day proved not so real to him.

This time when the stranger came, he was not in clothes that the village people wore. The stranger wore robes that were of fine linen and flowed as he walked. He had beautiful gold armlets on. His feet were in sandals even though there was snow on the ground. This time the box he held was ornamented with gold. The vial was bejeweled and the liquid sparkled like crushed diamonds but felt cool and smooth on his tongue. The stranger had a Light around him that filed the bedroom. He held out his hand and told the farmer to get out of bed and walk with him. The farmer did not question, never giving a thought he could not walk. He took the stranger's hand and found it warm. He pushed the blankets back, swung his legs over the edge of the bed, and stood up. He felt that he was locked into the eyes of the stranger. He could not have broken the gaze even if he had wanted to.

Now the stranger and the farmer were walking around the bed. The stranger asked the farmer if he were ready. The farmer nodded, not even wondering for what he was ready. He felt such peace he had not known before and felt love and caring emanate from the stranger, which he had never experienced before either. He kept his gaze on the stranger's eyes. If he had been looking elsewhere, he would have seen how they had walked through the wall of the bedroom and were now outside in the yard. There was snow on the ground, but they gave no notice to it. The farmer still wore his bedclothes. He felt no cold—only warmth and a gentle breeze. The stranger was telling him about many strange and wonderful events that would soon take place. All the time the farmer felt stronger and stronger. He noticed that his legs were striding forth as they walked around his farm and into the barn. He could understand what the animals were saying. He noticed that Mama Cat, their mouser, was complaining that her water dish was frozen over. He told her he would fix that soon.

Now he and the stranger were walking back to the house and had re-entered the bedroom. The stranger told the farmer that he was now well in all ways and that because of his many virtues, God had given him a gift—the gift of being able to converse with his beloved animals. The stranger then asked the farmer to stick out his tongue one last time as he put the two drops of cool liquid upon it. With that, the farmer fell into a deep sleep. When he awoke, he noticed that his family and the doctor were gathered around his bed. He was so surprised and asked what they all were doing in his bedroom?

Imagine how shocked he was when the doctor told him that he had only just then pronounced the farmer dead! The farmer, who never felt so alive in his life, did not know whether to laugh or to cry for joy, for he still remembered his beautiful experience with the stranger. As he laughed, he flung the bedcovers aside and bounced out of bed. *Praise be,* he cried. *I have had the most wonderful dream. However, before I tell you, I must dress and go give Mama Cat some fresh water, for she told me that the water in her dish is frozen.*

THE WANDERER—Djwhal Khul

I AM Djwhal Khul. There was a small village in ancient times nestled deep in the Himalayan Mountains. One day a stranger wandered into the village. All the villagers were soon in the road observing the stranger, for you see, everyone knew each other. Therefore, for a stranger to appear was very unusual and provided much excitement. The stranger was a man who was tall compared to the villagers. He had a ready smile and greeted the villagers warmly. He asked if he might obtain lodging with one of them. A lonely old widow said he might stay with her because her husband had died and she had no one to cook for anymore. She would enjoy his company. An arrangement for payment was made. The stranger would do some needed chores for the woman, bring in more wood, gather in the harvest from her small garden and just do what he saw was needed in the way of repairs.

Soon the woman and the stranger became fast friends. He enjoyed her cooking and she enjoyed his stories of his many adventures, for he had traveled everywhere. The villagers envied the woman, for they thought having a stranger reside with you was an honor in itself. Therefore, the woman invited as many people as her little house could hold to come in the evening hours after their chores and supper were completed. They then sat at the feet of the stranger and he told them of his travels beyond their village. They marveled at these tales, for their world consisted only of their small village. There were no phones, radios, or televisions in the village—for these inventions were still too new to be in such a remote village as this one.

One evening the stranger told them he would be leaving soon, before the winter snows set in. The villagers were quite upset, for the stranger had provided much amusement for the villagers. They felt stimulated after their evenings with him. They would talk among themselves about what they had been told. Life for them had come alive, and they vied for positions that would have them sitting closest to the man, for he radiated warmth and peace out to them. He told them he had journeyed everywhere as he felt he was directed by a higher Source to go to specific places. He did not explain why but conveyed he had been sent to this location. No one questioned him as to who had sent him.

Now his time with them was ending. He would be leaving at first light, he told them. The villagers were sad to have him go; they gathered around him even closer, touching him and parts of his garments. They just wanted to feel his peace and warmth for as long as they could.

As the sun broke through the clouds the next morning, the villagers gathered around the widow's house in order to wish the stranger a safe journey and to invite him to return. They waited and waited outside the door. Still the stranger did not appear. They decided they had better ask the widow what was taking him so long and why had he not come out? They timidly knocked on the door. There was no answer. They knocked again, this time louder. There was still no answer.

Since no one had locks on their doors, one woman came forward and pushed opened the door a few inches. She could smell that fresh bread had been baking. However, she neither heard nor saw anyone. She pushed the door open wider and called to the widow. There was no reply. Now the villagers were becoming agitated and all pushed through and entered the house. There were plates of fresh bread on the table with butter and jelly, cheese and hot tea. There was a bouquet of flowers on the table. All was in readiness for a festive meal of some kind, even though there was no one there.

They searched the two rooms and found no one. The two beds were freshly made with clean sheets. However, no one was to be found. They looked into trunks and at the hooks on the wall to see if anything had been taken, like a missing coat. All was as it should be. Now they were becoming quite excited. They were greatly puzzled as to where the occupants of the house were. They also noticed that the stranger's bedroll was still in the corner. They decided to go outside again to see if they had gone for a walk, although that would be quite odd, for the villagers had seen no one come and go.

They gathered outside now, confused and somewhat angry and fearful, for they felt this was indeed out of the ordinary. As their confusion grew, they began hearing voices coming from inside the small house. *How could this be?* They murmured. *We were just in there and there was no one there!* At about this time the old widow and the stranger appeared at the doorway. They were smiling and beckoning the villagers to come in, for they had prepared a repast for them and had been waiting for them.

The villagers crowded into the house once again. This time the food on the table seemed to have grown in abundance. There was plenty of food and tea for all of them. Everyone sat where they could and greatly enjoyed the hearty breakfast. However, the widow and stranger offered no explanation as to where they had been. In addition, the villagers noticed that the widow's gown seemed new and was of warm material that had embroidered flowers all over it with a matching shawl. The people had never seen such material. The stranger also had on new garments that were rich in color and of a warm material.

Finally after all had finished eating, the stranger asked them to gather around him once again for he had another story to tell them. The villagers nestled as close as they could get to him, again feeling his warmth and peace.

He told them that he had just come back from a far off place. He had taken the widow with him for she desired to see some of the wonders that he had spoken about. He told them that he was not really of their Earth any longer. He resided in different dimensions. He was able to come and go as he pleased. He could bring those who were ready with him. *Last night, the woman you know here as the widow, also was able to make that transition to the other dimension where all is living. She was with her dead husband for many hours having a grand reunion.* The stranger went on to tell them that the widow's husband had told her he had been waiting for her. She was to go back and tell the villagers they had nothing to fear from what is called *death,* for he was very much alive. The woman was shown how she could come and go in their world. She was shown how she could manifest the bountiful repast they had just enjoyed.

Now that my work is finished here, I will once again leave all of you, but I will be waiting for you when it is your time to come see me. I am called the Wanderer for that is my purpose—to wander the Earth telling people about the wonders I have seen and to bring them peace and love to fill their hearts. He told them about many strange and beautiful things they will find and that death is simply walking out the door of their house into a whole new world that awaits them.

After he had finished speaking, he looked at each one with such caring that the person thought only the two of them were in the room. With that, he stood up, went to his bedroll, picked it up, and walked through the door. The people rushed out of the house questioning and then exclaiming where the Wanderer had gone. He was just here and now no one could find him. Someone spoke up and said that he had seen him wave and then he just disappeared, instantly. They raced back into the house to question the widow, but she too had gone. The people knew she had left, for on the floor lay her velvet shawl, the one with all the flowers on it, and her rocker was still gently rocking.

A PARABLE—Jesus

I AM Jesus. One day when a woman tarried at the village well, she thought she heard a baby crying. The sound seemed to be coming from some bramble bushes that grew nearby. She went toward the crying sound. Sure enough, she found what was making the cry. A wee lamb seemed to be caught in the brambles. She gently soothed the animal and untangled it. She then looked around for its mother, but there were no other sheep around. She found this strange, but she knew she could not just leave the little lamb. In fact, as she started to walk away, the lamb followed her. With that, she swooped up the tiny animal and carried it back to her house.

Her husband was out tending a farmer's flock, and since she had no children, she decided she would keep the lamb and raise it as her own. She made a cozy corner for the lamb who promptly settled onto the soft cushion she had placed there and went to sleep. The woman was delighted, for she had lost a child at birth and had been very sad and lonely ever since. She got some milk and heated it and made up a makeshift bottle for the lamb which was a knotted cloth soaked with milk. When the lamb awoke, she gently placed the cloth in its mouth and watched it contentedly suck its fill.

When the woman's husband came home, he found his wife cuddling the tiny lamb, crooning to it and rocking it as if it were a human baby. The lamb with its soft white coat and large brown eyes looked at the man with such trust and contentment that the man did not have the heart to put it out of the house into the barn on such a cold night. Therefore, that was the beginning of a long, loving friendship. The lamb became part of the family.

Several months later and after the lamb had grown to its normal size, a farmer came to the couple's door and inquired after a lamb he had heard they had found. The couple invited the farmer in and proudly showed the farmer their beautiful sheep. The farmer exclaimed that that sheep was from one of his flock. He had lost the lamb, looked for it, and never had found it. He thought a wild animal had eaten it.

The couple was visibly upset, for they dearly loved their lamb and considered it theirs. They had nursed and raised it to be a fine looking sheep. However, they also knew deep down that they really did not own the sheep and that most likely it was from the farmer's flock. They did not know what to do. The farmer told them he appreciated their caring for his lamb and would be glad to compensate them for any expense. The couple declined the offer saying that the love they had received both in giving to the lamb and its giving back to them affection and companionship truly compensated them well enough.

The woman knelt, wrapped her arms around the sheep's neck, hugged and hugged it, thanking the sheep for her love and company and told the sheep that it would always be in their hearts. The woman made a collar from a bit of bright material so the lamb, now a grown sheep, would know how much she was loved and would be missed. With that, the farmer took the sheep back to its flock.

Now after the sheep and farmer had gone, the husband and his wife sat in front of their hEarth for most the night. They held hands and talked about their life. Moreover, they talked about how the sheep had truly been a gift from God, for now they felt healed from the loss of their stillborn baby and felt that God had sent the lamb to heal the couple's wounded hearts.

Would it surprise you Readers to know that the sheep returned to its flock and soon bore twin lambs of her own, while the lonely, once grief stricken couple also had a baby? I will not say they had twins, but all were healed of their lonely hearts—the lost lamb and the lost husband and mother.

The babies that God gives us to raise in order to help the soul evolve are not ours to own. They are 'lambs' put in our care. After they mature, we need to let them go so that they can serve their purpose and raise their own lambs. We will always carry them in our hearts, for as we prepare to let them go, we too evolve, each of us walking his/her own path Home.

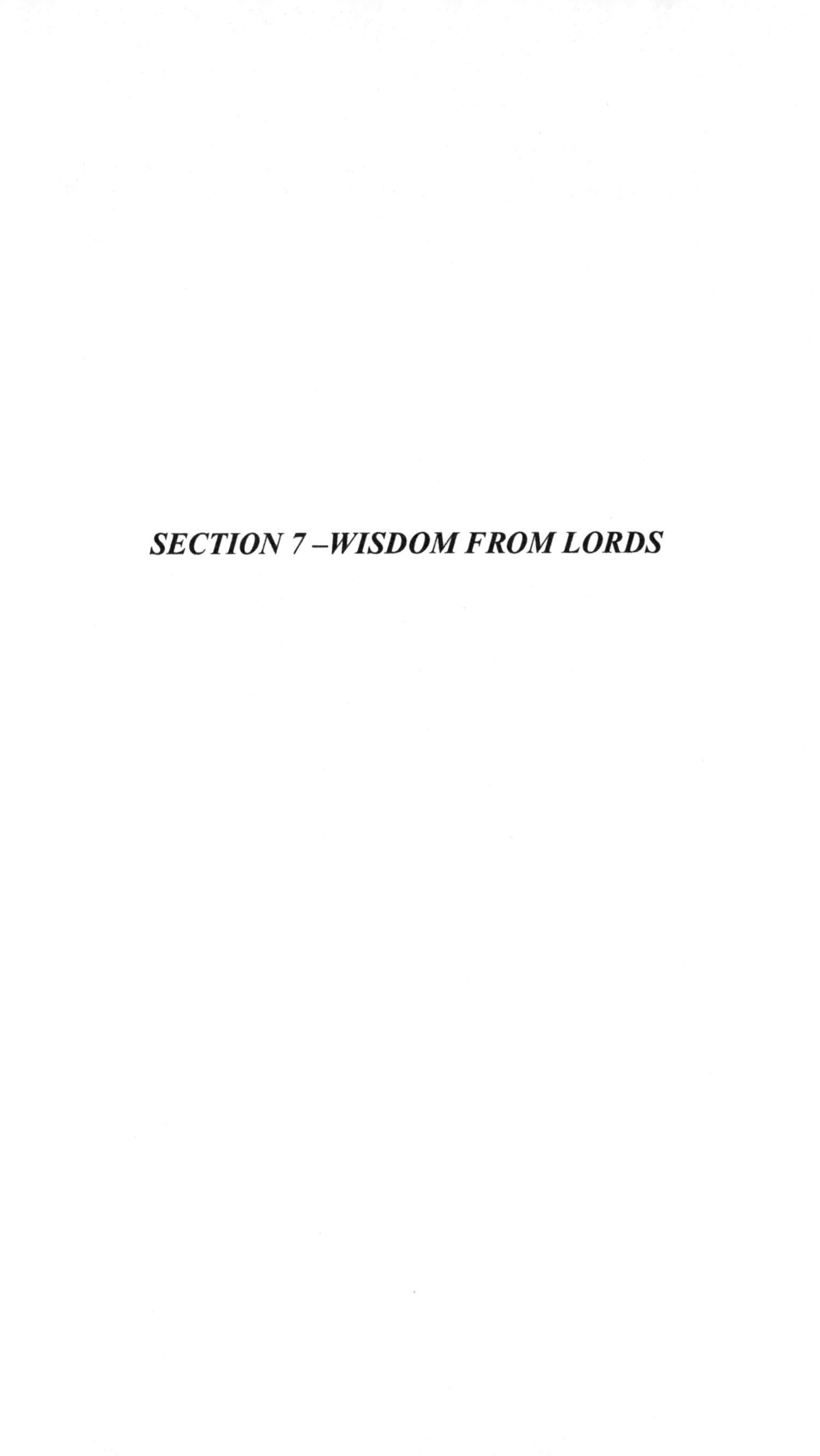

SECTION 7 –WISDOM FROM LORDS

LEAVING HOME—Jesus

I AM Jesus. When a soul is in embodiment, has a physical form, there are periods throughout that lifetime when he or she leaves home. There is that time when the young child starts pre-school, then kindergarten, then junior high, high school, and perhaps on to college. At each time period, the child, adolescent, or young adult leaves home. Each transition can be a traumatic event if the child has not been well counseled by its parent(s).

Picture what you call *Heaven* now. You are with your Heavenly Mother-Father. You are told how much you are loved and that the time draws near when you must go out into other worlds. Sometimes it is just that, other worlds. However, what I will refer to now is that the soul is sent to Earth where it will go to school and learn many lessons. Thus, this soul has left Home. Picture this Home as all loving. Everything you think is instantly known. Everything you wish for is granted. There is no want, disease, or stress of any kind.

Now you are in the body that God has given you. You have said your *goodbyes* to your first Home. Part of you is excited to see a new world and to experience new realities of the illusory kind. As an Earth-child, the veils fall. You have no recollection of your former Home. You are now in your Earth home. As the years progress and you grow and go through the different developmental stages, you experience fleeting happiness, much stress, and at times total confusion, as to the life you have chosen.

The point I am making, Reader, is that you have left your Heavenly Home and then your Earthly home many, many times. In fact, you have had this experience of leaving Home and home repeatedly. The feelings that you had when leaving your Heavenly Home are quite similar to leaving your Earth home. There is excitement, even anticipation. However, there can be also much sadness and even fear. It may seem strange to you to know that souls can feel fear also. However, it is a different kind of fear, more of trepidation, the fear of the unknown.

Here on Earth you have many of the same feelings you had at your other Home. People are apt to think that souls do not at times feel insecure. Earth people believe that all souls are impervious to new adventures in the Heavenlies. In addition, what may be the repercussions from moving out into other worlds? Earth people also will experience many emotions as they develop and move in and out of their journeys.

However, while on Earth, this becomes a time when the soul in embodiment has trials and tribulations, has growth opportunities, has testing of its morals and principles of clean living. Only on Earth is there a schoolhouse such as this that affords the soul the opportunities to advance in its consciousness.

In BOOK ONE, we spoke many times about how the soul was advancing up Jacob's ladder. ***Genesis 28:12*** *And he dreamed, and behold the ladder set up on the Earth, and the top of it reached to heaven; and behold the angels of God ascending and descending on it.* Angels in Jacob's dream went up and down the ladder, all of which were symbolic of souls going Home and then coming back to Earth to learn some more lessons. There is much learning in leaving your spiritual Home and then your Earth home. It is maturation in all areas of development. Not only is the body maturing, but the soul is growing also. It is learning both worlds, you see. After it leaves the Earth home and goes back to the Heavenly Home, it brings its learning adventures with it. There is great excitement when returning to your Heavenly Home.

Soon it is time again for the soul to venture forth. If the soul was still young and had not gone very far up Jacob's ladder, then the soul comes back to Earth to perfect its lessons repeatedly. If a soul is what is known as an *old soul*, millions, and maybe billions of years old, the soul leaves Home with instructions as to what it needs to do or accomplish while in service in the other worlds. There will still be periods of maturation, especially if the soul comes in through a physical birth. There are other ways of coming to Earth, but for now I am discussing being in a wee babe and going through all those phases of development.

Therefore, dear Readers, do realize when you leave your home for the workplace or for college, your soul has a mission. It is in service. It has a purpose. Humanity might think a soul's purpose must be grandiose—surely a great doctor, or statesperson. In reality, a soul's purpose can be a person who labors with his hands. Someone has to pick up the garbage. Someone has to dig ditches, work in the fields, reap the harvest, pick the fruits, and sand the icy roadways. These labor-type jobs can be a soul's purpose—a chance to learn many lessons. People, do you not think that a respected doctor or lawyer you admire has not had a life doing what you are doing, if in a menial job? Souls do not start at the top in anything! Souls must experience the whole spectrum in order to know *compassion* and to gain *wisdom.*

Leaving Home and leaving home carry pretty much the same dynamic. As I have said, there are feelings involved, excitement, for it is new. There can be anticipation of the journey, and there could be trepidation, because you are going into uncharted waters for yourself. Of course, there is a great deal of preparation on both sides of the veil. Parents and counselors advise what to expect. Your hand is held as long as possible and then the parent knows he/she is to let go—the soul must fly on its own, as a fledgling. The Earth-child must let go of Mom's and Dad's hands and now walk out into that world, that unknown space, whether Heaven or Earth. Both sets of parents bless their child and with great love watch the child as it grows into adulthood. There is much gratification when the child, now an adult, has found its purpose and is living its life as was intended. What glorious praise it receives on both sides of the veil. Leaving Home and leaving home are similar experiences. It is hoped that the Earth home has provided as much support and love for the child-adult as its Heavenly Home has done and continues to do so for that soul.

TO BELIEVE ONE'S TRUTH or ANOTHER'S—Jesus

I AM JESUS. Dear One, I wish to give you information that is not known to many. There arise at times opportunities for the soul in way of lessons that strengthen one's spiritual attributes. These lessons could be on *Faith, Patience,* and *Trust.* Nowhere else is there such an opportunity presented to the soul than when its own Truth needs reinforcing and even the act of defending. Many times during one's lifetime, the soul will be forced to choose between its Truth and another's. I say *forced* because a definite choice needs to be made about that particular dynamic. One could sit on a symbolic fence, but this becomes too stressful. One needs to make a decision one way or another. There is a persistent feeling of unrest. One ponders and ponders a situation, hoping the feeling will go away. Psychologists call this *cognitive dissonance*. Only when the person chooses a certain position does the feeling of dissonance recede.

It makes no difference if the choice errs on the side of Truth or not. The dynamic is simply so strong, that either of the two choices—one of truth, the other a lie—must be made. One's mind will not let a situation rest until that choice has been made. Once the choice of action has been decided, the little ego will struggle to keep the homeostasis—the status quo. No matter what further information comes forth, the ego will strongly assist the person to stay with the choice that was made previously, simply because it brought peace to the body.

This principle of having to choose between Truth and Lie is not as simple as it may seem to be. The belief systems a person carries are from long standing. If the person were to hear that a particular dynamic was no longer of Truth, the person would simply negate the new information as being unreliable—not anything to trust. Dear Readers, as you peruse this Book TWO, you may find that there were passages in the first book that were stated somewhat differently. Now you have a choice. Do you make the first book wrong? On the other hand, do you make an adjustment in your thinking pattern? Many times Teachers will say and teach different angles to a previous concept. They will change ever so slightly a particular dynamic or even the character in a subject. The change will elicit one's immediate response, whether to negate the previous material or to allow a new perspective to come forth.

Of course, Readers, I am speaking of one's Truth. What is true for you may not be Truth for another, especially if the person has a firm belief system in place. This becomes a particular problem for many of us in the Spiritual Hierarchy, for there have been many variations in many of the spiritual stories about us, no matter what the religious faith. The question then becomes, *how flexible are you*? Are you firmly entrenched in a particular way of thinking because you read it in a book for which you have a particular fondness? Some authors have done brilliant research on many past lives. Yet, they have erred. They have made the wrong conclusion and hooked some lineage to a figure that is actually linked to someone else. I know you are waiting for me to tell you who got it wrong. However, we prefer not to for the simple reason your own Truth must reveal the answer. You must feel it. Feel into that Truth from another person. Wait for your body's reaction. You will receive one, if your ego will let you.

Many times people do make an attempt to go to their own Truth, but the doubts take over—the little ego dictating your Truth—so that you are unable to hear your I AM Presence. All of you have the capability to hear and recognize your own Truth. You have the ability to make choices as to your Truth no matter how knowledgeable your latest informant is. If your belief system has been entrenched for many years, your little ego will not release its hold that easily, so that you can get to your Truth. It is at this time many people contact another, a *seer*, perhaps, that has the ability to separate the grains from the chaff. These *seers* are in a class by themselves, for they too may carry the stigma of a *psychic* or *fortuneteller*. However, I say to you that these *seers* of the higher spiritual training have pure and clear energies. They can help their client come to a clearer understanding; so that that person is now able to find his/her own Truth.

I wish now to address some of the ancient stories from the Biblical era. In the times of Abraham and Jacob, there was much oral history about these patriarchs. Abraham had a huge following that he led out into the desert in order to help people not make wrong choices about *sacrificing*. To this day, many people sacrifice their lives for another.

One sees this with caregivers, especially. If that is their purpose, they are following their Truth. If it is not their purpose, and they need to bring others into the family dynamic to help lift the burden from their shoulders from caring for someone, then they also are fulfilling their purpose—not to sacrifice their life. One could use the example where daughters were expected to sacrifice their happiness for an elderly parent in times gone by. Instead of bringing in outside care, the daughter was expected to stay unmarried and childless until the parent died. This could go on for ten or twenty years. Thus, it is a *sacrifice* for the daughter and a *take* on the parent's part. This would only be correct if it was the contract between the two, a contract that they agreed to before they were born. Therefore, Abraham started breaking up that dynamic of *self-sacrifice.*

You have Jacob and the stories of his sons, the most famous being of Joseph who was sold into slavery. This was a testing time for Joseph of the Coat of Many Colors. It was a test for Joseph every step of the way. He continually had to find his own Truth, whether it was interpreting dreams for Pharaoh, or in forgiving and bringing his family into Egypt. The Bible is full of symbolism. Almost every Biblical story has a symbolic interpretation. The story of Joseph being sold into slavery was the story of the Jews going into Egypt and becoming slaves to the Egyptians. It started with Joseph. It ended with Moses leading the people out of bondage and out of Egypt—the Exodus.

Much has been written and with great speculation as to who was who—what Biblical character was such and such in the stories? What character did he play, in what drama, only to appear again in another? I have had many lifetimes as different characters in the Bible before my Jesus-body. I brought different religions into being. I crisscrossed from the start of one to another. Authors may write that I was Buddha. Other authors write that I was Krishna. One wrote that I was Joseph of Egypt (*Edgar Cayce*). Another wrote that Joseph of Egypt was Moses and later was my father in my Jesus era (*Secret Places of the Lion, by George Hunt Williamson*). However, I say to you, we were all tied to the same Consciousness. Even Moses is portrayed as being a separate entity. I say to you, he was not. We were all one. I was as much a part of Moses as he was. He bore the name, but there was an aspect of me that was Moses.

Let us back up a bit. As most of you know, I also was Adam, the first man that the Bible proclaims. However, I was on other worlds before Adam. Therefore, aspects of that Consciousness was in each Biblical character thereafter. I could say I was *Joseph of Egypt, Moses, King David* and so forth, through the Biblical stories to the Jesus era. Many of you Readers had parts of yourself in famous figures. The Author had many aspects of herself throughout the Bible. One lifetime she would be someone's son. Another she would be someone's sister, as well as aspects of herself in the famous Biblical women. It is how the Spiritual World works. If the Father is bringing an energetic concept onto the planet as in the Exodus story that had its start in Abraham's time, the Higher Self can have many aspects, all in different time frames and sexes—past, present, and future—on-going. Therefore, seek your own Truth. If I say I am Jesus, know I am many other Beings also, bringing different religions to the Jews, Buddhists, and Christians.

People may wonder at this last remark; but if you will put the words in the context of being in many bodies and places all at the same time, I can say I was Moses, Joshua, Joseph of Egypt, and Jesus. All was on going. None of the statements is wrong when one views it all in the broader sense. You are so much more than just the name you bear now. You can be urchin, philanthropist, slave, and saint all at this NOW moment.

Broaden your belief systems to incorporate new ideas. Could some part of you be one of the many Marys in the Bible? There is every reason that substantiates that you could—that your Higher Self did have an aspect of itself in that person. It is a gigantic Universe. Why would you just be Bill in this one lifetime going on now? You would not. Touch your own truth, dear Readers. Loosen the tight grip your egos have on your belief systems. Your Truth lies in wait for you. Dare to change and touch it!

I AM Jesus called by many names, even beyond the **myriad** of names I was called in your Bible.

DID YOU SLEEP WELL?—Jesus

I AM Jesus. As each of you readers put your body to rest, to sleep after the day's activities, whether it was at your work place or at play, after you lay yourself down, sleep eventually overtakes you. It takes longer for some than others, but eventually the soul is able to slip out, put on its astral body, your exact replica of your flesh body, and then it is freedom for the soul. Some souls go to other planets; others visit relatives or friends; but all are very active.

Most souls go to that schoolhouse in the sky. Humanity may think that the school-house Earth is where all the action is. However, there are vast areas where souls gather to be taught and counseled during the night while the body sleeps. It may surprise you to know that **many of you go to the Light ships**, these great spaceships that are created from pure thought and Light, either for various teachings, or as an actual service of some kind. If you are a counselor on Earth, you could have a similar activity on board one of the ships.

These last sentences have most likely startled some of you. Perhaps you have not realized that there is a place for souls to be counseled. The counseling is on a spaceship of Light! The Beings that take on this Heavenly service are quite advanced. Nevertheless, if you are an initiate with a Point of Evolution (PoE) of 1.0 or so, the counselor assigned to you will be at least a 2.0. Those initiates who have reached the master stage of 5.0 and higher make a **choice** to come back to Earth in order to teach and to be a Wayshower on Earth. It could also astound you to know there are now masters of the 7.0, 8.2 and even higher PoE's, 15.1 and 22.0 walking the Earth. You would not know them particularly, except for their Consciousness and Light.

These masters walk your Earth as humans in every sense of the word. They are born into bodies and mature. They teach others by their examples. Some went to college; others did not. Some hold many degrees; others do not. You see, Readers, these great walking masters go where our Father sends them. Some are elderly; others are not. Some work in 9-5 jobs. Others do not; but work for the Father, they certainly do. Do you not think that living in this world, maintaining their Light, walking in Truth, being a Wayshower, an example, entails work? It most certainly does. Each of these masters must adhere to the laws of morality, practice *forgiveness*, and keep their own *faith* steady and pure. They are constantly being tested for their *patience, faith,* and *trust.*

Does this astound you that an Earth-walking master still has honing of his/her attributes? Most assuredly these masters do. Therefore, where do you think these great masters go when they put their body to sleep? They go back to work! They go to the benevolent spaceships and counsel others. They teach others who are still striving for consciousness. The point that I am bringing to your attention is that there are many masters walking your Earth now in human bodies. Their Light that shines forth is helping humanity. Just their presence helps to raise the vibrations of the planet.

It is the willingness of these masters to come to Earth and be of service that makes possible this dynamic of raising the Earth into the fourth and fifth dimensions. Some of you may be confused, for you may have read in other books that when a person reaches the 5-6-7th PoE levels that the karmic wheel of birth-death-rebirth has been broken. The person has now ascended and will no longer have a body. Ah, that is true. He or she may have ascended several times. However, **now** he/she may **choose** to be born again for a certain service. He/she will confer with the Father and then gladly go forth for another round of living on Earth. You see, Readers, just as in your society, those who attain high achievements are now in position to make positive differences to others—the Wayshowers.

Therefore, when the body sleeps, the souls are very active. It is usually between 1:00 and 3:00 AM, give or take a little on either side of the clock. People wonder about awakening around 3:00AM Well, school has just let out. Souls return for a short time, attend to the needs of their body, get it back to sleep, and either resume their service or go play. By that, I mean they can go and do whatever they wish. Most just come back to work. Think of your jaunt home to your body as having a "coffee break" for the soul. It is then back to work.

When I ask you how you slept, it was to give you information that your soul was **not** asleep. You were quite active learning or teaching. These great masters rarely rest while on the Light ships. Rest for them is contemplation in the solace of the many prayer rooms that are available on the ships for souls. The Father's energy and the Holy Spirit's Energy are prevalent in these rooms, and souls are invited to tarry a while in these sacred areas so that they may commune with their Father and soak in His Love and Light and Compassion.

Therefore, dear Readers, put your bodies to bed. Lay thee down. Sleep, dear body, and go forth to learn and study, browse the libraries, teach, counsel, pray, and contemplate, great souls. Enjoy your night, for tomorrow is another day in your body on school-house Earth, and you all know what trials and tribulations **that** could bring!

SO WHAT COMES NEXT?—Jesus

I AM Jesus. Beloved Readers, I last spoke of what you as souls did when you put your bodies to sleep. I wish to continue on that theme in this chapter. The Author is catching on to my titles that I mischievously name and then she finds I will speak on an entirely different theme than she expected. Well, today's lecture is also full of the unexpected.

I last left you happily fulfilling your duties or joys after you had put your body to sleep. You diligently apply yourself at your schoolhouse in the sky, with the many services you have taken on—most joyously, I might add. You then feel the pull of your body in the early morning hours around 3:00 AM or so. You zoom back and either go back to sleep or lie for hours more before giving up and arising for Earth's activities.

Have you wondered why you do not go back to sleep? You might think it is because your mind becomes active and you think about your present life's difficulties or pleasures. However, while this is true, your soul continues to be in and out of the body, for not all of it is ever in you at once. Your soul is a huge sphere of magnificent energies. You in the body are only a slight particle of the real you.

While people ponder the activity of the soul, few know what it is really doing. When a soul takes on a body, it has no sex per se, but a blend of the masculine and feminine principles. That is the Will and Power of God, the masculine, and the mother aspect, the intuitive, feminine side, which is the Holy Spirit Essence. Your soul carries these energies of God. Therefore, whenever the soul does its activity, it is bringing forth the masculine part of God, or the Divine Feminine of the Holy Spirit. Using a blend of the Mother-Father energies propels the soul forward in its endeavors.

If one keeps in mind you **are** a blend of these Energies, you **are** god, with your own personality so to speak, you may find you understand your nature more. How much more you can accomplish when you are god. I do not mean this as blasphemy, but as Truth. You carry the masculine, the Father, and the feminine, the Divine Mother. You are their child. They are your soul's Parents, but not in separate bodies like your Earth parents. You are a blend of your Earth-parents, as you know. On a soul level you are a blend of your Heavenly Parent that carries the two aspects of Itself we have come to know as God and the Holy Ghost—the One.

Therefore, your soul is a god in its own right. However, since it is younger than its Parents, Mother-Father God, it has much to learn before it can stand alone as God with a capital G. The soul has to learn, to grow, and to be stretched in that growth. Your Earth-school stretches the minds of your Earth-bodies. **Heaven's schools stretch the consciousness of the souls.**

I have titled this lecture, *So What Comes Next?* I wished to convey to you the importance of constant learning and growth! Souls do not just flit in and out of their bodies with no particular reason for doing so. They extend part of themselves in their body to bring *awareness* to that body. Since the majority of their energies are out of the body, the soul does not just sit on top of its body as one huge, helium balloon. It is constantly moving and growing. It is taking initiations, those next rungs up on Jacob's ladder. In the last chapter, I told you about the masters who are walking the Earth, even though long ago they had broken that birth-death-rebirth wheel—that seemingly endless cycle.

These great souls continue growing and expanding. They are reaching levels for which many souls are still striving. These masters are as active out of their body as when in it. In fact, they are more proficient, quicker on problem solving, clearer on seeing solutions, than when in their body. The point I am making is that your souls work constantly whether in or out of the body. They may be ministering to their several other bodies that are in other dimensions, in the future and/or parallel to this present time, as well.

Humanity tends to think within a somewhat narrow band. By confining itself within this small width of awareness, human beings solidify erroneous belief systems. They are unable to embrace new ideas. This seems to be especially true of the elderly. Unless they have been open to newer possibilities, they cordon themselves off from progressive, positive growth. They refuse to keep up with the times. They refuse to stretch themselves and learn computers, to learn how to e-mail, to search the Internet. Some are slow in accepting answering machines on their phone systems. There is a whole new generation that is hooked on technology. Cell phones have become the latest rage. They have long ago left the arena of being called a *gadget.* They can be a necessity and are a great resource for parent and child. These cell phones are a constant connection that is available to everyone now.

Thus, many seniors, the elderly, have not afforded themselves of modern technology. They are being rapidly left behind in the awareness of what is going on in their world. This is a stretch for oldsters. Technology has advanced so rapidly that elders are hard-pressed to keep up. I am not saying or implying that every elder who does not have a computer or cell phone is wrong. Everyone has the choice, the free will, as to how far or how great a stretch one wants to take.

It might interest you Readers to know that today's technology is in its infant stage of development. This is especially true with the cell phone industry. In the future, there will be phones that will be able to reach the astral planes. At first it will be the lower dimensions, but gradually people on Earth will be able to phone and talk to souls in the higher dimensions. There will be no wires, but a phone will be invented that will be able to tap into energy waves of the astral plane. Keep in mind everything is energy; therefore, there will be those souls whose purpose will be to bring forth the higher technologies. It would be a boost for humanity to be able to speak with a departed soul. It certainly would help uplift one's awareness, which will help raise the Earth's vibrations.

Therefore, when I ask, *So What Comes Next?* I am referring to what is planned for humanity. It is giving you a peep into the future. In BOOK ONE the Lord Djwhal Khul spoke of how the veil between Heaven and Earth will no longer exist. You will see the masters in their wondrous energies walking the Earth. You will be able to phone and talk to the other side just as easily as you can Europe today. One of the differences will be you will understand the language. You will not need an interpreter of any kind. In addition, the service will be faster, almost instantaneous. Therefore, dear Readers, what is next for you and your souls is continued growth and development in your life, whether on Earth or in Heaven. As the body develops, the soul develops rapidly. Have good cheer, Beloveds; there are infinite possibilities just on the horizon. So what are **you** going to do next?

TO BE ONE'S OWN SAVIOR—Maitreya, Sananda, Jesus

We are the Spiritual Trio: Maitreya, Sananda, and Jesus. Dear Readers, in the Biblical language of yesteryears, there were many stories about the *Savior*. Of course, we are speaking of Jesus, who was then the Christ. As we wrote in BOOK ONE, Maitreya was part of Jesus during his last three years, before his cross experience. I, Maitreya, say *last,* for after the crucifixion and his ascension, Jesus reappeared in a new form, but similar in appearance. His body retained the scars of the nails and spear. He could have erased those when he made this new form, but he chose to replicate those scars to provide evidence to his disciples and others throughout history, that he, Jesus, still lived.

After he reappeared, he met with his disciples, his beloved wife, Mary Magdalene, his family, and his friends. He spoke many times as to the reasons for the crucifixion. Jesus had decided that people did indeed need to know that there was salvation for them. So many of the people of that era were what Christians would call *sinners* in modern times. People were not being honest in their dealings with others over money. Women tended to cheat others at the market place if they could get away with it. Men were unfaithful to their wives. Women sold their favors to the highest bidder. Men tended to imbibe too much in the juice of the grape and many would appear at time of prayer, quite drunk, but by habit were able to mumble through the spiritual responses.

Therefore, there were your average sinners, as well as those more violent ones, who did not confess to believe in God, and who did rape and kill. We have just stated some of the ways the people of that Biblical era sinned. Now along comes Jesus. His Light fills his body. His love for people emanates forth, so that the people felt touched just by his presence. Jesus knew He needed to help raise the consciousness of these *sinners*. They needed help in getting in touch with their own hearts. Most the people of that era were unable to reach their I AM Presence in their heart. Most did not have the education that taught such things. Only those who were seeking

God, or the One, and Truth were able to reach their I AM Presence. Thus, after Jesus' crucifixion, it became apparent little had changed in the people's consciousness. Most were back into their old ways, patterns, habits, and addictions.

Jesus used the word *salvation* and *savior* many times while speaking to the crowds. He chose words that carried a certain connotation, that if they would seek God through him, Jesus, they would be able to enter God's Kingdom and receive *salvation* and *everlasting life*. During this modern era, those who go to church are still hearing that only through Jesus can one be saved.

We now wish to give you Readers another translation, a **new perspective for modern ears**. When one reads the Bible, there are many true statements, meaningful parables, and sweet passages. So much Truth and yet so much that could be interpreted with a different perspective. Most people know what *to love thy neighbor as yourself* means. It speaks of unity. It speaks of respect for others' beliefs. It speaks of allowing that neighbor to make his/her own choices on how to live life. There is a twist here however. If **you** do not respect yourself, care for yourself, love who you are, do you think you would afford your neighbor all those positive attitudes you would not give yourself? I think not. Therefore, when one is told to love your neighbor as you would love yourself, it is in the positive nature and not in your little ego of not being able to give to others simply because you cannot give to yourself.

We have noticed how difficult it seems to be for humanity to be generous and caring in its nature. There are times when humanity only gives during national crises, as during the 9-11 attacks on the Twin Towers in New York City and again with the tsunamis. There was such loss of life that people were able to overcome their own problems for a while, give, and share with others. Their *compassion was awakened.*

However, that concept of giving during a disaster of some kind does not bring *salvation* to the soul. That act cannot be accomplished by anyone else, except yourself, your own soul. So call upon God, Jesus, Buddha, and whoever else is in your spiritual belief system; I find this commendable. This dynamic becomes a helping hand of some kind. It is a resource. It is an act of awakening your *faith* and *trust.* It is you reaching for your own Truth. It is you, reaching out and using whatever means you have in your belief system inventory.

Most people have a starting point, a *beginning* as we have stated in this book. Hence, by taking that step to call upon your God, you have opened the door for help to step in. Now your open door allows others to come forth. You may find your help is in the form of a friend or neighbor, teacher, or spiritual leader. It allows new ideas to be embraced. One sees this in the New Age Thought that allows ideas to blossom that are **not** particularly written up in the Bible. This last statement can be upsetting for some. If you were brought up in a tradition that adheres only to what is written in the Bible, breaking that mold and bringing forth a new thought can be quite disconcerting. Nothing is more difficult than changing one's cornerstone, for it truly is cemented in, metaphorically speaking.

Readers, in order to change a belief structure, one needs to bring flexibility into his/her life. You can spot people who are so "cemented" into their ways, from which almost nothing will be able to change their minds. We are apt to call them *stubborn*. If you know of a person who is rigid in his/her life, know without a doubt that the person's belief systems too are nonflexible. Therefore, how can one bring a new concept into such rigid ears? It will be a slow process. First of all the person must start to **seek** a new idea. Secondly, the person must be willing to **accept** the new idea so that change can be made.

Thus, Readers, do you not see what a formidable task it becomes for the soul even to broach the concept that one does not **have** to embrace Jesus in order to be saved? A Truth here escapes the notice of most people. Since Jesus co-authored several of those Eastern religions, could not one think if he is a follower of Buddha or Krishna that he **had** embraced Jesus also? Do not the teachings have similar statements of *love* and *caring, forgiveness* and the right *walking of a path?* Is this not a beautiful thought that Christians could embrace? Ah, yes, it brings up the reincarnation concept. How Christians fight against the thought that they may have been born many times. People, Jesus taught on and wrote on *reincarnation.* It is real; you all have lived repeatedly. The author has had 53 lifetimes on this planet. Grant you that is a low number, as most people have at least twice that. However, each soul's endeavors are different. What takes one soul 100-200 lifetimes, another soul is able to bring the karmic wheel to a stop in less time. Jesus had 33 lifetimes. Again, keep in mind we are speaking of planet Earth. Many souls have had lives on several other planets besides Earth, including Jesus.

Therefore, Readers, being *saved* is **your** responsibility. It means your soul is working diligently, connecting to its body so that it can guide it to a more pure, clean, and honest life. ***Salvation simply means you are becoming more conscious.*** Your soul is *saving* itself. Jesus, God, and the different religions are a resource. They are a *way,* simply as a resource, **a** way. Jesus does not and cannot absolve your sins. He points the way—a Wayshower. He gives you examples; he gives you teachings in parables. However, your other religions do also. Every religion carries a Truth that is spiritual, mystical, philosophical, poetic, and educational. Granted you need to sift through some of the churches' renditions, some of the scribes' projections, but the beautiful parts are still intact. If by reading these varied scriptures and passages from the religion of your faith, no matter whether you are Buddhist, Jew, Catholic, Muslim, or Christian, and this provides you your resource that you feel is reliable, then live your life by those words. However, leave your energy-door open for flexibility to enter—to let different concepts in.

New Age Material is often passed by Traditionalists. It is scoffed at and placed in the category of the *flower children* of several years ago. The new ideas are thought to be too far out there. There were too many people talking about their past lives, smoking grass, and seemingly being irresponsible, to be taken seriously. The many churchgoers just could not accept the new ideas of past lives and speaking with the Masters.

The New Age Movement brought a new **beginning** to Christian thought. It has taken thirty plus years to be more acceptable, but have you noticed that God's Methodology is rarely a swift occurrence? He knows His people are slow to change. He knew that the New Age Concept would take years before it would become part of the cultural attitudes of many people. This occurrence of such an energy that manifested on Earth was to bring change in people's belief structures. It was hoped the new energy would start new beginnings in the lives and thought forms of humanity. We view this as a fact now. The New Age Movement is a reality and has stirred the beliefs of people, helped them leave their rigid thinking. It was and is a *Beginning.*

As we have stated in the title of this chapter, *To Be One's Own Savior,* it is these kinds of Beginnings—the willingness to change one's belief structures—that create your path for becoming your own *savior.* You still need your connection to the Father, and you need your connection to your mighty I AM Presence in your heart. It would be the ideal to be connected to the many masters who are available to you, not just Jesus, if your particular religion does not embrace him. However, in order to be your **own** *savior* you need *consciousness*. Consciousness, a spiritual awareness, is built into being saved. **Being saved merely means being 100% conscious.** Religions wish you to believe only their faith will bring salvation. Truth is lacking here. For a person to believe in a particular religion and think he/she is now saved is not total Truth. The soul needs to gain consciousness. When it is fully conscious, it is *love* and *truth*. Therefore, it has **earned** its own salvation. That, however, is such a Christian term. Let us refrain from using that word in modern times. Let us speak in terms of *Consciousness*, *Truth* and *Love.* That is all one needs. The rest just takes care of itself. You will ascend and be with God. If you wish to use the word *Kingdom*, you can then **know** you have entered His Kingdom where there will be great rejoicing.

Dear Readers, only **you** can save you! It is done through diligent work on the part of the soul. Moreover, as it is needed, it is done through many lifetimes in order to hone the soul until it is 100% conscious and its own master. It is then able to communicate directly with the God of the Heavens and any of the myriad of masters who are available, constantly willing to commune with you and to share many enjoyable moments. We bless you.

TO BE or NOT TO BE—Jesus

I AM Jesus. Dear Readers, I have given you a title of another small lecture I will be giving you, but is this title not a teaser? What could it possibly mean—*To Be or Not To Be?* Do you think it might have something to do with your consciousness in order to make that deep connection to God, your Father? So many times humanity becomes caught up in its busyness. It does not even think that what it does or does not do has anything to do with consciousness. People are apt to categorize *consciousness* as being semi-comatose in a hospital.

However, dear ones, I am speaking of your capacity for a deeper connection with your soul, and that then leads you further on the pathway towards God. Everyone has a God-cell placed by the Father in his or her heart. When you were created, you were given His energy, just like with your Earth-parents. All of humanity carries a God-cell, as does the soul. This, what looks to be unseen with a microscope, is planted in your body's chakra system in the heart area. This cell helps activate your love for the Father as you mature. As a senior, an oldster, elder, your God-cell is quite mature and enlarged although it still cannot be seen under a microscope.

Hence, this God-cell, deeply imbedded in the heart chakra center, gives you the opportunity to draw closer to God. As the chakras develop, so does this Cell. Not all humanity believes in the chakras; but I say to you, your body would not be alive if it did not have these energy centers. Remember, I have said *all is energy*. Well, the chakras are energy centers; they are circles of energy that pulsate, each bearing its own color, vibration, and tone. There are many books you may find in your libraries whose authors teach extensively on the chakra systems. The point I wish to make here is that the chakra system is not just an Eastern tradition, but also an actual esoteric system of the body; and God put a cell of Himself in the heart center. These centers are attached to the spine of the physical body, but only clairvoyant eyes can see them.

Your God-cell enables you to remember and reconnect with Him. We have stated there are many paths to God. Your God-cell facilitates your walking your path for coming to Him. You realize that all is symbolic and many metaphors are used as explanations. However, the *path* is simply a conscious belief system that will lead you onward and back to God.

In your history, churches were the usual way to God. However, the church fathers tended to be overzealous and made the path strict and controlling. They took away people's freedom to make positive choices—to use their free will. People always had the devil held over their heads to fear, instead of God's Love and Light. Consequently, we could say that one of the paths to God **was** through control and fear. If church leaders scared their parishioners enough, they would no longer sin. As I have told you before, sin is in the eyes of the beholder. By curtailing dancing all in the name of God, and believing that the devil lurked behind every punch bowl, people were not making their own choices to seek God. They were no better off than in Biblical times where many prayed to the many gods for protection. As the church leaders pontificated on the devil, the innocent children shrank away from God in fear.

Nowhere is this more evident than in your Polynesian Islands when the zealous missionaries of Jesus' Teachings would storm the beaches in their inappropriate clothing made for northern parts of the world and force the natives who were barely clothed to put on this cumbersome apparel in order to thwart the devil.

I now wish to convey to you, Readers, that since all of you are ascending (and we will only be addressing ascending, not descending, if you are leading a clean and God-filled life), you will keep ascending. What we are really focusing on is *consciousness*—your level of consciousness that has you climbing that symbolic ladder.

In centuries of lore, there were creatures on your Earth that were mythical in history, but real in actuality. This would be during the Lemuria era, even before Atlantis. Souls chose to learn how animals thought—to know animal nature. Therefore, they lowered their Light and entered into animal energy. They mated and took on forms that were part animal and part human, as we have stated in BOOK ONE. When souls chose to blend with the Animal Kingdom, they did gain what they were seeking—knowledge of animals, what they thought and felt—but at the same time, they lost a part of themselves. They lost that higher consciousness that raised them above the Animal Kingdom.

Keep in mind, souls chose to seek animal wisdom. However, it was a terrible gamble. Many of those souls were arrogant in their own beliefs. They thought they were better than animals; therefore, they would always be able to rise above them, would not lose their Light, and would always be attached to God. What a grave error in judgment.

What these adventurous souls did not ascertain was that when one becomes entrapped, one **loses** consciousness. One does not become more highly developed. One actually grows less so spiritually. However, there is a dichotomy here. They lost a great deal of their spiritual consciousness. They did gain knowledge and wisdom of the Animal Kingdom, but at what price?

Souls that played this game of mythical proportions of being half-human and half-animal found they had to end cycle with that game and then climb back up the ladder of consciousness. How were they going to do this? As we have said in BOOK ONE in the chapter, *Humans and Beasts*, God brought a great flood—before Noah's time—which did wipe out not only these mythical-type creatures, but also many of the giants that roamed the Earth with your prehistoric animals. Now this took care of the immediate problem, but there continued to be a bleed-through with many humans being born with animal appendages. Edgar Cayce speaks of this when he talks about Atlantis. Bodies still carried the genetics of those myth-like creatures. The souls had a big problem on their hands.

God stepped in and brought in more Truth for the souls to help them regain their spiritual progress, as well as delineate more strongly between animals and humans. Thus, this abomination of mating and crossbreeding outside of your species' kingdom would never happen on Earth again. Can you imagine the struggle the souls now had that had made this ill-advised choice of mating and breeding with animals? These souls lost so much more than they ever had hoped to gain from the Animal Kingdom. I am speaking of thousands and thousands of years, plus lifetime after lifetime of trying to rebuild their lost consciousness—a formidable task.

However strange as it may seem, and here is the dichotomy, the wisdom they learned from joining the Animal Kingdom was never lost to them. They carried that ability to commune with animals, to listen and know what they are feeling, to be able to go to that animal energy by thought and to manipulate it. These souls were able to go to that animal's energy band and control the animal by thought. Many of your Winged Pharaohs of Egypt had this ability and would have great cats sitting by their thrones. Therefore, the animal wisdom gained was tremendous; but at what price to the soul, for that too was tremendous!

Many of humanity today were those adventurous souls. They have the ability to tune into animals and train them well. Many of your horse whisperers, your wild animal trainers, gained their abilities from those ancient times and practices. However, it is at this point I feel I need to warn you, Readers, not to judge. You too may have been one of those souls who put aspects of themselves into animals or crossbred with the Animal Kingdom. Remember, we are speaking of thousands of years ago. You no longer are that Being, but you do carry those memories deep inside of you.

Therefore, Readers, be aware of the impact your choices have upon your consciousness. Always ask yourself if the choice you want to make enhances your consciousness. Everything is energy. Therefore, every act you do, every thought you have, has an energetic impact on your consciousness. We suggest you look and listen before you leap into action on anything. While there is no such thing as an accident (for you will learn one way or another by giving yourself time to pause, contemplate, and ask for guidance of your I AM Presence), you may find that your choice is indeed a positive one that enhances you to be more conscious. *To Be or Not to Be (Conscious)* is really a most serious decision, whether the soul is in or out of its body.

THE ECLECTICISM of BELIEF SYSTEMS—Jesus

I AM Jesus. In the past I have stated many times that, *all is an illusion*. Your real world is in the Heavenlies—the higher dimensions. You may be surprised to know there are many dimensions beyond what various writers have proclaimed as forty-nine. There are dimensions not written about. I have seen where people are told they are at the twelfth dimension that is considered the throne room. I do not fully agree. The Throne of God is actually in even higher dimensions. Let us say it is at least in triple digit numbers.

Humanity is so quick to grab on to a writer's numbers simply because he/she seems so knowledgeable. Perhaps that person has been told by masters a particular number; but People, I am saying that forty-nine seems like a very low number to me. One must place these numbers in their correct context. There are forty-nine dimensions; but there are also double those numbers! We are talking about quantum physics and sacred geometry, different Universes and worlds. None of these Universes has the same number of dimensions, nor do the different worlds in them. Therefore, be aware, Beloveds, that for you to grasp and hold on to a certain number is not accurate. Remember flexibility. If only physicists and your scientists would accept that there are more dimensions than the ten or twelve on which they seem to place their equations, then they could stop confining themselves.

Let us take psychology for example. Last century psychology went from learning about your body's drives and ego to the theory that Freud was not completely accurate, for it was the body's animal reactions that was truth. After Behaviorism, came Humanistic Psychology, the whole person and unconditional love. Psychology was now branching out in all directions, with Gestalt, or Primal Screams, motivating people to scream into their pillows or in their cars with their windows rolled up. Throughout psychology's growing pains, Carl Jung was teaching people they could not forget the soul. Abraham Maslow brought in self-actualization. Both Carl Jung and Maslow are considered the grandfathers of the widely popular Transpersonal Psychology, the integration of mind, body, and spirit. This psychology recognizes that we indeed have altered states of consciousness and that we can move beyond ego into those higher dimensions. Now psychology is making great strides in the right direction. One must **not** take only one person's theory and let none of the others in. Truth be known, psychology does have its own maturation process. (*This Author's doctorate is in Transpersonal Psychology. 2011)*

It grew through those first steps from ego-drives, to body, to the whole person, to combining it with the spiritual soul, to going beyond ego. There was more reality out in the Universe than just one point of view. All needs to be integrated on its own merits. Each of those pioneers of psychology added a facet of truth to it. They created the foundation so that other theorists could branch off, but still keep their own connection to the basic theories.

Therefore, in science, physics, and sacred geometry, theorists need to be receptive to new possibilities. What they think is an *absolute* cannot be total truth. Just as they think an equation has been created to explain some phenomenon, someone else will come along with a newer equation that proves something else. Consequently, when New Agers embrace the premise there are absolutely forty-nine dimensions, I say to you *forty-nine and counting!* There are infinite dimensions in space of which not even we Masters know. Frankly, exploring those outer dimensions can be rather intimidating to us too. I would feel a bit of trepidation, I must say, if I decided to go exploring beyond known dimensions and boundaries. One needs to keep an open mind.

In our etheric world, we see many strange and marvelous things that you on Earth would not even be able to comprehend. Your physicists and astronomers have just barely touched the surface, especially when exploring black holes. A phenomenon where gravity sucks into itself is a remarkable sight. Therefore, dear Readers, do not narrow yourselves to certain belief systems. Always leave an open door for another possibility to enter.

You know it reminds me a bit of pastors of one church taking a particular position on God and Me, Jesus, and proclaiming that this is the way of it—how Teachings stand. Then another pastor will decide that particular interpretation is inaccurate and one must practice religion this way in order to be a Methodist, Presbyterian,

Unitarian, Pentecostal, Lutheran, Catholic, Mormon, plus all the outcroppings from those religions where just Christ is the name of the church—so many interpretations of my words.

However, there is that saying, *different strokes for different folks,* which I find quite apropos. It is noteworthy to know that all the religions mentioned honor God, the Father, and Me. The different interpretations, creeds, and rules are what separate. That is what is hurtful for humanity—the separation. All of these religions create a separation among people. Why could there not be just one thought on spirituality and religion? Well someday, Readers, that is exactly what will happen. All of this myriad of different religious sects will no longer be. There will come a time when religion is more even in its thinking. There will not be such delineation on what one ought to believe, think, and do, versus another's religion. Years ago, religions controlled the masses more than they do now. As people started to attend church less and less, the pastors felt their control slipping away.

Consequently, religious practices became less constrictive. People were allowed to eat what they wished when they wished. There still is a religious belief that fish instead of meat needs to be eaten on a particular day, but all of that was the churches controlling people and many were controlling through fear. In the new spiritual practice, this kind of control will no longer exist. It will be the person's free will whether he/she wants to eat seafood on a particular day, or on any day, or at anytime, if at all.

Many people have opted for a vegetarian diet. That too is within the belief structure of people. Some people do very well on a vegetarian diet; others have bodies that need a varied amount of protein. There are certain enzymes that one needs for energy expansion that can only be obtained through a light meat of some kind. This last remark will not sit well with true vegetarians; but to repeat, there **are** enzymes that are needed at times and can only be obtained through meat! I know many vegetarians sanction their eating of no meat, eggs, gelatin, and so forth; but that is a spiritual practice that they have embraced and a very strong belief system. Many of your spiritual practices and religions have some belief systems that are written and spoken about in very pure statements.

It is still the choice of the practitioner to embrace what he/she has been taught.

I am stating, Readers, that one's belief system is as strong as the flexibility that you have incorporated into it. If you hear of a new idea, it then becomes your choice as to whether you will give the idea a try-out. Some find the idea is just what they had been searching for. Others find it is not quite right for them; they lose interest; or the practice requires too much of their attention. Consequently, it becomes too much trouble. Therefore, dear Readers, I would urge you to just be an open vessel. Try out new ideas and see if they work for you. If you need to change a lifestyle or eating habit, give your attention to it. Keep in mind bodies do not take rapidly to change. They need to be nudged into a new way of being. One needs to persevere. After a number of weeks, re-evaluate. I would suggest that you give any new *beginning* at least a six to eight week trial run. If you find you are not being consistent or just keep forgetting to do the practice, chances are it won't be your path and you will need to embrace another idea.

I suggest that you never make another person wrong if he/she gets excited and enthused about a *beginning* that person is making. Whatever is going on, he/she is being soul led; or he/she would not be feeling so much joy and excitement. Remember that bodies are not logical; they tend not to like change and can be quite inflexible. The soul must instigate the new ideas. It is a goal of the soul to be well integrated with its body, as souls carry the mind. The body's brain is more like a computer. It does not have the mind as such but does carry out the soul's instructions. Your body is wise and is your best friend. Treat it as such. Listen to it; talk to it. It will communicate very well for you with goose bumps and tears of joy or sorrow. It will also show you its unhappiness through its anger and/or depression. Use your body as a barometer for your immediate environment. It will tell you if your new *beginning* will be one to develop or one of which to let go.

Religions all carry their particular messages. All have an element of truth. Whether to be a vegetarian is for you to decide. It has its benefits also. It is up to both your body and soul to agree if this is your path or not. Free will, People, gives you the right to make your own choices. Whatever you are wishing to do; whatever progress and advancement your soul is wanting to make, all will merge and come together, some sooner than later. The main point I wish you to take away with you from this chapter is all eclectic ideas and beliefs that are presented to us each lifetime are a growth opportunity.

The way psychology and its theories have advanced, the way physicists question the number and dynamics of dimensions, the way different religions expound their own interpretation of God and Jesus, all of these carry elements of truth; but **not one** is complete in itself. Each needs the other to build upon in order to advance its theories. Keep an open mind. Allow new ideas in. Allow yourself to let go of those outdated beliefs that no longer serve you. **Be eclectic** in your belief structure. Dare to persevere and change.

CREATION—Maitreya, Sananda, Jesus

We are Maitreya, Sananda, and Jesus. This chapter will be on *Creation,* a loaded topic for sure. When most people hear about *Creation,* they immediately think, *now that has to be about evolution.* However, we feel humanity has read all about the Creation theories. We will just add our opinion and say that both theories hold truth, for there are people who evolved from the Animal Kingdom. Nevertheless, the more highly-evolved Beings came from the spiritual aspect of Adam. People also came from other planets and star systems. I am sure you Readers have heard the term, *star seeds.* Well much of humanity is star seed—a Being that came from other planets. The Hebrews are such a grouping. They brought in the Laws and were not indigenous to the planet. Suffice for now; we will leave concepts of creation to religions and to the Evolutionists.

What we do wish to address is what souls create. What has been the creation in your lives? In the past, many souls were reincarnated in order to grow, clean up their karma, grow, unconsciously create more karma, and grow. One can begin to see how that wheel of birth-death-rebirth-death is perpetuated repeatedly. It is really about the evolution of the soul, the advancement up the rungs of Jacob's ladder, and hopefully Home to God. However, as you know, on paper it looks to be a simple task. Keep steadfast, persevere, and fill yourself with God's Presence.

As most of humanity has discovered, what looks to be a simple task in theory can become formidable in reality. It is the body and its wants and needs, its ego, habits, compulsions, anxieties, vast range of emotions, and energy fluctuations that make what seemed a simple path to be one that had many twists and turns.

One of the main reasons for the struggle that souls encounter is that they have difficulty with their *creating.* What they have in their lives, they created knowingly or unknowingly. Now we understand you Readers may be exclaiming that it was your karma and lessons that have put you where you are today. That is true. What you have in your life today most likely **is** what you created in your last lifetime; or the life before that, or before that one even. Your creations do follow you from lifetime to lifetime. They really do show you what predicaments you had gotten yourself into years and centuries before.

Consequently, in this lifetime you will encounter old pathways that need resurfacing, to use a metaphor. You may look around you, see people with so much money, with so many possessions you wonder how they can manage such abundance. They rarely can. They have to hire business managers just to help them to manage and cope with all their money, investments, and attachments. This is what we would like to call to your attention. Just because someone is what you may think *outrageously wealthy*, it does **not** mean the person is having a free ride this lifetime. The person's wealth is a huge lesson the soul has taken on in order to learn a myriad of things. For example, the soul may wish to learn how to give to others, how not to hoard, how to stay free of greed, how to receive, and how to give back to God, to name but a few. Many times great wealth can be a great burden as well. It is not easy for the soul. Chances are the soul has had to rotate from a life of wealth to one of poverty and then back to wealth. This type of rotation can take several lifetimes, according to what the soul has created around great wealth, either positively or negatively during those lifetimes.

Many times people are born into extreme poverty. They then take on that energy of *poverty* and find they always have money problems and have great difficulty giving to themselves. If a body thinks it has nothing and never will have anything, chances are the person will not, to put it bluntly! The soul chose that lifetime for it afforded a great opportunity for advancement if the soul's personality did not succumb to a poverty mentality.

There are highly-evolved Beings that literally are unable to be around poverty energy. They find the feeling of that energy so heavy and devoid of life that they can barely function around it. Picture someone walking through a beautiful meadow. Then the person comes to a place that is not inviting. It does not beckon to him; so the person walks around and away from the area. The energy there was too cloying, with no evidence of tranquility and joy. Consequently, the area is avoided. People who are stuck in their poverty mentality usually cannot draw to them people of Light—only if a person of

Light comes in service, a caretaker position, perhaps. These can be your social workers—the problem solvers.

People in poverty might object to what we have said and exclaim that if others are more highly evolved, would they not want to come and help raise the person of poverty up and out of that condition? We say *we cannot save you!* Only you on a soul level can move you out of poverty. Let us back up a bit. Souls that are born into poverty have **requested** this, or they have **created** this from a past life transgression. Now the soul has a life of extreme poverty. What are the choices here? At first glance, they seem nil. However, *poverty* can be a state of mind. A person can have little money, be quite poor, but **not** be in poverty.

The person who is poor usually knows how to ask for help, knows how to use available resources, does not **believe** he/she is poverty-stricken. The soul may be taking classes in order to better its education. This person will always be able to strive forward eventually and make a better life for him/herself. This type of person does not think in terms of poverty. This person does not focus on how little money he/she has and what is lacking in life. On the other hand, people with a poverty mentality always believe life has done it to them. They are victims to their circumstances. They are born pessimists. To them the glass is always half empty.

Therefore, what can we add in order to help people who are in poverty turn it around? Indeed, it may be their karmic task to turn a poverty-stricken life positive. One of the simplest ways—and you know we always go for what is simple—is not to let the idea you are in poverty creep in. It is similar to *reframing* a thought, as therapists would say. As soon as you entertain the idea you are in poverty, you are to say **NO** to it. That is all, just a **NO** and then reframe or recreate that thought in order to make it a positive. For example, if you harbor the thought you will always be in poverty, say to yourself, ***only*** *if I choose to be.* You see, Reader, **a mental state is by choice of thoughts**. When you say No to an idea before it is formed and you change the notion to a positive choice, you have not allowed that thought to form.

One of the dangers for people in poverty is the tendency to sink into despair. They create more and more negative thoughts until they have this big cloud hanging over them. It is a cloud of all their negative thoughts and ideas. Therefore, it is essential you not let these negative thoughts manifest. Catch them a bit at a time—say, three-fourths the way, then half way, one fourth way, and finally you will catch them at the first negative word you think. There is a good statement one can say—*do not go there!* That is a very productive utterance. It stops you from entering into a negative space. Simply do not tolerate that thought. Do not go there!

Poverty is insidious in that it creeps into one's mentality and settles in. We have said people have many lessons concerning money and one of the hardest is being born into a family that has little. They are monetarily poor, but can be rich in Spirit. Alternatively, are they in poverty on all levels? It has been our observation that people with a poverty mentality are usually in poverty spiritually also. Their soul is not that connected to the body. The body has little soul supervision and is habit-ridden and ego-driven. The ego dictates what to do and where to go.

Conversely, people who may be poor have material lack, but many times, they are quite spiritual and continually give thanks and appreciation for what they do have. Poor people can receive. Poverty people receive nothing, only take, and usually take what does not belong to them. They steal and lie, but mostly lie to themselves for they do not approach life in a positive way, but only in a victim way. They can mouth that that is not true. They can profess they are not being a victim, but that is not usually a truthful, heartfelt statement. Many poverty-minded people know what to say and what is expected of them, but the words do not ring true.

Amazingly, people who carry poverty energy can look like they do not. They dress fairly well, but their energy belies the fact that they think they are in poverty. This is a difficult concept to get across to people. Poor people may look poor, have to scrimp and save, but they do not carry the poverty energy. On the other hand, people with the poverty energy can actually have more than a poor person. They may have more food in the refrigerator, frequently eat out at fast food restaurants, but they seldom have a feeling of peace about money. They can even hoard money and still feel and act as if they are poverty-stricken.

Therefore, dear Readers, we are speaking of your creations in this chapter. What have you created in your life around money? Are you wealthy, poor, in poverty, or just comfortable? Each of those four categories can be created in your life by you. Your soul has brought in these lessons, most likely from past lives. These are lessons from which you are still gleaning the wisdom. You will interchange positions concerning money lifetime after lifetime. You may learn both ends of the spectrum. Even the masters who are walking your Earth today who we have spoken about still choose lives where the question of money is present. There are Masters who are quite wealthy, masters who are comfortable, and masters who have chosen to be poor. Each of these masters has a particular purpose for his/her choice. The struggle may be a challenge but is not **the** challenge for them. **The** challenge is to reach a certain level of humanity that is on your monetary level and to be the Wayshower on how to live life. Many of these masters will be gifted by God with large sums of money when the austerity period has been completed. In a way, it is their lesson in *faith, patience,* and *trust*. Thus, the main reason is not karmic—it is the job description for the particular service to which the master has agreed.

Consequently, Readers, know there are many reasons for one's economical life. For the average person, the reasons are lessons to learn and karma to overcome, for it is due to your creations. Do not judge your fellow laborer in life, for he/she may be a master who has agreed to come to Earth and live in a similar environment such as yours, in order, perhaps, to show you by example how to raise yourself out of the lower economical strata. The master just could be God's answer to your prayers for help. Since your lesson needs to be experienced by you, the master only can show you a way, if you will but listen, observe, and receive the direction to which you are being led. Let this be one of your creations also—beginning a new way to approach life and walking a different path toward Home.

(*Money is one of the most difficult lessons a soul takes on to learn, for money has so many facets to it—entrapment, greed, possession, to name but a few. These lessons in money are spread out over several lifetimes: "rich man, poor man, beggar-man, thief . . ."* 2011)

METAMORPHOSIS—Djwhal Khul

I AM Djwhal Khul—also known to you as the *Tibetan*. In years gone by, there were people on the planet who worshipped many inanimate objects as well as living parts of Nature, such as the trees and animals. These people knew there was something bigger than themselves but could not define the concept. What they had was a deep reverence for the Earth. They practiced rituals with song and dance, giving praise to their different deities of the land.

In those ancient times, the word for God was not known. However, they had names for their many gods of the Earth. In all spiritual, religious, and heathen practices, there is an element of truth. What these people knew was there was a Higher Energy than they living in their sacred areas and objects. One of the most known gods was Pele, Goddess of Volcanoes. The people knew this goddess was all-powerful. They knew when she was angry and they thought they knew how to appease her. They picked a young virgin girl and gave her as a sacrifice to Pele.

Now what they did not realize was that the Goddess Pele did not want their children thrown into her fire. What she did want was a particular energy. She was seeking the energy of *balance.* This may seem strange to you Readers to think that **fire and volcanoes are living entities**, but they are. They belong to the Elemental and Mineral Kingdoms with their own intelligence.

Meanwhile, while people were practicing their rituals of appeasement, the gods and goddesses were seeking *balance* for the planet. At times, as in the case of Pele, the volcanoes belched, blew and let off pressure that had been building underground. You see, Readers, while volcanoes can be destructive, they serve a much needed purpose. They act as smoke stacks for the Earth. They help the Earth release a build-up of excess vapor and energy. They erupt and spew forth in an awesome display of activity, which releases and discharges much pressure. However, in ancient times people who lived near the volcanoes always viewed this fiery display as a sign they had transgressed in some way. Down through generations the practice of appeasement was in the form of a human sacrifice. We of course understand now that that was not a positive choice by the natives, but it was a belief system well entrenched in them.

Many centuries later people put volcanic eruptions more into the category of a natural phenomenon. Thus, human sacrifices finally were discontinued. It took the evolution of the soul in order to no longer play this game. Meanwhile, Pele continued to spew forth with or without the sacrifices. People became wiser and built their villages in less vulnerable locations. However, even today there are villages being developed too close to mountains that could erupt, which could destroy the village with great loss of life.

For example, people living too near Mt. Rainier have been warned that the mountain is in danger of erupting, maybe not just like Mt. St. Helens, but also certainly with great destruction and loss of life. The villagers near Mt. Rainer are in deep denial. Having volcano-eruption drills for the schoolchildren is like handing each child a cup for when a dam might break! The concept is not realistic. It is a form of Russian roulette. People believe the eruption of Mt. Rainier just will not happen in their lifetime. We say to that, *hmm . . . heed the warning!*

By now, Readers may be questioning what has the discussion of volcanoes have to do with *beginnings?* Do you not think these were concepts of *beginnings* when people no longer sacrificed? That certainly was a tremendous beginning for a change in consciousness for the soul. If you would stop a moment and realize that, any change marks a *beginning*. New Agers even have that saying *it has begun!* Of course the meaning here is that as the planet locks into the fourth dimension, all must change—people, places and things. When the planet seeks balance, it will see to it that certain changes must be made. While God leads the souls to evolve and thus change their consciousness, the planet moves forward also and makes her changes in the weather patterns, and new formation of her topography, as the plates shift. Volcanoes will spew forth, the Earth's crust will shake, and the waters will rush in. This is the planet's way of bringing balance to herself, a metamorphosis.

As people's consciousness is raised to a higher degree, their negative thought forms are transmuted. People will want to care for their world. People will become more involved with the ecological system, for it must change. There are so many pollutants from automobiles to industry to gas snowmobiles, lawn mowers and leaf blowers. All emit gases harmful to the planet. In addition, the pollutants from your hair salons continue. The aerosol cans are still preferred to the pump in order to dispense hair spray. All of this creates a cloud that hangs over the planet.

It may happen after the cleansing period that there will be changes in how people use machinery. Long speeding trains will travel on air. Automobiles will be electrified and will have their own battery charging mechanism. Thus, cars will be able to travel great distances without pulling once into a filling station for gas. When they do, it will be to recharge their battery. The former gas stations will convert to electric power grids. Cars will be able to pull in and while the driver has a brief respite, the person's car will be recharged, all in a matter of less than an hour.

Oil will be a commodity of the past. Those of the mid-east countries will fight this new direction, for their money will no longer flow as their oil did. The oil then will be able to continue its real purpose, to lubricate the Earth. Oil products for cosmetics will no longer be used. Your petroleum jelly will seem outdated—in the category of snake oil from your pioneer days.

Most people would like to keep the world as they know it. They are open to new inventions like the cell phone, as long as these inventions do not infringe on other conveniences, such as their gas-guzzling cars. It is when someone has received the new invention and is trying to market it, that he/she runs into trouble. Then the big auto companies fight the new ideas. The hairsprays, creams, and lubricants for myriad purposes create big money for the big companies. They are not apt to take willingly to a new inventor whose product is a complete changeover from another product. As long as companies' finances are involved, they will not be open to any new idea that rocks their boat, so to speak. They are more willing to spend millions on their lawyers and the legal battles than on trying a complete metamorphosis of their own product. As we see it, if the company is American, it is the almighty dollar that really dictates the progress of any new idea, whether for the good of the people and/or environment. Nothing is a stronger incentive than the silver dollar.

Imagine the mid-eastern countries where the demarcation between the *haves* and the *have-nots* is so noticeable. These potentates have thousands of feet of garage space just to house their lavish Rolls Royces, many that are bulletproof. Are these people of the desert going to step aside and not produce any more oil simply because the demand for oil in the world is no longer there? They will fight to protect their way of life. Therefore, what is one to do? Well, Reader, the good news is Mother Earth will no longer put off what **she** wishes to do. She is steadily evolving and reaching for the next dimension. Thus, one could say that these next fifty years will be her growing pains. Most people of the 3D world would have made their transitions to the astral planes or other planets by then.

The consciousness of the people will have risen, as the souls are able to bring in more highly developed bodies. Keep in mind the more evolved your body is, the more consciousness souls are able to bring in. Think in terms of automobiles. If you own an old clunker that sputters and leaks oil and does not go very fast on its four cylinders, can you imagine what a car will do that is new, powerful, and cleanly maintained? Your bodies are very much the same way. They will evolve and become more efficient. How would you like to remember most of what you have ever read? How would you like to eat what you like and not have to take antacids or pills to calm down the acid-making mechanisms? How would you like to have such acute vision that you will be able to see birds nestled in trees half a block away? All of this is coming as the body's DNA is updated. Remember, each body has a Divine Blueprint of itself. It resides in the first chakra area. God made you perfect in every way. You have the papers to prove it, metaphorically speaking, in your energy center. (*As we evolve, our blueprints change. We could be on our third blueprint for this lifetime even! 2011)*

Consequently, dear Readers, there is much hope for your Earth and humanity. Keep in mind when one speaks of a *beginning* that it implies a change will occur at the same time. Therefore, in order to incorporate these changes, your world has to undergo very important *beginnings* in all areas: Nature, people, and not only your environment, but also much of what you take for granted in the way of your conveniences. All will go through a metamorphosis. The finished product will be glorious for you all. Accept your beginnings and changes and find the positive in whatever occurs. Remember, in order to grow, the Earth must have her changes. Some will be from volcanoes, Earthquakes, and tsunamis. Some changes will be with your weather, but oh how fresh everything smells and how bright everything looks after a spring rain! Do not approach your *beginnings* in fear, for there is a reason behind the chaos. Do you not think the purpose might be to raise your and the planet's consciousness so that all can come into balance?

THE MASTERS' FIRST CONTACT—Sananda

I AM Sananda. Many of you Readers will wonder why one person is picked to receive our thoughts versus another, or versus you perhaps. Beloveds, we would like nothing better than to speak to you from the mental plane; but dear ones, have you questioned yourself that maybe we have tried? We, hundreds of times—too numerous to put a number to—have entered the mental body of many of you, but could not get your attention. Let us take the example of a switchboard operator. Fifty years ago, there were no cell phones. There were huge switchboards and an operator sat in front of them directing the phone calls that came in by plugging in one of those long rubber hoses. Now the person calling and the person receiving the call were connected.

It is very similar to what I am doing at this very moment. The Author's internal switchboard is lit up, ready and waiting for my call. She has stilled herself and set the stage by saying a prayer, so that any communication will come through the spiritual energy of prayer. She sits patiently, keeping her active mind as still as possible. I, at my end, am alerted that a person is opened to receive. I will not go into all the facts of how we have made contact with her. Suffice to know it was by her diligence, intention, perseverance, clean and pure energy, and opened chakras that we are able to connect.

Once we see that a student, a chela, is ready and waiting to communicate with us in the higher dimensions, we step forward. Of course, the first contact at our level will be from the person's master teacher(s). In the Author's case, there is more than one of us. I, Sananda, initially contacted her, by coming close enough to stroke her cheek a couple of times. At the same time, I was strongly repeating a short sentence. I repeated it to break through her thoughts, for she had no idea what was going to happen. At the same time I was touching her cheek, I observed her chakras, especially the heart chakra. I observed her emotional body. I observed her entire body watching for any sign that she was not ready to walk this path. What I observed was she was ready. She just did not know it yet, for she had a strong belief system concerning channeling that she needed to work through and release.

If one is told for many years not to channel, and being the good student that she is who listened to her teachers (for she had some difficulty in recognizing that the limitation she had adhered to was for her own protection), she would not be so apt to set those teachings aside and start channeling. All of her chakras were wide open. In fact, her teachers would monitor them and would close them a bit so that her emotional body could be more prepared. What she did not know was the control of her channeling was by her Higher Self and not the teachers at that time. Any adjustment to her chakras was always done with her permission and trust.

Therefore, in order to break through the body's resistance to channeling, we had to allow the idea to germinate and to give her time. We gave her two years. During that time, we would come and just talk to her while she wrote our words in her journal. She gradually would tell people she had received a message or two, but generally, she kept the fact that she channeled us private. You see, Readers, how your belief systems play a role also in whether we come and get through to you, to make that first contact.

Consequently, you are watched ever so closely, whether you realize it or not, in order to see your progress and whether now would be the time to make contact. I imagine most of you Readers have heard that when you are ready, your teacher will come. Well, this is what we are doing—watching and waiting. We expect that those of you who read this chapter just may start to practice *still times* in order to ready yourselves if you have not already done so. Come, we surely will when you are ready!

The Author found that that first contact could be an awesome experience—for it is the body that will react to our energies. Most people will experience goose bumps and chills. It is their body acknowledging that there is someone in their energy field—their space. Keep in mind we do not enter anyone's field unless we are invited in. Of course, in this case her Higher Self gave the permission. The Author's body felt shaky and quite tearful, for our energy goes to one's heart chakra for a greater connection. All the time the chills and goose bumps are occurring with tears and sniffles too, we are speaking mentally and she is conversing and questioning our presence, asking who we are and so forth. We purposely avoided our name at first in order to give her the chance to **seek** who we are. One ought never to allow others into your space without knowing with whom you are speaking, although I am aware, some people are taught it does not matter. Most likely, they were sitting in a well-protected group, protected by the masters who were the only ones that would be entering the students' field. However, when you, Reader, are pursuing this path on your own, so to speak, be careful and **know** whom you are channeling.

Another experience the Author had was when I switched pronouns from me to We. She caught that instantly and wanted to know about the *we*. I told her that many times we come not singularly, but with others. We can blend our energies with each other and become a We versus an I. You will notice in this book, many times we come as the Trio: Maitreya, Sananda, and Jesus; or Jesus, Maitreya, and Sananda. The order in which the names are said has little relevance to the reader. When you make a smoothie blender drink, it makes little difference in what order you put the orange juice, banana, and peach into the blender. You flip the switch and all is one. When we blend our energies, we too are One.

Now let us go back to the first contact from a master. You may have been contacted by entities of lower vibrations long before we made contact with you. This was your learning process, the opening and clearing of your chakras. Your lessons were at times difficult, may have been scary even, if you attracted to you an undesirable entity. You would have learned when channeling whether you were to share your body with the entity, or just channel telepathically. This entailed your being able to go into an altered state, called a *trance* by some, open your clairaudience, and be in your mental body, as well as in your heart. Your third eye will also be well developed. All the chakras in the head area will be energized and working as a unit.

As you have developed your chakra centers, your Light quotient also has risen. You have climbed new rungs up Jacob's ladder. Whether you are aware of it or not, your Light beckons to the master that you are ready. I also want to remind you that this is not the first lifetime that you have channeled. You have had many lifetimes where you have been able to hear us and have us share your body. We have made contact with you many lifetimes earlier. Would it surprise you to know we just may have known each other even before Lemuria or Atlantis? Hmmm, I thought it might.

Consequently, our making first contact in this year of 2005, I could also say 1005 and count backwards to the thousands and millions of years ago that we knew you. This lifetime is but a little blip on the radar screen, for there are all the lives you have had on other planets as well. Broaden your horizons. Let go of those old belief systems of having lived only once. They are very incorrect. You are **not** that young in soul. I can assure you!

To end our narration, whether we make first contact with you is up to you. Is it your purpose this lifetime to just do your thing and never meditate? Is it your purpose to meditate and ride the inner planes to learn about God's Kingdom? Is it your purpose to still your body and develop your telepathy so you and I can converse? Is it your soul's purpose and agreement with God to write books telepathically? There are so many variations to each of your purposes. I hope that you have followed your soul's purpose and are happily engaged in that. Perhaps it is part of your purpose to make contact with us this lifetime. We know what purpose you have chosen. However, it is up to you to tell us! Dear Reader, always follow your heart and soul's purpose. You will know if you still yourself long enough so that your I AM Presence can lead you. Whatever your choices are, we watch you, guide you, and bless you.

MASCULINE and FEMININE PRINCIPALS-

Sananda

I AM Sananda. Readers, if you have read all of these chapters to this point, you may be wondering when he is going to speak of some of the more controversial aspects that humanity faces today. As you probably know by now, Jesus, Maitreya, and I are truly a blend and at times speak as one entity. However, each of us has his own personality, and we carry the masculine and feminine Principals within each of us. As you have read in previous chapters, when you reach your mastership, it means you have blended those energies. Your masculine energy is *Will* and *Power* and your feminine energy is *Intuition* and *Creativity*.

In years past, the energies were more polarized. Men were very masculine, using little of their feminine energies, what one could say as being the softer side of man. Conversely, women were very feminine, using little of their masculine principal. Now when God created man and woman, He purposely put those two energies into the body. It would then be up to the soul as to which energy to make dominant, no matter what gender the body was. In the early years of the last century, men were copying women by the use of extravagant dress—heavy velvets, laces and jewels. They wore the long stockings to show off their legs.

Meanwhile the women, not of the court, dressed more simply, in an austere way. They did not show their legs; they had simple dress designs with maybe ribbons and a bit of lace. Remember, these women were not of royalty and the upper classes, but the average down-to-Earth woman.

Now what were these dynamics in play that had men dressing like women and the women dressing in a more somber, no-frills way? It all stemmed from the energies that were dominant in the body. The men used more of their feminine principal and less of their masculine principal. Thus, these energies were not in balance. Again I remind you I am not speaking of gender, for although these men were quite feminine in their use of the energy, they all were very much men in their sexual habits. Although there were many homosexuals in that era, they were not as open about it as they are today.

Therefore, what creates this overbalance of one principal versus the other? The soul manipulates the body from which it can live its purpose. Many souls found that bringing balance to these two energies, masculine Will and feminine Intuition, or left brain and right brain, was not an easy task. Several mitigating circumstances would greatly influence the progress of this blending. Much of the problem lay in outside influences—the era one was born into, the religious scene and the political status at that time.

As I have said, the early part of the last century and even before that, men of the court were vying for women's attentions by copying women in dress and manner. When that soul had too much of the feminine principal flowing in its male body, it was difficult to bring the body into balance. The women suffragettes on the other hand revved up their masculine-principal energy in order to break through the male dominance of politics. The suffragettes wanted the vote in America. They matched the men's energy. The term *feminist* is a misnomer in my opinion. That term suggests they were more feminine, while the opposite was truth. They used their masculine energy in a strong way, in order to win the right for women to vote.

To reiterate for you, Readers, for this dynamic may be new to you, God gave the body both the masculine and feminine energies. It is electrical in nature with the masculine energy being from the positive pole and the negative being the feminine electrical surge. God made the masculine, positive energy *Will* and *Power.* The feminine negative electrical energy is *Intuition* and *Creativity.* Both of these energies are part of the body in the heart chakra and brain lobes. The soul carries both also. Let go of the belief that we are speaking of good and bad. It is energy. How you **use** the energies connotes whether your choices have made your experience a good or bad one, if you wish to use those terms. Those of you with a psychology background will have no trouble with this concept of the two energies, for Carl Jung made it quite clear in his Jungian psychology works when he named the masculine energy *animus,* and the feminine energy *anima*.

Let us come back to the present and the large numbers of homosexuals—gays and lesbians who have come out of the closet.

There are several reasons for homosexuality. First, is homosexuality innate in the body? For some it is and for some it is a human choice. The personality chooses the alternative lifestyle. For others, the soul chooses the lifestyle. It chose a body whose energies would decree the preference of the same sex relationship and/or partnership.

The soul is ever evolving. Since Earth is a planet of duality, the *pairs of opposites* as Jung would say, the soul in its eternal search for wisdom and advancement **chooses** to experience all facets of homosexuality. In one lifetime, it chooses a male body and is gay. In another lifetime, the soul chooses a body that will be lesbian. Many times when a soul has had these various gay past lives and lifestyles and then chooses a body that does not have these yearnings to be with a same sex person in the present life, the soul could have bi-sexual encounters. However, the soul will most likely settle on one partner of the opposite sex for the present lifetime.

Conversely, there are many people in the gay community who choose an opposite sex partner, marry and have children, and then are drawn to those of the same sex once again. Most likely, souls who are ending the homosexual cycle from previous lives and the clearing of the belief systems still find this dynamic a dilemma.

There are instances where males and females choose a same sex partner. The lifestyle is a free will **choice,** not because the body dictates this because of hormonal imbalances. Nor does the soul choose this. In these cases, the soul may not be that connected to its body, so that the personality pretty much does what it wishes to do. In many cases, the parenting was not of a higher quality, so that the family unit was dysfunctional. Hence, the personality chose those of the same sex for safety and nurturing, seeking what it felt it had not received from its own parents.

Therefore, Readers, watch your judgments against the homosexual community. It is a melting pot of past life alternative lifestyles; a soul **choosing** the experience and the lessons one learns; the soul readjusting its energies and bringing into balance the masculine and feminine Principals. Many times souls have found also that a homosexual body can bring forth innate artistry that they were unable to touch in other lifetimes.

Religions have been especially critical of the homosexual. Those religions that have opened their doors for homosexuals to be spiritual leaders are then judged by other religions as being blasphemous. There is so much judgment of souls that are learning different lessons and evolving. Not everyone is on the same rung of Jacob's ladder. You may have not played your homosexual games yet; or you may have completed them. God's Kingdom is all about balance, and above all *love*.

If you, Readers, could just stay in your heart and have compassion. Do not judge what you may perceive as not your way, but know your fellow neighbor has chosen his or her own set of lessons and purposes. If you can let go of stereotypical belief systems of what you perceive as a right or wrong way of living life—if you could do all the above—you may find that you have climbed higher on Jacob's ladder and garnered much wisdom.

(Note: I have used the word ***principal*** *when speaking of the masculine and feminine aspect for it is an* ***alive*** *energy, versus' principle,' which is not animate but a doctrine.)*

AFTER the FACT—Sananda

I AM Sananda. I can well imagine, Readers, your puzzlement as to what I will discourse on with such a title, *After the Fact.* Take but a moment and think about the many times you may have grumbled to yourself, *if I had only had that information* ***before*** *I had acted.* This is thinking in terms of *after the fact*. Now what occurs when a person realizes that he or she indeed did not have all of the facts? Why would one go ahead with a decision when one did not have a clear picture of how to proceed?

There can be various reasons. One can be the soul was not that connected to the body. Consequently, the personality made the decision. Another reason could be the body was not being guided. The ego just stipulated what choice to make. Hence, there is a great howling on the side of the personality when it realizes another choice could have been more advantageous, perhaps more fruitful. What do you, Reader, think has happened? I will not keep you guessing any longer. Your **soul** carried the solution as to what decision to make. Your soul simply was not minding its store, or in this case its body.

What humanity many times does not realize is that the soul needs to be present for any choice that affects you. I am not speaking about choices whether to buy a yogurt cone or such. That can be left to the personality. However, the soul brings in the choices as to what direction to pursue for any problem or endeavor. If you found that your choice was not the best one, after the fact, it merely means your soul either was not that connected to its body, or the personality jumped before it inspected all the places to jump to, or the soul had not finished investigating the choices about the problem. Remember, there is no set rule as to when a choice is to be made.

You may know immediately what you want to do, or you may wish to take your time. Souls are unique. Many jump ahead to do something with little hesitation. Others are more cautious by nature and take a longer time to reach a decision as to what choice to make. Imagine the dismay of the personality when it finds its choice was premature. You have heard people groan, *if only I knew then what I know now!* All is after the fact

Therefore, dear ones, know there are mainly those three reasons why you utter in dismay when you have not chosen wisely: **One**, your soul was not that close; **two**, your personality did not wait for guidance; and **three** your body just took over. Throughout your lifetime, you will run into this problem of having to address your choice after the fact. It is a soul's lesson. It is a lesson to guide its body, to be present in the body and to step forth decisively and not leap in with both feet. Humanity is apt to approach its problems in one mode or another—to step or leap. Let it be a clue for you. If you are eager to leap ahead on something, pause a moment and discern who is making the decision—soul, personality, or body? It just may help you from having to acknowledge your choice was not the best.

I leave you for now, Readers, with this idea to ponder upon, *who is in control in **your** life, soul or body?* Interesting question, is it not?

REFLECTIONS on the PAPACY—Jesus, Sananda

I AM Jesus. As this chapter is being written, the pope is in the hospital for the second time, after undergoing a tracheotomy for breathing problems. I will not say at this time whether this is his time for passing, but I will say that he has a great soul who knows his purpose, as well as his timing for his transition. In the Catholic history of the church, there have been many popes. All were great souls and sent by the Father to look over and guide a certain sect of people. All did the best they knew how. As with any human endeavor, each man had his own personality, ego, body habits, and, of course, soul.

In the history of popes, all the men struggled with their position behind the scenes. There were power plays put into practice before each pope took office. There was great effort on each pope's part to bring the power factions under his control. Some succeeded, but most did not. While the cardinals and bishops were polite and said the correct things, there were still the power games going on behind the pope's back. One can get a better concept, perhaps, if you look at America's political history.

Many of America's presidents came into office with certain ideals, but gradually succumbed to pressures of political activists and huge company lobbyists. Presidents found out quickly how to play the Washington, D.C., game, if they had not known before. Going to the endless working-type parties, lunches, cocktail parties, dinners, and one of the most popular, breakfasts, afforded many opportunities for political wrangling.

Now let us look at Vatican City. It is similar to the political scene in Washington. The ceremonies can be compared also to those of royalty—the deference and protocols are strictly adhered to. Do we wear long sleeves, gloves, take gloves off when shaking hands or not? There are so many ways to show respect for the office. All ceremonial gestures have a certain meaning. If the dignitaries are not properly counseled, instructed, and rehearsed, snafus can and do take place, which the recipient then takes as an affront, insult and so forth. Actually, it could be just plain ignorance because no one told the visitor about that particular protocol. Hence, there are many intrigues and political struggles for prominence and control, which continue down through generations of presidencies, kings, queens, and popes.

In the present year of 2005, this pope will make his transition when God ordains it. The public not of the Catholic faith think the pope ought to abdicate because of his frail health. Catholics pray long and hard and want him to continue as their pope. However, those closest to the pope are witness to his decline in health. They too believe he ought to abdicate, but no one dares to tell him. However, people, it truly is the pope's Higher Self and God who will counsel the soul and then sever the cord to his body. This man is full of love for God. He has done well in his position.

The present pope was born into this position. He knew before he was born that he would be elected pope. Hence, what the public may not realize is that God selects the pope before birth! Of course, the free will can negate this choice; but so far, all the popes have heeded their calling and walked their path that led them to the highest office in the Vatican. What magnificent souls these men have. If you would stop and think about it, all popes have control of a vast number of peoples all over the world. Each one of these Catholics at one time or another says his name repeatedly, sends him prayers, and asks for healings. They trust him as a living god. Moreover, indeed, in his own right, he is. These men are high initiates, but it may surprise you to know there are masters on Earth right now who are more evolved. Most are in human bodies and most do not really know the extent of their spiritual greatness. However, in the pope's genealogy there are previous Biblical lifetimes and several lives of martyrdom and sainthood.

Popes who come into office eventually head to the historical archives. Each wants to read or have someone read to him about historical events, especially information on the Christ. Of course, there are priests who know every inch of those archives and many who are fine linguists, who can read the many scrolls that are preserved there. In addition, they can translate them verbally upon request. Many of the priests have read my Teachings and have read my manuscripts on *reincarnation.* I keep hoping that one of those popes will make these writings known, but it has not happened yet. However, the next pope is destined to make these announcements.

As I have stated in our books, one of my disciples will be the next pope. It seems only fitting that he would be the one to share my original Teachings since he played a prominent role as one of my disciples. His name will be announced all in good time. As an interesting side note, his present body will not look like his Biblical body. He chose another body with a different stature and intellectual capacities.

The fear most Catholics experience at the death of their pope is that the next one will make many changes or will not fulfill the people's needs in some way. Of course this is a possibility, but not very probable. The next pope will make changes, but the changes will be for the newer generation. He will start loosening some of the tight hold the church has had on its people. Some of the edicts are outmoded and will either be rewritten or done away with.

There will be people who will be against change. Most of that kind of dissention will be from the clergy—those in the Vatican. The new pope also will break up some of the existing power plays and control that have to do not only with creeds, but also with the monetary system. The Vatican has great wealth and does not share much of it. There are so many areas where Catholics need churches that have modern amenities. It would surprise people to know that in poor countries, the small churches have no running water, let alone sanitary conveniences. The clergy are not adequately paid. Some priests barely have enough money to buy food and necessities for themselves. What I am saying is there is no balance here. The poor countries have poor churches with underpaid clergy who are led to feel disloyal or arrogant if they ask for an increase in their allowances and expenses. Meanwhile in Vatican City the bishops and cardinals walk, pray, and gain weight from their many elaborate meals.

The new pope will be guided to make changes in order to bring more of a balance to the system. The present pope has done the best as he could for the time being. He has traveled widely and has seen first-hand what he was allowed to see. However, it has been centuries since a pope was able to get dust on his shoes.

What happens after a pope dies? Many popes have their life's review just as every soul does. They then go on to greet relatives and friends from long ago. They no longer are thought of as a pope. I will not say they become one of the *common folk,* but their past life of exaltation has completed. They soon forget that life, as do others about them. If they are highly evolved, meaning their Point of Evolution (PoE) number is at least 6.0 or higher, the souls meet then with God and the other masters to strategize as to what would be the next step in bringing the Father's Plan ever closer.

Keep in mind not all people who hold high positions are at the master level yet. Many of America's presidents are not. Your founding fathers were. The same is true of kings and queens. They are given that high position for **that** lifetime; or there could be other lifetimes where the person was born as the young prince or princess that was murdered. The following lifetime the young royals come in again to a royal family. This time they could become a king or queen. However, this does not mean they are at the master level yet. Whenever you ponder the status of someone, Readers, look at what they have accomplished in their lifetime. I can assure you, a master does not have an unproductive life. He or she can be born into a moderate-income family, not of royalty. Nevertheless, the person has accomplished so much in his/her life that it leaves no doubt as to his/her mastership. **At this time, there are no masters in any of the royals throughout the world.** (*However, Princess Diana was either a Lady Master or becoming one, for her soul's purpose was to break up the solidity and the outdated belief systems of England's royalty. Was not her divorce a direct slap at that system that had one royal abdicating because the love of his life, Wally Simpson, was a gay American divorcee and he would never have been allowed to marry her? 2011)*

In other words, a high position in the world does not dictate mastership. The person is an initiate but is not ready for the fifth initiation. In the same vein, several of your popes did obtain their masterships, but not all of them. Therefore, to get back to the present, when the present pope makes his transition, the new pope will be my disciple and will be a master. He will have his veils as most humans do, but he will confer with me, and I will continue guiding him so that certain changes can be made, for there are much needed changes, especially in the allocation of funds, that need implementing.

As a final message to Catholics, your present pope has served his purpose as well as his office with much integrity and dedication. He has earned the people's devotion. This is not his last lifetime on Earth for him, a hard belief system to break through. Popes do not like to think they might come again to Earth and serve in the lower ranks. However, once you have reached the pinnacle of any life-game you have chosen, like the pope, you most likely would not come back into a Vatican life again. You will take a life that allows you to marry and have children. You could even have a different kind of spiritual life. You could opt for a more New Age outlook and go to a non-denominational church or chapel. You could even start your own church.

Therefore, Readers, do not presuppose that a former pope will come back instantly. There could be fifty or one hundred years or more interim between lives. It is predicated on whatever and wherever your services are needed. It is not a soul just popping into a *rest-life*. Souls at a pope's level will have several opportunities to further the Father's Plan. It is a glorious time for souls. The opportunity for spiritual growth is endless and many souls return to Earth as soon as they and their soul group are fully re-united in the Heavenlies and each has agreed to its new role.

I AM Sananda. In years past when there were your world wars, souls came back to Earth to be a part of that great strife and struggle against evil. It may seem strange to you that souls would be born just so they could die in a war, but so much more was at stake. Each soul came with the intention to fight evil, to give one's life for good. This was a tremendous gain for souls, for it was re-enforcing their *faith* and beliefs in God. During this time of WWII, that pope lived in a country that was part of that evil. It took much spiritual stamina to uphold the standards of Catholicism and not be a pawn to the ruling government of Italy. That Pope **was** a master.

Therefore, Readers, be discerning. Is your head of a church a master showing you the way; or is he a great soul learning his lessons of how to lead people with love and not from control? If you discern you are in a spiritual community that is back-biting and not walking the talk, if protestant, leave that environment. If the priests are not practicing the highest of morals in your Catholic church, report the transgressions and then leave. Your salvation is **your** responsibility. **Loyalty is not always a positive choice to make, for it can keep you locked into a negative position.**

If the position you have chosen to be a part of, whether your place of work or place of worship, has turned negative with cheating, stealing, sexual harassment, exploitation and molestation, to remain loyal is acquiescence. Remember what we have said about **silence and acquiescence being an agreement to a lie. Loyalty is in the same category**. You confront the situation, state your reasons, and get out. What has gone on with Catholic priests and their inappropriate behavior with minors is an abomination in our opinion. The church just shuffled the perpetrators around. It would send its problem priest or nun to another order. Let them deal with it. Nothing was solved or brought to restitution. This must change swiftly in the churches.

Congregations are slow to embrace changes a new Pope will bring. However, the immediate changes will be with the next pope. There will be sweeping changes as far as the morality of the priests and nuns are concerned. The church is so afraid of losing priests that it has just shuffled its bad seeds around. No more will these sex-offender-priests be allowed. They will be defrocked, excommunicated, and turned over to the police. There is a dichotomy here—the more those priests defamed their station in God's service, the more parishioners became disillusioned and left the church and faith. When the bad seeds are removed, and when new rules and regulations are put in place, people will come back to the faith! Men will opt to be priests and truly will hear the voice of God once more. The church will never be the same again. Nothing that is reorganized is ever the same. It is to make it better and stronger, cleaner and more pure. After this present pope makes his transition and the new pope is in place, the internal changes will be swift.

Many priests will be asked to resign, or retire or will be just plain ousted. A new *beginning* is on the horizon for the Catholic Church—one that again has the respect and love of its people. As history has shown us, whenever something is due to change—the decline of the Roman Empire is always a good example—there is a period of decay, a death of the old, an ending of cycle. This is what is going on in the Catholic Church. People are seeing the decay. The new pope will bring in the rebirth, the new *beginning* for the

Catholics. His changes will be sweeping the **internal** structure of the Church clean so that the Church will once again shine as a pure jewel and become Truth.

(*Pope John Paul II died, April 2, 2005)*

THE EFFECTS of CHRIST CONSCIOUSNESS—Sananda

I AM Sananda. As the world reaches for higher levels of the fourth and into the fifth dimensions, many advanced souls will be strengthening their desire for *Christ Consciousness.* That is a loaded term. The soul strives for more consciousness and attains this more and more with each embodiment. After a soul attains certain awareness, the consciousness subtly changes into what is known as *Christ Consciousness.* It means the soul's level of consciousness is becoming closer to what Jesus Christ experienced and brought onto the planet.

The dynamic of having one's consciousness at the level of the Christ means the soul has reached a high level of attainment, one of *truth* and *love.* The advancing person is quite emotional and feels at times as if his/her heart is so full of love that there is no room for more. Now this is a fallacy, for there is no such thing as having too much love in one's body or soul. The person now becomes quite demonstrative in that he or she can tear up over anything that is associated with *love*. They can look at Earth's wee animals cavorting in the forest and tear up with love for Nature. They can be in meditation and have periods of sobbing as the masters come forth. They are so attuned and bonded to their master teachers that the person feels their presence immediately with a rush of tears. They start to recognize that we are always with our chela; so much so that if the person in living his/her life encounters a raw point that is going to be challenging, the person will feel our presence even stronger and burst into tears. Such is the birthing of Christ Consciousness.

Each time the body is reacting to our presence, for we move in ever more strongly. It is the stretching of the heart chakra; hence the feeling of fullness. The tearing up and sobbing is all part of the acknowledging of the sweetness of the Christ Energy. **You are touching *love* and *truth* in its purity.** When the student is at this stage, it is glorious to behold, for the Light he/she then carries is like a rainbow of sunbursts. The colors are so magnificent.

Now what really is the importance of this Christ Consciousness? Why is it so desirable? It all has to do with raising one's vibratory rate and frequencies. The Light quotient rises; the soul is attaining advanced initiations—flying up Jacob's ladder; the advancement is at such a rapid pace. Christ Consciousness is **important** because it means the soul is now ready for even higher advancement. It means the person can speak to, converse with, and know God well. It is the ability to come to your I AM Presence. Why is Christ Consciousness **desirable**—what makes it special? Because you are no longer Earth bound. You are not only self-actualized, **you are God-realized**! God sent His sparklets of souls out into the Universe so that they could grow and become gods in their own right. A God-realized soul while in embodiment is at the height of one's attainment. Its energy is clean and pure; its colors are bright; the person is full of Light, and above all else realizes he/she is *love*. What a glorious Ultimate Experience indeed!

All souls come into their body with several purposes. Most are to learn more wisdom on a particular subject or dynamic. After that there is to be a service to humanity of some kind. However, the purpose that all souls strive for is Christ Consciousness. To obtain that in one's lifetime is the greatest attainment of all. Once a soul has achieved Christ Consciousness fully, not just the beginnings of it, but to its ultimate level, the soul is able to accomplish so much more in life. The soul knows where to go in order to shine its Light. Whenever there is a need for something, God sends in His Light bearers. Not all have reached Christ Consciousness, but most are striving for it.

The birthing process for Christ Consciousness may sound painful, for the person cries so easily; but it is a sweet kind of pain. One seeks this feeling more and more. When one is God-realized, the person now carries the Consciousness that Christ did in that Biblical experience and still does. The Lord Maitreya is Head of the Office of the Christ and is the World Teacher. He was instrumental in the Master Jesus becoming the Christ. All of the Ascended Masters carry this Christ Consciousness. All are God-realized.

Each master walking the Earth today as a human Being has attained the Christ Consciousness level—the God-realization level—in each embodiment. Keep in mind most of these masters' veils are still in place. They may know they are masters but they do not **really** know their greatness. It is by attaining the Christ Consciousness again that the realization of who they actually are filters in. It is part of the Father's Plan to have masters walk on Earth being Wayshowers. Consequently, a master must regain his former consciousness—his Christ Consciousness—the ability to be a walking Christ.

Therefore, the constant tearfulness is not just a painful situation. It is a glorious one, for it conveys to the teacher that the student is experiencing birthing pains. It is the chrysalis becoming a butterfly. There is nothing greater than that, to be God-realized and full of Christ Consciousness. We salute you!

In years past, not much was said or written about Christ Consciousness. It was thought to be unattainable in one's lifetime. The veils were well in place, so much so that many of the walking masters in embodiment would die before obtaining their Christ Consciousness that they had attained in previous lives. People wonder at why there seems to be such a repetition of everything life after life. In the lives of the initiates, they are to re-embrace each previous initiation, integrate them before God allows them to proceed further. We have written of this previously. The same dynamic applies to obtaining Christ Consciousness. It must be reached **each** lifetime. If the master does not quite obtain that level of awareness for whatever reason before he makes his transition, the master simply returns and strives again.

It may seem ironical that a master has attained the status where he/she no longer **needs** to be reborn. However, it is by **choice** that the master will return to Earth in order to embrace that height of awareness, the Christ consciousness. Now this is usually when the master comes onto the planet through its mother's birth canal as a baby. If a master chooses that type of planetary entry, he/she must embrace all the previous initiations and the levels of consciousness that go with it.

However, the master could choose just to appear on Earth and manifest an Earth-body. This way he/she would carry all of the consciousness and abilities with him or her. There would be no veils. The master would simply appear in all his or her glory. There have been many times, too numerous to give a number to, where both the Lords Maitreya and Jesus have walked your Earth in disguises. They create forms that would shock most people if they rigidly adhere to old belief systems of always seeing Jesus in their minds as some of the old portrait painters portrayed him. When he and Maitreya suddenly appear in or out of crowds, their disguises are apt to be similar to that group of people. Many times on TV, commentators show people walking down the streets of New York, for example. One of those men **or** women could be Jesus or Maitreya. They are more apt, however, to be at certain spiritual lectures or churches and be just one of the crowd there. Hence, do not be fooled by their appearance, for they carry their Christ Consciousness fully.

Humanity often is puzzled as to the purpose of all this New Age stuff, as they see it. It is difficult for people to see beyond the veils. It is similar to Catch 22. How can one know there is a higher consciousness to strive for if one's own consciousness does not have that awareness! This has puzzled people for centuries. Opening of the chakras helps in bringing consciousness. How can one love one's neighbor when one's heart chakra is closed off and the person has no love of self? One cannot. How can an intellectual believe in Ascended Masters when one's left brain over-dominates its right brain of intuition—the feminine principal? It cannot. How can one share when one's energies are in the lower centers of control, sexual promiscuity, and lust? One cannot, for **the lust for power and control, controls the person who is controlling**!

Therefore, addressing the Catch 22 question, how can one become more conscious when one is **un**conscious? Moreover, I am not referring to a medical state, but the lack of spiritual awareness. The answer lies in the development of the chakra system, especially the heart chakra. The answer lies in the soul's connection to its body. In addition, an added ingredient, one needs flexibility and the willingness to alter outdated belief systems; transmute them or let them go.

This may seem like a tall order if one is reading this kind of information for the first time. However, keep in mind that evolution is also involved—lifetimes are involved, many of them. If all has proceeded as planned by the soul (and we know that is a big **IF**), if all went like clockwork for that soul, it will have completed its life with new awareness and wisdom. It then takes another life and hopes to grow even more. Some lifetimes the soul slides down a little. Most of you know that saying, *two steps forward, and three steps backward,* wiping out all your advancement and then some. This is true for souls re-incarnating. Each lifetime's goal is to be able to open the chakras and increase the awareness. Eventually, the lifetimes are those where consciousness has risen to the point where one takes initiations and is able to bring into balance one's physical, emotional, mental, and spiritual bodies.

Once that happens in a particular lifetime, the advancement is rapid. The soul's goals now incorporate garnering as much consciousness as possible to reach Christ Consciousness. Those that do attain this in one lifetime then wish to come to Earth several more times in order to reach the Christ Consciousness repeatedly. Each time a master is able to reach this Christ way of being, the master's energy helps others raise their awareness. All of this helps Earth with her vibratory rate, which helps raise her into the higher dimensions. Everyone then benefits from the master's achievement: the master, humanity, and Earth.

Henceforth, dear Readers, keep striving for awareness, so that one day you too may walk as Christ did. Keep in mind we are not speaking of religion, not even Christianity. We are speaking of energy of the purest *love, truth, and Light.* It is energy from God for all man/ womankind. It is for you, Readers. It is the Ultimate Experience of being fully conscious and most assuredly the path to God.

(Politicians are quite susceptible to greed and lust. A high office stimulates the second chakra of creativity, and sexual appetites increase. The person loses integrity and accepts unauthorized company perks and/or seeks the sexual thrill of the shadow part of the Internet. 2011)

***(Sequence to achieve Christ Consciousness: Earth-self _ Christ-Self _ God-Self _ I AM Presence.** 2011)*

DEATH IS but a STEP AWAY—Sananda

I AM Sananda. Good morning, dear Readers. I am going to discourse today on what humanity perceives as *death*. Some people might wish to avoid reading this chapter, for it could be scary for them. When I say, *death is but a step away,* I mean each moment there is a part of you that dies. On a physical level, the cells in your body are dying, so that new ones can spring forth. Your body replaces cells at an amazing rate. When you have reached that stage where you can control every cell in your body, you will be able to stay and look forever young or at any age you wish to remain. Now, as you journey through life, your body ages and then dies. However, I am sure you have heard that as soon as a baby is born, it has started dying. There will be cells that slough off and die. It can be in the area of the umbilical cord. Mothers cannot wait for it to drop off and slough off so they can immerse their baby wholly in a warm bath versus sponge baths.

However, cells at the umbilical cord are not the only areas. Every cell has a certain life span of its own, depending on what purpose it is serving. Is the purpose being a cell for an organ, muscle, skin, bones, or blood? There are also all the cells in the head area, brain, glands, eyes and hair. By now, you ought to have an understanding as to what I am imparting to you. Not one of those cells in those various areas lives forever, although the body can live to be an octogenarian and beyond. Therefore, with each step you take in life, there is a part of you dying. However, there also is a part of you that is rejuvenating, or we could say being reborn, as you create new cells.

So far, I have been speaking of the physical body. Can the same be said of the emotional body? Look back in time and remember how your emotions were then, especially at puberty time. You were on an emotional roller coaster as your hormones kicked in. Your emotions were erratic and hard to control. You could be in a rage one minute and burst into tears the next. Thus, the emotional body was growing, adjusting, and maturing. I could say your emotional body also went through a death cycle in order to be the calm and stable person you are today. Some people take longer than others to bring stability to their emotions, but age has a way of honing the emotional body.

Next, there is one's mental body. Is death one step away here? If you think about it, the death cycle for the mental body can be in your belief systems. Do you still hang on to erroneous belief systems that are now a lie? Do you have so many old beliefs that **could** be put into the death cycle? It becomes trickier when we speak of the mental body for it is a rather complex body. However, to simplify this concept, let us just think of the mental body as being your belief systems. Of course, this would encompass memory and intellect. Some of your beliefs are from childhood. You have the memory of them, but the intellect that formed them was immature.

You had little reasoning abilities and were very programmable. You took on what you picked up from your parents, siblings, teachers, and peers—none of which makes the beliefs necessarily correct. The people may have been well meaning, but their beliefs were not always true for you. Therefore, you are carrying around these lies in your mental body. These need to be put into the death cycle, so that the release allows new beliefs to enter. This concept is rather abstract, for it involves so much of you that is psychologically driven. However, there are areas in the mental body that can be and ought to be but a step away from death.

Reader, we now approach your spiritual body. Is death but a step away here? It most assuredly is! This is where people need to adjust their thoughts and not mix in what **you** think is spiritual with the spiritual body. Whatever you **think** is spiritual means you are in your mental body—the belief systems. In your spiritual body, we are referring to soul—that nebulous part of you that people find hard to grasp and define. I am sure, Readers, you have heard that the soul never dies, for it is eternal. That is Truth. Therefore, what is there in the spiritual body that is but one step away from death? Suppose the soul never makes it back to God. Is not that a death? As the soul evolves, there are always choices it must make. If it chooses to go toward evil—remember this planet is created with duality—if the soul chooses to become dark, then has it not killed its own Light? Has it not put its Light into the death cycle? **Since the soul has free will, every choice it makes that is not of the Light has killed its own Light!**

Say you are growing a beautiful plant that requires a great deal of light. You instead choose to experiment and put it in a windowless basement. You water and feed it, but the plant starts to wilt and will die if you do not move it to a window or outdoors. Many times souls experiment. They go toward darkness and hang out with the wrong crowd. They get into addictive drugs and alcohol. With each choice the soul makes to experiment with the dark side of life, it is killing its own Light. Hence, the soul is changing and becoming dark. The soul is but one step away from death.

I can hear all the exclamations; but you said *the soul has eternal life!* That I did and it does. However, there are different modes of life for the soul, just as there are for a physical life. When a soul has killed its Light, it has become metamorphosed into a puppet of evil or becomes evil. In the meantime the Overself experiences a great loss, for a part of its energy is now lost to it. To reiterate, **a dark soul has killed its own Light**. That is the meaning of *death is but one step away.* One false step, one evil choice, and you have brought death to your Light. Your spiritual body is no longer evolving and walking toward God. It has chosen another path and has suffered greatly because of its choices.

Therefore, dear Readers, always be aware of your advancement. Go to a *seer* if you are unable to evaluate yourself. Do not spend a whole lifetime doing your thing and then at your life's review find that if only you had chosen a different path your life would have been less wasted. Actually, you may have learned a great deal, but it will not necessarily raise your Light Quotient. There are excellent *seers* who are capable of giving you your Light percentage. I encourage students to have an update at least once a year, if not twice a year. Think of this as one of God's resources that He has made available to humanity.

I will close this chapter now by giving you this to reflect upon. *I am God's child, whether I am an adult or not; whether I believe this or not, does not matter. What does matter are my choices in life. Each choice reflects my state of consciousness.* Seek the Light, my friends. Everything else will fall into place for you: *Joy, Peace*, and *Abundance.* Heaven is truly your Home. That is where your Truth and Light reside. Moreover, lest you forget, all can be found in your own heart.

A CALL for MERCY—Sananda

I AM Sananda. Readers, have you ever given thought as to that dynamic when one calls on God for *mercy*? I am sure you have heard or read about people exclaiming, *Oh, God, have mercy on me!* What do you think that implies? What are you **really** asking for? Actually, this is an area of philosophy. Great thinkers have pondered this. What **is** one asking for?

Most people, when they ask God to be merciful, want some affliction to be removed from them. There is a hardship in life. Alternatively, people are asking God to alleviate a severe illness. Now let us examine that word *mercy*. People say, *for mercy sake, look at such and such*. People utter the word as part of their modern language and are apt to say this over some trivial happenstance they are observing outside of themselves, or that is happening to them. People want and ask God to be merciful.

However, when people gather their thoughts asking God to be merciful, what is the supposition, Reader? The supposition is that by asking for *mercy,* the person is asking God to stop **punishing** them! Every utterance that associates *mercy* with God implies God is meting out a punishment of some kind. Most people do not associate asking for God's mercy as asking Him to quit punishing them. Now what I am lighting up for you is that **God does not punish, ever! You** have brought upon yourself some affliction. Keep in mind *Cause* and *Effect*, or karma. What you do and say to people, the choices you make all have an effect of some kind, either in a positive or negative way.

Let us look at the idea of *mercy* more closely. Clergymen often speak of God being a *merciful* God, one who will take it easy on you, punish you less if you call upon Him. There certainly are mixed messages here. First off, of course one can call upon God for help, but secondly, **not** to have Him punish you less! Readers, do separate punishment from God. Do not make this association.

When the scribes were writing down Biblical oral history, many times they would make an interpretation from their own projections. They would write what they **thought** a particular saying meant, not what it actually meant. Therefore, the word *mercy* picked up connotations that simply were not true. ***Mercy* is a spiritual term associated with God. It means *forgiveness.* When God shows *mercy,* He is forgiving you for your humanness**. It does not mean you will not still have the *cause and effect* principal apply to you, but God forgives your transgression. He is *merciful.* He forgives.

So often people think that every word that is uttered in the Bible is verbatim of what was said and what actually happened. I do hope you realize, Readers, that this is not accurate. **Many of the concepts are correct. The direct quotes can be suspect.** In your Christian Bible, Jesus told many stories. They were parables, very similar to the parable he gave in Section 2 of this book. He made up simple stories that served as examples that would help people grasp what he was teaching. People of that era were not well educated. Most that he taught could barely read or write; they used an X to sign their names.

You can imagine how rudimentary any new concept would need to be. Every teaching had to be put forth in the simplest manner possible. Yet in this generation, people are still trying to decipher the real meaning of each of Jesus' words. Therefore, you can imagine trying to explain *mercy.* Since most people then were just getting the concept that there was only one God, and since most of the people thought of the many other little gods as being capable of great wrath and punishment, one can see how *mercy* became associated with alleviating punishment. There are people today who still believe God punishes.

Some of your Evangelists, as they expound their thoughts on the danger of sin, tell their parishioners that they will be punished and burn in Hell. I will not go into that concept at this time, but there is the underlying concept that the sinners are being punished and need to ask God for *mercy. Mercy* and *punishment* **have** become opposite sides of the same coin to many people. *Mercy* and *punishment* do not wear the same face, any more than *love* and *hate* do. That is what I hope you have gotten from this chapter.

Mercy has no dark face on its coin. It **is** *forgiveness* given with *love, compassion* and a great deal of *caring* by God. When you ask for *mercy,* you are asking for *forgiveness* for what **your** choices have led you to, **not** for what God has done to you. He **is** *merciful,* with *pure love.* Call upon Him to help you lift the burden you have placed upon your shoulders. You also can be merciful to yourself. Forgiveness must always start with you, by forgiving yourself, being merciful to yourself, before you can **receive** *mercy* and *forgiveness* from God.

A DAY to REMEMBER—Djwhal Khul

I AM Djwhal Khul. Dear Reader, how many times throughout your life have you said to yourself, *this is a day to remember*? What marks this day to be a special day? All through the ages there are periods in time that proclaim it a special date in history. Of course, politically in America those dates could be the assassinations of Presidents Abraham Lincoln and John Kennedy and Dr. Martin Luther King. There can be global dates of historical significance with World War II, the beginning as well as the ending of it. Christianity certainly would claim the crucifixion of Jesus as being a day to remember. Therefore, humanity tends to remember the tragic moments, as they become a part of history.

However, there are significant glorious moments such as coronations, the ordination of a new pope, royal weddings and for the movie industry, the Academy Awards. All of these events provide joy and entertainment for all the participants and the observers.

As I was contemplating a lecture for BOOK TWO, I was struck by the fact that humanity has not had many joyous moments of a global nature lately. In America, the emphasis seems to be on security so much of the time. There is airport security; security in your cars against hijackers; security in your school, for students bring guns to school; security in your courts, for just this morning a judge was shot to death in his courtroom. There is security in your homes against rapists, robbers, murderers, and security for your own identity. It seems to me that the pendulum has swung from *freedom, peace,* and *joy* to fear of perpetrators and the need for added vigilance and protection in every phase of life.

I pose a question to you, Readers. If you were able to step back in time, say fifty years ago, would you feel any more secure? Granted there was no identity theft, although people could have their passports stolen. In your cities, people were still cautious as to whom to let into their apartments and homes. Cars were still stolen. Airplane travel was less stressful as there were few electronic checkpoints. One just presented a ticket and you were let aboard the aircraft. So what has **really** changed?

FEAR! Fear has crept into the hearts of humanity. No longer can lovers feel safe while parked in their automobiles in secluded necking areas. Every night on TV fear is reinforced in people's hearts by showing and reporting the atrocities of war, or shootings in courts, or murders in the local news. Most of humanity does not realize that fear begets fear. A dark energy feeds on itself. The more people are in fear, the stronger the fear can be, the more pervasive it can become.

As we in the Heavenlies in our higher dimensions look at Earth, we can see literally this dark cloud of energy permeating Earth. Most of you have seen sci-fi movies. A greenish, gray mist starts to creep and curl among the tombstones in a cemetery. That is how this dark energy looks. We can observe pockets in your cities where the fear energy hovers like smog. We can see how it has moved from the cities out into the suburbs and into small towns. Fear is not the only dark energy permeating humankind, for there is greed, selfishness, lust, and a proliferation of abnormal sex games, with the availability of pornography on the Internet. All of these lower chakra energies create this pea-soup smog. Fear feels right at home in such an atmosphere. Obviously, spiritual consciousness is grossly lacking in these areas of degradation and unclean living. As America becomes more polarized toward fear and is caught up in the government policies geared toward security and the fight against terrorism, it becomes more and more out of balance.

What is happening then on an energy level that brings this imbalance about? There are two reasons right off that I can speak about. First, of course, is your free will. People use their free will to make ego-driven decisions versus listening to their Higher Self guiding them. With your present Bush government in America, there are prolific amounts of decisions being made from pure ego that affect the world. Secondly, as the planet strives for the higher dimensions, the old energy of negative aspects, already mentioned, needs to be shifted, transmuted, and released. There usually is chaos before a dramatic change occurs. It is at such times that souls need to work extra hard in order to keep their body balanced.

When you view the violence reported on TV, the out-of-balance perpetrators are negative, ego-driven, and lacking in soul guidance, or making choices that lead to darkness and evil. The fear you see in humanity is the result of this chaos. It is the stormy day before spring arrives. However, one ought not to just accept a chaotic life.

I am sure you have heard that phrase of *attaining peace that surpasses all understanding*. It is that feeling that you are watched over and protected no matter what comes your way. You still will have to problem-solve. Life will not be handed to you without any challenges or strife, but you carry an inner knowing that all truly is well with your soul. Some people say it is their guardian angels looking after them. On the other hand, God's Grace creates the inner peaceful environment. Actually, both perceptions are Truth. Angels work quite closely with God and you.

I also wish to impart to you that, as I wrote in BOOK ONE my closing statement, it was not until I had ascended that I realized I had not fully appreciated my life on Earth, for I had my head in the spiritual clouds. My goal of ascension became a passion, which I could have accomplished differently. I did not **truly** appreciate my life. I mean truly love being in a body and experiencing the art of living. Yes, I acknowledge I wrote many books with the cooperation of those great channels, Madam Blavatsky and Alice Bailey, but I had little appreciation that I could walk among Nature's beauty in the world.

Consequently, dear Readers, when I named this chapter, *A Day to Remember*, what I really wished to convey to you is to remember each of your days. Give thanks to God and Nature for the beauty of each day. One way to start this, if you have not already done so, is to write in your journal or diary each day. Write about the joyful things in your life. Give thanks to your Father. This need not be a religious exercise. God lives in your heart. Your religion or no religion does not matter. He has His cell in your heart. He is even in the atheist's heart unbeknownst to him or her.

Make each day a day to remember. Life is so full of wonders. Seek the joys of it. Appreciate your gift of life so that you too will experience that peace that surpasses all understanding. Everyone can attain this. Maybe **this** will be your day to remember!

DISAPPOINTMENTS—Sananda

I AM Sananda. Readers, as one travels one's paths throughout life, one encounters many disappointments. They in themselves become lessons. These lessons to learn can range from *anger and victimhood to patience, faith,* and *trust*. Understand that *disappointments* are losses in themselves. If one accepts that premise, then one can acknowledge that there will be a subsequent grief process. It is the letting go of something or someone. At this time I am not making a reference to death of people, but a loss of a job perhaps, or a relationship; loss in that a certain business proposal was not accepted. There are losses or disappointments whenever we have received a rejection of some kind.

The task then becomes how one is going to handle the disappointment. People are becoming wiser in knowing that many times a rejection of any kind can be an opportunity for new doors to open. Many times, we have seen depicted on television a story where the star is an author who puts the manuscript in the mail and then waits for months for either the acceptance letter, or more likely, the rejection letter. The movie story then unfolds around how the writer either stops writing and becomes a drunk, or keeps writing and sending the manuscript to other publishers. Eventually, some publisher accepts the material and a book is launched. However, the growing pains for the body and soul are tough indeed.

Even though a writer tells him or herself that he or she will just send the manuscript to someone else, the process takes its toll. Now the disappointments mount up. They compound each other. You have losses on top of losses. It is difficult to keep a positive outlook when you keep being rejected. So often the rejections are from fear by the publisher. They fear liability if they publish anything too controversial. They do not want a disgruntled reader who might take offense from a particular written subject and sue. Many people will sue over anything these days and a publishing house is a prime target. Another factor for the rejection is the editor's free will. If he or she thinks a book is too controversial, the person will just reject it. I would say free will plays a major role in having one's work published or not. Lastly, what was the energy of the author; was there a glitch because the author really did not want the book published?

Therefore, what is a budding author supposed to do? How does one fight the system? First off, **never** give up. Keep writing. Write a sequel to the rejected book. Write a second sequel, a third, a fourth. Just keep plugging away. You see, Readers, there is a purpose for one's creations. Let us take an author as our example again. Maybe that author's soul's purpose **is** to write several books. If the person gives up upon receiving a rejection letter, then the person is not fulfilling his/her purpose. Rarely is writing several books, or even just one, a whimsy! There is a purpose for such an undertaking. Granted the purpose can be for the learning of lessons, but usually there is a higher reason at stake.

Some writers find their books are stories from their past lives. The higher purpose here is karmic. They are **meant** to write these books in order to bring information to the public on how a certain century was enacted. It may seem like historical fiction; but in reality the story was real, just the names of the characters have been changed. Has the author been commissioned by God to write certain books? Would this not entail a higher purpose? Can these books be rejected by a publisher even if they have been blessed by God? They certainly can be—free will, remember.

Consequently, beloved Readers, if you have had these experiences of encountering such disappointments, know they are an opportunity to decide whether to sink or learn to swim. It is an opportunity to persevere and remain steadfast; not to be the victim; to attempt to learn what you could have done better; to take the opportunity to edit your work more, if you are an author. Above all else, keep in mind your **intention.** What is your intention now? I certainly hope you will continue your work. You see, we never know—maybe the revised edition will be a best seller! Keep your intention focused on a positive outcome. You are creating. What you create with intention has already manifested in other dimensions. Your intention and positive nature will bring your creation into being. Now that is a thought worth pondering!

WHEN TO LET THE BODY DIE—Sananda

I AM Sananda. It has been in your news recently about whether to let a person (the name needs to remain anonymous) die from malnutrition and dehydration or whether to insert again a feeding tube. This is a complex situation. Remember there are no accidents. Hence, what is going on with the soul in this case of so many twists and turns?

Let us address the soul's contract first. When the soul made this decision to create this condition so it could gain the wisdom from it, both husband and wife on a soul level agreed to this present-day scenario. We will speak more on that later. In the same vein, the souls who were to be the parents and siblings were involved also in working out this game plan before they were born.

Now what was the lesson that this **soul** wanted to learn? It was a lesson of how to die—not become entrapped in the unconscious body. As much as Christians and the parents wish it were so, the body will not recover. In this, the medical profession is correct. Therefore, at this time we also do not think the body will recover.

I wish to address another possibility. If another soul wished to take over the unconscious body, be a walk-in, there could possibly be a change in the person's condition, for the new soul would be bringing in a different agenda. The new soul might desire learning how to live in such a state and how to activate the body once again. This a master could do, if he wanted to use a grown body for some reason. However, it is not very likely. Therefore, as of now, it looks to be the person's **soul** that has the problem. It cannot abdicate and then hope to be saved from this sad situation by having a master walk-in and rejuvenate the body. That is not the agreement.

What is the danger for this soul? As I have stated, it is one of *entrapment*. When a body is kept on life support for years, two things usually have happened. One, the soul just abdicates, ups and leaves its body. It is still attached by the silver cord, but it is so far from it that it can literally forget it has a body in a vegetative state. Two, the soul is entrapped inside the unconscious body. One could use the term, *stuck*. The soul is stuck in its body. It cannot leave. Which one of these two conditions did this soul create? Ah, Reader, that is for you to discern and for us to know. I will give you a hint though. Have you ever looked into the eyes of a body that is unconscious? There is no life in them. The soul has gone.

Now the family and other well-meaning people say the person can still recover, that the doctors misdiagnosed and that the body does respond. Sadly, we believe the medical diagnosis is correct in this case. The body's autonomic nervous system has the body reacting—breathing on its own, turning its head. These are reflexes and not soul consciousness.

Let us address the fact the family wishes to have the feeding tube re-inserted again. All that would do is keep the **body** alive. Will the soul evacuate more easily if it is stuck in the fed-body? We think not. Would the soul who has long left, return and take up connecting to its body again? That is even a more firm **no**. Therefore, the soul will not progress in evolution no matter whether it is in **or** out of the body.

There are so many well-meaning people involved, for they believe in saving not only the soul, but a body. As your president has said, if one cannot decide the correct road to take, then choose life. He has a good assessment as far as his limited information takes him. What the people cannot accept and still struggle over is when to let a person die. They have such a belief structure that does not allow any other possibility. True spirituality does not condemn a person for stating no machines for life support if the medical situation is such that machines become simply lessons in futility. The argument is made that it is different if the machines are to keep the lung and heart functioning, versus a tube for sustenance and water. It really does not matter.

Ah, people, spirituality also must have a large portion of common sense in the equation. We from our dimensions concur in letting a body die, if the soul's lessons are completed and the Higher Self is finished garnering all it wishes from that body. On a positive perspective, that is the only way the entrapped soul **can** escape, and it still will need help from its teachers to do so. As for the soul that chooses to split versus staying with its body, it could still come back to check out the circumstances and find out the body had died fifty years previously. Hmmm, that would be an interesting life's review to monitor!

Now let us address the family. They are trying to keep their adult-child alive. Of course, we cannot judge them. They have greatly suffered over the years. The pain and shock of this whole dynamic must be devastating to them. They will never come to accept the death if the body dies from starvation.

The spouse grieves. Is he wrong and despicable for wanting his wife to die? One needs to address some issues here. For instance, what was their contract? Was he to stand by her for years and years? Maybe he innately knows that he did not agree to that. Maybe his contract allows him to remarry. Did his contract allow divorce? You see, people, a situation like this is far more complex than it just looks to be on the physical, for there is so much in the spiritual world that has to do with the couple's and family's pre-birth agreements. For what did each player sign on? What duration did each player agree to? There are so many issues involved.

Therefore, whether a judge signs a paper to re-insert a feeding tube or not, do not condemn the judge. You do not have the **whole** picture. Whether the husband is wrong or not for wanting another wife and children, do not condemn him; you do not have the **whole** picture. Lastly, do not judge and condemn the family for fighting for their adult-child's life. You do not have the **whole** picture!

The title of this chapter is *When to Let the Body Die.* I hope I have brought to your attention that there **is** no easy answer. Not all the facts are on the table. As for future cases of when to stop the machines or food and water, no one can comfortably make that decision. You simply do not have **all** the information, physically or spiritually. The best we can offer you is to seek out a reputable *seer.* Unfortunately, too many Christians and others debunk such an act.

I have spoken to you about whether the soul has vacated its unconscious body and is in another dimension or it is stuck in its unconscious body. I have told you about various contracts between the players—pre-birth agreements. If you feel qualified to counsel people on these aspects, do so. However, if you have no conscious information on these dynamics in the spiritual world, we suggest you hold your judgments. You may discern and make a personal assessment; but chances are you only are seeing half the story. The other half of the story rests in our world.

JESUS SPEAKS—Jesus

I AM Jesus. Good morning, my dear one. Ah, such sweet tears. How could I not come to you on this most propitious day of long ago? (*I had been meditating on Good Friday and thinking about Jesus' crucifixion, which brought tears to my eyes. He is referring to this.*) Remember, my beloved, I was able to control the pain. I had many years in India being trained by the yogis there. I was able to rise above it all. One of the main difficulties of course is controlling the emotional body. This I was able to do by just being in that no-pain state. However, imagine struggling with carrying the cross and knowing what it represented!

I was able to keep my focus on God. I knew it was He carrying that cross. It is only natural that the crown of thorns would hurt, but that too I was able to rise above. **I did not let fear enter in or touch me in any way**. I also had turned my will over to the Father so that He was then able to help me a great deal with the energies that swirled around me. Keep in mind that the energies of the Romans and others who wished me dead were simply the result of ignorance. These people did not have much awareness. To them a person being crucified deserved it.

A similar dynamic has come down through the ages. The French used the guillotine as the ultimate punishment, and crowds would gather to watch the blade come down and lop off the person's head. There then were great roars of glee—a circus atmosphere. Vendors were out selling their wares. In your pioneer days in America, the villagers would gather to watch the hangings.

Therefore, the atmosphere at Golgotha was not much different. There was a fascination for people at watching death do its work. That is what the majority of the crowd anticipated. However, there were pockets of people who were severely grieved, for they sensed that this was not the usual happenstance—something that they did not understand nor could formulate words for was happening. Some thought it was the Messiah being crucified. Others thought that he could not be the Messiah, for surely he would have saved himself. They did not realize that while I was not the Messiah at that time, there was some dynamic in play before their eyes. **They felt the Presence of God, for truly I say to you that that whole hill became Holy Ground**.

Meanwhile, I concentrated on staying in the upper chakras, communing constantly with Maitreya, my beloved Teacher. I could not see my Mary or mother in the crowd. I saw only angels. As I looked over the distant crowd, I saw a golden Light. Everything was in a haze, for I was not really seeing through the physical eyes. I saw through my third eye, the Ajna. In addition, I was not in the third dimension, so that I truly was in two worlds of Heaven and Earth. I had clear memory of everything. I was quite conscious in that way, but paid little attention to the nails in my hands and feet, nor the spear that later poked my side. I noted them, but I was not there.

As many grief counselors note, their clients can dissociate easily from the emotional pain of the body. Psychologists call that dynamic *dissociation.* I suppose I could use that term in describing my mental state. However, I think it more accurate to say that I was in an altered state of deep meditation that I learned in my travels in India where I studied with the master yogis. They are able to be in those higher dimensions easily.

Therefore, beloved, I appreciate your tears of grief for me, but I managed to live as you can attest to right now. You have that saying, *we do what we have to do!* I had chosen to awaken humanity by that method of crucifixion. I could have chosen another era but those ancient times seemed to be more suited for bringing new information forward—to change people's belief systems. Humanity seemed to be grinding its wheels in the same rut of war, pillage, inequality, and certainly little respect for women.

Women were placed into categories: a mother for your children, a beautiful woman to give you pleasure, and/or a woman as a maid, servant, nurse, or nanny. Little thought was given to have women equal in mental capacities, teachers, and sacred companions throughout one's life. Those are some reasons I came when I did. I wanted *love* to be awakened in a more pure form, to be able to *love thy neighbor.* Well, my dear ones, you can see how 2000 plus years later it has all turned out. We in your Heavens are still *working the piece,* as some of you might say. Thus as we once again celebrate my *ascension* and *resurrection,* keep in mind humanity still does not know all of it. They would like to think they do. They have had over 2000 years to study it, but there are pieces of the puzzle still missing for most of humanity.

So many people condemn me still, for their different religious beliefs do not include much truth of me. They expound we are one with God, but they are unable to truly believe that yet. Some day, beloveds, we will truly be One, not only in Spirit but also in people's consciousness and actions.

Until then, dear people, my love flows through you, just waiting for the day you recognize this. That you will then say *thank you* and offer your love in return, so that I too might thank you!

I AM Jesus this Good Friday, March 25, 2005.

(The Master originally was speaking to me for a journal notation. At the end he told me to make the above a chapter for BOOK TWO. For those who have read BOOK ONE, you will note he has embellished the material on his cross experiences in this chapter.)

(And in BOOK FOUR, Realities of the Crucifixion, *the description of his experiences change yet again. 2011)*

EASTER THOUGHTS—Jesus, Maitreya, Sananda

We are the Trio: Jesus, Maitreya, and Sananda. We come this beautiful Easter morning to give you some words of hope for your future. Many people will read this after Easter has passed, but the words will be timeless so that you can take them into your hearts and let them stir your inner memories when you were pure soul and in the Heavenly Spheres.

Our dear Readers, on this Easter morn there are so many people sitting in churches. There are so many gathered in Vatican City waiting for words from their pope. There are many gathered in Florida praying for the dying woman and for the child who is dead. There are people all over the world thinking of Jesus and the *resurrection*.

This is a beautiful time of year—the birth of spring and the birth of humankind. We of course are speaking of the *resurrection* of humanity as a whole. Do you not see that humanity is experiencing *resurrection* as we speak? What do we mean by that? It is a rebirth of consciousness—a rebirth for the soul. As the soul gains a rebirth of energies, so does the body gain a rebirth in its cells. The subconscious is stirred, causing old memories to surface. Old belief structures are transmuted or let go. It is letting go of the old energy that has held you back. It is an inner work that you will be engaged in for the next several months and even years for some.

The seniors of humanity have long absorbed their past adventures and inner journeys through life. They sit and daydream—muse on their performances that could have been improved upon—been more caring, less selfish, less ego-driven. Have you noticed that seniors are either quite rigid in their old belief structures or they realize those beliefs no longer serve them? It is *water under the bridge*, as the saying goes. Seniors begin to appreciate what they once had and took for granted. They appreciate the agility of the body they once had and their youthful looks. Yet rarely would they want to trade the wisdom they have accrued for their youth again. They groan when they reminisce about the pain in their teenage years. Those growing, psychological pains can be devastating for teenagers. You also had the hormone changes with the acne bumps all over your face. It then becomes a toss-up for the senior as to what era is the better—youth's agility and youthful looks, plus all the downside of psychological scars, or the senior's stability, wisdom and common sense. You see, Readers, each stage of a person's journey has its trials and tribulations. Such is life—especially if you have chosen school-house-Earth for your evolution of soul.

What we have been speaking to you about is *resurrection.* It is *ascension* and *resurrection* rolled into one. It is a rebirth into a higher consciousness. We say **re**birth for you had your original birth as a baby-body. You had your original birth as soul from the Mother-Father. Each time you reincarnate, it is a new birth for the body, but a **re**birth for the soul. It is a rise in consciousness. It therefore becomes a *resurrection* in itself.

People are apt to take a word and think that it cannot be used in other ways, even as a metaphor. Of course, we are referring to the English language. The Hebrew language cannot be changed in any way or it will have a different meaning. There are languages where the word is spelled the same but the **intonation** gives the meaning—Vietnamese for one. Hence, dear ones, the words *resurrection* and *ascension* can be used interchangeably. We are ascending every minute—raising consciousness. We are being resurrected in those moments. We are being reborn into a different consciousness.

Now when Jesus experienced his *resurrection*, it was described as the body being translated, taken up and brought out of death. Well, by now it is hoped some of humanity will understand that **Jesus did not die on the cross**. His body had been severely ravaged by beatings, the crucifixion, the hanging on the cross with the nails barely supporting the weight of his body. **However, he did not die.** Any other man would have died, especially with the last cruel affront of thrusting the spear into his side. Nevertheless, dear ones, if you can rise above your belief systems of thinking he died on the cross and see it for what it was, **he lived**!

The real story was that a human being lived despite that torture—that a man lived through that. **That** is one of the miracles. Another miracle is that he did ascend with his body while in the tomb, leaving his shroud. **That** was a miracle. Another miracle is that he left his shroud intact for all to see. **That** was a miracle.

The final miracle was that he **descended**. **That** was a miracle. The Bible has different time lines for when he *ascended* and *resurrected*. Suffice to say, he ascended in the tomb with his body and came back in a slightly different form, meaning his body was now more one of Light than flesh and blood; but he still carried the healed scars. He would look solid to others but carried the scars on purpose, for his body had indeed been resurrected in that he was free to come and go to Heaven and return to Earth—in and out of the dimensions at will.

In the New Testament, Jesus tells the people that they too will be able to do the things he did, and even do greater things than he. He was referring to people being able to heal others, to manifest their own loaves and fishes, to calm the elements, and to ascend and become resurrected in the greater sense of the new birth of the soul. We are speaking of course of Christ Consciousness, God-realization, and the ability to come and go—to travel in and out of dimensions.

Therefore, even though you will read this after Easter, please let these words into your consciousness. Let them rejuvenate your agility to think new thoughts. Just as seniors wished they could have the agility of their youth again, here is your excellent opportunity to have agility of mind. Change that belief structure. Let it be more fluid. Take the information we have given you for your resurrection. Once you are able to do that, you have opened yourself to possibilities of thought you have never contemplated, or even allowed a spark of change to come through. **Be not a cement block**. Be agile again. Use your wisdom, if you are a senior, to guide you to new thought. If you are in your youth, stay open. Do not make such snap judgments about Truth. Listen to your inner heart, those of you who are in that category of thirty-something. Life is about change. Use the concept of *resurrection* as a rebirth into a new level of consciousness and dare to change.

We are the Trio and we bless you this Easter morn 2005.

(Hello my precious one, I have dropped by to make a few comments on the work that you are doing on making the three books into one. I know it is difficult for you at times, as you see the information change before your eyes. Just know that everything changes, even information that was given to you for a previous book.

You see all information is on a continuum and hence, it changes as humanity marches forward. Much of humanity was not able to receive information that was so far removed from what they had been taught. Now up through the years, people are in a different space. They are more open to change and therefore, they can now receive deeper information. There are layers within layers, you see. Keep adding a little text here and there that brings people more up to date. It gives them the opportunity to catch up. Greetings, Jesus. 2011)

DEATH of a GREAT SAINT—Sananda

I AM Sananda. Dear Readers, we thought it only appropriate that I come to you to express the great joy we experienced in the return of your blessed Pope John Paul II. There was great anticipation of his arrival in our dimension. He was a dear soul in embodiment, who loved God and the Christ with every cell in his body. He was full of Light and his passing over was a lesson in how to die with *love* and *forgiveness* in your heart, a lesson for all his followers, as well as humanity.

His death was peaceful and joyous. He came to us with such anticipation and carried his love of the Father deeply in his heart, as he parted the veils and saw the Christ waiting for him. He **knew**, you see, he would see his Lord. He carried absolutely **no doubt** to that fact.

The death of this saint makes it difficult for many to embrace a new pope. For the younger generation, it is all that they have known. The pictures of him are carried in their hearts. However, they will soon learn to love and follow the new pope. He has a huge heart also, and a wonderful sense of humor. He will tread softly but will wield an awesome rod of power. He will not be afraid to use it either, for he knows that God has given him the power to do so, as well as the honor.

The lines are already being drawn among the cardinals. There are little clicks and hierarchies expanding. Each cardinal inwardly hopes he will be chosen as the new pope. Those who are being more honest will know who is better qualified. One thing they have in common is **they each carry the belief that God chooses the pope**. So even when they vote and arguments break out, **they do know God's hand is on the head of the chosen one.**

Jesus has written in different chapters of these books that the new pope will be one of his disciples. This is an exciting time. However, one must keep in mind that while your past lives do influence your present one, if you choose a new body type from the one you had in your Biblical days, then you will have different characteristics and mannerisms. So keep that in mind, Readers, as you attempt to discern which of the Biblical disciples the new pope is.

All of the popes in the past have had lives that led them to the Vatican. They had to take on almost every spectrum of a particular human life. That saying *Rich-man, poor-man, beggar-man, thief, doctor, lawyer, merchant, chief* is very true. One needs to add to that saint and sinner. Of course, a thief could be the sinner. If you have been a saint from a past life, that in reality is not greatly desired by most. Saints become saints many times through martyrdoms. You professed your love for God as you were being burned at the stake. In those ancient times, the righteous, religious leaders viewed great men and women as sinful, or witches. In their ignorance, they thought death by fire was what was warranted if the person did things out of the ordinary from what church fathers approved. Little did the zealous church leaders know that many times they were burning a future saint, one who would be martyred and placed into the very position the church claimed was being blasphemed.

Pope John Paul II was martyred several times in his past lives. He was already a saint. **In fact, he would pray to a particular saint for an intervention of some kind, not knowing he was praying to himself**! In addition, his prayer would be answered. You might ponder this.

Therefore, we of the Spiritual Hierarchy are paying our respects to the physical memory of a great man. We pay homage to the saint who fulfilled his purpose, served the Father all of his life, and died with dignity and in God's Grace, April 2, 2005. We salute you, Great Saint!

SECTION 8—BRINGING TO A CLOSE #2

CLOSING STATEMENT—Sananda

I AM Sananda. Dear Readers, we have come to the end of our journey together. BOOK TWO was to show you the many *beginnings* that incorporate life—the many times you had to persevere, for it was a new beginning for you in some endeavor. Just reading this book was a beginning in itself.

In eons past, there have been many wars. There would then follow a few years of peace until another leader decided he wanted more land to call his own. Of course, I am speaking of countries, but even in your pioneer days, there were bankers who accrued much property through foreclosures. The little people were the ones to suffer.

In modern times, it is your huge companies cheating their investors. It seems as if many of your CEOs are never satisfied. They have an insatiable quest for more acquisitions. That is why they are hired. They are good at what they do—gain power.

How many times is the lesser god cheated by those who walk over people in order to make it to the top where they can gain more power? People use their free will to seek power. Your first Ray is Will and Power. However, it is to be used in a positive way, not to destroy people. It is the masculine principal using the Will of God to further one's purpose.

In years past, reaching deep into history, people felt everything was theirs for the taking. It was the survival of the fittest. Of course, there was some truth in this; but that did not make it altogether correct. It seemed as if widows were prime prey, for they were helpless in a man's world. They fought a good fight as best they could, but eventually they had to give in to the land baron. They sold their valuable property at an unfair price and moved away. The world seemed up for grabs for whoever wanted to make the first power move.

Today America is at war once again (*Iraq*). This need not have happened. This was not a positive way of advancing *democracy*. Democracy is all about *for the people and by the people*, to give the people a say in how their lives are to unfold. When you have a government who takes a nation like America into war under the false pretenses of looking for weapons of mass destruction, while all along the subterfuge is another's oil, democracy is being demonstrated in a warped way.

For a presidential candidate (*Bush*) to profess a love of Jesus and God and then his every act decry the hypocrisy of his statements is sad to behold indeed. We have stated elsewhere that America's president **was not destined**. **He was not the candidate that God had chosen.** Senator Kerry was God's choice of candidates. However, there is a warped belief among Christian structure that does not embrace Catholics. This is absurd in our opinion. Senator Kerry was as honest as most candidates can be with the information given to him by his advisors. He has a love of God and a belief in the Trinity that is actually at a deeper level than the incumbent's is. Senator Kerry has a fuller and deeper heart than the incumbent. **He** was the chosen one. Yet the Christian Fundamentalists were swayed to vote for your present president for he had been *born again*. Well, with that kind of reasoning, would Senator Kerry have gotten more votes if he had left his Catholic church and converted to say a Methodist, or Presbyterian? It is such hypocrisy in our opinion.

Now let me also address the votes. When I looked at the map of the United States, I saw the red and blue states depicted. The votes for the incumbent dominated the whole Midwest, the Bible belt. However, Readers, the voting was not honest. There were lost votes, on purpose I might add. There were votes counted more than once, and there were votes erased, reversed, and given to the Republicans, whereas the Democrats were entitled to those votes. President Bush did win the popular vote, again mostly from the Christian faction wrongly led by religious leaders. Conversely, Senator Kerry was to win the electoral votes that were fraudulently stolen from him and cast for the incumbent.

History will tell the true story eventually. Lies are usually uncovered, but maybe not for years yet. Meanwhile America's government has led her to the war that was planned way before the election took place. You have noticed, I am sure, the decline in America's stature. She no longer has the prestige she has enjoyed in the past. Your President Bush has made many errors in judgment, not only nationally but also globally. America's reputation for honesty and democracy has been severely eroded. It will take years to stem this slide of destructive acts and thoughts. In addition, have you noticed, Readers, how the negative forces are feeding on all the chaos—the violence is escalating? (*Some say that Cheney was the real power behind Bush. 2011).*

Therefore, Readers, dare to change your belief structures. Just because you **think** Jesus and God have proclaimed one state of affairs does not make it actually so. Keep in mind that both God and His Spiritual Hierarchy are *love* and *truth.* We would have chosen *peace, sharing*, and *loving thy neighbor* as the standard of choice. Question your belief structures. Put those that no longer serve you in the death cycle. Form new beliefs based on the highest Teachings. Treat each of your endeavors as a new *beginning.* We look forward to meeting you again in BOOK THREE. Blessings.

CLOSING STATEMENT—Jesus

I AM Jesus. Dear ones, if you are reading the closing statements, then you know BOOK TWO has been completed. It was with great joy we have continuously come over these last three months to impart our Teachings. Please, Readers, take the time to ingest the information in this book. While it can be read from cover to cover in a day's or night's time, we suggest you pace yourself and read just one or two lectures each day. That way it gives you time to reflect on the knowledge being given to you. For some of you, you will flip over the pages seeking those chapters that speak to you. You are then apt to not retrace your steps, so that there would be chapters not read. In fact, you may be reading this closing statement now before reading the book. Ah, gotcha!

Thereby, dear Readers, you will miss some of the pertinent information, for the titles of the lectures do not really end up being the subject matter you thought it would be. *Have You Said Your Prayers Today* (reference BOOK ONE) is an example that comes to mind. There is a reason for this—the title not matching your preconceived thought. You see, every time you read a chapter that has a title different from what you presupposed, it lights up one of your belief systems! Now have we not been tricky? We had such fun with naming the chapters.

Let us now comment on some of the content of BOOK TWO. Again, you found mini-lectures. We purposely chose to comment and teach on current issues—the current affairs. By doing that, we were again drawing to your attention that Spirituality has many facets. One of them is garnering knowledge and wisdom. As people are in tune with what is going on around them, they then have choices to make. Most of the choices pertain to not judging, but using discernment. It is not an easy task to rise above the horror pictures you see on TV, or alternatively, to rise above the news the media is reporting. In your world, you are constantly bombarded with news about war, car accidents, murders in residential settings, and school shootings. It becomes a major lesson in how not to become judgmental when you hear and view the television replays of the various crime scenes.

However, you are on Earth. You are a soul that has **chosen** this lifetime for your growth and evolution. Maybe the lesson you have asked for is how to survive **or** die in war. Maybe the lesson you chose was how to function in school with drugs so available and gangs wanting you to lower your consciousness to their level. Maybe the lesson was how to live to be a senior and be productive and continuously seeking growth. Maybe your lesson is to learn to be nonjudgmental. You certainly chose a good time-line for that lesson!

Therefore, Readers, by our speaking about different issues that humanity faces today and/or muses over its history, or reaches for New Age Thought, we spark you. Our energy flows throughout these books. In BOOK ONE, we probed some of your belief structures—some myths that still exist about me. In BOOK TWO, we addressed *beginnings.* Each chapter had a beginning of something in it. It could be a beginning in a character's life, such as depicted in the *Beginnings* section, or there were *beginnings* woven throughout the lectures. Go back, thumb through those chapters, and see if you can pull out where a particular dynamic is a beginning of something.

Each chapter invites you to change your belief structure in order to let another idea germinate—a new and different way to look at things. You will have to reflect on some of the chapters, but a *beginning* for a new thought rests in those chapters for you to discover. Now is that not a unique idea for you in reading this book? Therefore, can that not be a beginning for you? It is our hope and our intention that it is so.

BOOK THREE is also on the immediate horizon. Since the Author has the number three strongly placed in her energy field and her belief system, BOOK THREE will be completed approximately three months hence. Now when we say it is completed in three months, the Author and we are referring to the telepathic transmission part. There usually follows about a month more in order to edit, send the work to be copyrighted, and to get the manuscript ready for distribution in one form or another. In addition, I wish to concur that at this time it makes little difference how the material is presented, whether in manuscript or bound-book form, or even email. The fact that the work goes out is what is important. Wisdom and teachings always need to fan out to humanity. It would serve no purpose to hoard this work. In this, the Author has a strong sense of integrity.

Gifts are meant to be shared. We give the Author our gift of wisdom and teachings. We use her gift of being able to receive telepathically. She then sends the words out to humanity—shares with people both gifts, hers and ours. In that way we all are gratified. We in the Spiritual Hierarchy **need you,** dear ones, to help us carry out our work. In this we thank the Author and we thank you, Readers. May we meet again in BOOK THREE.

CLOSING STATEMENT—Djwhal Khul

I AM Djwhal Khul. When the Author first started receiving our words last September 2004, little did she realize she would be receiving closing statements on our **second** book in April 2005. It has been a most joyous time for all concerned. We salute the Author for her dedication and for the joy she emits, as she offers the finished product to the outside world. She does not realize how many people will be touched by her efforts.

This second book is about *beginnings,* and it seems only appropriate to tell you Readers that our next book will begin shortly. The theme will remain hidden for now, but we who are participating in formulating the book have taken great joy in doing so. Readers, you may not know that for us formulating books for those dear souls to channel is a respite for us. As the world grows more chaotic, as Earth strives to advance to a higher dimension, we are involved in helping in any way we can. There is constant vigilance required and the adjusting of energies in order to help Mother Earth. When we can switch gears and speak mentally to those who can hear us and have offered their services, it is a rest period for us, a mini-vacation, so to speak—a respite. Consequently, we come with great joy to the Author in order to conclude this book and to alert her to the third one yet to be written.

Enjoy these written words, Readers, the many teachings in this book. It is a book to be handed to others, but also a book to keep in one's heart. I greet all of you Readers. I hope you have enjoyed these writings as much as we have enjoyed giving them to you. There will be more.

I AM Djwhal Khul, and I thank the Author for her joyous service. Blessings.

CLOSING STATEMENT—GOD

My dear daughter, ***I AM your Father***. I have come to give you My blessing on this your second book. It truly is an accomplishment for all concerned. Dear one, do give credit to where credit is due also—you. I thank you for your service to Me. The days ahead will be quite joyous for you, for you walk in My Grace, and you are greatly protected from the stress from living in your world.

Many centuries ago, humanity had not raised its awareness much. People were worshipping all manner of objects trying to connect with what was missing in their lives. Little did they know their answers lay in their hearts. People searched for that inner peace outside of them.

In this new century, I hope that My people will now find Me in their hearts—will draw ever closer. There will come a time when most of humanity will be integrated with Heaven—the Heavenly Spheres. They will observe the masters walking the Earth and they will know Me better. There are many astounding inventions I wish to bring for the people. My hope and plan is that Earth truly will be like Heaven.

Dear Readers, you have just read this BOOK TWO. Know that each word carries the masters' energies and now carries Mine. **I bless this Author, this glorious book and each word is now infused with my Love and Light and Peace.** May you absorb this energy to the fullest.

I greet you. I AM Your Lord. Good day.

FURTHER MUSINGS #2

We are **so** *pleased you have taken on this assignment. We congratulate you, our sister. I AM Jesus.*

As I, the Author, prepare myself to write the Epilogue for BOOK TWO, I realize more that the Masters really do need people like you, Readers, and me to carry out their words — to keep their wisdom flowing outward. I was not even in my *still time*, but about to sit at my computer again, after lovingly touching the copies of BOOK ONE I had yet to deliver, when I felt this familiar emotion well up inside me. I knew one of the Masters wanted to speak. The above sentences are the result.

In BOOK TWO, I did not add a section on *Dreams* in an Appendix. I will wait for feedback on BOOK ONE in order to see if the Readers felt that enhanced the book or not. However, one dream I have had recently is where there is a man who calls me, *Sweetheart*. He is advising me and as we part, I exclaim, *He is the most beautiful man I have ever met*! I awoke knowing it was the Lord Jesus.

In another dream I had, I pick up a box and in it are two rings with huge diamonds. They are surrounded by smaller diamonds. I interpret the two rings as being our two books. The smaller diamonds that surround the large stones could represent the twenty-two to twenty-three lectures that are in each book.

I presented BOOK ONE to the Wednesday Metaphysical Study Group I attend, facilitated by Mary Helen Wichmann. The presentation was well received with many people placing orders for the book. The room seemed to be electrified by the unseen presence of several of the Masters—come to observe how their words were received, perhaps. I narrated my experiences of my *beginnings* with the Masters and read to the group one of the chapters from BOOK TWO that I am still editing. The group seemed eager to hear these Teachings. It brought such joy to my heart.

Again, this evening of April 8, 2005, the Masters were very close. I felt their love as they touched my heart. I can only trust they are leading me onward. To what and where I do not fully know, except for the fact the Masters are keeping me busy once again on BOOK THREE. The veils are parting for me and I can only wait patiently for the grand unveilings!

BOOK THREE COVER TEXT

THE ULTIMATE EXPERIENCE
The Many Paths to GOD

BOOK THREE

Verling CHAKO Priest, PhD

RIGHTS PROTECTED #3

THE ULTIMATE EXPERIENCE SYNOPSIS THREE

There are **twenty-four** mini-lectures in this third book. Many of the lectures emphasize what the Masters refer to as *historical karma*—humankind's karma which we all need to help transmute. The Lord Sananda states *America was founded with God's Grace. Throughout the centuries, humanity has eroded that.*

Lord Djwhal Khul tells the Reader that souls are given a body in order to help it develop and grow—*not to downgrade it, but to* ***upgrade*** *it.*

Lord Jesus reflects on His life in Biblical times, that it was *life in the slow lane, versus today's fast lane*. He talks about our possessions. *Do they possess us?* He speaks about the soul and its *life-streams* that it is bringing forth from past lives in order to integrate into our present one.

Lord Sanat Kumara brings to Readers' attention that their names carry a particular equation. If one changes his or her name, the equation and frequency has also changed. He tells how Earth is entering more into chaos and how this affects the Heavenlies.

Lord Confucius reflects on the Oriental mind—its quickness at being able to problem-solve with an innate ability to survive. *It is within the Oriental mind that there is orderliness to the world.*

Archangel Metatron states that wings for an angel are more of a *dress code.*

The Lord Maitreya in his Opening Remarks dictates more details *about the Author* than she is comfortable in hearing. His humor is infectious, however.

The Lord Kuthumi speaks on *how the Earth stood still for a nano-second when the Master Jesus was crucified, for* ***love*** *had been killed (symbolically).* The Closing Statement by God closes the book.

PRELIMINARY REMARKS #3

Dear Readers,.

I previously had written for BOOKS ONE and TWO how three years ago (August, 2002) Lord Sananda had made first contact. He physically stroked my cheek a few times. I did not see him. I only felt his soft caress. He mentally spoke with me but did not refer to my writing any books. It was not until two years later (September 2004) that Jesus told me to *pick up your pen, dear one, and write what you hear me say . . .* The Lords were steadfast on their part and brought forth their views and Teachings on a variety of subjects almost day after day, week after week. However, some days they did not speak. That was to teach me *patience, faith, and trust*, I was told.

I since have been told by Lord Sananda that our books are my *mission* now. I also have come to realize that when God gives you a mission, He has a purpose for it. The purpose is not always obvious to us. I know that the books' purpose is to trigger in Readers those belief systems that need changing or releasing. However, that is not necessarily **my** purpose or His purpose in giving me this mission I am privileged to receive. His purpose has yet to be revealed to me.

Therefore, Readers, there will be a *BOOK FOUR. I have a sense it will bear the same title, but the format may be changed. Meanwhile, do enjoy BOOK THREE. Even if the material seems familiar to you, trust that the Lords have reasons for repeating some of their words. Trust that there may be a different *spin* on their words than you anticipated. Lastly, trust that the Lords' energies are in every word. People vary in their reactions to the books. Each one will experience the energy in a unique way that is just for that Reader. Trust your body's sensory perception, perhaps with goose bumps and tears. It will tell you when you are receiving the energies. As with all books, there will be those Readers who do not resonate with the books. However, maybe they will pick up a future book and find they embrace that one. Each person's timing is unique. At this time, I am only the *messenger.* Here is BOOK THREE with our blessings.

CHAKO

(*BOOK FOUR is titled *Realities of the Crucifixion*.)

HEART WORDS #3

I dedicate this third book to

My beloved Teachers, the

Masters of Wisdom, and to

God, with whom all things are possible.

"And Jesus looking upon them saith,
With men, it is impossible, but not with God:
For with God all things are possible (Mark 10:27)."

KUDOS #3

My first acknowledgment must be to God and the Ascended Masters: Jesus, Sananda, Maitreya, Djwhal Khul, and Kuthumi who are my Teachers. They have provided the context of our book with not only their personal stories, but also their wisdom on many issues that face humanity today. I thank them and feel blessed to have them in my life. I thank the Lord Confucius with his revelations of the Oriental mind. I thank Lord Sanat Kumara and Archangel Metatron. I am honored to have them come and give their words of wisdom for this book.

I give loving thanks with a great appreciation to my oldest daughter, Susan Verling Miller O'Brien, for all the computer work that she did. No matter how many corrections were made, she cheerfully accepted the changes and diligently sat at her laptop computer hour after hour. We spent much time in emailing the book's file back and forth so that she could place the chapters into the book as I finished typing and editing them. The Masters gave us free rein and much latitude, in what I call our *grunt* work. Susan was invaluable indeed in this endeavor. She and her husband were in California for the summer months. Being able to email the material directly to Susan helped facilitate the completion of this book. Thank you, dear heart, for giving some of your vacation time in order to be of service in this joint endeavor.

All authors need a proofreader. I have Heather Clarke. My eyes and brain do not always agree on what is typed. Many times, I have been surprised to find a word that is not the one for that particular sentence. The computer let the word pass through spell-check because it was spelled correctly—*here* and *hear*, for example. However, I required another word. This is what Heather does best. Her eyes and brain are synchronized (*smile*). Therefore, Heather, I thank you for your skills. You have alleviated much frustration for me.

I wish to thank you Readers for your kind remarks and your enthusiasms for the books. It is such a joy to read your email telling how the energies of the books are affecting you so uniquely and in such positive ways. I truly appreciate your feedback.

I thank all of you Readers who have bought these books. I do hope you enjoy them as much as I have in bringing them to you.

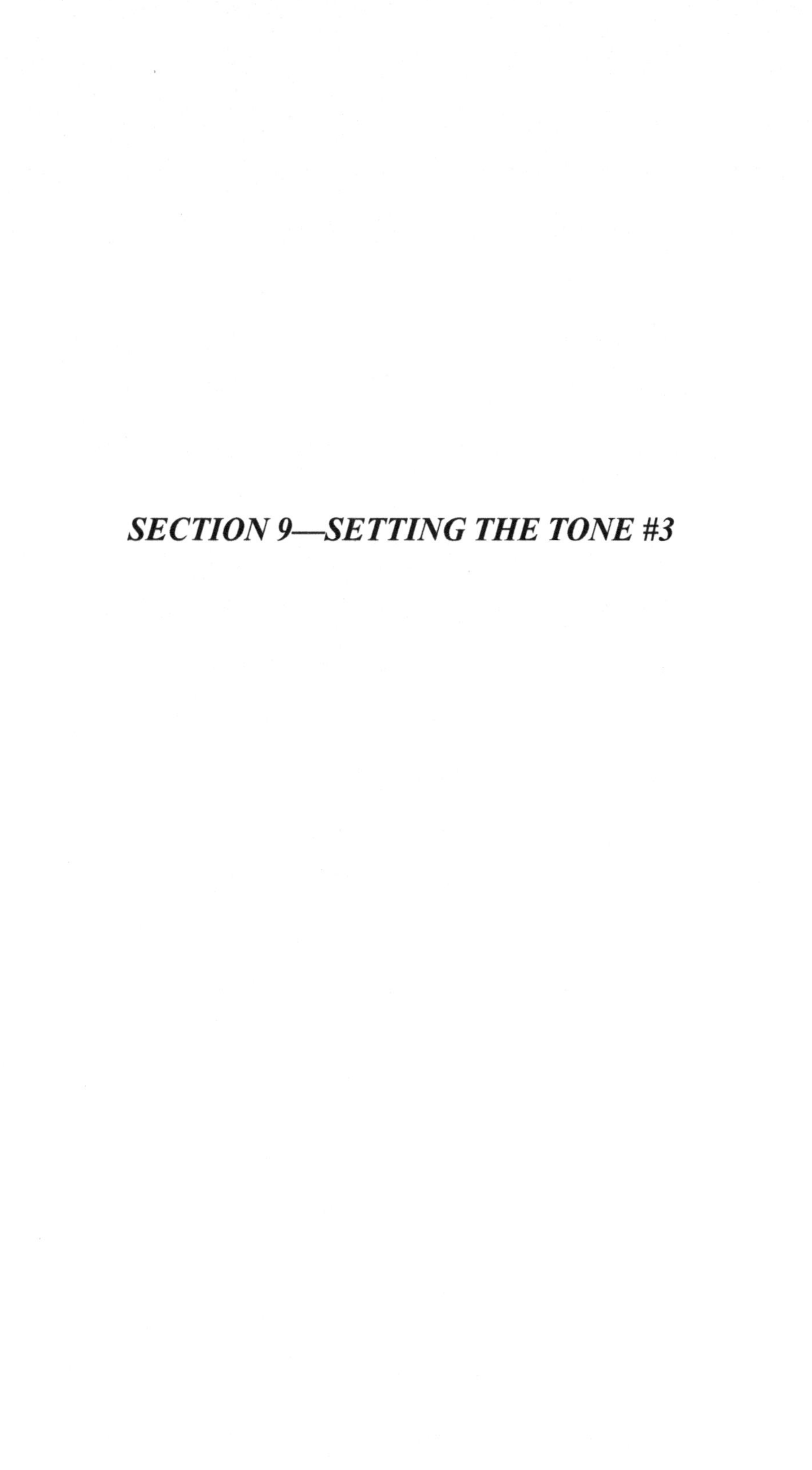

SECTION 9—SETTING THE TONE #3

OPENING REMARKS—Sananda, Djwhal Khul, Jesus, Maitreya

I AM Sananda. Readers, we come to you for the third time to give you information that perhaps will not only be informative but will prove delightful for you also.

In the beginning, as the Bible starts out, the planet Earth was sparsely populated and still in its infancy, as far as its firmaments were concerned. Water covered a great deal of the land, which was joined in larger degrees than it is today. We will call this period *prehistoric,* for there were many different forms of prehistoric creatures on the planet during that time.

There were dinosaurs, the Red giants, and the little people from the Elemental Kingdom that could be seen with human eyesight. If one looked at a flower, one could see that elemental fairy sitting on a petal, perhaps. The giants on the other hand, as they became more solid, were more noticeable, and they did not particularly watch where they stepped or sat; so many an elf's house was flattened when the giants roamed the forests.

Now a Reader might ask what would be the purpose in having the little people and the giants? Strange as it may seem, both served Mother Earth and Mother Nature in magnificent ways. The little people tended to Nature's beauty. All the colors of the rainbow were instilled in Nature's plants and vegetation. The plants provided the colors, smells and sounds, for as the wind blew the flowers and the tree branches would sway, their sound would carry on the winds for miles around. In creation there needs to be sound and Light for something to be created, and there needs to be odors—a smell—so that animals and humans could be led as to what to eat or to not eat. Bees, for example, are led to flowers by their smell. It does not take bees long to find food at a picnic, nor ants.

The giants also had color. Their skin was in shades of red. Hence, they were called the *Red Giants*. They came from a different planet and carried many genetic encodements with them. They were very intelligent and had huge brains. They also had huge bodies, many times taller than your modern basketball players. Therefore, when

Moses sent Joshua and other tribes across the Jordan to clear the way for the Israelites, there was great fear, as the people encountered the remnants of these giants. Eventually, that race died off; but the fairies, elves—the little people—just became invisible to the naked eye. As the density of the Earth increased, the ability to see these finer, diaphanous energies decreased also.

As the world started to change and different peoples populated it, the Laws were then brought in by the Hebrews who came from another planet also. The Laws brought structure for the people, which enabled them to bring in more of their soul. Humanity that long ago was still pretty much into survival. Now when we say *survival,* it incorporates all levels. It is not just survival of the body, but how one interacted with each other. People were quite narcissistic, materialistic and into a great deal of comparison. They would vie to have more wealth than their neighbor did. There were caste systems—not as in India, but levels of people of the *haves* and the *have-nots*. If a person was in the category of having many material possessions and owned many animals, they were looked up to. In that long ago time, people with wealth were not necessarily good people. We can use King Herod as an example. Not all the riches in the world would make this king a good person!

Consequently, there were greater imbalances than ever before. When Jesus came to the planet in the Jesus era, he was quite aware that something drastic needed to take place—something extraordinary had to happen in order to instigate a new growth that would lead the people spiritually—to enable them to move out of their body-games of *sex, lust for power,* and *greed*.

Readers may wonder why I have ventured to use the word *sex*. It has so many connotations attached to it, of which most are negative. If one is correctly sexual, then the act is not only one for procreation and the release of pent-up energy, but for joy as well. I will refrain from saying *pleasure* for the average person equates that with promiscuity—too much pleasure. However, **for those of a higher awareness, sex is an act of loving, caring, creating, and a sharing of two bodies**. While the bodies shared their love, the souls shared the joy.

Conversely, when people did not have the proper respect for women, when men used women just for bearing their children, when men then sought loose women to give them what they sought—pleasure—then the soul could not grow consciously. It was continually being pulled down into the lower awareness. It became a spiral effect. Consequently, when souls saw how entrapped they could become, they just opted to stay out of their bodies. It seemed far safer to be out of one's body than in it!

It really was a *Catch 22*. If the soul **entered** somewhat fully into its body—and that would only be about 10-15% in that era—the soul would become stuck in the body's lower-type energies. On the other hand, if the **soul stayed out** of its body, the **body** ran the life and the soul still did not grow in the right direction. Consequently, souls were having a real dilemma on their hands. What to do?

Jesus saw what was taking place on Earth and decided it was better now than later to step in and give humanity a boost upward. His tales of walking among the people, teaching, healing, raising the dead, crucifixion, ascending, and the resurrection are all Truth. He was a Wayshower. He taught by example. Everything he did he taught to his disciples. He kept telling people that everything he did they could do even better.

Amazingly, the people did not believe that they too could accomplish what they thought of as *miracles*. They did not have the vocabulary, the mind-set, in order for Jesus to teach them what the miracles were or how they came about. For example, take a cook—your garden-variety cook. She has her flour that she has ground from the wheat she has harvested. She has her particular ingredients she adds to the dough. She dumps a batch of it on her kneading stone and rolls and slaps it into round loaves. Now if someone had said to her to put the ingredients into this bread machine and let it alone until she hears the beep that tells her the bread has been kneaded, risen, punched down, raised and baked all within three to four hours without her hands touching it, she would have not believed you. That kind of miracle was not in her reality. Therefore, when Jesus told his disciples and followers, he would show them the way to do as he does, the people simply could not fathom of what he was teaching. They came **to watch** his miracles happen and not so much to try to do them themselves. They just enjoyed listening to his voice and basking in his energies.

His voice carried much energy: *Strength, caring, compassion, Truth*, and at times, *anger*. Oh, could he show anger! But it was always a reaction to something that was truly incorrect to his mind. He would then come to realize it was a case of semantics or just plain ignorance on the part of the people. He would then change his emotions instantly. He had total control that way. Consequently, he came to show the way, not only to his disciples but also to his many followers. By this time, there would be hundreds of people that would gather to hear him speak. Your movies do a fairly good job of portraying those gatherings.

However, as we have said, people who heard the Master's words did not always understand them. He attempted to make the words represent a certain concept, but if that idea was new to people, they just could not grasp the full meaning. Jesus found he had to repeat the words over and over. He would try new ways to present his ideas and finally settled on the *parable.* This seemed to be the easiest for people to understand. Remember, these people were mostly not well educated. Some could read and write. Many could not. But even the learned rabbis had a difficult time in trying to understand what Jesus was saying. He would say things to them of which they had never heard.

If the rabbis had belief systems that they felt could not be changed, then anything they heard from a young man would just be considered too far out there, so to speak. Remember, it was the Jews, the one hundred Original Hebrews that brought in the Laws. These Laws were now part of the genetic makeup of the Jews. Therefore, if any new idea was proposed that was different from their inherent wisdom and learning, they simply could not accept those radical, new teachings.

In BOOK THREE, what we will present will be areas of concern in humanity today. We will also tie in many times some of the Biblical or planet's history in order to give you Readers the why-of-it. How one concept came about? What is its history? **This BOOK THREE's purpose then will be to tie into the present generation's belief structures and how they have manifested down through the ages**. Most of humanity does not realize how much of what they believe is passed on down from generation to generation—one's past history. We would like to see humanity make new history by embracing new concepts. It will not happen overnight, but there always needs to be a beginning somewhere.

The Presenters for BOOK THREE will be me, Sananda, Jesus, Maitreya, Djwhal Khul, and one or two other Lords (*Sanat Kumara*) who wish to contribute some of their knowledge and wisdom. **These are Lords ancient beyond time**. Even we will be interested to hear what they are going to say. We are raising the bar in this third book—raising the depth of knowledge for you. We waited, for we wanted to see how our words of knowledge would be received in the first two books. From our point of observation, it looks to be a wildfire just about ready to blaze forth. We are so gratified that there are people eagerly waiting to read our words. It is so gratifying and we give you Readers our deepest appreciation and again to the Author for her perseverance and dedication. With that said, I will step back now so that another may continue this Introduction chapter.

I AM Djwhal Khul. Good morning to all of you. I was asked to speak once again. Of course, I am most delighted to do so. Dear Readers, you have read the two previous books by now. We hear that you are greatly enjoying our words, as well as our energies that permeate the words. This at times is a difficult concept for new Readers to grasp—that our energies linger on in the words, long after we have declared the book finished. Let me elucidate further and maybe this will help you understand this principal.

All is energy, as most of you know by now. Therefore, as the Author writes down the words she is hearing through her mental body, our energy is coming and blending into that body. She then brings the energy of the words into her physical body and on down into her hands and fingers. All are blended. We are in that part of her aura; hence her body feels and reacts with goose bumps. The energy stays in the words for we have not withdrawn it. (This is **not** *automatic writing*, but mental telepathy.) God's energies are in your Bibles and the Torah. The words are sacred because the Most High's energies permeate the words. Now let us proceed.

Many years ago of your last century or so, I ascended. I had worked diligently writing books through my magnificent chelas, Madam Blavatsky and Alice Bailey. There were others, but these are the most known in these times. I told them many esoteric mysteries.

However, you see, I gave them information far beyond what the average person could understand. It was too much too soon. Thereby, there is a huge chunk of humanity that just has not heard of these writings, or found them too difficult to comprehend. I, therefore, decided to put information in a more simple way. People do not retain vast amounts of knowledge when it is so esoteric. A little bit of knowledge goes a long way. It was for some of these reasons that we purposely have kept the rhetoric simple in these books. We are demystifying it and hopefully people will take away some of the concepts in this simplified manner.

I wish to give you some knowledge now that is in your esoteric books amidst much more information. Since we have been discussing knowledge and wisdom, let us address knowledge of the energies that permeate one's energy field. By now you Readers know there is an energy field around the body that is referred to as the *aura.* There is this aura of different colors of Lights. Each color depicts a different condition in your body. There are many books that one can buy on this subject. There are energy vortices that twirl in certain directions. These of course are your chakras. There are chakras that come out from the spine to the front of the body. There are chakras in the body organs. There are chakras in your hands and feet. There is a chakra under the feet and chakras over your head. At this point in time most of you have twelve major chakras.

Again, you can read about these in other writings. I am stepping down information in order to make it less pedantic. All that I have been telling you is to lead you toward knowledge of your soul's work. It is the soul that has the capability to develop fully its body's chakra system—its energy centers. If a soul does not take its responsibility seriously enough, the body is left to its own devices and we all know how that can turn out! One does not want just an unguided, almost soul-less body running around. The soul must take responsibility for its gift of a body.

You see, Readers, when a soul is given the privilege of a body, a body that will help the soul's growth, then the soul is literally agreeing to its responsibility. I cannot impress upon you enough what a privilege it is even to receive a body. There literally are souls lined up to receive a body. One could almost put it into the category, *take a number, please.* Masters that are incarnating at will have first choice. Many times, they just repeat their body from the previous life, for it is well developed for their purposes. They use the same Genetic Entity. Those souls of higher awareness just carry their Genetic Entity with them from life to life—as many times as they wish. The average person must wait to be assigned a Genetic Entity, an entity that **is** the body and carries all the encodements. Therefore, when souls are given a body, it is with the understanding that they will help it to develop and grow—**not to downgrade it, but to upgrade it**.

In previous centuries, souls were not as advanced as they are today. Now that is not to say today's souls are well advanced either, for they are not. There are just **more** souls that have raised their vibratory rate but are not necessarily high initiates. In the first two books, we spoke of one's Point of Evolution (PoE) that depicts the soul's progress up Jacob's ladder—one's initiation status. Well, in the present generation, the PoE levels of the souls that have incarnated now are still barely touching the first initiation. That is to say the souls of today, while more advanced than in previous generations, have PoE numbers still only of 1.0—2.0, if that! That is a low number in my estimation.

I had told you there are now more advanced souls on the planet than ever before. I am speaking of souls who have been born with a 6.0—7.0 initiation level and who, through embracing the previous levels and integrating all of them, have been able to move forward to 8.0, to 15.0, to 22.0 and even beyond. This may astound you readers, for you would have thought these souls would no longer have to have lives. They don't! They have continued Earth-lives by choice. I previously have spoken about this. The information may be a repeat for some of you, but necessary in order to have everyone on the same page, so to speak.

Now that I have caught you up, re-addressed some of the previous material in the other two books, let me continue this discourse for a while. Picture those souls who are at the 6—22 initiation levels and beyond. They too have their veils still in place. Most do not have full realization of their mastership. Most do not realize their greatness. Therefore, in that respect, they are very similar to their fellow country—men/women. However, what sets them apart is **what** they have accomplished in their lifetime. Most of these great walking-Earth masters have created a resume that would seem daunting to the average person. I do not mean they are necessarily famous, although some are, from their endeavors. They are just very productive people. They are walking-masters. This is the Father's Plan, a part of it where the veils are to be lifted so that masters will know who they are and so will the people they meet. The purpose of that is so humanity will see how they too could do some of the same activities. I would say all masters are Wayshowers—all masters who walk the Earth, that is.

Therefore, let us back up a bit in this narration. The point I wish to make is to bring to readers' attention that they too could be walking-masters—Wayshowers. It could be interesting for you to note just what did you accomplish in order to attain such a spiritual height? It is time, Readers, to know your worth. Most people who will be led or drawn to read these books are really searching for knowledge of Self. Each time you pick up a book such as ours, you are pondering where your belief structure fits in. What role did you select to play as you set up your life? What goals did you bring in? Have you completed your goals? Did you walk your talk? All of these kinds of introspective queries are in the category of soul searching. Lump them together and it is you searching for knowledge about you—about Self. I have capitalized Self to show it is your Higher Self of which you want more knowledge.

Consequently, you take Earth lives repeatedly. You reach the point where that karmic wheel of birth-death-rebirth is broken—a term frequently used to depict you no longer have to be born onto this planet. However, in your newly designated title of *master*, you **select** to come to Earth repeatedly, even though karmically you have finished. Yet, there is always more to learn. You choose more intricate and more difficult games of life on Earth. Now you want to hone the skills of the soul, as well as the body you have chosen to create over and over again. Of course, each lifetime is not just for you, for that would be too self-serving. You are here by choice to serve the Father. Therefore, you confer with Him and incorporate what He is wishing to experience with what you wish to learn or to refine. There is now a nice balance of giving and receiving.

Thus, dear Readers, this lifetime could be a honing of your skills. Many times a Reader may not realize if something—an act or skill—comes easily to you that chances are it is not your first time in having this skill. Many doctors who are specialists in their fields, an oncologist for example, have had many lifetimes perfecting themselves. First, they will have had several lifetimes experiencing cancer. Sometimes they died and at other times, they were able to overcome it, whether by means of medical procedures or holistically.

In ancient times, it was the people's use of highly evolved *healers* and *seers* that helped them heal themselves. After several lifetimes of that lesson, they became an alchemist and then a doctor in subsequent lifetimes. Each life they became more proficient in their field. You can well imagine a doctor in the 1800's having little to do with one's healing of cancer. Usually, the patient died, but the soul learned about how people suffered, and how it felt **not** to be able to help them. Consequently, an oncologist in modern day has earned the prestige of his/her specialty. Moreover, of course, this dynamic applies to all specialists in all fields in all the games of life—(*psychologists, musicians, actors, writers, etc.*)

It has come to our attention that many souls have good intentions of upgrading their bodies when they first take a body, but then somewhere along life's path, they lose track of their purpose for coming to Earth. They let their body take over. The souls find their bodies become addicted to not only drugs, but to certain unhealthy foods and drinks. It is a known fact that many of today's youths are obese. These young people have not been properly guided at home, in my opinion. Many of these youths are what you call, *latch key kids*. Both of their parents work; or if they are living with a single parent, that parent is not present for long enough hours at home. There is too much television allowed where the young adults are greatly influenced by the food and snack commercials. The parent(s) many times comes home tired from long hours at work. He/she just throws some fast-prepared foods together; or stops and picks up pizza or a value meal somewhere. These meals, while filling, are so processed, full of fats and sodium, and the drinks are so full of sugar that they just perpetuate the obesity of the children.

You know, Readers, what you are seeing is lack of soul guidance. The soul has chosen a difficult life; to be a single parent is especially trying. Therefore, as the body slowly takes over, the soul is guiding it less and less. The action for the soul is that it is more interesting to be out of the body than in it. The soul can even be visiting another planet, versus minding its own perimeter of energy—its body.

Therefore, one can see how a soul can get off track and fail or even forget to guide its body. If the soul is far enough away, it can just plain forget it has a body! This, unfortunately, is what we in our spiritual dimensions are seeing more and more. Of course, the solution is for the soul to take more responsibility and be willing to be fully present in order to guide its body. Now we realize that there are those Readers that find this information incredulous, even doubtful, if hearing this for the first time. I would say that those of you reading our books are quite responsible and are advancing nicely. Well, many of you **are** walking masters! The point then becomes, what has happened to the rest of humanity? Why have they not caught up—gone higher up Jacob's ladder? Why are they not taking initiations in even greater numbers? Ah, they are carrying a heavy load of their past history karma, you see.

Each soul, when it takes a body, has also agreed to some of the karma that stems from the planet's history! (***75% of karma is humanity's; 25% is the souls'.***) This might surprise you to know you are not only working your own piece, as the saying goes, but the karmic pieces of your ancestors, as well. Let us approach this from the viewpoint of diseases on the planet. Do you realize that some of your diseases are indigenous to the planet? Take tuberculosis. It is a ravaging disease of one's lungs. It stems from the bacteria that were in the dust spores that came onto this planet. Now this may be unthinkable; but it is true. Your many potent diseases, while indigenous, arrived on the planet from other species.

You see, Readers, when the planet was formed, all was pure. However, as the dust spores settled on Earth, there were particles that held these different bacterial diseases. As different species came to the planet, they many times carried their own bacterium that was not harmful to them. They were Light bodies, but as they became more solid, their cells then became cells for their Earth bodies. At first, there was no harm done; but as these bodies were buried, they started contaminating the Earth. Now these bacteria started manifesting as diseases. You all have heard we have what is called *good* and *bad bacteria* in our bodies. Well, what was once not a harmful bacterium has now became deadly.

A good example could be when the white settlers of America brought their deadly diseases to the Indians who had never had that bacterium. They became very ill and died from these diseases that were unknown to the natives. (*Measles was especially deadly.)* Keep in mind this happened centuries ago and then millions of years before that. That is why we say that tuberculosis is indigenous to the planet, for it has been here since the planet's beginning. People do not realize that there can be whole planets that are populated with people who carry entirely different types of illnesses. Some of your flesh-eating bacteria come from these planets. That is why spaceships landing—coming and going—could be deadly and not because of abductions necessarily, but because of the contamination with the bacteria and viruses. That is also why people have been warned about spacecraft that are not of Light and pure thought. **Our Light ships carry no diseases, or bacteria, or viruses.** We of Light and Love are of the higher vibration than say, tuberculosis. The frequencies of this disease are much lower and therefore could not survive in the higher vibrations of the ships of Light. **No Lord of Light carries diseases of any kind.**

I know for some of you Readers the thought of any micro-organism coming to Earth seems quite astonishing. However, your space in the Universe is teaming with life of all kinds. Most cannot be seen by the naked eye. There are winds and water, dust spores, all active in the vast areas of the Universe. As I have said, viruses and bacteria float on these particles of dust. Now when you think of dust in your world, you picture dust that collects on your automobile or furniture. I am speaking of dust that is so miniscule that it would take microscopes of enormous capabilities to magnify in order to see these particles. In fact, I do not believe your scientists have seen or have had the capabilities to see the space particles that can carry so much life from the outer reaches of your world and other planets. If you put it into the perspective that all is energy in your world and the Universes, you might be able to perceive these miniscule particles that carry much life moving throughout space—carried on the solar winds.

Therefore, Readers, as Earth raises her vibrations, these diseases of humankind and the planet will be eradicated. They will no longer be able to survive in the higher frequencies. That certainly is a positive reason to upgrade the planet. You are then helping to eradicate the diseases that humanity has kept perpetuating by its own lower consciousness. Raise your consciousness; it helps raise the planet's vibration that eradicates indigenous diseases, and then you have helped alleviate the historical, karmic debt to the planet—what a bright future that will be.

Consequently, Readers, each soul who incarnates has agreed to take on some of that debt. Diseases are only one facet of the debt. It is a daunting task, but one that must be accomplished in order for Heaven to blend with Earth. It can and will be done!

(When Jesus and Mary Magdalene came upon the Earth, they came with no personal karma. One of their missions, however, was to upgrade the DNA of humanity. Therefore, they worked with the 75% of humanity's karma. 2011.)

I AM Jesus. Readers, we meet once again in our third book of thoughts, Teachings, wisdoms, stories, and studies. This book will have a deeper presentation for you. While we will address issues that face humanity today, we will give you also some of the reasons, as we see it, for humanity's reactions and beliefs.

Many centuries ago, there were wars. There was pillage. The victors would storm a village and take what they wanted of the spoils. They took most able-bodied men for male servants and slaves. They took young girls for their pleasures and then cast them aside when they became pregnant. They took whatever wealth they could find. This is what wars were all about, not only the plundering and rapes, but also the conquest, power over and servitude of the peoples. A king wanted power. A king wanted to control the people through fear. These kings had huge egos that must be constantly fed. They were into greed, so that only vast storage rooms of their gold and bejeweled objects could bring them some satisfaction. They covered themselves and their many women concubines in jewels. However, as with anything that satiates one, whether it was one's gold plates and goblets, or one's jewels; or if in modern times, one's collection of classic automobiles, the excitement of one's possessions dims. The person is no longer awed or delighted by extravagant jewels. You have pictures of many sultans being draped in strings of gigantic pearls with jewels the size of hen's eggs attached to their headbands. Again, if one has this over-abundance of anything, it no longer brings one the pleasure it once did. Therefore, kings and queens, sultans and rulers were hard-pressed as to where to find their next excitement.

War seemed to be the answer. It is difficult in modern times to comprehend fully how killing and conquering could be the ultimate excitement for these rulers. However, it was. You see, Readers, I am speaking of power—the energy of power. The Father gave free will to the souls. Some of the souls who were of the first Ray of Will and Power started abusing this power. As Djwhal Khul has stated in the previous books, all the Rays are dualistic in that they have the positive as well as negative aspects of their qualities and essence. Consequently, rulers who are using this Ray in a negative way are never satisfied. Power begets power. Once one enters that energy band in a negative way, one is never satisfied. Power is food for these kinds of rulers of ancient days, as well as for those in modern times.

Consequently, the rulers would become insatiable and would want more and more of everything: land, villages, countries, and wealth in jewels or the commodities of the land, which could be slaves or beautiful women. If you were born into these countries, it did not pay to be beautiful whether a woman or man! Your beauty was your downfall to heartbreak and violence. However, as you know, many adventurous souls opted for that kind of experience— to be conquered and enslaved in whatever way their conqueror desired.

Subsequently, these long-ago-times, these lower awareness-times were brought about by man/woman's lust for power and control over people. The souls that chose those lifetimes died and either were famous in their atrocities—your King Herod for one—or were not that big a fish in their pond so they did not make a historical name for themselves. However, **the legacy they did leave was their karmic debt to that area**. Many times, there was great devastation to Nature. The conquering armies killed off the animals that could be eaten and to provide warmth from their skins in order to feed and clothe their troops. Trees were felled for not only firewood, but also to be used to build bridges and battering rams and huge gates for their compounds. Vegetation was killed in order to be able to see more clearly the surrounding area. Therefore, this became karma for humankind.

Now humanity wonders why there are such drastic Earth changes from Mother Nature and Mother Earth. The energy of these wars and devastation of the land during that time is greatly negative. There are pockets all over this planet that have karmic history. Therefore, as Djwhal Khul told you, souls that incarnate agree to take a piece of this karma on—what we are calling *historical karma*, meaning karma that is not necessarily theirs from recent past lives, but theirs nevertheless as they trace their genealogical line that far back in history.

Consequently, dear Readers, as you read BOOK THREE, know we are giving you a glimpse into **your** ancient history. You may have been the soldier in Herod's camp. You may have been the maiden who fought for her virginity by killing her captive. You might have been the beautiful male that was made a eunuch and provided pleasure to bored officials. You may have been the butcher who carved up the many animals for their skins alone. There are so many facets to history. People may wonder where the positive aspects were. Indeed, there were in your *healers*; there were in your *seers*. However, dear ones, they were then burned or put in stocks or beheaded, because they were of the Light. Alternatively, another of you Readers could have had that lifetime as their perpetrator.

Therefore, what I am imparting to you is the fact you indeed have *historical karma*. However, to leave you on a positive note, dear Readers, look how far you have risen! As you read this chapter, take time to muse over our words. Accept the possibility you may have been the plunderer. Then forgive yourself. This is very important. Forgive yourself before you ask the Father for His Mercy. Remember what we have said previously that asking for *mercy* is to ask for *forgiveness*—not to ask Him to stop punishing you! Take joy in the fact you are no longer that denser aspect of yourself. You have come a long way toward Home, Beloveds. Rejoice!

I AM Maitreya. Dear Readers, it is such joy to us that you so eagerly await our words. You know we could be at this for many a year if it were feasible. There is so much to tell. Where to begin? First,

I do wish to give our gratitude to the Author for her willingness to be our channel. There are many people throughout the world receiving different messages from us. We go to those channels in different countries to reach those in that particular culture. Remember, we have spoken before about *different strokes for different folks*. That is precisely what we do. We mold our dictation to suit the times and presence of those Readers, speaking to them in terminology they will understand. It may surprise you to know we channel in almost every country in the world. Now grant you we do not split ourselves into all those parts in order to channel. We have the ability to locate our energies in different spots at the same time. The term is *bi-location*—to be in two places at once. Well, you can multiply that several times, as we are able to be all over your map, the saying goes. Many times, of course, it is not our actual form but a hologram of us if we wish to be seen. However, it is quite simple to pop in and out of people's mental bodies in order to say a few words.

The people we pick and who agree to be channels for us must have a great deal of integrity, with love in their hearts, Light in their energy fields and Truth in their soul. It sounds quite simple but when we start approaching different candidates to be channels, we find they may have a component or two that is not developed enough. Usually, a person can have *love* and *Light*, but their *integrity* and *Truth* may not be as strong. Thus, it is not as easy, as it first appears—to find a chela, a student, a fellow Wayshower who has developed all four of those attributes *Love, Light, Integrity,* and *Truth*. People might have good intentions and fervently would love to channel us, but it would not be productive for either of us, for they would not be fully prepared.

It has taken this Author over thirty years to come to the point she is now in her development. It has taken her the last five years to strengthen her attributes and to overcome old programming that no longer served her. During that time, there was also the strengthening of her emotional body. Her mental body was quite advanced, but the emotional body needed to catch up. Her life's game plan and her personal trials and tribulations needed closure—to end cycle. She has been honed on many levels. She does not talk about those times, for they are *water under the bridge*, as she would say. Suffice to know she has had many of the illnesses, diseases, surgeries that have plagued womankind today. She has had her share and more of grief. This entire phase she has brought to resolution with conscious, deliberate attention to her spiritual path. She has spent hours and hours in introspection clearing and processing the old Truths. She has readied herself well.

She is finely tuned now, so that she can receive our knowledge, wisdom, and Teachings, for they are hers also. Your term *been there, done that* does indeed describe her life in almost every phase one could imagine. We therefore carry the greatest respect for her, thank her, and salute her. One of these times we just might give you a peep at some of her past lives that have molded her to the superbly, fine-tuned individual she is today.

You can imagine, Reader, how she struggles to stay true to our words, as she transcribes this channeling. You see she has trained her three beautiful daughters that *beauty is as beauty does. Therefore, watch your egos*. She is telling me right now that her daughters will be saying *that's ego, Mom. Delete that*! We are telling her, *no, you are not to touch one word of this discourse*! Of course, we are saying this with humor; but it is amusing to watch her hesitate over our compliments sometimes. Ah, but it is true. Enough said now, or she will just close up her channeling shop!

I Am Maitreya, your World Teacher. We have finished these opening remarks in the introductory chapter.

(*This segment by Lord Maitreya is a challenge for me to accept his words and include them here. He added a couple more little remarks. "Readers like to know personal bits about Authors. Not everyone gets such a profound description of herself."*)

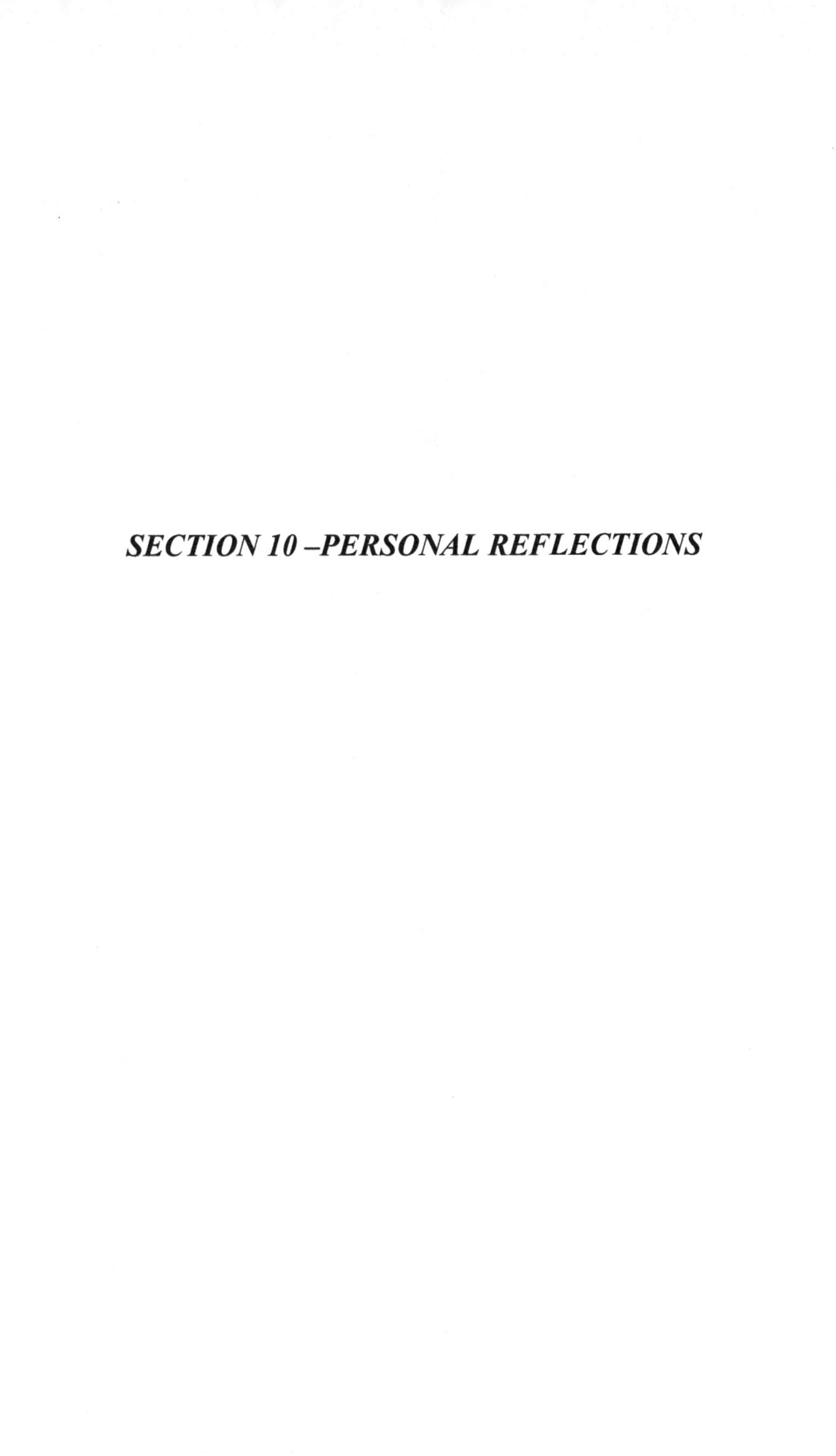

SECTION 10 –PERSONAL REFLECTIONS

LIFE in the SLOW LANE—Jesus

I AM Jesus. When I was a young lad of twelve or so, I knew my time had come to lay aside childish play and concentrate more on my Father's work. Therefore, I started making mental lists of the various steps I would have to take. It has been noted in your Bible how I would go to the Temple and admonish the moneychangers and those who sold doves. However, at the same time I noted that not much was being done about cleaning up the area after my explosion of wrath. I felt anger and incredulous amazement that the men carried no awareness of how they were downgrading the energies of the Temple.

The Temple was a glorious edifice. Solomon had followed his instructions from God to the letter. All the cubic feet that were measured off were specifically adhered to. The woodcarvings, the gold trims, all portrayed the elegance, opulence and wonderment of the Father's World. The Temple was perfect in design, in architecture and furnishings. It was perfect as the Most High is perfect. Therefore, when the rabbis allowed the entrances, porticoes, the large gathering places to become places of commerce, it was just astounding to me. Could they not see how they polluted the energy? Could they not feel how there were areas that were desecrated? This was God's House and the people were allowed to defile it.

What is not written in your Bible is that nothing changed! Doves were still sold and money was still being exchanged. I had tried to suggest they could use another area, a courtyard further away. But I was just looked upon as *Mary's precocious son. You know he's not from here. They are leaving soon. Do not worry about him. He is not that educated in our ways, the ways of the people of the Temple.* Thus, I was dismissed. I found this attitude somewhat strange, for I thought rabbis were much closer to God than the average person was. They knew the Laws and would give long teachings from the Torah.

Therefore, Reader, I felt confused and somewhat puzzled. How does one approach a problem when the people you wish to approach do not have the awareness you do? As I look back at that time in history, it always becomes clear to me what a formidable task I had set to accomplish. To bring this account to modern times, take your Fundamentalists. They think they are accurate as to the exact interpretation of the Bible no matter from what creed. They listen to the pontificating of their pastors; they partake in the rituals; they attend church each Sunday—maybe even twice and once on Wednesday. But has their little ego—the personality—changed for the better?

They may have made better choices on caring for their body. They may had made some positive choices on some of their habits, but their awareness has not changed all that much. They still have their judgments and prejudices. They do not seem to catch what they are doing when they mentally or verbally attack another's looks or manner. They do not realize they are being hypocritical. Hence, if one were to take the Fundamentalist Christian and put him or her in the same room with the Orthodox Jew, each sect would feel he has been contaminated! What has changed? It is still just another era where there is non-tolerance, either of another's beliefs or behaviors, or looks, and/or dress code. What has happened here that creates such hypocrisy in people?

We think it stems from one's level of consciousness—how far the person has climbed up Jacob's ladder. People, **it is one's awareness and connections of the soul to its body that bring change.** Let us go back to the days of Solomon's Temple. The people of that time **were** a mixture of cultures in the market place. There were your Jews, Palestinians, people from Jordan and other countries, and of course, there were the Romans. All were selling and buying wares and foods at the markets and in the bazaars. All intermingled with mistrust of everyone else. Women bought what was needed and left. The men tarried and smoked. The women did their gatherings at the wells. Men did their gatherings at the places of worship. There was little trust of one's neighbors.

Trust was placed in families. The Jewish family unit was very strong with the wife-mother being the dominant figure. She was the one who ruled the house and disciplined the children. She was the one who taught them how to tend to their father, to respect him for being the head of their household. In social gatherings the women did the cleaning of the house, the preparation of the food, the baking of bread, the trips to the wells for water, and the women were the ones who served the meal to the father and waited on the men at the table.

The point I wish to make is, you have a saying, *the woman wears the pants in the family*—that was true of the Jewish families. The men talked of many things, their animals, crops, and interpretations of the Torah and the Laws. But if a Jewish household was running smoothly, it was because of the women's adeptness at being able to maneuver the men into their way of enacting. However, when the young boys reached Jewish manhood, the fathers would take over the training of their sons. If the family was educated, then the sons were enrolled in the synagogues in order to instill the proper teaching of the Laws. Therefore, the education was left to the discretion of the father. However, many a mother gave her children *home schooling*, especially the girls. Not all humanity realizes just how learned my mother was, for she was well taught by the Essenes. She taught us sacred geometry and even astrology. On the other hand, if the family were well to do, the children would come under the tutelage of the rabbis.

Therefore, Readers, each time in history there are different elements of life in play. Living in the 21st century is living in the *fast lane* compared to 2000 years ago. We were in the *slow lane* then. History serves a purpose. It keeps us connected to the evolution of humanity. I agree we are not to stay in the past but be in the NOW instead. However, one can revisit the past through historical tours, either by going to museums, or by reading books, or just with your mental musings. By remembering your past history—and you all have had a part in making history—by remembering it, you are recognizing how far you have come—how much you have grown as a soul. **These are soul reflections.** At times, this can be quite a healthy act—to reflect on one's past. You are part of the greater whole. Look at what you went through to get to this point. Is it not a tremendous accomplishment? When you have finished your contemplation of the past, forgive yourself for any of your transgressions, and then come to the present. Be in the NOW; be in the moment, and then continue on your path.

HAVE YOU SEEN YOUR REFLECTION TODAY?—Djwhal Khul

I AM Djwhal Khul: In the many years of the past, humanity had its growing pains. It still has, but the growth is at a different pace. The pain is at a different level. In days of lore, humanity did not experience much soul. Now when I make such an observation, it is because humanity was being led by its ego and body most the time. You know, Readers, one is apt to think the body struggles just to stay alive, but the soul also is struggling. The struggle for the soul is keeping all in balance—its body and the soul's expectations and intentions. You see, Readers, souls come into their body with so much expectation. They want to do such and such. They are so eager. They bring in much karma to clear.

Picture a person carrying a huge sack. In that sack are all manner of karmic pieces, or dynamics. Perhaps the soul thinks it can learn to play certain instruments, be an artist, be an intellectual thinker, marry and have a family, take on some of the genetic dispositions of its parents, and on it goes. I am only half way through one's list. Therefore, it becomes a problem when the soul is in a body and all its karmic pieces start to manifest, for he or she has brought them into play. Now the soul finds it does not know how to control its body that has an artistic bent. Artists have so many ideas that come in and out of their thoughts rapidly, that one can observe that artists are cooking on all five burners at once!

An artist's temperament tends to be scattered and it is hard for some to develop intellectually. They seem to be all right-creative-intuitive brain! It amazes us to watch this phenomenon. Look at your past artistic masters. Mozart is a good example. The music just poured forth from him day and night. His artistic ability was so strong that he could not balance himself emotionally. Now it is no secret that he was a master in embodiment, as were many of his peers. Therefore, souls tend to be overzealous in what they take on, or bring with them. All souls are counseled before birth and cautioned not to take on too much karma; but souls do not always listen to their elders, as you know.

Thereby, we watched humanity struggle for balance. There were whole groups of brilliant artists that came forth to create music, as well as to create paintings that are priceless in today's market. Stradivarius made his violin. I hear it brought over a million dollars at a recent auction. However, he was never a wealthy man. None of these great artists was. There seemed to be a code against having wealth at the same time one was creating beauty for humanity. There seemed to be the suggestion that artists had to suffer in order to write the famous poem, paint the picture, write the music—all with periods of great want and suffering for these persons. It was a phenomenon throughout history—one must suffer in order to succeed in life or in death—to be a martyr. It was a group consciousness in which souls were born. One needs to suffer. This in turn will produce great works and great acclaim, they thought.

I have titled this reflection on history in this chapter, *Have You Seen Your Reflection Today?* What were those great souls with such talents reflecting? Why were so many having such difficult lives? The answer lies in humanity's concept and erroneous beliefs that nothing comes easily to anyone. There must always be hard work and struggle. Well, there is some truth there. One indeed must work hard and be diligent; but one does **not need** to suffer in doing so. It is a belief system that has carried over from past lives for most of humanity. Remember our telling you that there is karmic history with humanity. Much of the idea one must suffer in order to achieve comes from your religions. There are religious practices this day where people flail their bodies with whips until they are dripping with blood—all for atonement. One must suffer for one's sins.

Alternatively, one must suffer in order to have visions of God. On the other hand, one must suffer if one is to be a great artist. One must have a most difficult life and this pain and suffering will allow the artistic creativity to emerge. Can you see, Readers, where suffering is synonymous with achievement?

In Christianity, Christ is purported to have suffered on the cross. His purpose showed people of those times that one could ascend, be resurrected, and overcome adversity. He had many other purposes, but I am speaking of suffering right now. Therefore, **we can see how suffering seemed to be synonymous with achieving.** The various religions just kept the mind-set reinforced throughout the ages, as a strong way to control the people. If people were suffering, was it not good for the soul? How many times have you heard that erroneous adage?

Therefore, we can see how many of these difficult situations in life are perpetuated generation after generation. Just because people repeat this concept for centuries does not necessarily make it correct. The concept that one has to suffer in order to advance has been going on for centuries. People are so used to accepting this that young children take it for granted. Children just *suffer through it* in silence. That does not make the situation correct. Many times all that children need to do is to communicate to their parents or teachers and the situation could be remedied. However, they suffer in silence. Consequently, one can see how deeply the concept of suffering has infused the bodies. One might be wondering where the soul is while its body is suffering so. Sometimes the soul is not present to a great extent. Life had gotten out of hand, so the soul opted not to be in its body that much. Thus, it would not have to deal with the situation.

These souls are not all that advanced. They are probably in that bracket of only 10-15% Light Quotient. Other souls are working diligently in their body but are reeling from the difficulties they are encountering. Many times the *historical karma* for which they have signed on has proven more difficult than their personal karma they brought with them. They are floundering. These souls are more advanced, maybe with Light Quotients of between 15-25%. One can empathize with these souls. Life is a beautiful gift from the Father, but that does not necessarily make it a *walk in the park* either. There is such great planning, implementation, and work involved.

Therefore, when we ask about your *reflection,* we are really addressing what **you** are reflecting—with what historical karma you are struggling. It might be of benefit for each of you Readers to ponder this. Each person on the planet is *working on* some specific area, part of the puzzle that concerns humanity in a great way. The Father has His Plan out on the drawing board, so to speak. You have one of the pieces that when you transmute it and clean it up, you have done service to God and have furthered His Plan. Each part, no matter whether it is of miniscule size, is of the greatest importance. God does not judge by size. The finished perfection brings Him joy.

People may want an example in order to gain perspective. For a soul to take a body and find how to balance its life, to love others, to share and give to others, to not suffer and be the victim is the greatest joy for the Father. Historical karma is a tremendous undertaking, if one looks at the whole. However, if one soul can do its part with just a small portion of that karma, and then another soul also accomplishes its task, and then another, and on it goes until one day the task has been completed. What a glorious time that will be. To be able to put a check mark that that part of God's Plan is complete and to know you have done your part to make it so—that is what makes life worth living. The law of Cause and Effect has been completed.

REFLECTIONS on HISTORICAL KARMA—Sananda

I AM Sananda. I have had many centuries to replay those Biblical lives in my mind. I do not dwell on them, but I still remember those that have special meaning for me. Of course, Reader, you realize I can read the records and view any of my past lives as I wish. I can project myself there, observe, and watch as a bystander. I would be in holographic form, but would appear real to people. I would disguise myself so that I would just become one of the crowd.

One of my favorite times to revisit was during my years in Egypt. Walking among those great pyramids was awesome even centuries ago. I could wander the Halls. I could read the records secreted deep down in vast libraries where many records from Lemuria and Atlantis are interned to this day. History always fascinates me—to watch the evolution of humanity, how it has transpired, the greatness of it and the bottom dregs of its barrel. As you know, souls experience both ends of the spectrum, so one sees the very lowest of struggling souls to the highest achievers.

Now what I am leading up to is that history is never completed. In your lives, parents have children. That is not the end of it, for those children have children. You have that saying *time marches onward*. That is how history is formed.

In our dimensions, we have records you have come to know as the *Akashic Records*. These records are an actual recording of each soul's actions and thoughts. This may surprise you in that **countries also have their Akashic Records**. As your founding fathers established what was known as America and later the United States, a group-mind was formed. It then had its own consciousness. Every act by America, every thought by its citizens is recorded. One can go to the Hall of Records and read all about the rise of America. In your world, it would be similar to watching a moving picture show. The difference would be it would take a person the same length of time to view America as it did to create it. One is not going to flip a switch and delete whole sections on the World Wars. However, one can fast forward, as the saying goes. Alternatively, you can program what past you wish to view. Also, keep in mind souls that view different countries and their records are usually in the spiritual planes. They most likely are researching something of interest.

Therefore, I can still replay the records of Egyptian times—visit Egypt's records. Many of you know Egypt was the center for many of the sacred rites of passage and initiations. Students were taught how to leave their bodies for an extended period. In fact, that was one of the initiation rites for Winged Pharaohs. They were called *Winged Pharaohs* because they were able to leave (fly out) of their body, leave it in animated suspension, do whatever they were doing in other dimensions and then return to their body. Of course, this initiation rite killed many a body much to the dismay of the candidate when it could not re-enter its deceased body. There would be priests that watched over the body, but bodies still died if there was not enough life force running through them. Initiates would try repeatedly until they had mastered that rite. Of course being a Winged Pharaoh was very handy when one wanted to observe what its warring neighbors were planning. Therefore, I enjoyed going back to those pasts in history.

Your Master Jesus had his initiations in Egypt but several other writers have written of those times. Suffice to know that this Son of God was not just a stationary Being as he was in his Buddha life. Jesus walked every mile of his country, sailed to different countries, and rode camels around Egypt, as he did in India. He was not sedentary by any means.

Therefore, know dear Readers, that your every thought and action is recorded not only on your personal records, but also for the country in which you live. You can see then how one becomes part of *historical karma*, as we have said. It is important for humanity to know this. If you have traveled a great deal, spending years in foreign lands as the Author has, then know she has a piece of that country's historical karma to help transmute. Whatever happened while you were in another country, whether you were just asleep when the country experienced some trauma, you are still a part of that dynamic for that is where your body was at that time.

With that, I will close these reflections until we meet again within these pages.

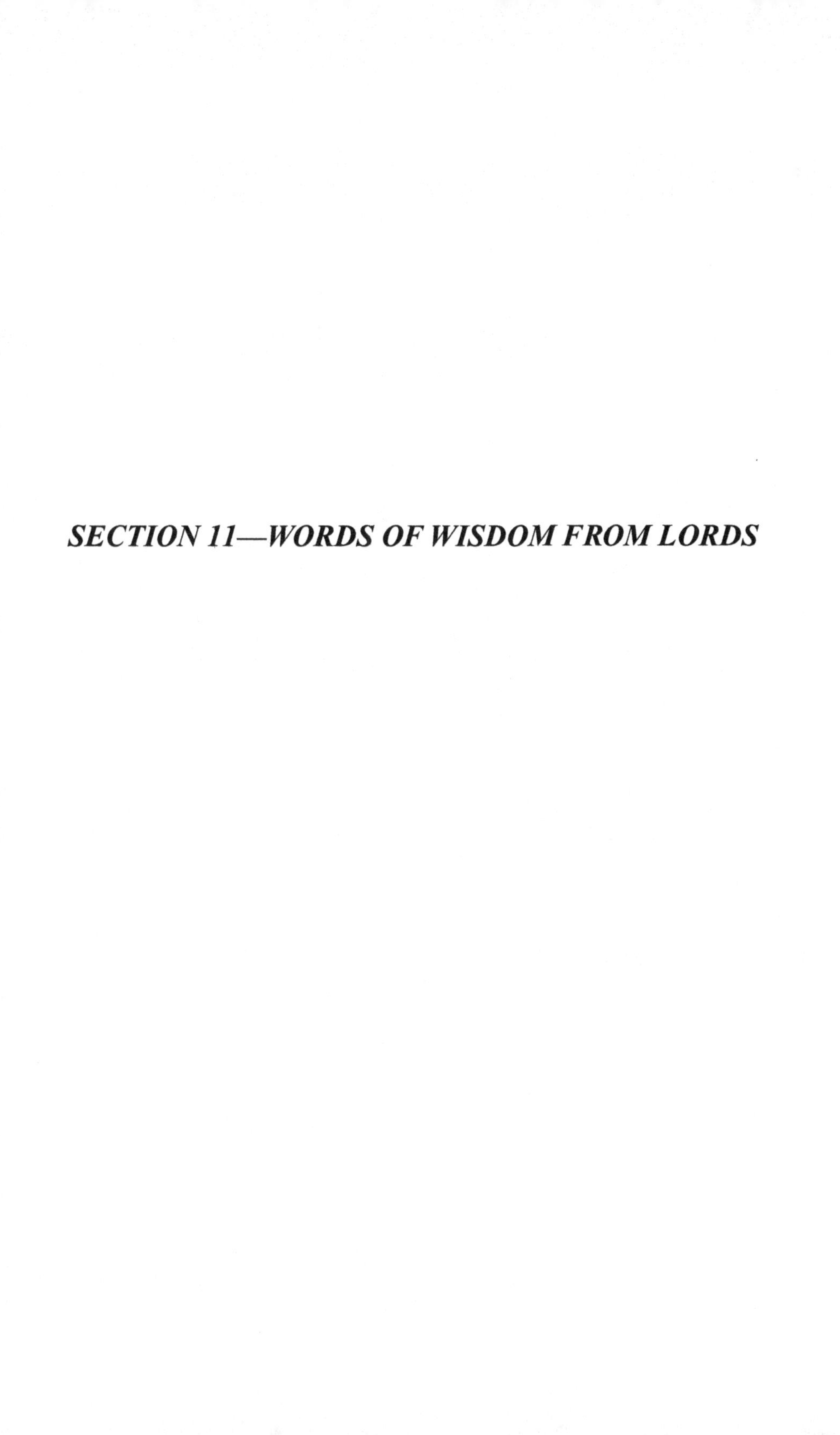

SECTION 11—WORDS OF WISDOM FROM LORDS

FOOD for THOUGHT from the PLANETARY LOGOS—Sanat Kumara

I AM Sanat Kumara, known in your world as the **Lord of the World, the Planetary Logos**. Some of you may wish further information. *Kumara* is an honorary title for Teacher. Sananda is also a Kumara, as are many of the Lords. However, I am at this moment the Kumara of your planet. I am the planet's Logos, the energies of Will and Power. I am able to ingest many of the energies of your higher Beings, those of you with the finer vibrations and those of you who have reached ever-higher initiations. Once you have done so, your energies become a part of me—as part of my chakra system. This is enough about me for now. What is important is what I wish to impart to you. This will be a small lecture, but great in wisdom.

Throughout many millenniums, before your planet was formed, I was. I was an energy born of God, just as you are. I evolved just as you are doing, Readers. The difference, however, is that I did not evolve on planet Earth, for I was one of the Creators of your planet. I come from different worlds, and yes, even a different Universe. You see, Readers, nothing is secret in what you refer to as the *Heavenlies*. When the Father is expressing His desire for a new planet to be formed so that souls could have the use of their free will in whatever direction they choose, we in other worlds and Universes hear of this—know it. All is energy, as you have been told many times. Therefore, do you not see how even God's thoughts are known to those of us who still have the ability to hear His thoughts? You see, dear Readers that is part of humanity's problem. The people no longer hear their Father! Therefore, when we in other worlds and Universes hear the Father express His desire, His wish, we who hear come forth. We volunteer. *We will help you, Father*, we exclaim.

I say *we* for there is never just one of us. Remember your Trinity in your religions. There are always more than one and usually three or more for such huge projects as creating a planet. Therefore, others and I conferred with your God. I call Him **your** God, for He is named in other ways in our Universes and worlds. He carries many Names.

Some of those Names have over a hundred or so letters. Some of those Names have no letters, but only sounds. Each Name carries a different vibration and frequency. The Names, all of them, are not indiscriminately given out. There are reasons for this, all having to do with the vibrations. If a dark soul wished to do evil, he could do so by using one of your God's Names while creating. One calls upon God when creating. It becomes part of the sound. There are intricate, sacred geometric equations in all of the Father's Names. Therefore, not everyone has **earned** the privilege of knowing Him with such intimacy.

You see, Readers, one must earn the advancements. You on Earth strive to advance from one job to another, or one department to another, or one initiation to another. You earn these advancements, not through lies and the misuse of power—not to ride over someone with subterfuge and lack of integrity. However, many a person has risen to high places in your government, in political circles, in work places this way; but keep in mind this is now. This is one lifetime. After the person has died and has had his or her life's review, the high prestige one experienced in that lifetime is erased. It dissipates and is no more, for the achievement was not with honesty and integrity. Therefore, what the soul experienced in that life was a waste, as far as any spiritual advancement. The soul did learn how **not** to achieve, however.

Hence, when I speak of the Names of God being kept private, for only those who have achieved with **integrity** are to know His Names, this is why. In addition, there is the same fact in play where one of lower consciousness and Light cannot know or see the higher. Only those of the finer frequencies and Light can even understand the equations in God's Names in order to recognize the formulas.

It may be of interest to you readers to know that each of your names holds formulations. Numerology is the closest to depicting this fact. Each letter holds a number. However, even numerology does not give the whole picture. Each of your names is encoded in the Bible. God formulated the equation and put the names into His Book. It matters not which Book, whether Christian Bible or Torah. Your names are there.

A New Age school of thought has people changing their given names. They could be born a *Patricia* and change the name to

Angel, or *Crystal*, or *Star*. These are whimsical and endearing, but are merely metaphors for the person. Be very careful in changing your name, for when you do, you are leaving behind part of your equation. You cannot change your equation when Patricia is in the Bible or Book of Life, whereas Star or Crystal is not.

It has come to our observation that people seem to shorten their names. They no longer answer to Susan, but are Sue or Suz. Whenever you abbreviate her name, you are abbreviating her formula of energy. This does not do a great deal of harm, but it is making her less than she is. Some people say of Lord Djwhal Khul, *DK*. That too lessens who He is, this great Lord of the second Ray. In addition, he has agreed to allow his name to be used as an example. So please, Readers, be aware when you shorten people's names. You are not using their complete geometric formula, which of course depicts their essence. You are making them less of who they are.

When I was in my youth, and indeed, I too was young of heart, Readers, I was learning my lessons just as all of you are today. Now grant you this would be billions of years ago, for I am rather ancient. However, I too had to grow once I left the Father's Domain. I was, as I have said, in another Universe than yours. The dimensions there, while similar to yours, do not have the same vibrations as the planet we are all in now. The frequencies of the sphere I was on were at a higher vibration. They resonate and move outward at a more rapid rate than this one does. What happens then is that everything develops more rapidly. The souls advance more quickly and more is accomplished. Let us see if I can give you an example.

Now remember your childhood nursery tale of Jack and the Beanstalk—that he finds a seed, plants it and the stalk miraculously grows many feet each day. Well, every cell and energy in the Universe where I developed does the same thing. Any creative thought is instantly finished. You might be wondering what the purpose would be to have a Universe vibrating at such a rapid speed—to accomplish creation at a more rapid pace. You on Planet Earth realize how long it takes any evolution to manifest. Any change on this planet takes years and years. All the plant, mineral, animal, and human kingdoms take centuries to evolve. Grant you some are faster than others are—a man versus a rock, for example. You can make your own calculation as to which will change faster. The rock will still be changing into its purpose, while man has come and gone back to dust. Therefore, there are different worlds and Universes that vibrate at different levels. I am not speaking of time necessarily, but I merely use time as an analogy for you.

Therefore, those energies and souls like myself, developed in a Universe that evolved more rapidly than your Universe. Of course, I was also in a world in that Universe, a certain sphere. The point I make is there are different energies, vibrations, frequencies in each of the worlds and Universes outside of your own. I have told you Earth is slow to change, but she **is** advancing. Earth is moving into the finer vibration and frequencies. What this will do is make it easier for souls to evolve. Remember, I told you how fast evolution was in the Universe and world in which I grew up. Well now, your Earth is shifting her gears. She is revving up and is moving with increased speed. Everything is speeding up. You will find that many of your new children coming on to this planet—you may call them Indigo, or Crystal, or Children from the Great Central Sun—these magnificent Beings vibrate at a higher rate. Their motors are racing, to put it in racecar lingo. Therefore, just their presence helps Earth rev **her** motors.

Parents are hard-pressed to keep up with their unique children. Most parents of these children are what were previously known as the *New Agers*. Now they are in their thirties or older. They have children from worlds that they did not experience. They, the parents, do not have the knowledge and wisdom of these new children of the Great Central Sun yet, for instance. They are learning to parent these children as their **children teach them**! That is how evolution works. The Author was born to parents who were very old, learned, advanced souls. She in turn brought in old souls and a New Ager. They in turn brought in brilliant-minded souls. Some are New Agers as their parents are, others are the Indigo and then the higher Sun Children, and on it goes. Each generation upgrades the energies. Thus, Earth can upgrade hers.

It may surprise you to learn not everyone is from this world. Your New Agers are not; your Indigo-Crystal children are not from where the New Agers came from; and now you have children from even more different energies of the Great Central Sun—the very heart of your Creator. What magnificent children these are. They are brilliant in mind, strong in their will, strong in their emotions, and strong in body. However, there are parts of them that need honing. Some do not know of animals that much. Some of them do not know how to control the body's emotional body. They may have strong emotions but still have to learn how to control them and when it is or is not appropriate to use them.

Therefore, Readers, while Earth is evolving, even the more highly evolved have come to Earth not only to help her, but also to experience Earth's many, varied games of life. You may see these brilliant children having a difficult time in schools, if schools have not adjusted their curricular activities to accommodate the new and different minds of these different energy-programmed bodies. These children will play hard and then need rest. They have endurance but know when it is time to let down their motors, so to speak—to slow down and rest.

Your present schools allow little time for rest and recreation. Even your sports have become so competitive that students are stressed out just trying out, or they feel they must take drugs in order to beef up their muscles. What is not being properly taught to them is the **body's timing** for development of muscle mass. Moreover, it is different for young girls. Your children are sexually developing more quickly in body, mind, and belief structures—way before the emotional body has become stable. Put sexuality on top of having to have muscles for sports of all kinds, and there is little room for stability. Teenage suicide is on the rise. Again, the body has to stabilize its hormones. In addition, its emotions and its mental abilities are still forming. Too much too soon seems to be the norm for these adolescents—these new-minded high-energy souls.

Many a soul is seeking counsel, for even with its best intent of wanting to upgrade its body, the body control is getting away from these puzzled souls. Many simply do not know what to do, or how to control their bodies. A good example could be a person who acquires a beautiful horse. The horse is of high energy—what you might call high spirited. It rears and breaks rein, gallops when it is supposed to canter, breaks into a canter when it is supposed to trot, and mostly refuses to walk unless it has completely been exhausted to the point it will follow the rider's commands docilely. That could describe these high-energy souls in bodies for the first time. They do not quite know how to control them and are giving their exhausted parents many a sleepless night. You are then experiencing evolution of a planet, a body, and a soul. It becomes an awesome experience for all.

I will close this small discourse. I have given you Readers just a glimpse of the Father's Domain. I will come another time in order to give information outside of your planet. My purpose in doing so is to give you an opportunity to gather new information. When you receive new information, new for you perhaps, it will become a catalyst for change, if you will let it.

Good day to you all.

ONE'S BODY of LIGHT—Sananda

I AM Sananda. Throughout the ages, many people have heard or read about their having a Body of Light and are creating this Light Body with every incarnation. People have heard they have what is also known as a Light quotient. It is how one's Light Body is measured. Since humanity is still evolving, its Light Body is also.

When God created the soul, He knew the new soul could not handle a full quotient of His Light, meaning 100%. The new soul simply would waste it. Now it may seem strange to you that souls cannot carry 100% Light, but I am speaking about the **evolution** of the soul. To give you an example, suppose you were a six-month-old baby. Would the parents shine a collagen lamp straight into the babe's eyes? They would not, for too much light would blind the child. It would be the same with the parents gazing into the sun. They would be blinded. Now you have your Heavenly Father who gives out small percentages of His Light to His souls. However, they must **grow** in consciousness before He gives them another infusion or portion of Light. You may ask how a soul wastes its Light. He wastes his Light by not using it!

Your Light quotient correlates to your level of consciousness. No matter what your Light quotient is, that is your consciousness level. Humanity on a whole does not have a great deal of Light. There of course are pockets of Light on the planet where there are groups of people with higher consciousness; but overall, humanity's Light is low indeed. Light quotients range from 1—100%. Some of the new children entering the planet already have Light quotients of 35—50%. That is unheard of compared to one hundred years ago. Most of today's souls are not fully awake. Their quotients are still around 10—25%. Your Masters in embodiment carry Light quotients from 75—100%. It is because of the veils in place that they do not fully realize their Light. As they awaken more, their Light quotient rises. Masters who have their Light quotients in the 80—95% range are far and above humanity. Yet if one were to meet a master of that higher level, you most likely would not notice anything different about the person as you walked by. It is in the interaction that you will feel masters' Light, for they will radiate *love* and *caring*. They may express their emotions strongly and honestly. You will not have to guess in order to know from where they are coming. If a situation rises where the master must be decisive, you will see that too. There will be no display of self-pity; nor will the master play the victim. His or Her level of consciousness affords Him or Her deep perception that most do not yet have.

Now I have stated a master's Light quotient can be in the 90's, but not 100%. What is the reason for this since God is the one who metes out His Light with every rise of a master's achievement? In BOOK ONE, I spoke of Christ Consciousness. A master with a Light that measures 100% is God-realized. She or he has attained Christ Consciousness. Hence, we can say that ***Christ Consciousness is synonymous to a 100% Light quotient.*** Therefore, Readers, you can see how far humanity needs to advance its awareness.

Let us now address where one's Light Body resides. Is it in our actual physical body? Is there a sheath around it that is full of this Light? Is the Light in the astral body; the body one floats away in after your body is asleep? Does the soul carry the Light? These questions all carry an element of Truth. Let's address these queries one at a time.

Your Light does permeate your physical body. It is what keeps your body from being so solid. Your chakras become brighter as you bring more Light into the body. So Light is stored in the body, if you wish to use this picture, and it becomes part of the opening of your chakras.

Is there a sheath for the Light—an envelope for God to put His Light into? The soul does have a sheath around it. This sheath becomes your Light Body. When the soul is first created by God, this layer is small; but through the many incarnations and growth of the soul, its body of Light expands until it too takes shape and can be a separate form. This is different from a twin flame. It is **not** the soul separating, but a tremendous build-up of its Light. Since everything is energy, the Light Body is also pure energy. Right now Jesus and I, Sananda, can be separate and be two different forms; but we are the same soul! We are two different personalities with one soul. This is different from a twin flame. **Twin flames are the splitting of the original soul. A Light Body is a sharing of a soul.** Twin flames split off and go their separate ways. That soul may not encounter its flame for centuries. A Light Body does not split the soul's energy. A Light Body is formed by the one soul's Light. One could ask who comes first, the chicken or the egg? There is no first. All is Light and Energy. Jesus and I have always been One. He is an aspect of me and I am an aspect of Him. We are One.

The Light also becomes a part of your astral body. Your astral body develops and grows, as do your other bodies. All is evolving; all is energy. It becomes the task of the soul to bring consciousness to its physical body. As it does so, the astral body depicts this by reflecting the Light from the physical. Therefore, your astral body also emits Light.

By now, Reader, you may surmise that the soul carries a great deal of Light—so much so that it is not able to bring all of its Light into the body. We have spoken before about the soul having just a small part of itself in the body. The rest of the soul remains outside of its body. To reiterate, the Light Body is formed by God pouring forth His Light into the soul. The Light is collected in a diaphanous sheath. It is similar to an envelope, but that does not adequately explain the containment. How does one contain the sun? You cannot, for it flares forth in its brilliance. Yet there is a structure not seen by the naked eye. There are fine filament threads of energy of pure Light that give structure to the sun. Each soul carries its own Light tapestry, which builds and blazes forth with each Light infusion from God.

Masters in their full brilliance could light up a city block if they chose to. However, most masters in embodiment with some veils still in place have not realized their full 100% Light quotient; but they will light up a room for those with clairvoyant sight.

Some of you Readers may be puzzled, for if Jesus and I are one, why has there not been more written about Sananda's past lives? I have had numerous past lives. **Jesus had thirty-three**. I have had fewer. My name was not recorded in those lifetimes so people would not know of me. You may be a Bill or Betsy in this life, but your true identity is not made known. I do not wish to state my lifetimes, for they are past history. However, for your knowledge, most masters will have had Earth lives, for there is so much to experience on this planet. That is why they keep re-incarnating at will, because they choose to either be of service to the Father to perform some task, or to hone their own abilities. Earth is a challenge for everyone no matter at what level he or she is.

THE DAY AFTER—Maitreya, Sananda, Jesus

We are the Trio: Maitreya, Sananda, and Jesus. In the many eons that passed since the crucifixion, people still kept to their old ways. Nothing much that looked to be on a positive level seemed to change. The changes were mostly negative. Wars continued. Women remained the lesser gods. They were used for bearing children and carrying on the bloodlines, or for pleasure. People had a difficult time being motivated to raise their consciousness.

The new thought, what was called *Christianity*, took a negative bent. Men were so used to being in power; they just took hold of a new opportunity to grab onto a new power and control others by it. The interesting fact was that the dynamic of Christianity was similar to a prairie wildfire that caught the flame of zealots and burned out of control across the prairies of men's ambitions. The zealots fanned the blaze and watched the fire dissolve the people's consciousness in front of their eyes. People gave away their personal heart-power to whoever wielded the larger stick. Of course, Readers, you recognize all the metaphors we are using. Christianity seemed to be this huge conflagration. It consumed whole countries. Kings and queens, princes and princesses were killed, dethroned, murdered in order to keep the ruler of a Christian faith on the throne or off the throne.

Such were the birthing pains of the new order of how to worship God in every facet of humankind. Of course, Jesus was long ascended, but we observed what was happening. Jesus made a vow that he would stay on the planet until humankind had acquired higher consciousness. He knew not everyone would be able to reach a Christ Consciousness, but he knew that for humanity to raise its vibrations so that a new consciousness would take place was not completely an unattainable task. He knew that eventually, as the Earth moved forward, so would humankind. When a soul, such as Jesus the Christ, takes on a certain task, he sees it to the glorious end. He does not stop his input of energy just because the task is taking longer than hoped. He pledges his energy to fulfill what he has started.

Therefore, *the day after* the crucifixion carried much expectation for all concerned. The Holy Family was still reeling from the horror of it all. The people could talk of nothing else. The Heavens were still dark, threatening, as a reminder to people of what had been done to this Son of God. The Earth rumbled in protest of the dark energies. The Romans tried to make *the day after* just like any other working day. Pontius Pilate stayed secluded, feeling the pangs of guilt. The rabbis talked furiously, justifying their actions of persecuting one of their own. They drew upon their righteousness and read their spiritual passages in order to bring solace to their worried hearts. There was not one person in that area that was not affected.

Why are we bringing this up again? We make note of this in order to bring to your attention once more **that much of this tragic play had been set in motion before the players were born!** Prophets prophesized centuries ago that the Messiah would come and be persecuted. Readers, this tragic drama that humanity experienced was planned and orchestrated by the Father and Jesus, who was not called by that name, but was known as Yeshua. His Mother Mary, his Father Joseph, all of the disciples and yes, even Judas and Pontius Pilate were instructed and shown their roles. However, what many may not realize is that **there were different endings planned** also. Any changes would be because humanity's consciousness had raised, or one of the players changed the script by choosing another way to interact while in embodiment. Even Yeshua could have changed the path of history if he had chosen differently some of the options that were open to him. He need not have proceeded to bring this drama to the stage. He did have other choices, but they involved **rebirths** for many of the people of the original play. **He made the choice that he did in order to bring forth the new dynamic in his lifetime.**

The original script called for more players to be involved, not just him. However, they were killed by evil men, so that Yeshua made the choice to proceed on his own. **It is similar to building a house on four pillars. Three pillars are destroyed. Can just one pillar still hold up the house?** Yeshua, after much contemplation and communion with the Father, decided to forge ahead. It took tremendous strength of will on his part and steadfastness to see it through. The outcome may have been different in that the new religion would not have started with such a dark legacy. However, remember, if he were shown this play in action before he was born, would he not have seen the alternative paths also? Of course he did, for he knew what was in store for Earth if he chose another direction.

He knew that the dark side of humankind would become dominant. He knew that the original plan for humanity was no longer feasible when the other players had been prematurely killed. Therefore, he chose **his** way. He felt that humanity was dark and not moving toward the Light very much. He felt that by allowing himself to be crucified, that that could provide the catalyst to lift people out of their stupor and to get them moving again.

Well, it certainly proved to be a catalyst all right. People moved in both directions—up and down, if one wishes to use that terminology. Some people were lifted more toward God. Others, as we have said at the beginning of this chapter, jumped at the chance to gain power. Jesus' crucifixion made one either more Holy or less Holy. Consequently, there was great change throughout the centuries—some for the better and other changes for the worse. People sought the closeness to God in the nunneries and people sought power in the Inquisitions and Crusades. Such were the many repercussions that were born from the decisions by the Son of God—God's Methodologies in action.

Therefore, Readers, as you stand in judgment of others, whether of people or their religious beliefs, remember what we have said about *historical karma*. Each of you has signed on for a piece of this, to help transmute the negative and to move the planet forward. You are all part of *The Day After*. You have chosen to be born repeatedly, to experience the many facets of life. Watch your many choices and know each choice will bring a different ending. **Be not the victim to your choice, but be the victor.**

CONFUCIUS SAYS—Confucius

I AM Confucius. Our dear sister, I am known in the other worlds by different names, but the one I will use for this book is *Confucius.* **Djwhal Khul is an aspect of me**. I was for the Oriental mind in those eons of times. However, I see that almost every fortune cookie bears one of my sayings. At least the writers of the cookies think those were my words.

I taught on a variety of subjects but mainly strove to reach the minds of the Orientals. That ethnic group, as most of you readers are aware, has finely-tuned minds. Even the peasants had cunning with analytical minds. The well-educated persons excelled at mathematics. In those far off times, however, women were not thought to be worthy of an education. The upper classes were taught to write and to read what was given to them. However, their training was more on how to please the males. Women were taught the proper dress and good manners, what to say and what not to say.

Therefore, when I came into my own, I taught on several levels. Jesus used *parables*, little stories to which people could relate. I chose a similar fashion in that I wrote *little sentences or phrases* that would stimulate the minds, from a peasant to royalty. Now most of the lower classes could not read or write in those ancient times, so my teachings became oral in tradition. Soon people were saying my little phrases in their everyday lives. They would quote what I had said. In that way they passed on the teachings to their children and they to their children to even today, for people will say *Confucius says . . .* That was the best way to reach the Oriental mind, for people would take the meanings to heart and then actually start practicing what was said. *Confucius says to give to yourself* ***not*** *what you would give to your dog*. It would make the people think what **had** been given to the dog. Some got it and others would ask for the meaning from friends and relatives. There would be debates, arguments and much laughter.

One day, when I was contemplating how to get a particular teaching into a short sentence, I heard much noise and arguments out toward the servants' quarters. I sent one of my housemen out to investigate. He came back telling me that the cooks were all arguing about how to state what I had said. One heard it one way; another heard a different rendition; so I went to the kitchen, which brought a sudden silence to the room. The masters of households rarely visited the kitchen in those ancient times. I asked them what their dilemma was. They told me that they did not know how to use the saying for they felt it must be for a man and others felt it was for a woman. They did not see how both males and females could benefit from a particular passage. Some felt I only spoke for males. They did not see how my writings were for everyone. All could benefit.

As humanity develops in today's world, there is still that inequality, the demarcations between male and female. The blending of the two Principals still needs to happen in most of humanity. Many times the world seems to be a man's world, as I have heard many people exclaim. It is perceived like that because the masculine principal still dominates in the world. You see, as long as there is duality in your world, humanity will be one or the other principal. It is rare to find people in balance with those two Principals, no matter what gender. (*Sananda addresses these Principals in BOOK TWO*). It usually is because souls are still learning their lessons. They want to experience what it is that drives men or women to react as they do. In the Oriental mind, the male principal is quite dominant. It will be centuries yet before there is equality in this ethnic group.

Another phenomenon is that in certain cultures, the male dominance must be protected. A male must act like a man in all matters. The male must never show weakness or his gentler side while out in his world. It is up to the women he may surround himself with to keep that myth alive.

I believe in your Western culture—it was taught in your pioneer days—that men could not show tears. No emotions that could be described as a weakness were allowed. Your movies would emphasize this fact by showing the young male actor being instructed not to show his tears even though he may be standing near his mother's grave. This act of not showing emotion has done a great deal of emotional harm.

The youngster grew up and did not allow himself to have strong feelings. Many times, he was a cauldron of steaming anger. It was through his brawling in bars, his killing of others, that he was able to release the heavy emotions that were pent up for so long. That is where wife and child beatings came into play—the release of anger. Hence, in the Oriental body, true emotions also were not allowed to surface. Men had concubines. These they could treat in any manner they wished. If they came in an angry mood to their kept woman, she was slapped around, while the wife was spared.

Therefore, dear Readers, here I am once again. I have visited your world in various forms. I have even been Caucasian and Black. However, I seem best suited to the Oriental body. It is that body I understand the best. Now I no longer have bodies. Djwhal Khul was my last body. If you know the many books he wrote as the Tibetan, you know me. I have come to you readers so that you too might know there are aspects of you that have ascended after having excelled at whatever you had chosen. **All souls have many aspects of themselves that they do not know**. Souls in bodies do not know of their greatness. However, Readers, it is time. It is time to reclaim who you are in the fullest degree. You will be greatly surprised at the depth of you, at your lineage. It is impressive; I can assure you. It has been my pleasure to visit you. I AM Confucius.

DO YOUR POSSESSIONS POSSESS YOU?—Jesus

I AM Jesus. What do you have in life that no longer serves you? What are you hanging onto, Readers? We have come many times in these books to tell you about past histories on different subjects. We then are speaking of the past. When we say *past,* it means just that. It has passed. Whatever was happening that day, year, or century has passed. When you yourself pass to the other side, you will find that your whole life is in the past. It is no more. What is amazing is you will soon forget you even had it! That is why one's life-review is immediate; otherwise, one would just forget all about that life. People, when alive, do not remember the Heavenlies. Souls in other dimensions do not remember their life on Earth. One could say there are veils on both sides of the dimensions. Of course, those souls of higher frequencies are able to read their records at will and retain everything they so wish. Those of the lesser frequencies just enjoy where they are and make little effort to gain more awareness during that time.

When the time comes for souls to incarnate again, the souls go to the various halls for instruction, counseling, and teachings. They spend a great deal of time with those who are in spirit and of their soul group. They review their plans for a new life, designate who will play what role, who they will meet, and so forth. They are shown the material possessions they will have and their economical stratum. They are shown what educational level for which they are to strive. They are shown, also, what illnesses and weak dispositions of their body they will have to adjust. When all is in readiness, they venture forth as eager souls with great expectations and intentions. Therefore, they begin an Earth-life once again. Many souls re-incarnate several hundreds of times. It is not always because they have not broken the re-birth wheel, but because they come in order to be of service once again. Therefore, when you hear of people who have had two hundred, to four hundred, to a thousand lifetimes, do not jump to judgment that they are a *slow learner*. There are masters that have work to do and come to Earth repeatedly to be of service.

Consequently, say you are a soul in an Earth-body and of moderate income. You have acquired certain possessions over the many years that you have lived. Are you still as attached to your possessions as you were, say ten years ago? Alternatively, do you just keep adding on to what you have? Do you want to liberate some of your space? On the other hand, is it becoming more cluttered?

There is a phenomenon that has one acquiring objects for comfort, for utility, for beauty, for satisfaction, for impression, and for greed. Each of these categories draws a certain energy to it—a sameness. As you read over that list, are there areas of which you, Reader, could now let go? Do you really need more books of all kinds? Do you really need more crystal goblets, silver place settings, candelabras, and all the possessions one uses in order to set a beautiful table? Some people buy knick-knacks or collector-items of teacups and spoons. All of these objects fall into the category of possessions. **Do your possessions possess you?** How many times have you entered a home and found the tables are covered in little objects—vases, picture-frames, and candles. The walls too may have groupings of pictures, and mirrors. In some homes, it is aesthetic. In other homes, it is clutter.

You might be wondering by now where this chapter is leading. I have talked about *re-incarnation, the veils, and possessions*. The point I am making is that since the soul almost immediately forgets its life once its body dies, why does the person acquire so many objects during that lifetime? You see, Readers, **a soul in embodiment is seeking what it cannot remember!** It has a sense of *peace* and *tranquility*. It has a sense of *beauty*. Consequently, if it surrounds itself with what it **thinks** will bring it these states of being, it will feel more at home in its body.

However, as you know, bodies do not carry logic. A body has little sense of balance with one's possessions. If the personality wants more of something, it buys more. Therefore, before one knows it, one is surrounded by too much, or perhaps by too little. There is no balance. Many times, you will hear the elderly exclaim they do not want any more *stuff.* They gladly embrace downsizing. They move to smaller homes and have garage sales in order to pass on their possessions to someone else. The problem arises when people are unable to let go. They may even rent small storage facilities in order to retain the overflow of their possessions. They may have moved to smaller quarters, but their possessions are still with them—just in a different location!

Can you imagine what the astral planes would look like by now if a soul were able to bring one armload of its possessions through the tunnel? God's beautiful area He has prepared for souls would become similar to a gigantic antique warehouse. Interestingly enough, a soul can manifest any object it wishes just by intention of thought. It does not **have** to bring any possession with it, even if it were possible.

In the many years since your Biblical times, people seemed to practice their old ways of acquiring possessions. There were those who had more than enough material objects and those who just barely had a table and chair. They were satisfied with so little. In those austere times for some and opulent times for others, people were not aware they needed to share. They were generous at times among their own family, but rarely did they attempt to share with the less fortunate. Even though the people would worship God, they were unable to implement the teachings outside of their own environment.

Reader, do you not see how this lack of sharing became karma that was passed on down through the ages—hence it became part of the *historical karma*. Nothing is more pleasing to the Father than when people or countries share. You have been told that God experiences humanity through His people. Every time you think and/or do something, He knows this and experiences the many trials and successes of humankind. Therefore, the lack of sharing that became your historical karma greatly troubles Him. He noted those of you with possessions in abundance who just rolled the overflow into rental lockers, instead of driving a load of it to say, Goodwill.

We are aware also that common sense and practicability need to be incorporated here. However, we say to you to take those possessions that no longer serve you and give them away. Maybe your collection of stuffed animals could bring joy to children to whom many spiritual organizations have the ability to distribute your donations. When a person has so much, stop and think what you can get rid of—pass on to those that would enjoy it. **You are passing on what once brought you pleasure and now can bring pleasure to others.**

Consequently, the point I wish to impart with you is whether your possessions still serve a purpose. Is it time to let some of them go? On the other hand, **do your possessions possess you? That is worth pondering!**

WAKE UP AMERICA—Sananda

I AM Sananda. In the past few months, there has been an increase in killings in your world. The wars continue unabated. It is as though the darker part of souls has taken over. It used to be that murders, car bombs, and so forth, were so rare people could not believe it when the violence happened. Nowadays, it seems to be the norm—so much murder these days.

People wonder when it will end. How will it end? What will bring the ending to these atrocities? What has happened when people take other's sacred books, their Bibles and desecrate them? Where has the respect for other's beliefs gone? In other words, what has gone awry? Ah, Readers, we too wonder at the meanness of little people. We shake our heads in wonderment at the stupidity and uncaring acts of others.

We have not spoken out on these atrocious acts until now—the acts where a young woman degrades a prisoner, where military people think up ideas of degradation. It is just astounding to us the level that humanity has sunk. There are so many good people in the world diligently striving to be of service in the Father's work. There are tremendous Beings adjusting energies, watching over the Earth, and working very hard. Then there is the lower rung of humanity, with little awareness or caring. It is sad to see.

We in the Spiritual Realms see your world as it is in all of its cruel reality. There will come a time when humanity will pay dearly for its lack of consciousness and its cruel acts to its fellow neighbors, whether the people are in Palestine, Israel, Iraq, or in America. All people are your neighbors in the sense that Jesus said in those Biblical days *to love thy neighbor*. Regrettably, people who will buy this third book are not of the less aware kind. They are striving for Christ Consciousness. Therefore, we in the Spiritual Hierarchy have a real dilemma on our hands. As you know, neither God nor we can step in and alter the circumstances for humankind. Any change must come from your free will and heart. All we can do is wait and watch.

Now I know this short discourse is a *downer* for you Readers, but I wanted you to know we do know what is transpiring on Earth. We see the repercussions before you do. We knew that when your government made the decision to declare war on Iraq that that would release the darker energies long before liberating any of the people of Light. It is in that category where one turns over a large rock and finds any matter of creatures, large or small, snake or grasshopper, ant or ladybug. All existed in their hidden world.

Nevertheless, once the rock was overturned, the act released everything that was hidden from view. These are metaphors, as you know, but the point I am making is America's attack brought out and unleashed, the ugly energies that lay dormant in people no matter on whose side they were. People made judgment calls, were ill advised, and took action. When you think of it, many of the service people are too young for much wisdom and their superiors are into too much power. Therefore, the dark forces have been unleashed and have grown in strength.

When your government thought it would liberate Iraq, it did major damage to your country. It will take another administration in order to curb the rising tide of destruction for America. When the excess of a hurricane howls, when houses go flying in tornadoes, when carjacking, identity theft, murders, drive-by shooting all escalate, you will be watching the sinking of America. It is as if she is in quicksand with no way up. That is how powerful negative thought-forms can be. That is the by-product of an unnecessary war. When a motive for war is for another country's resource, then the very foundation is warped. There is no way this war can be called *bringing democracy to Iraq*. Anything that is not predicated on Truth will be warped and not have a successful ending. That war will continue for as long as Mother Earth will allow it. By that, we mean, only natural disasters will end that greedy decision by a group of darker energies. It makes no difference if they profess their belief in God and the Bible. We do not look at what comes out their mouths, but only at their actions. *Actions speak louder than words.* That statement is a truism here.

It has come to our attention that people are either complacent over their government's actions, or they have lost their voice. **Congress is the people's voice**. Many times when an elected official gains office, he or she may talk a lot about one's constituency, but then the person gets more and more into personal power and loses track as to who voted him or her into office. We believe what is happening is that Congress too is polarized. As the Earth is polarized into Light or dark, so is Congress. The Republicans join with the president. The Democrats try in every way possible to defeat his purposes. Moreover, rightly so, because so many of the edicts that stem from the Oval Office are not of Truth, but power. President Bush calls it his bank account. Since he had the majority of the popular vote, he feels that regarding any of his ideas, the public also will want the same thing.

However, as the poll numbers show, the president is losing his popularity. His mistakes in judgment are many. He nominates people around him to the various offices, but he chooses only people he knows will agree with him. He says he is the people's president, but he does not walk his talk. He is finding it more and more difficult to get his ideas accepted. He has been pushing the change in Social Security, and indeed, some of it does need restating and redefining. However, the proposal he has presented is full of potentially disastrous financial effects for people. It is doubtful if anything of merit will come of the president's Social Security ideas—his ideals.

People of America, you have entered a period in time where much that was good will dim and much that was dark will become darker. Maitreya, that great Lord who holds the Office of the Christ, has stated in BOOK ONE that restitution needs to come to America. There is always chaos before the dawn of peace breaks through. What most people do not realize is that America must reach for God once again. **America was founded with God's Grace. Throughout the centuries, humanity has eroded that**. Power and greed have taken over the hearts of so many of the people. Your Congress has a few strong Lights—those who still carry the Light, but on the whole the dark energies are taking over. Congress makes many compromises—*we will vote for what you want if you will give us what we want*. There is little balance, only political games of intrigue.

Most Congressmen or women are too wrapped up in the power of their office. If you are a junior member, you must adhere to your elders and play their game. That will earn you in time the right to do likewise to any newcomers. Few listen to the juniors. No elder entertains the thought he or she could be wrong. There is little balance of power, therefore.

Dear Readers, you are living in grave and dire times. Do keep aware of your checks and balances—**your** spiritual bank account. It is easier now than ever to be led astray. Keep your focus on who you are, not in body, but in soul! Walk in your Light with caring for your neighbor. Be careful about becoming too wrapped up in the news media. Know they too have their guidelines. Keep touching your Truth and walk with God at your side.

I have stated clearly what this government has done—the harm to humanity and the lying cover-ups and justifiers. **Nothing can bring restitution to your government, oh America, but a change in administration and policy**. The damage is irreparable. Pray hard and steadfastly, America. The Captain of **your** ship is driving you onto the rocks!

SEX—Jesus

I AM Jesus. Hello once again, Readers, you might be wondering when we are going to run out of ideas for lectures; but, dear people, there are still so many subjects on which we could discourse. Therefore, I have chosen a subject that Readers love to read about but dare not to speak about to the Son of God! Dear Readers, we are going to speak of ***sex.*** This Author had to take a breath when she heard that topic! However, there are so many misconceptions about *sex*. We thought it was about time to bring up the subject.

When God created you, the soul, He incorporated different energies into the soul. When He made the body, He again incorporated different energies. We have already spoken about the masculine and feminine Principals in BOOK TWO. Now let us carry that a few steps further and speak of *sex*. Many of you might think that sex only occurs with bodies on Earth. Well, here is the shocker for some of you**. Souls have sex also in the upper dimensions**. Many of you might remember the times you have had what one may call a satisfactory, sexual release. Others have rarely experienced that while in a body, perhaps.

In the Heavenlies, there are no bodies, of course. There are only souls, or spirits, as you might say. Now here is a curious query. Do you think that the sexual urge only is possible with a body? Do you think that souls come to Earth for that only is where they can have sex? Where do you think sex stems from? Since the Father gave sex organs to the body, sex urges for the species to pro-create, why would souls in spirit-form be no different? You have that saying *as above, so below*. Therefore, do you not think that sex in the Heavenlies was instigated long before there were bodies, and long before there was Planet Earth?

All right, I hope I have sparked your imaginations by now, for **we in the Heavenlies are still sexual!** Now that certainly is a loaded statement. Either many Readers will slam this book shut, or it may be well dog-eared before this chapter is completed. I do hope you are enjoying my humor, for it is always fun to come forward and shock people out of their complacent belief systems.

You realize that while I am presenting this topic in a humorous fashion, I am serious, as I give you these Truths. The Father created what you term *sex* for various reasons. Catholics, especially of long ago times, tried to curb the sex impulses in humankind. They preached abstinence. Sex was for procreation only, never for pleasure and joy—but certainly not promiscuously. In that, they are correct—sex is never to be promiscuous, for it will keep one's consciousness in the lower centers.

However, when no contraceptives were or are allowed of any kind, that decreed that sex was only for procreation. That is a fallacy that has been passed on down through the centuries. **God did not restrict bodies in that way**. **Pure, clean sex is a wonderful gift that God has given everyone**. Do you not think that having sex until it reaches the orgasmic state is not a release of energy? Why would He give bodies this act if it were not to be used to its fullest intent? Bodies have the ability to release pent-up gases for example. Even your tiny babies are tapped gently on their backs until they give forth a burp, much to the delight of their mothers and which affords many a giggle for their siblings. Therefore, when God created bodies, every orifice had a purpose. Every act has a purpose. Hence, when I say to you that sex releases pent-up energies, that is one of its purposes, other than just procreation.

The restrictions that your spiritual leaders have placed on you concerning your sexual behaviors have stifled you and caused guilt for many a young person. Of course, I am speaking of natural acts and not about rapes, incest, and sex-acts with animals. I believe you understand now what I am telling you**. There ought to be no guilt associated with clean sex, whether for release of pent-up energy or pleasure. None!** This is always a difficult subject for clergy to address, for they feel they must adhere to what their particular creed dictates, which is usually that sex is only for pro-creation. I hope I have alleviated your concerns by now. God gave bodies this ability for sex in the deepest sense of the word.

However, as you know by now, we are speaking of second chakra energies in bodies. This energy center can make or break you. What I mean by that is the soul must connect this center with the heart center so that there can be correctness within the energies. That connection will ensure that sex is also from the heart and not just from lust. It also helps the soul not to become entrapped in that lower energy center. Everyone uses the second chakra, sexual energy for creativity. You not only create your babies from this energy, but you use this energy in creating your homes, your employment—anything that you create, you use second chakra energy. Therefore, you can see how there can be an energy build-up that needs release every so often.

Now let us address *sex* in the Heavenlies. If human bodies come together and join in the sexual union, souls also come together and join energies. However, their final climax is like a sunburst of energies flowing through them. There is not the dynamic where one partner withholds from the other, so only one reaches a satisfactory finish. With souls, the explosion is simultaneous and the joy is more than you will ever experience in a body. For those Readers who have had what they thought was a true love, pleasure, and joy release, multiply that a hundred fold and you may have a wee concept of what true sex is in the Heavenlies.

Where is sex appropriate? In your Earth plane, there is a time and place for everything. Couples make love in their bedrooms. In ancient times, those were the only places that were acceptable. Nowadays, couples have sex wherever they believe there is some privacy. I will not go into the various places people have sex. Your news media and television portray these phenomena explicitly. Therefore, let us speak of when it is appropriate in Heaven.

Bear in mind that, while sex can be spontaneous for couples, there still is the correct time and place. I need not tell you that for your Earth lives. There are times when the joining of souls is not correct in the Heavenlies either. To give you an example, many times when a master has new students who have not been fully trained yet, the student with love in its heart throws him/herself into the arms of its teacher, not realizing the impact. The student forgets protocol and decorum. He or she is just so thrilled to see the master. As on Earth, there is a difference between warm bear hugs of joy. Conversely, a warm embrace could carry an invitation with it. I think souls forget that there is protocol, a certain standard one adheres to whether on Earth or in the Heavenlies.

Just as one would not greet an Earthly teacher on a sexual level, a soul ought not to greet its Heavenly Teacher in a sexual embrace.

It may surprise you to know little is different between the two worlds when one addresses what action is correct between students and teachers, whether on Earth or in the Heavenlies. That is just the structure God has created.

One might wonder that if one were at a high enough level to meet one's teacher, why a soul would not know this protocol. I can only say this dynamic between students and teachers, the correctness of it, is no different in our world versus Earth. Some souls are just more spontaneous than others are. After you have let this concept sink in, you may be wondering as to when it is appropriate for souls of higher dimensions to have sex. In our dimensions, we too have private areas. You may not call them *bedrooms* exactly, but there are areas that are ours—our sanctuary. It is a place of our creation. Remember, we can create instantly any environment we wish.

Sometimes we create a place in a deep forest with waterfalls. The trees are real and afford cool shade. The sound of water is soothing. We create a setting for our union. At times our unions can be more spontaneous, but only when alone. **A soul's union is considered a sacred act**. It is the coming together of two souls in their fullness of colors and energies. Human eyes could see no form and at times, there is no form, just a joining, and a merging of energies. At other times, we may come together in our cosmic, etheric forms. Nevertheless, keep in mind, it is not the form that makes the difference, but the energies.

On the astral planes, souls that have recently passed over retain their astral forms. That is how they see each other. They will have sex in **replays** of their sexual experiences while on Earth. It is all they know. As they advance in consciousness, and they drop their astral bodies, they will begin experiencing true sex—how it is supposed to be.

Now I pose a question to you Readers. Why do you think the sexual union is important—is as important in our worlds as it seems to be in yours? Why did the Father put such emphasis on the union of two bodies or souls? Dear ones, it is so you would remember Him and the Divine Mother—Father-Mother God. As we have said, all is energy. When two of anything come together, there is a union. Fire and steel make molten metal that is then shaped into any form you wish. Man's seed comes into a woman's egg. This union brings forth a child. You can think of all manner of unions. Artists join colors to produce another color. This merging of energies is the way everything is created. Some energies when they come together cause massive explosions, whether one is speaking of weapons of mass destruction, or the explosion of matter that brings forth star systems. The union of energies, no matter what kind of energy, brings an explosion, a release. This can be when two bodies come together to an orgasmic climax. This can be when two souls come together in a brilliant sunburst of energies. It is electrical in nature. It is the grand finale of life at both ends of the spectrum—body and soul. Nothing is finer than that. The experience is beyond describing.

God gave us a wee taste of Him in these explosive acts. Each time we come together in a union, we are to remember God. As He experiences His creations through us, we experience Him in the ultimate act of creating! Grant you, what you on Earth experience is miniscule compared to what really is—this union involved is a sacred act. He has given us a tremendous gift, for He has shown us and allowed us to experience Him and the Divine Mother in a most intimate way.

PROPHETS—Jesus

I AM Jesus. Readers, in the past, many great prophets roamed the Earth. They are well chronicled in your sacred books. However, there were also prophets that were not recorded. They since have gone on to other heights. The point I wish to make was there were many more people in those distant times who prophesized. They were able to hear God's thoughts as clearly as this Author is hearing mine. This phenomenon of communing with God telepathically has continued to this day.

Many of your Evangelists hear God or me, Jesus, or talk to angels. The modern day prophets hear much more than they dare to speak. They monitor themselves quite closely. However, the thread that these modern prophets have that weaves them together is they can and do speak with God. Some actually hear a voice, but most just hear the words being spoken, as they telepathically receive them.

Prophets have always served a purpose throughout many a millennium. Prophets usually warn people of an approaching doom. However, they also bring glad tidings. Many of your prophets today are referred to either in the religious sense, or in a psychic sense—a soothsayer. Many psychics earn certificates pronouncing them as Reverends. That title bears fewer stigmas, although society still places judgments on the psychic Evangelist.

Therefore, prophets still are plentiful in today's society. Every creed has its own prophet. In fact, there are modern prophets who become caught in their egos. They branch off from traditional churches in order to practice the religion under their own interpretations. We see this happening with the Mormons. All we can say for that blessed sect is to beware, people, when sexual energies are dictating the decrees. The leader sends young boys out onto the streets after they have reached puberty, for fear that they might marry a young virgin that the men too have their eyes on, in order to add to their multiple wives. This is stretching credibility!

To obtain a coveted object or person at the detriment of another is very incorrect. To practice this ego-based decree, no matter how another suffers, is an abomination in the Eyes of God. There is no

Truth here and the leader is leading his flock by **control, fear**, and **sex—never a good combination!** We have written a chapter on *Sex*.

This modern version of polygamy practiced by a fragmented branch of Mormons is an example where some religions have become polarized and need redefining. You are seeing the crumbling of a church structure. The Catholic Church has started its decay by the coming to light of the sexual abuse by priests. Now you are seeing the Mormon Church that will have to step in and redefine its practices.

In Christianity, the many protestant churches hold too strict a control over the people. When churches dictate how one may live one's life according only to their creeds, then there needs to be change. I have stated in the other books that change will come to the many churches. It must, for what has happened is that more and more pastors lay their personal interpretations on the congregation. Each pastor thinks he or she is the one carrying my Teachings correctly.

In the long ago eras, Christianity took many evil twists and turns. Paganism also had its *day in the sun*, as the saying goes. What pastors saw as the faithless was in actuality people at a more heart-felt energy for the planet than the pastors held. People worshipped gods and goddesses, the sun and moon. While they did not **think** there was or **knew** there was a God, they did know there was Mother Earth. They knew in their hearts that there was something greater than they were. Some people thought that greatness resided in animals—the *sacred cow* for instance. No matter how starving the people were, they would not eat the meat of the *sacred cow*.

When the prophets and seers (those psychics of higher vibrations and clarity) and oracles spoke their Truths, people listened and attempted to follow the directives. However, as history has proven, more people viewed prophets as eccentrics. I must admit they were in most cases. These people led extreme lives. Since they were so in tuned with God's Energy, they were hard pressed to keep both feet on the ground. Many were more in Heaven than on Earth. They kept themselves somewhat grounded by walking the land. Your present-day prophets have a most difficult time staying grounded. There are people who work directly with different star systems. You will find that they spend many hours sleeping day and night, for that is when they are gathering their information. They are able to retain this information and bring it into their body in vivid detail. These seers were oracles in past lives. They lived in far-reached places—some lived in caves, or temples perched on mountaintops.

The higher-placed the locations, the higher were the frequencies. Being away from the density of people enabled the oracle to maintain his/her high vibration. This in turn enabled the person to reach for the higher contact of the many gods and goddesses whose energies were indeed real. Ancients may have carried the worshipping of these deities to the extreme. However, for the mentality of society in those times, these deities did serve their purposes. They gave people something in which to believe. They gave them *hope* where many times their lives were quite dark. It may surprise you Readers to know that these gods and goddesses are very much alive to this day. They of course are ascended, such as we are. They are beautiful still to behold and carry exquisite energies. They are relieved they no longer are worshipped, for they never wanted that. They were a forerunner for all of us. (*Lady Jezebel comes to mind. 2011)*

You see, each facet of history plays a part. These ancient gods and goddesses provided people a way—gave them ideals for which to strive. Now of course some of the gods were excessive in their energies—Bacchus, the god of wine and revelry, for one. However, even he served a purpose—a celebration and joy of the grape harvest. The people carried the celebration into drunkenness, not he.

Therefore, Readers the many prophets brought information from God. They still do. However, how many people listen or take it seriously? I am afraid not as many as you might think. As I end this chapter, I would like to leave you this message. How many of you talk to God every day, let alone listen for a reply? Communing with God is having a conversation. **One needs to talk to Him in order to have Him converse with you!** Ponder this.

A TESTING of FAITH—Sananda, Maitreya, Jesus

We are Sananda, Maitreya, and Jesus. We blend our energies this morning in order to bring you a higher vibration that will reside in our words for these books. Just as a light bulb can shine at 100 watts, it can shine at 150 watts, and 200 watts. While our combination is greater than a 200-watt light bulb, we thought this analogy might give you Readers a better perspective of what happens when masters blend their energies.

There has always been that pause for discernment when one person has ideas with which another does not agree. People are hard-pressed to allow others their own ideas. Take an author for example. Authors struggle to be true to their work. They take the added precaution of not reading other authors' writings on the same subject in order not to compromise their own work, unless they are doing research. Authors who channel their material have an added burden to carry, for there are other people who channel on the same subject, but whose work might differ. They differ not only in words—the wordage—but also in energy. What many Readers do not realize is that **many times the energies they are feeling are from the Rays that that author carries**. If one author's soul is on the second Ray of love and wisdom and another author's soul is on the fourth Ray of harmony through conflict, Readers will pick up the Ray energies of the two authors and experience the energies differently.

If the authors are advanced enough so that their monads have drawn closer in order to be the guide of the soul, Readers will pick up that monad's energy in the book. Readers may see geometric designs mixed with a color, if the Reader has developed that clairvoyant gift. The Reader, for example, may confuse the color red they see with sensuality or anger, when actually the Reader is seeing the monad's color from the first Ray of God's Will, Power, and Leadership. The subatomic particles one sees are the sacred geometry formulas. Therefore, what is actually happening? The Reader accurately perceived the first Ray essence plus the sacred geometry that permeated the book. (*This was reported for BOOK ONE from various Readers.*)

Another Reader may feel energy emanating from the book as her hands start to vibrate when first touching the book. The person is feeling the combined blend of energies of the masters. Remember our telling you we are similar to a 200-watt light bulb, but more powerful. Imagine that not only is there this blended Light, but the energies of the Rays in the books. Now if the author is truly advanced, and **if the books have been blessed by God, then the Divine Shekinah, the Holy Spirit, is also part of the books' energies.** By now, you must realize we are speaking of this Author. She has been getting feedback on what various Readers are feeling and seeing in BOOK ONE.

However, in the same vein, she has come to realize that our words we have given her do not always stand side by side with what other authors have written on similar subjects. Now it becomes a *test of faith*. Does she go within and see **her** Truth, or does she give over her seniority of her space to another author just because that person seems more knowledgeable in writing?

This inner struggle for Truth becomes an ever-increasing phenomenon with advancement in consciousness. One would think the higher one demonstrates his or her expertise, the more certain the person would become of his or her own Truth. However, dear Readers, the opposite seems to be the norm. Now do keep in mind we are not speaking about the *ego* here. We are speaking of people who are high achievers and have their egos under control. We are speaking of individuals who may carry that seed of doubt of their own Truth versus another's. We are speaking of people who have **chosen** to return to Earth as a mission for the Father. These people have broken the karmic wheel of birth-death-rebirth. They now have a choice whether to come back to Earth or go on to other planets, as we have said. Hence, each time one of these great souls makes the choice to return to Earth, there is always a mission from the Father involved. Of course, the soul can choose to do other things beyond its mission also. That is why they look to be and are such high achievers. It is because they are not only doing the Father's works, but their own side trips, so to speak, as well.

Consequently, you have some great souls who accomplish much in their life. However, keep in mind they come in with the veils in place also. They come in with initiation after initiation they must replay and integrate. Moreover, they will **still** have self-doubts. That is why God keeps testing their faith in whatever way He can**. The higher these great Beings achieve, the faster the tests come**. It gets so the person feels the testing must be finished. *Surely, there is nothing left to test!* Then unexpectedly, someone will attack the person's Truth in some way—maybe just having channeled something that differs from what the person had been given. So on it goes.

Each time there seems to be a discrepancy, either in what you Readers are reading, have heard, and so forth, you too need to pause and reflect and discern where the Truth lies. What one person sees as light blue, another may see as aquamarine. Here is the puzzler. Both hold Truth. We have stated to this Author that we have not come to her to bring false information. **We do not carry lie energy, for that kind of energy is lower and denser. It has no love-frequency in it. Consequently, it is impossible for us to carry that vibration. Hence, when we speak to this Author, it is with Truth.**

Those of you who can see and feel energies and sacred geometry have seen the Truth and have felt the Breeze of the Shekinah. There is no greater validation than that. These books carry the potency of our God's Light. May you receive these energies to their fullest intentions, for there is healing, peace, love, and Light in each word. We will now close this discourse. We ask the editor and Author to be extra sensitive to deleting any of these sentences, so as not to lessen the impact. We step back now as the Trio.

(*Other authors have channeled Biblical history that differs from what was given to me. I believe the Masters are referring to this. The color red, the sacred geometry, the hand vibrations and tingling, the gentle Breeze of the Shekinah was reported to me by separate Readers of BOOK ONE.)*

SIMON SAYS—Jesus

I AM Jesus. I would like this morning to speak on a subject people think about, but then pay little to no thought afterwards. In years past, most people could neither read nor write. They had to learn by oral notations. Anything that came through someone else could be suspect, for people would embellish a particular news report. They would put their own projections and interpretations to it. It reminds me of your childhood game of *Simon says* . . . A person whispered what Simon allegedly had said. By the time the last person had received the saying, it would be quite garbled from the original much to the hilarious shouts of glee from the participants. A short sentence was now a caricature of its original. Therefore, Readers you can see how much faith I have in oral history. Now to give due respect where respect is earned, some of the scribes were very meticulous and did make the reports as verbatim as they could.

However, even those writings became polluted, for the church fathers would change a word here and there, if they did not like the sound of a certain passage. Many times their own fears would rise to the surface, so that changes were made in order to alleviate not only their fear of the material, but fear for the people.

The Spanish Inquisition was a dark time in history. The Inquisitors had become so righteous in thinking their interpretation of The Word was the only correct one. They sentenced many a person to death just because the person refused to recant what he or she believed. Therefore, most religions went through periods of adjustment. Hence, the many branches of religions were born. As a particular leader received a certain revelation, he would start a new sect. There were always available followers. As people themselves became disillusioned, they would follow a new leader with new ideas and interpretations.

Now their leaders usually had received new revelations. Many received true visions. The leaders were quite correct in following their purpose. However, since all were striving for consciousness, even the leaders of new sects did not always get it all right. It was *Simon says* . . . all over again. However, they followed their hearts, so that a different take on Christianity occurred, a new creed was developed, and a new sect was born. **History is, fortunately, a great lie-breaker, for it is through history that Truth becomes known**—the light of dawn of a new era. What was put out as Truth in the past was no longer true.

In my life as Jesus, or more accurately, Yeshua, I traveled extensively into countries where many in modern times may have never been—what you call Great Britain, Ireland, Scotland, France, the Himalayas, India, and Egypt, plus the smaller countries closer to home. At all of those foreign places, I studied great mysteries taught in what you would call the *Mystery Schools*. I went through extreme initiations of which most of humanity has little concept or knowledge. All of the many initiations were for the purpose of the Ultimate Experience—the Crucifixion, Resurrection, and Ascension. It was during those times in foreign lands studying with masters of the highest abilities that enabled me to conquer over death. I was able to control my vital signs until only a whisper of life force was left in the body. This ability enabled me to withstand the hours on the cross. If one is in a deep altered state, one can lie on a bed of nails, such as Indian yogis can. They are able to enter this altered state quickly, deeply, and stay in that state for as long as they wish.

Such was my training—I too could withstand nails and thorns, and even a spear thrust, with but barely a sigh. I simply felt little to none of what was excruciating pain for my brother sufferers on crosses of their own on either side of me. Many Evangelists pontificate on my suffering. Dear Readers, **I did not suffer!** My body did not suffer.

There were so many unseen angels ready to rush in to help me if I had asked. However, I was what one might say *oblivious to any pain*. On the other hand, there is always some sensation, for you are speaking of a body. For example, many people of New Age Thought have been able to walk across burning coals while in an altered state and have only the sensation of walking on warm popcorn. They have been able to maintain their altered state so that the coals did not burn them. I was in an even deeper state on the cross.

I have spoken of the Winged Pharaohs, those initiates who were able to keep their body alive in the sarcophagus, while they on a soul level took wing and left their body for three days. During that time, someone could put pins or nails into the body and it would not react. However, it is upon the soul's return that much work has to occur—when the resurrection must occur in order for the body to keep on living.

All of this has been written about many times before in your esoteric books. However, there is always a new reader where it might be news to him or her. Suffice to know, and the point I really wish to convey to you, is that resurrection is a very true phenomenon. It was not just for me in my era, but to this day. It is for everyone. The great yogis in India resurrect their bodies each time they return from a deep altered state. People of today are resurrecting their body more than they realize. As cells replenish themselves, as one's DNA strands increase to twelve and even more, as new chakras are added, all of these body changes are in the category of *resurrection.*

Therefore, when Simon says Jesus did not suffer on the cross, receive this teaching. When Simon says Jesus was resurrected, receive this information clearly. When Simon says you, Reader, can do what Jesus did in initiations, believe this. When Simon says you too can be a Wayshower and walk in Jesus' sandals, receive this. Bring these Teachings into your body as Truth. Above all else, when Simon says you are *Love, Light,* and *Truth*, believe that with all of your heart and soul.

I AM the fictitious Simon, and the much alive Jesus.

A MESSAGE for TODAY—Sananda

I AM Sananda. In days of lore, way before man and creatures roamed the Earth, there was nothing but the firmament, the fauna and flora, and energies swirling around. These energies were creating much of the foundation for the planet. There were Beings of extraordinary Light, creativity and beauty creating what humankind now takes for granted—your beautiful planet.

The co-creators of this planet Earth had a synchronized plan. They were architects of the highest and true sense. They did not just cause an explosion of energies and then wait for the dust to settle. They knew at each moment what was required and how to attain this. The Bible speaks often of the co-creators, but few people realize the reference is to the Angelic and Elemental Kingdoms. Probably the angel most people know, besides Archangel Michael, is the Archangel Metatron. He holds the atomic structure of the planet in his Light. You Readers have heard of sacred geometry—meaning geometric designs, matrices, circles, triangles, and cubes, all coalescing and creating structure wherever the intent is made manifest. *Metatron*—his name alone conveys these geometric designs and **electrons**.

What many Readers may not know is that most of us started as angels. As our souls developed, some of us stayed with Archangel Metatron, studied, and learned from him. He taught us how to use God's Light that is available to all of us. He taught us how to utilize the Light and how to create using intention, Light and sacred geometry. One could say we became apprentices to Metatron, to put it simply. Of course, we are speaking of millions of years. We have told you before what a lengthy process is evolution. While we stayed in Metatron's sphere of Light, we learned and evolved until it became time for us *caterpillars* to become *butterflies*. This we did. Souls then had choices. They could go to Enoch's sphere and spend eons of time studying with Enoch. They could go to Melchizedek and study with him or both ad infinitum. Souls were evermore evolving, but they evolved by learning how to manipulate energies, and as they absorbed more of God's Light, the souls grew in consciousness.

In today's world, people still join the Order of Melchizedek in order to learn the spiritual mysteries he taught. However, any Melchizedek School of today is a greatly watered-down version of the original. It may be of interest for you Readers to know that most everyone who is guided to read these books has historical karma—positive karma—having been a student, an aspirant of those exquisite Beings—Metatron, Melchizedek, and Enoch. It is also interesting to note that since you started as angels—when God thought you into existence—you evolved and then went on to different planets. Keep in mind you were pure energy and Light. You were diaphanous and one could see straight through you, although you still had a form. You were not just a blob, but your form was more like an elongated sphere—some were even more rounded than others. Your size did not necessarily depict your power and strength, however.

You could be the size of a French beauty spot worn by women in order to add extra glamour to them centuries ago. However, the tiny dots I am referring to are Beings who carry tremendous energy and intelligence. They can take form as they wish or maintain their miniscule size. People often wonder when they first turn off the lights at night and see pinpoints of Light moving hither and yon. These are particles of energy and most have a living consciousness to the nth degree.

What humanity needs to come to realize is that energy exists in everything. Just because a tree has been cut down, the wood is used for a cabin, and then to burn fires, the energy is still in the wood. It may be in a transmuted form, but the wooden stool still is energy. Therefore, if humanity can remember this, then it would not seem too incredulous to view an orb in the sky as a point of energy, whether a star or planet.

Let us take that a step further and say the light in the sky or any area you are looking at is a point of energy-consciousness. If there is Light, there is energy. If there is energy, there is consciousness. If there is consciousness, there is life. If there is life, there is connectedness to the One. If there is connectedness as I have just stated, then there is God in every pinpoint of energy-consciousness. Now the point of this list of ***if(s)*** was to advance the knowledge to you, if you had not known before, that we truly are all One and connected. It is impossible to be otherwise.

Centuries ago, religious leaders had so many debates over whose interpretations were correct. The Jews debated their Teachings in the Torah. The Catholics debated over Jesus' Teachings, leaving out much pertinent material, either because they did not understand it, or because it seemed too threatening to them. After all, they were not about to lose their ironclad control of the people by revealing Jesus' Teachings on the many initiations he and Mary Magdalene had received from the various mystery schools at which they studied. The Christians also censored greatly their Master's Teachings. Saint Paul attempted to widen the interpretation of the Teachings, but even he did not have all the information that was taught to the others long before Saint Paul literally saw the Light. (*He was the Chohan Hilarion.)*

It is not to say that those men like Saint Paul were not appreciated for their great writings, for they were. Again, their information was limited. When Jesus came to teach and lead a small group of humankind into the Light of higher consciousness, even he did not fully know the way Christians would respond. He knew that his own disciples struggled. Therefore, he also knew that other people in the world away from him most likely would not get what he was teaching either. If one said to you, *I AM the Light of the World*, would you fully understand his meaning? If you cannot truly say you know, then you can imagine how much more difficult for people with denser energies back in those far off times. People just did not get it.

Actually, people are tripped up by the simplicity of the statement. I had stated we are all energy, interconnected and connected to God. **If He is the Light of the World, are you not also the Light of the World?** He is Light. You are Light, for you are energy. Also, note he did not say he was **in** the world, but **of** the world. Since you are pure energy and Light also, you are connected to and therefore, a part of God. For one to be **in** the world, your awareness and energies are denser, and it becomes more difficult to keep your conscious connection with God.

Therefore, what Jesus was telling people was his Light was not **of** that denser quality that happens when people are in their lower centers and just surviving **in** the world. He often called to people to *follow me!* He was asking the people to note the examples he was giving them and to be a Wayshower that he was. *Follow my example*, he was saying.

In modern times, we can use many of the same phrases or messages that Jesus gave forth. Since you are Light energies, you too, Readers can say, I *AM the Light of the World.* You too can say *I AM **of** the World*, not in the world. As I have suggested, those in the world are in their base emotions. They are lying, cheating, and stealing what they covet. It makes no difference if they are a street-wise gang member or a CEO doing white-collar crime of cheating the investors. All of those people are examples of being in the world. Just as souls have what is known as the *dark side of the soul*, the world has its dark side—those **in** the world. Conversely, you of Light are not in the world but of it.

Someday the planet herself will regain her recorded purity, but even then, there will be the pluralities. Humanity makes this difference. As long as there is duality and free will, even during the time of the thousand years of peace, there will still be skirmishes between peoples. Perhaps thinking of children squabbling in a sandbox may be easier for Readers to grasp what I am telling you.

I will pose a question: How many of you siblings fight among yourselves? Here is another question. How many married couples have a good screaming match? I can carry this further into the workplace and ask when you had the last heated disagreement with your co-workers or boss? You see, it is human nature to squabble. It is a country's nature not to trust its neighbors fully and feels its borders must be protected. Consequently, Readers, there will not be total peace on Earth for many centuries. The only way that could happen is when each person has raised his or her vibrations and consciousness and has made advancement in the Light Quotient and Points of Evolution (PoE)—initiation levels.

Therefore, Readers I have imparted to you that you are Light. You are energy and you stem from God. It is **you** that has felt you were separated from Him. It has come to our attention that there are people of today who still believe one need fear God. We say ***never.*** God does not judge you. Therefore, He does not punish you for your transgressions. It is again *cause and effect* with you judging yourself and you bringing restitution to yourself. Remember, dear Readers, your historical karma runs deep. While you may no longer have recollection of your past misdeeds, it is all written on your records. Jesus did forgive you your transgressions. However, you still will have to bring into balance, make restitution for your misdeeds. It is not God punishing you. It is simply you living the *Law of Cause and Effect*. That is God's Law. That is God's Commandment. However, you only have yourself to fear, if you wish to keep that concept. We would rather you fear nothing and live your life in God's Grace. You will find then you will fear nothing, not even yourself

We bring closure to this chapter by saying; *you of the Light are **of** the world. You in your dark polarity are **in** the world.* Reach for your Light. Be a Wayshower, and then you too can say, *follow me!*

(*I questioned the Lord's version of the words **of** and **in** the world, for the Bible reverses this. He wanted his explanatory remarks to stand as is.)*

GARDEN of EDEN—Sananda

I AM Sananda. Many lifetimes ago, I walked your Earth, not as Jesus, but in another form. This was in those ancient times when the Earth was still forming. I wanted to know how man could maintain himself—how he would survive. This period was before Lemuria. Humanity thinks that Jesus born of Mary had not lived before. People who are more aware know I had thirty-three lifetimes in which I experienced Earth and learned what I needed to know in order to have the culmination of all my Earth lives come forward in that last glorious life that you have come to realize was Jesus and the crucifixion.

Therefore, in the beginning of my thirty-three lives on Earth, **I came onto the planet as Adam**. The Bible-scribes have maligned me by writing how I sinned when I took the apple from Eve, and how Eve sinned by giving me the apple—the forbidden fruit from the Tree of Knowledge. However, whenever there is a myth established of such disproportion, know that there will be half-truths mixed in with Truths. God did make me after His Own Image. He projected me onto the Earth. **I was a manifestation of the Divine Blueprint of man.** It was God's intent to create a likeness of Him on Earth. He wanted Sons just as any parent does. At the same time the Divine Mother, the Feminine Aspect of God, wanted a likeness of Her. Therefore, They created a woman. Now in order for humans to be able to distinguish between the two forms, my Heavenly Parents gave the woman breasts and mammary ducks so that her body would make the nourishment that could feed the couple's children.

The Bible says that God took a rib from Adam, in order to form Eve, which was metaphoric in nature. Since God and the Divine Mother are one—Father-Mother God—They together created Adam and Eve. Adam's rib represented the fact that Adam and Eve came from the one God—Father-Mother God. Adam and Eve were One, just as Father-Mother God is one Person.

Therefore, we have Adam and Eve, in flesh and blood, manifested and materialized as the **externalization** of our Heavenly Father-Mother. The rib taken from Adam was the clue that Eve then was the Divine Mother Aspect. Now here is another thought. Since Adam represented the male Aspect of God, and Eve represented the female Aspect of God—or we could say the masculine and feminine Principals of Father-Mother God—Adam and Eve then epitomized God—complete in their wholeness.

The Bible goes on to say that a serpent urged Eve to eat the fruit—the forbidden fruit—and to give Adam some. Let us pause here. Again these are metaphors for what future humanity would be learning. Every child is born naked. It certainly could not pass through the birth canal with shirt and diapers. However, in Adam and Eve's case, the nakedness was symbolic of the purity and innocence of the couple. God, according to the Bible, told them not to eat the fruit from this one tree. Again, that is symbolic, for the Tree represented knowledge of being **in** the world, versus being **of** the world with your consciousness in the upper centers. Symbolically**, when Adam and Eve ate the forbidden fruit, they then gained the knowledge of the lower aspects of the world**. Supposedly, they were embarrassed by their nakedness—again symbolic.

How many of you Readers have dreams where you are walking around naked, feel embarrassed, and try to cover up? Alternatively, you may be half-naked and it does not seem to matter? Those kinds of dreams are quite archetypal. Most people have dreams where they are naked. These are dreams for you to analyze. These dreams depict whether you are hiding something from others or yourself. These naked-type dreams are a great tool used by your soul to bring information to your consciousness, as to how open you are, or how you are hiding behind clothes and your half-truths or lies.

Therefore, symbolically, Adam and Eve now knew what the dark side of a soul could be. **They knew lies, blame, shame, and guilt**. **These would be the *sins* that humanity would come to know**—and must face in order to learn, be tested, and to grow. The Bible makes this Fall quite dramatic, where in actuality, it was symbolic of humanity's future journey. One is born with innocence (nakedness), but as the babe develops, he or she loses Light, or it dims because the person is now clothed in denser energy and the person learns to lie, then becomes the effect and turns to blame, in order to assuage his or her wounds—then that leads to shame, and guilt. She or he is now a victim. Every person portrays the Adam and

Eve story and has his/her own personal Garden of Eden, with the lying serpent called the *ego*. **Your ego is your serpent that judges and then perpetuates your *sins.***

During this time, the developing of your Earth, there were other bodies of peoples. There were people who had come and eventually evolved from the Animal Kingdom. You would call them cave men, for they mostly lived in caves in order to escape the elements and wild animals. There would also be pockets of people called Sky people, for they came from other planets. At first, they came in their Light bodies, but they became more solid when they started mating with the denser peoples of the planet. Other Sky people just played out their games of life that were not of a positive nature that they had played in other star systems. Consequently, through the millenniums, the different peoples started populating the Earth.

Now, of course, God was watching closely. He wanted man-woman to be more pure, to be in His likeness. He postulated that if the planet was going to be the symbolic Garden of Eden, a world where Heaven and Earth could be one, then humanity needed to be upgraded. If Earth were to be populated in His Image, then there needed to be the first man and woman—prototypes of perfection. Hence, Adam and Eve were created in physical body form. They did have children, for that was their purpose. The Bible does describe all of that with all of its *begets,* which many a scholar has groaned over, as he or she pursued the study of Genesis.

Now this brings me to where we began this chapter. I have stated before that the Bible states many Truths. I have also said that the oral history was not always accurate, nor did the scribes write the history verbatim. Therefore, there are many fallacies from most of these great stories. Some say there were no separate man and woman named *Adam* and *Eve*. Some say these two people were symbolic of races or nations. However, I say that both sayings hold Truth. There were groups of people that I have just described—cave people, Sky people, and animal people. They would be comprised of groups of many people. However, there also were the two perfect human beings you know as *Adam* and *Eve.*

God has a purpose for everything He does. We have called it *God's Methodology*. Therefore, **everything that the Bible tells of Adam and Eve was supposed to happen.** One could call it a *set-up*! Adam and Eve had been instructed before they came to the planet what roles they were to play. I have told you how their bodies were projected upon Earth. However, their **souls** were of God. They had the Veils of Forgetfulness applied to them just as humanity does. Just as Jesus and his whole cast of players came to Earth to play their parts, so did Adam and Eve. This was part of the Plan, in order to get the bodies out of stagnation, mating with the Daughters of Man, and into a higher consciousness. Know that there is a purpose for everything that God orchestrates. The Adam and Eve story in the Garden of Eden was one of God's greater Symphonies—all according to His Will. Each participant played his or her notes to perfection.

THE USE of PENDULUMS—Sananda

I AM Sananda. Pendulums have a long history. They have been used as supernatural tools for centuries. Originally, crystals were tied on chains in some fashion. People observed how the crystal would sway in different directions in response to different thoughts. Therefore, crystals were used clear back in Lemuria for divining purposes. As people became more skilled in the use of crystals and grew in consciousness, they came to realize they could utilize crystals in all manner of supernatural practices. They found that crystals strung on a loose thong of some kind became quite a handy tool, for it seemed to have a consciousness. Those of higher training knew the power in crystals and that they indeed did contain consciousness. If one knew how to read a crystal correctly, it would give you information to questions you would ask.

Now when they discovered they could harness a crystal for dousing, or for finding objects and for divining, they also discovered the crystal could sway in *yes* or *no* directions. People started playing with the pendulum and having fun with this esoteric tool. They did not have the awareness to know one does not use an esoteric tool just for fun—any more than one would use a Ouija Board for *yes* or *no* answers. The reason for this is that it dilutes the energy. It downgrades it just by the person's consciousness. Consequently, it is not always accurate.

Nevertheless, a person in modern times has trained him or herself to use a pendulum. Nowadays, anything that can be held up and has movement in order to sway in different directions can be called a *pendulum*. If one has an area of expertise, one can use any object in case one has left her pendulum at home and wants a quick answer on something. Keys on a key chain can be used, if one needs the answer in a hurry. Some people use their jewelry crosses. Others use a favorite gold locket—whatever works for you.

A phenomenon that can happen, however, is that if people are not that evolved in consciousness, although they may not realize this, they still do not have control of their own space. They can have any dead Tom, Dick, or Harry flitting by, checking out the astral, seeing you in action, and come to play with you. They will swing your pendulum. Since you do not have the awareness to direct your angels to watch over your space, you really do not know who is in it! **Therefore, these factors become definitive reasons for the wide fluctuation between numbers when you are asking for percentages—your own subconscious influencing the pendulum and the fly-by-night energies invading your space**. These people, instead of judging books by their covers, so to speak, would be better off holding the book to their heart and letting their body tell them Truth by goose bumps or tears, versus their pendulum. Pendulums in the hands of conscious and advanced people are a wonderful tool, however.

What sets them apart from the average pendulum user is they **know** a pendulum reading on someone else's material can never be 100% Truth, even if they themselves have channeled it. This is so, simply because not anything received **outside** of you can be total Truth. It can register in the higher digits for Truth, but not be total Truth, for that is the domain of your I AM Presence. You are the one that holds total Truth for you.

WAR and ITS MANY OPPORTUNITIES for CHANGE—Trio

We are Maitreya, Sananda, and Jesus. This last Memorial Day brought up many memories for the older generation. There were many television movies of World War II, the various intrigues plus the famous generals. It may surprise you to know that your famous generals Patton, Eisenhower, and Bradley were high initiates. Stop to think about it. World War II was a time in history where thousands of lives were lost, while the warring countries of Japan and Germany failed. Why do you think God sent in the great military leaders? These had been great generals, political leaders, and warriors in previous past lives from Atlantis, Egypt, Biblical times into the twentieth century.

God always has warriors He can count on. It is a certain energy, *warrior energy*, which these great military people carried. There was a huge shift for the planet from the World Wars. It brought forth great inventions and the refining of existing machinery. Just as NASA has developed vacuum-packed foods and other products for space-travel that has made its way to the market, the different wars advanced aircraft, ships, tanks, and guns.

These new inventions and the updating of the old brought a new enterprise for America. People had jobs working fast and furiously on assembly lines. It brought equality for women not experienced before this. Women took over the many jobs that used to be just for men. Women learned how to rivet bolts, pack parachutes, and assemble gun parts. Almost every job that a man was doing before the wars, women were now filling in those spaces, as the men went off to war.

Thus wars, while dreadful in and of themselves, do bring an economy boost for the winning country. They tend to bankrupt the country that loses the war, however. God gave people their free will. Thus, when humanity's free will turns to warring, God uses the energies created in order to bring on much needed change—the chaos before peace can reign.

We noted that the younger generation, which consists of the New Age children, has no conscious memory of war yet. They have not fought in one until now with the advent of the Iraq war. That war, while devastating to the loved ones left behind, pales in comparison to the World Wars. The Viet Nam war was another different war. It was not a winnable war due to the hostile environment. It was similar to asking a dolphin to come out of the water and fight a snake in the jungle. Not only did American soldiers not know jungle fighting, they were severely tested in weather conditions.

Caucasians, African Americans, Hispanics, and other ethnic groups who fought are not acclimated to jungle climate. There was no way soldiers could combat the humidity, insects, reptiles, and the jungle snares that the clever Oriental minds—the Viet Cong and North Vietnamese—knew for trapping the unsuspecting soldiers. The loss of life was tremendous. Your president Johnson ought to have pulled out the troops long before he did. Legacies are not always easy to accept and carry. However, these wars become a methodology that can bring in a new era.

People may be interested to know that many of the young people who were killed had fought and died in the previous wars. It was an opportunity for souls to play the war game again. Maybe one person previously had lost his courage. Now he was able to find it this time around. Maybe a person had sacrificed his life to save someone else. Now both players have come again and exchanged roles so that the *savior* in one war can be the *saved* in another war. Do you see, Readers, how wars always provide opportunities for souls? It may not seem like a glorious opportunity to join an outfit just so you can experience the many hardships and dangerous assignments.

Let us not forget also the hours of tedious boredom while you wait to hear what the next call for duty will be. Think also about the heartache involved as a military person thinks of home and the family he or she left behind, maybe a new spouse or a new baby. These are such hardships for bodies. Meanwhile, souls are busy trying to bring balance to their bodies. When the body finally falls into an exhausted sleep, the soul can slip away to the astral planes for much needed guidance.

If you choose a body to transmute some karma you have chosen, you will need much guidance. It is a tremendous growth opportunity for souls and most are determined to make the most of it. You see wars of these magnitudes do not happen every seven years, say. These wars most likely only occur in your one lifetime. However, the twentieth century had the two World Wars, Korean War, the Vietnam War, **and** the Iraq War. In between those wars, there were the skirmishes when helping other countries in their wars—like Afghanistan.

Therefore, wars come and go, taking bodies with them. The souls sign on for these experiences, many having warred in other centuries. The point we are making is God changes energies, brings in new ways of doing things with new inventions These then become great opportunities for souls to grow, take initiations, have tests of faith, patience, and courage. They are tested in their faith to the Father, in their patience while doing their service, and in the courage of their bodies. War brings out the attributes and virtues of body and soul.

At the same time, war is hell on Earth and many people cannot cope emotionally with the atrocities they see. Young people grow up fast in wars. One of the most difficult tasks is to keep your heart from shutting down. That is where the soul must be present, for while war can kill a body, it can be a devastating setback for the soul. There is so much work to be done—so much balance to be kept on both sides of the veil.

However, when the conquering hero comes home, there is great rejoicing in all dimensions. Just as service men and women get medals for their valor, souls, when they return Home, get a different type of acknowledgment. They receive God's Thank You for their service to humanity. Hearing God thank you for a job well done is one of the greatest honors one could ever receive, for the love one feels at that moment **is** the Ultimate Experience.

AN ARCHANGEL'S POINT of VIEW—Archangel Metatron

I AM Metatron, the Archangel of God's Kingdom. Hello, dear soul. You were with me when you were emerging from your cocoon as the beautiful butterfly you are now. We are speaking of billions of years ago. We thought it about time to have an Archangel be part of your books also. Let us begin.

Billions of years ago, the Archangels were. They have been from the beginning with what you know as your Supreme Being. I am privileged to hold your God's Highest Stream of Energy within my Being. I am the creator of electrons. I am electrical energy in essence. That is why if I entered your body other than your mental body, you would feel as though you were being charged, as my electric shocks would soar through you. By only coming to your mental body, your physical body will not be harmed in any way.

Most people do not realize they come from the Angelic Realm. However, when the Father thinks souls into existence, they carry the energies of angels. You know that angels can only help you when you direct them by asking for certain protection, perhaps. Many people, if they are conscious of having angels, simply ask their angels to protect their family, house, car, and so forth. Many times your angels know what needs extra protection before you do. Since you have asked for their help in the past, they will step in and help in your immediate future if need be. Many a car crash has been minimized by the presence of your angels.

As a person progresses, so does your angel advance. People of less awareness will have only one or two angels—the one you call your *guardian angel*. More advanced people have more angels assigned to them for various purposes. Angels must evolve in ability also, you see. One might say *you grow together*.

Billions of years ago, I was. I too had to evolve. I did not have control of my full potential. I was given different assignments by the Father. When I was successful in that endeavor, I would be given a more advanced—more difficult task. One day, which is not in the same time as your Earth days, the Father decided I had been tested and honed to the point He could trust me with more of His Energies. Therefore, I climbed up the ladder also. I am still growing and developing, for one can never stop. It would be stagnation if I did and that would not only harm me, but everyone with whom I am involved.

People on Earth have a tendency to fall into two categories—the *doers* and the *non-producers*. The *doers* accomplish much. The *non-producers* accomplish little and just *tread water,* as the saying goes. What some souls may not realize is if you waste your lifetime, you must come again and replay much that you had tried to avoid. It has been written many times what a privilege it is for souls to be given a body. Well, Readers, it is a privilege for angels to be assigned to a soul and its body! Since there are so many of us, we eagerly await our Earth assignments. One of our most enjoyable tasks is to be assigned to twins. If you think the parents are in for *double trouble*, you ought to see us hopping around. Actually, I am making light of this—we do take our assignments seriously. In the case of multiple births, there will always be more than one angel to help protect that soul's bodies.

Even though we may be assigned to a body to protect it, we have other duties. We watch not only the body but also the soul. Many souls, even if an *old soul,* still need us angels. It is God's way of always watching over his flock of angels. People think we flit around with great wings. That is a myth, actually. We are shown with wings, and many times we will manifest wings simply because it is expected. However, we do not have wings. The Cherubim and Seraphim have wings, but only if they wish to be seen that way. It is not really expected. Wings were noted by scribes in the Bible. They helped people to be able to recognize a supernatural Being. If Gabriel just came to you wearing the clothes of that era, He would not be recognized. If He wore His wings, then the person would know it was God's Messenger. Therefore, **wings are almost in the category of a *dress code*.** I certainly do not wear wings on the bridge of one of Commander Ashtar's ships. We are usually tall in stature, approximately eight feet tall. If we added wings to that angel, put ten of them in a room, there would be little room in which to maneuver. I am having fun with you, but I did want to let you know that wings are more part of mythology than reality.

I will step back now, Readers. I do hope to chat with you again. The Author has been told that after her body goes to sleep, she more often than not is with Lord Sananda and me on his Light ship. We have had some humorous times.

With that, I bless you with the Light of the Most High. I AM Metatron, Archangel of God, the Father. Amen!

EVERY SEVEN YEARS . . . —Sananda

I AM Sananda. Readers, after many eons of time, humanity has advanced itself to the point where the masters really can make contact with many of you in order to give out our Teachings. We have noticed the age bracket for interest in us still seems to be in the senior years, and I am placing fifty-something in that grouping. We have told you before that it is on your fiftieth birthday you begin to reap your wisdom. You have all heard, I am sure, how your lives change every seven years. There is a new direction. Well, 7 x 7 = 49. Hence, on the fiftieth year, your wisdom starts *downloading*, to use a computer term.

Of course, nothing is that cut and dried, but if you look back on your life, no matter what age you are now, you will see the subtle changes that have manifested every seven years. Sometimes the changes are in the health of the body. Other times, changes are at the workplace. Other changes might be people who re-enter college in order to obtain the higher learning they were deprived of earlier in life due to child bearing, finances, and so forth. Some people are freed up to make changes in their life after a parent has passed away.

Therefore, when you come to your forty ninth-fiftieth birthday, you finally come into your own wisdom—or make great strides toward it. Now the Reader may be wondering why one has to wait so long to become wise. Why cannot a youth be wise? I think you all remember those times when you were a youth. You were *impatient* for things to happen. In addition, you did not always *trust* your soul to be aware of its body and to guide you. Lastly, you did not carry that much *faith* that your life had a wonderful future. Hence, we are speaking of *patience, trust, and faith*. Now these attributes are to be honed, to be activated, and to be strengthened. Since that youthful exuberance is somewhat tempered by age, you are better able to listen to your guidance now.

There are, therefore, those changes that the body must go through—the maturation process. However, Readers, the soul too is maturing while in its body. Let us say the soul is refining its other bodies—emotional, mental, and spiritual bodies. Of course, in Earth years, most souls are older and matured. Nevertheless, each lifetime brings a refinement to the soul that can only be obtained through a body on Earth. However, those of you of more advanced initiations come back with other agendas. Maybe you wish to refine your *patience, trust, and faith* to even higher standards. Maybe you wish to be even more *courageous*. Maybe you wish to be *tested* during wartime conditions. Maybe you wish to become *stronger* in your *empathy* and *compassion*. You see, Readers, how even masters keep striving for more and more perfection of their traits. Therefore, with each seven-year period, there is a new direction toward something.

This Author had no idea she would be writing books, especially books she has telepathically channeled from many masters. Yet, her life subtly changed. She went through years of trials and tribulation, tests beyond belief of most people. She had no idea what was coming. She just kept walking her path, wherever it led. She rarely questioned *why me*, until she was first contacted by me. It never occurred to her she had climbed so far.

Therefore, the point I am making is that every seven years the soul leads the body onward. You *take life as it comes*—an astute saying. Before you realize it, you are at that halfway point of fifty-something. You have come into your wisdom. Now your path may feel similar to that moving walkway in an airport. Everything seems to speed up. Farmers often notice how their mules start speeding up as they near the barn. Well, Readers, souls also know when they are nearing the barn, or in this case Home. They work doubly hard attempting to get all of their projects finished that were on the *drawing board*, so to speak. However, many times, if the body has not had proper attention, or if genetic health issues appear, the plans do not always come to fruition.

It is always important, dear Readers, to use your fiftieth year as one in which you pause for a bit and contemplate what your next goal will be. Some of you will find that you are winding down your drive for material gains and only wish to concentrate on spiritual matters. Others have worked so hard in order to make a living and raise the family that they want to play for a while. They may start to travel more. Keep in mind that almost every act one does in one's senior years has a purpose. A purpose could be to just play and not have to work so hard. However, each soul will have its own way of closing its chapter on those first fifty years. If you carry that awareness, you can observe your friends, or relatives, as to what they have planned for the next seven years. It is always quite illuminating to watch a soul and discern what it is contemplating next.

Therefore, for those Readers who are past fifty and approaching their sixties, you might find what those souls are up to is even easier to discern, if you know at what you are looking. It is really quite simple. Just ask yourself how productive is he or she? Do you see him or her still being in service in some way? That is always an excellent clue when the soul is still active and being the Light of the World.

I will close now with this on which to ponder: What have I accomplished in my fifty years and is it completed? What have I always wanted to do and have not had the time to do it? Well, all you beloved seniors, now is your time. You have fulfilled your purposes with family and extended family. Now you can fulfill your real purpose for being!

THE EFFECTS of CHAOS in the HEAVENLIES—Sanat Kumara

I AM Sanat Kumara. Today I wish to speak about the Heavenlies, as you refer to the wondrous vibrations outside of your sphere known as Earth. You understand, Readers, that your planet is not the only sphere in your Universe. You know that other planets influence your Earth. However, I wonder if you know that each Universe influences another, just like planets do. Every energy throughout these Heavens influences every other energy. I will not give names, for it will mean little to you. However, suffice to know your Universe is not alone in the Heavenlies.

In fact, see if this will help you visualize this mental picture: you have a body. Think of it as a Universe. The body has limbs, fingers, and toes. These could represent other planets and star systems. Your organs could represent spheres of existence within these systems and on it goes. Everything is connected. Everything is energy that needs to be kept in balance. When one part becomes off balanced, chaos is the result. For a body, that would manifest as an illness, or a health condition of some kind. For planets, that imbalance would manifest in changes for that planet. On Earth, one would say *Earth changes*. On another planet, say Mars, it would be referenced as *Mars changes*.

There was a time when there was water and life, as you know it on Mars. Now it is no longer an inviting, hospitable planet, although it still has Beings on it. They just are not in forms you would recognize. Also, just as in Earth, there are Entities living deep within Mars' structure—what you would call *underground.* These Beings have adapted to Mars' atmosphere. They are busy monitoring their planet and are connected to the Galactic Space Command.

Therefore, Readers, as your NASA keeps sending out its space ships in hopes of creating a productive space station that one sees portrayed in your television screenplays, its purpose is not always benevolent. There are scientists who help evolve these space ships. However, the technology is not there yet. One could say it compares to a grammar school science project. The leap for achieving a spaceship such as the Galactic Command has is still centuries away. Many of your scientists are excited about space travel. They fervently wish to explore space.

However, other scientists of the dark side only want to have control of the planet. If they were allowed, they would have more than one station and have them manned with some type of weaponry to be able to point it at a particular nation and say, *we've got you covered!* There will always be men who bask in the ultimate power of control. Now why am I telling you this? As I have stated, the planets and Universes are all connected with each other. Therefore, if your planet Earth becomes imbalanced to the point of scientists wanting control of it, that then brings the other planets out of balance also. It then affects the Universe and that fans out. Now you have chaos.

In the months to come and in the next few years, especially, Earth will enter more into chaos. This always happens before imbalances are corrected. Some of the chaos will dissipate as humanity's consciousness is raised. However, how does one bring balance back to the other planets that are the effect of Earth's imbalance? Ah, this is what poses a tremendous problem for all. What it calls for is an adjustment throughout the Heavenlies. One off-balanced planet has affected all the other planets and the Universe that houses them. Dear friends, this is what we all have known would be happening.

Let us use another analogy. Take a bathtub filled with some water. Put balls or spheres of different sizes into the water. Now put your hand in and swish it back and forth. When you withdraw your hand, the spheres are in different positions than they originally were. Well, dear Readers, when Earth reaches her full chaos, it will cause this chain reaction that will move the planets into different positions in the Heavenlies. Astrologers will need to design new charts, for what planet influenced its neighbor before will no longer be true. It will be as if God has redesigned Heaven. Your astronomers will be greatly perplexed for where once they could spot Venus at a particular point; she will no longer be there. That too will be part of the chaos—astronomers not seeing what they used to see in the sky.

On the other hand, astrologers are more apt to embrace New Age Thought. They may have heard that a change will be forthcoming as to the new positioning of the planets. They may know what to expect and will make their adjustments. Their *readings of the stars* for their clients will be exciting for them. Strange as it might seem, even though the planets may have moved into different positions, they will still influence people pretty much in the same way as before. People in Virgo will still be meticulous and well organized, but they may find they could also carry traits of another planet they had not previously carried, for the cusps will all be changed also. Therefore, astrologers will have their work cut out for them.

Readers, do not be dismayed over hearing that the planets will change positions. This rotation has happened before, you see. People are apt to think every happening of significance is new—that this is the first time. If one has many lifetimes, one may have had a lifetime where the dynamic is repeated, such as it is today. The Heavens will seem to move. However, it merely will be different planets shifting a bit.

Now some people who have heard of this phenomenon wonder how long something this tremendous will take. Do they just wake up some day and find the Morning Star is in a different position? On the other hand, do they gradually notice that the Morning Star seems to be a bit lower than it was? Therefore, I will tell you that the shift has already begun! You are living in this momentous miracle now. It will take more years to accomplish this, but all planets will be in their right positions during most of your lifetimes. So do not worry that you will be tossed out of your bed upside down because Earth has gone into a different orbit. I know, various writers have written that this can happen in a twinkling of an eye. We do not see it happening that quickly. I think that some speculators are mixing up the Earth turning on its axis with planet changes in the Heavenlies.

Let me come up with an example for you. Take an orange and in some clever way, put a string through it so it comes out both ends. Now tie the two ends together. You now have a sphere that moves its axis but has not necessarily moved its orbit. This is how we feel the change will be. Of course, any change of Earth's axis will cause weather and Earth changes.

Now what will cause the Earth to shift into different positions in the Heavenlies, other than a change of its axis? This shift will be caused by the change in gravitational pulls. Rocket ships that are sent by NASA into outer space require extreme power by their rockets in order to break away from Earth's gravitational pull. As a ship approaches another planet—we will say Mars since that probe had a successful landing on Mars—the ship will be drawn into the gravitational pull of that planet. Now here is the puzzler. Each of the planets you can see through telescopes has its own gravitational pull. However, what causes this gravity? Where does it come from? It comes from its neighbor. Now I know this may seem a strange concept to you Readers if you are hearing it for the first time. However, **the magnetic force in the Universe creates the gravitational pull for each planet**. When something happens to upset this equilibrium, the planets are affected. You have seen sci-fi movies where the force field has weakened so that a malevolent ship can enter the force field and do harm to the futuristic city. In your modern day world, it is humanity's consciousness that represents the "malevolent ship," which weakens Earth's force field.

Humanity's environmental pollution has affected the ozone layers. They act as her shield against the sun's harmful rays. As Earth's shield is damaged, so are her force field, her gravity, and her magnetic field. Since all the planets are connected to each other, when Earth's fields weaken, all of her neighbors are affected also. She is a beautiful Soul, with a huge heart that has suffered the harmful ways of humanity long enough. In fact, she has been so desecrated for so long, she did not know whether she would sustain or deplete life.

However, she has made her decision. The fact that she is striving forth into the fourth and fifth dimensions will validate that. Earth needs to do some house cleaning. She will shake the *fleas* off her back in the form of Earthquakes. She will give herself a good *cleansing* with the healing waters of floods and her oceans coming ashore. She will strengthen her gravitational pull with the help of her planet neighbors.

Some day when you are traveling in a spaceship either in your dreams or in your waking journeys, you will view your planet Earth as the jewel she is among her neighbors and not as some distant spot in the Universe for fear she might be too destructive. Better put, the Beings she allowed in might be too destructive to have close by. Instead of the outcast, she is now a mature planet in her own right. Beings of lower consciousness will no longer be tolerated on Earth's pristine shores. This planet will then be the planet that has Heaven on her doorstep—where masters come eagerly to call and walk her shores.

I AM Sanat Kumara.

THE DAY the EARTH STOOD STILL—Kuthumi

I AM Kuthumi. Dear Readers, many of you may have read about the *Day the Earth Stood Still* when your Lord Jesus was crucified. However, many of you may feel this is a legend or even a myth. I say to you that indeed there was a moment in time when all stopped. It was as though even the in-breath of the Most High paused for that slight second in time. The crucifixion of the Son of Man was of course true. However, there was great symbolic meaning to much of it also. I will be addressing that part for this section.

In your own experience, when an *accident* befalls someone (yes, we know there are no accidents, but for our purposes we will use that word), the act is so sudden and unexpected that it belies one's belief that such a thing could happen. In that instant, if you are close to the person or persons involved, there is that short period of time when you hold your breath and are not even conscious that you have done so. You stop whatever you were doing. There is a pause. You are in another reality, literally. Your world as it affects you has stopped.

Now multiply that a hundred fold for the crucifixion of the Lord Jesus. His time, while very symbolic, was so utterly incredulous that people were not only horrified but were stopped in their actions. The disbelief that swirled around people fanned out. The Heavens actually paused for what you would call a nanosecond. Then the Heavens roared and the Earth shook and rumbled. You see, this great injustice affected the living planet. All the Elementals of fire, air, wind, and water reacted. His assimilated *death* affected the entire kingdoms of not only the human race, but the plant and animal kingdoms also.

It has been written in noteworthy books that your Lord's death was really a deep sleep. He did not die but was in an altered state. However, this very condition was not just a passing chance. Jesus had prepared himself throughout that lifetime in studying with high initiates and yogis on how to reach that state of near death and yet maintain a thread of life. (*Similar to a Winged Pharaoh of Egypt. 2011)*

Of course, his Teachers and the Father monitored him closely, instructed him spiritually, and helped him fully. Jesus had full awareness and consciousness, even though his body was deeply tranced. Jesus knew what he must do, where he needed to travel in those upper planes and dimensions. At that time, he fully came into his own and acclaimed his sovereignship of this Universe he had created. He acknowledged he was God in his own right. He embraced all that he was. All of this was going on as his body was limply hanging on the cross and had the final insult of the spear being thrust into his side.

Hence, while Jesus was experiencing on a physical level and in an altered state all that the Bible states, the world was also being affected mightily. I have stated that all was symbolic, since the Christ did not die on the cross. However, what I have not stated is that this grand finale of Jesus' life was meant to be. He took it upon himself to bring to humankind the new Teachings about *death, resurrection, and ascension*. Humanity still does not fully understand this concept. It does not realize that one can approach this metaphorically through almost any aspect of one's life. Humanity does not understand that any living thing from insects, animals, plants, to humans must die in some form or another in order to be resurrected. Even your nonliving things like relationships, business adventures—all born of someone's creation—live and then die.

Therefore, Jesus' "death" (and let us put that in quotation marks) played a significant role for humankind's consciousness. He had such love for humanity. While he was born of the flesh, he still was able to sustain his deep love for everyone. It was not just a gesture, for he truly loved everyone and everything. When a great soul such as Jesus entered your world, he was able to keep those veils of forgetfulness from slipping. **He knew he was *love***. He knew, therefore, that he was one with every creature on Earth**. He created this Universe**.

Therefore, he knew that everything in his Universe was connected to each other. Since he created from *love*, whatever he created was also *love.* Hence, he truly loved everyone he saw. Now someone might ask, what about snakes? Did he create those also? No, he did not. Those were brought forth from the *fallen angels* in order to create evil. Since everyone has free will, he did not control all of the creatures in his Universe.

There is an inference that since Jesus "died" on the cross, he "died" for the sins of humanity. The more correct interpretation would be he was showing humanity how death is a cycle that can be overcome. Humanity has many sins, if you wish to use that term. It is not crucifixion on a cross that absolves one from his or her sins. It is humanity's ability to *love thy neighbor*. Let us back up a bit. If all the people who had joined that mob-mentality had truly loved each other such as the Christ did, there would have been no need to crucify anyone. What one does to another in cruel acts comes back to haunt that person for lifetimes.

Therefore, **the Earth stood still, for *love* had been withdrawn from the world**. Think about it. If the majority withdraws *love*, the dark side of the soul prevails. When that pocket of people had committed that horrendous act, even if it was fulfilling scripture, at that nanosecond of Jesus' *death*, *love*—his *love*—was withdrawn from the world. People reacted by holding their breath. The Earth stopped functioning and breathing for that instance in time, literally. **The crucifixion showed people what the reactions or repercussions would be like when God's *love* is withdrawn even for a nanosecond**. Since Jesus was God at the time of his death on the cross, and since he was pure *love,* when humankind killed him, they destroyed *love*—just for that nanosecond. Think about that, Reader—when there was no *love* on Earth.

However, please keep in mind I am speaking symbolically. **Jesus did not die on the cross**, but at the hour that his body ought to have been pronounced dead, **when the Heavens roared and the Earth rocked, that was what the world would be like if there were no *love* on the planet again. It would stop Earth for that brief time, and plunge it into eternal darkness and chaos. That was the greater lesson Jesus was demonstrating**. There is nothing greater than *love*. There is only darkness and chaos without it. Ponder this, dear Readers.

I AM Kuthumi, the Christ's Teacher and his greatest admirer and friend.

JESUS and MARY—Jesus

I AM Jesus. Dear friends and readers of this book, we will be drawing this material to a close once again. However, I wished to discourse just a bit more on my life as Jesus. As we have said in the previous two books, I was spreading the Word of God to love without judgment. That is what I was referring to mostly—to *love your neighbor, as you would love yourself*. However, since humanity judges not only each other, but also one's self, that teaching is difficult to adhere to for most people.

Some days in those ancient times, life was pleasant and full of surprises. I remember visiting one of my many relatives. Many of us had gathered for singing, dancing, and camaraderie. The house pets were under people's feet most the time, for they too liked to be part of the festivities. The women had spent several days in preparing food, expecting a large gathering for it was a special occasion, a wedding feast. **It was the wedding of my beloved Mary Magdalene and me**.

I imagine most of you readers who have read these books already know that I married the true love of my life, my spiritual helpmate, my double in all respects. **We were betrothed before we were born**. We were meant for each other forever, for my Mary was truly the Light of the World also. Let us picture this special day. Mary was glorious with her long, curly hair intertwined with flowers. She wore a white gown of finely woven material. She wore a girdle, what you would call a belt, which draped from hip to hip at an angle. The girdle was in multicolored braids and had different colored beads woven into the fabric that caught the light as she moved. Her eyes sparkled and there was a radiant smile on her lips. She had a small dimple at the corner of her mouth that would undulate, in and out, making her mouth appear to be dancing also. She was my deepest *love.*

I wore the costume of the day. I had on flowing pants with an embroidered tunic. It had been embroidered by my *love*. It was customary for the bride to embroider her husband's marriage tunic. I too wore a girdle-belt at my hips. However, mine was of pliable leather, deeply embossed and heavily tooled in design. We both wore new, but simply designed sandals. I wore no body ornaments. However, my Mary wore earrings.

Therefore, there I was in a fine tunic and my Mary in her wedding dress. There was the typical wedding ceremony with the various rituals involved. The ceremony was read in Hebrew, but afterwards we spoke Aramaic. The Bible has a story of my turning water into wine. This is so. It was purported to be my first miracle. I say to you, having my Mary become my wife was truly the miracle of that day. I had not expected to marry.

Most books written on Biblical history do not portray my marriage. There seems to be a belief that if Jesus were married, he could not be pronounced the Messiah—be a God. As I look back on those times, it seems rather incredulous to me that my marriage was kept so hidden—at least in the writings. Since most of my life was written about after I had ascended, came back, fathered children, and made my transition at a ripe old age, the writers just left out the human details. They wanted to revere me and keep me inaccessible. I was supposed to be kept some place up in the sky where people could look **upwards** in order to find me.

Well, dear readers, I am somewhere up in the sky now, but I still walk among you. You just do not recognize me when I am walking as one of the *common folk*. Ah, readers, such is the power of one's belief systems. Such is the power of the church's programming and the oft times incorrect interpretations of me. Lastly, such is the power of parents' belief systems on their children. The myths keep being perpetuated. Do you think you could release some of them now? The Jesus era was so long ago. I did marry. *I married Mary Magdalene who was as pure in spirit as she was in body. She had never sinned in any way. She was Light and Love and she was my heartbeat.* We loved; we married; we had children. Our progeny lives on. However, keep in mind we had other lifetimes where we loved, married, and had children. Those progeny live on also. Where and who are they? You mighta.

(People are apt to deify the children of Jesus and Mary Magdalene. One hears of the "bloodline" that must remain intact at all cost. However, as Jesus points out, he had other children in other

lifetimes. Joseph of Egypt comes to mind. Does it not make sense that all of these souls have reincarnated repeatedly, changed their form, their sexuality, and no longer have Jesus as their parent? That bloodline was compromised eons ago. It is called "evolution.")

LIFE—STREAMS of the SOUL—Jesus

I AM Jesus. As souls developed and had their different incarnations on Earth as well as on other planets, they left behind many times what are called *life-streams*. These particles of the soul's energy were not integrated with the soul at the time of death in order to bring all of itself Home. Now we realize some of you are familiar with this concept of life-streams, while the majority of you Readers are not.

Let us give you some examples. When a body dies, the soul gathers up all of its information, its energies and brings it all Home. However, there are instances where the death was not correct. Again, this may appear to be an unusual dynamic and unheard of for most people. However, **not all deaths are correctly achieved**. By that, we mean the deaths of the body happened according to the medical model all right, but the soul's involvement was not correctly done. The soul could be scattered, fragmented for whatever reasons. Sometimes if the body is heavily abused by drugs, the soul cannot die correctly. Sometimes in the very elderly and medically incapacitated, the soul is fragmented. It has streams of itself hither and yon—sometimes in other time frames and dimensions. Consequently, at the time of death, the soul literally has abandoned-streams of itself—*life-streams*.

Now what starts to happen after repeated lifetimes is that the soul finds that it has life-streams all over the world and in different dimensions. You may have heard that you have many selves. Well, those are life-streams. They need to be integrated until all of you come together once again. **These streams of energy are you**. They may have been particles of male or female. We are speaking of energies. Therefore, these energies are androgynous. They may hold one of the masculine or feminine Principals more dominant, but they are androgynous. It makes no difference what sex your present body is now. These pieces or life-streams will integrate into your present body. Sometimes the life-streams are higher frequencies of you. Therefore, you might experience its re-entry as a higher *walk-in,* which is not a true *walk-in* (where another entity enters a body that the present inhabitant has agreed to vacate and has turned over to you for various reasons). Therefore, your life-streams can be of the higher frequencies or of the higher, finer Self.

Another reason life-streams are left behind when the soul makes its transition during death is when the soul leaves a particle of itself on purpose. **Many souls of higher frequencies leave life-streams of energy in sacred spots for safekeeping.*** There are sacred areas all over the world—Sedona, Arizona; Mt. Shasta, California; England, Ireland, Scotland, France, Australia, Egypt and the Himalayas to name but a few. Many souls had past lives in those places and left life-streams of them there. You might be wondering why souls would do that.

One of the main reasons is that that life-stream helps maintain the energies in those sacred areas. Unfortunately, the dark energies have done the same thing—left streams of them on the planet also. It is not only the Earth that has your life-streams, past, present and future, but different planets that you have been to also. People might think this to be a negative dynamic, to leave parts of you behind and sometimes it is, but it is what souls do. Many times, it is for positive reasons to help maintain the energy of those particular spots.

Let me pose this question to you. How many of you still have life-streams in those megalithic stones of Stonehenge. Those highly energized streams of you were deliberately placed in those stones in order to help maintain the vibrations of that sacred spot and to facilitate the stones' purpose. Some of you are still there, although many are not. Think of it this way. If you have traveled to those sacred areas in this lifetime, you were most likely gathering up those streams of your soul for you to integrate. How many of you experience sadness or depression after a lengthy, significant journey? Do you think it might be that that particular part of you might feel sadness, might feel lonely for what it has left behind? Ponder this.

Now let us come to present time. You have chosen a life when the Earth is raising her vibrations and moving into other dimensions. You were told this was the time to gather into yourself all those (well not really all, for you could not do that in one lifetime) life-streams that you had lovingly or not so lovingly (if they were the dark parts of you) left behind. **Now** was the lifetime for you to integrate those parts of yourself. Colleges have re-entry programs—well, People, so do souls. This is the lifetime (if you have not already done so) to bring yourselves back to you—your personal re-entry program.

There are more *walk-ins* than ever before being reported. I would say these are soul fragments—life-streams—being integrated, more than likely.

Consequently, people are having a struggle on their hands, for many times the life-stream that is blending has a tendency to be more dominant, before the symbolic dust tends to settle. These life-streams of the positive kind carry much strength and a sense of purpose. They will come in, integrate, address the present karma, and parent the children in different ways, perhaps. Many divorce, for the game plan has changed and the integrating soul knows that the former spouse has a new and oft times exciting life and a new marriage partner waiting for him or her, perhaps.

However, soul-streams can also carry the darker parts of you. You may find you are more argumentative, arrogant, abrasive, and quick to anger—all of this needs to be transmuted and integrated with you. Therefore, Readers, you can see what souls have chosen for this lifetime—the grand integration process of these soul's life-streams from the highly developed spiritual-streams to one's egotistical darker-selves. All must and needs to be integrated. This is an on-going situation. Souls will find lives are difficult, but they keep coming back repeatedly in order to reclaim those missing links. Remember, we are speaking of your energy, your Light. What a glorious sight you will be when your Tree of Life is fully lit—just like a Christmas tree full of different colored light bulbs, each depicting parts of you. What a remarkable sight, indeed. I bless you.

(*This Author left a life-stream in the King's chamber in the Giza pyramid in Egypt eons ago when the planet was going through a dark phase and Beings of Light had to vacate Earth. The huge stones that lined the walls of the chamber, and which were alive, kept the life-streams safe until the Beings of Light could return and reclaim their past energies. When Chako re-visited the pyramid in 1990, she regained that part of her. The name of her Light-stream was So-**Su**-She-Sa, which incorporated the names of her three daughters today: So=Sandra; **Su**=Susan; She=Verling; and Sa=Sara. When the Author tried to use her Chako name, the stone-Being insisted on the name, Verling, the name that was given to her at birth. In other words, the coding for Chako did not match the coding of the life-stream of Verling. Hmm, picky, picky—smile. 2011.)*

THE DAY before YESTERDAY—Sananda

I AM Sananda. Dear Readers, throughout the advancing years, humanity has often said, *the day before yesterday.* What is the true meaning of that phrase? As I have previously stated, I carry a great deal of interest in history—past, present, and future. You might be wondering how anything in the future could be in a history category. Well, keep in mind that past, present, and future are all ongoing. They are timeframes that blend into each other. It is very similar to your globe. You in the West are in the present, while those in the East Coast are in **your** past, for they have already viewed the rising sun. Where would the future be then? That could be south of the equator. Australia could represent your future time, as it is so many hours and even a day ahead of America. Therefore, when you use that term *the day before yesterday,* it really depends from what area you are viewing all of this. If you are on the East Coast, you might think the West Coast is your past time dimension, for you have already seen the sunrise.

Many of you Readers travel the different time dimensions in your sleep. Many of you get lost in those vast time dimensions. The soul literally loses track of time—where it has traveled. Fortunately for you, your higher Teachers are right on your tail and come to find you and bring you back to your body. Time travel is very tricky. You have often heard where there is no time away from Earth. I would say there is no time the way **you** have experienced it. However, each dimension carries its own timeframe.

We traverse them repeatedly, as we maneuver our ships through them. You understand that since thought is what acts as the *glue* for our Light ships, we must all share the responsibility for *right thought.* Of course, I am simplifying this greatly, but in order to maneuver one's ships in and out of different dimensions, we need to remain cognizant of the different levels of time in those dimensions. Some dimensions carry your past. Think of history, when people were evolving from the lower frequency centers. Most of humanity was in that lower vibration of the first and second dimensions. Think back to Biblical times—those dimensions were more dense and in the past.

The Earth is moving more fully into the fourth dimension. Therefore, the third dimension carries the past. The fourth carries the present and the fifth dimension carries the future. Hence, those dimensions have their own time—frames. One of the predicaments that befalls humanity is that it is not always capable of staying in the present. All dimensions are ongoing and blending with each other. How many life-streams (note the lecture on *Life-Streams of the Soul)* do you have in those different periods? As those streams of soul-life come forward in order to integrate, they must be able to make that transition into the present dimension. Keep in mind that the dimensions can correlate to your chakras. The fourth chakra is your heart center. The fourth dimension uses that vibration and on up the line. Many of you operate in the fifth dimension without full awareness of so doing. That dimension carries a higher frequency and the use of your mental body's telepathic abilities.

Throughout history, there has been the struggle for humanity to raise its vibratory rate. That struggle was because the Earth had not raised **her** vibrations. It is quite difficult to develop finer frequencies when all around you—your environment—is of the denser energies. Nowadays, there are no excuses for anyone, for it is simply a matter of choice. Are you advancing up that ladder, or are you sitting on a lower rung and refusing to budge—to change? It really is up to you—your free will choice.

Thereby, when you make a statement about *the day before yesterday*, some dynamic has occurred. Keep in mind you have a choice to move beyond that—be in present time, but striving for a higher dimension. *Try it. You might like it*, as the saying goes.

We see your Light. When are **you** going to see it and claim it as your own? When are you going to turn off the electric lights at night and yet see a light glowing brightly behind you, as though there is a spotlight on you? That is your Light Body glowing. Try as you may, you cannot make it go away until your eyes adjust to the darkness and you are no longer seeing it with your third eye. It is not an optical illusion, for you can cover a portion of it with your hand and not see it. Take your hand away, and your head area seems to have a light at the back of it. You could not take it away—only hide it from yourself momentarily. It is a remarkable sight.

I will bring this chapter to a close, dear Reader. Ponder this. In what dimension are **you** residing?

WHY DO WE CONTEMPLATE?—Sananda

I AM Sananda. Dear Readers, you all, I am sure, have heard or read how the religious fathers spent hours on their knees in contemplation. This is a time for one to question one's beliefs and attitudes. Many times the church fathers had their inner struggles just as you all do. They, however, struggled over their beliefs of what and who was God. They wondered how He could be so invisible. Now this was many years and even centuries ago. There were so many teachings about God.

The Spanish Inquisition had its own set of ideas about God. They incorporated anything **they** prescribed as sinful and embraced the belief that God would not tolerate such blasphemy, such as an Innocent who proclaimed he or she heard God's Thoughts and even His Voice. This is a case where Christianity took a sharp bend in the road—a horrid, warped viewpoint in its Teachings. It was not the Teachings of Jesus, but the interpretations that left Truth and invented sinful perspectives. If a person, such as this Author, were to tell others she could converse with God in her thoughts, that would be considered blasphemous in those times.

No one was exempt. Your only protection would be if you were part of the clergy. Even then, the more saintly brothers kept their conversations with God a private matter. Therefore, prayer time grew to be a time of not only meditation to put you into an altered state so that you could talk with God, but prayer time became contemplation time also. Many people have their own ideas on what is meant by *contemplation*. We like and adhere to the idea that ***contemplation is your questioning your connection with God***. Are you walking the right path? Are you walking your talk, being a Wayshower, an example of *loving thy neighbor*? As you sit and contemplate, do you question where you are going with your spiritual life? Have you paid more attention to it in recent months? Are you setting aside time to be still, so that you can hear God? Have you contemplated your future? Do you feel at peace? Do you feel joy? These are all subjects about which one can contemplate.

These are times when you, the personality in the body, can connect more profoundly with your soul. Keep in mind; **your ego does not converse with God. It is your soul, always**. Now that ego-part of you can carry on the illusion that God is conversing with you, but that is merely an illusion. True connection with God has no ego involvement, for **ego is not capable of Truth**. Now that is worth contemplating—ego and Truth. Whenever you speak with anyone, Truth will not be present with ego. They can run parallel courses, but they can never be one dynamic, for **ego is invariably the illusion, the lie.**

What else can one contemplate? If it is in the religious context, it will be about God. However, there are relationships, either personal or of the business kind. People in Truth are straightforward. One does not have to guess as to his or her meaning on a particular subject. I will say that the relationship one has at the work place can be one of the most difficult to experience. There you have a wide variety of people all doing their best to survive in the working world. Political in-house intrigues and emotions run high. It is so easy—a trap, actually—to be caught up into the politics of that organization. How to rise above it all and remain cheerful can be a most difficult challenge for many people. Again, it is the pull of the ego that demands your being involved in some way. Before you know it, you are on a downhill slide and ousted from the various cliques, or you find you have few real friends who you can trust.

If you had practiced *meditation and contemplation* time, you might find that the more difficult times of life become more bearable. You might find that you received revelations of thought that help you make ego-less decisions. You might find you feel more at peace and have less stress in your life. You might find that you actually are conversing with God. He does hear you when you are in Truth. Therefore, Readers, these are some of the reasons for *contemplation.* Not only does it help us problem-solve, but it brings *joy* and *peace* to us also.

Hence, *contemplation* surely is a path to God—a most simple one to walk. I urge you, Beloveds, to practice *contemplation* in your lives. It is the path to your I AM Presence, your Truth, the God of your heart.

I AM Sananda.

GOD BLESS AMERICA—Sananda

I AM Sananda. As I sit and contemplate what might bring joy to humanity, peace to those of broken hearts, hope to those in anguish for various reasons, I am struck by how souls do persevere—how they remain steadfast in their purposes. It was not so long ago, at least to us in our world, where there was strife of great proportions among different factions of the world. As America draws near to celebrating her Independence Day of July 4, 2005, those long ago events of America's winning her independence from England in 1776 seem far in the distance of long ago.

However, we in the Spiritual Planes view this struggle between the old and the new countries as one of growth and evolution, not only on the physical level, but on the spiritual level as well. England has a grand history and culture, but her control became too oppressive, for the people wanted more freedom in all ways. Ironically, after a new country has grown, such as America has, she also falls back on what she had been karmically programmed from her parent country—more control.

It is difficult at times for people to make that connection—that karma, *historical karma,* follows people and countries in which the people live. If one country has not addressed its dark-side past—brought it to the consciousness of the people—the karma just keeps occurring repeatedly. Therefore, dear Readers, every time your government seems to be struggling over its decisions as to what to do, how to do it, whom to appoint to what position, know that you are watching historical karma play out. I have told you previously, that I am what you might call a *history buff.* History has always fascinated me, for it shows the karmic patterns so clearly.

One of the patterns others and I have observed is that America always seems to rise to the occasion that is required. I am referring to helping others. America is looked to for help in combating diseases, for example. Many doctors give of their time and expense of flying to different countries and conducting surgeries that are many times life saving. They perform operations on children who have been born with a cleft palate, perhaps. They dispense medicines in order to ward off the diseases that run rampant when sanitary conditions are at the lowest.

Other people go forth and help the communities in building houses for those who would most likely never own a house. Others go to the elderly and do repairs and restorations with paint and new electrical wiring and plumbing.

All of these people are *working the historical karma*, as the saying goes. Every time you hear that someone has gone to help someone else or a country in a major way, know there is karma being activated. Whether the previous karma is dark or not makes no difference. What the person or nation is doing is now transmuting that karmic debt into Light. You see, Readers, this is what stops karma from perpetuating itself. You have transmuted it. It is finished.

Many times when people view violence on television, and there is certainly enough from which to choose, the violence will trigger memories of one's past and past lives. Those who enjoy those dark programs are watching as though from a home movie of how they used to be. Women many times can catch a glimpse of themselves, if watching an old Western. There are the saloon girls, scantily clad for that era, and the genteel women with their parasols, gloves, lace, and bustles—not a bare ankle is shown. Women who view these movies are seeing several of their past-life plays. Remember, a soul experiences both ends of a spectrum, from the saloon girl to the preacher's wife. She has tried out all of those lives—knows them well. The same applies to the men—from preachers to robbers, from sheriffs to the drunkards. That is what fascinates people. They are watching a moving picture of themselves—their past lives and/or their present life. Therefore, it is not only the people, but also the governments, and the country whose karma is an open book.

America on her Independence Day will once again address her historical memories. You will know that in that long ago period, you also were playing out a drama. It makes no matter whose side you were on. You played both sides eventually. Some settled in England, for that is where most of their karma lay. Some settled in America, for those souls wished to be a part of founding a new nation that was independent from its parent country. You know, Readers, even that act of wanting independence from a parent country is no different from wanting independence from one's birth parents. That is where God's gift of free will comes into play so strongly. It helps as a catalyst. It catapults us out and away from the parent. It is a wonderful gift for evolving the soul. However, as you all have found out eventually, the free will is a tool that can be misused. Many an ill deed is done because of the dark ego making the decisions, abusing the free will.

Therefore, America, we of the Spiritual Hierarchy, salute you, for you are independent. You indeed have earned the right to celebrate your special birthday. Happy 4th of July, America! May you continue to grow and prosper, as long as you keep this in your heart—**God Bless America**!

We are the Spiritual Hierarchy sending you this greeting for your special day.

PREDICTION-UPDATES 2005—Masters of Wisdom

I AM Jesus. There appears to be a feeding frenzy going on on the Internet. So many people are reporting dreams, having visions—all doom and gloom. Therefore, we of the Masters of Wisdom felt we also needed to come forth and hopefully bring calm to the chaos and alleviate some of the fear that is starting to permeate the ethers. I will talk on a few subjects and then other Masters will come forth and speak of what he is seeing. Let us begin.

Gasoline: The high price people have had to pay at the pump for gasoline will remain for most the year. This gasoline status is a gouging of people's purses. **There is no gas shortage**. The high prices are being perpetuated by the subterfuge of your government and those outside of the United States. You call it a *cartel.* There indeed are countries that control the gasoline and oil for the whole world. When you, America, elected a government-family, (*Bush*) which includes your vice president (*Cheney*), whose sole interest is increasing its wealth while in power, oil and gasoline become the priorities.

Keep in mind that almost any bill that Congress puts forth has the backing of your government, for the bill in some way unknown to the public will increase the coffers of the reigning families. Therefore, gas and oil prices will remain pretty much where they are at right now, the high end. The news media often reports of a drop of a penny or two in gas prices. That is again a subterfuge in order for people to think prices are inching downward. It means nothing. When ten dollars only buys less than five gallons of regular gas and has for several months, there is little about which to be jubilant. The present range for gas is pretty much set in stone for the rest of the year. If there is any change, it will be higher most likely. *I will step back now for another commentator.*

I AM Djwhal Khul. As I look more closely at your world, bringing your timeframe closer, I see where there is much fear on a global scale. People are so frightened now with imagined pictures of a giant tsunami, as was experienced in the Indian Ocean in 2004. I come to put your mind, America, at ease.

Tsunamis: There will be no tsunami of giant proportions for the rest of 2005 for America. Keep in mind we are just speaking of the remaining months of 2005. America will experience large tsunamis eventually, but just not this year. (*And then there was the monster tsunami in Japan, wiping out villages and people in 2011.)* Also, keep in mind, whenever there is a quake at sea, no matter where the epicenter is, there will be a wave effect. Dropping a pebble in a pond and watching the gentle waves undulate outward is a good example. Therefore, a wave effect is always a certainty with ocean quakes. However, there is always a correlation with how large the quake is and how far it is from landfall. Islands like the Hawaiian Islands are more vulnerable than the Bay Area of California would ever be. Consequently, Readers, keep a proper perspective and be rational in your concepts when you hear of quakes and tsunamis. Of course, people with boats and yachts moored here and there need to be vigilant and move their boats to higher ground if the warnings give them enough time. *Another master will step forward.*

I AM Kuthumi: I do wish to alert people that even though your weather will be violent at times (*2005-2006*), as we come into the tornado and hurricane season, there will be many delightful days. There will be rain for some of the drier spots, which is always good news for all concerned. There will be plenty of sunshine for those states further north. They are apt still to experience colder temperatures. (*And in 2011 there were many, extra violent tornadoes and loss of life in some states and tremendous floods in others.)*

Insects: What you term as *pests* will be more prevalent. Those of you around vacation lakes will notice an abundance of mosquitoes. They will seem to appear ever earlier and stay later. In other words, the whine of mosquitoes will be quite constant. In addition, those areas that draw ants will have more of an infestation than usual. The point I am making is that as the Earth goes through her growth cycles, so do the insects. Everything and every insect are affected. The effect could manifest as extinction for some species, but also manifests in proliferation for others. (*In Arizona that I know of there has been an increase infestation of scorpions due to the Earth's* *cleansing of her discord through different timelines, mainly Egypt. 2011)*

In the remainder of 2005 and through 2006, you will find that there will no longer be time where you can just lay back, *veg out*, as the saying goes, and not be affected by the world around you. Sananda gave you an excellent chapter on being the Light of the World, but **do not be in it,** for there is much chaos manifesting. There will be areas that will go darker so they can be transmuted into Light. Know this in your hearts, Readers. Maintain your Light and be a beacon to the world. I step back now. *(This last paragraph is still apropos for today. 2011)*

I AM Metatron. This section is for bringing Readers up to date on some of the predictions and even prophecies that self-proclaimed prophets are making. First off, Readers, know that it is your heart and your will that will carry you forever onward. **No matter if bridges are falling in quakes. No matter if trees are falling around you in storms; know you have the ability to be in the right spot at the right time. Walk in God's Grace and know you are protected.** You could walk through a hailstorm and not be touched if you carried that faith. Therefore, when I say to you that the shores of America will be washed clean, know you are guided whether to have a beach party or not. Maybe you will be required someplace else and have to cancel going to the beach. Therefore, you were in the right place at the right time when the tsunami came ashore. It will happen, but not this year. Major quakes will happen in America and especially on the West Coast, but not this year. **There will be quakes and even a bad one, but it will not be the major one, the *big one*—not yet anyway**. Therefore, Readers, listen to your body for its guidance. If it is feeling poorly, listen and react accordingly—stay home! *I leave you now for one more wishes to speak.*

I AM Confucius. I could not pass up the opportunity to speak for there are so many of my dear Oriental peoples located on the coast of California. **It is within the Oriental mind that there is *orderliness* to the world**. In that orderliness, chaos is not seen. **The Oriental mind proclaims that any chaos is the result of humankind's lack**

of order. Now true, as with most cultures, the youth of a particular culture strives to live outside of its inherent beliefs. The Oriental youth, if he or she is influenced by peers who are into gangs and wrong ways of living, loses momentarily his or her cultural morals and instincts. However, no matter how these youths attempt to blend outside of their culture, those values of respect for their elders and their sense of order prevail. They will return to right thinking as they mature. It is innate with them. They cannot think and live outside of this box, so that saying goes, for long. Hence, the Oriental peoples, especially on the West Coast, still carry how to maintain calmness in chaos.

If the Caucasian wishes to learn how to survive in chaos, look toward the Oriental for guidance. Jesus said *follow me*. Well, if an Oriental tells you to follow him or her, believe that you will be led to safety during dangerous times. You can use this concept figuratively or symbolically. The Oriental mind is quite cunning, as well as quick acting. These peoples on the West coast may and will die—but only because they are led Home. However, the majority will survive. If you on the West Coast see or hear of Orientals moving out of state, it might be a clue for you to follow their example.

The Orientals have an innate ability to survive. Why do you think there are so many of them in China? It certainly is not because of a nurturing government. These, my beloved people, know how to survive in all ways—physically, emotionally, and spiritually. Look how Feng Shui has swept the United States in popularity. Before that, it was acupuncture. Now acupuncture is an acceptable treatment for pain. That is a physical reality. Feng Shui is a spiritual concept of maintaining the correct flow of energies in the home or office. Right energies, right mind—orderliness.

Therefore, dear Readers, take a leaf out of the Oriental's Book of Knowledge and apply it in your life. The Earth is evolving at an even faster rate as of now. Times will be chaotic. Practice a little Tai Chi for the emotional body. Your Oriental brothers and sisters have many practices that humanity could emulate. God gave each culture certain concepts—mind sets—just for that culture. However, another culture could share its wealth of wisdom, if you would but ask and observe.

I am Confucius. This closes these commentaries.

(This transmission was given to me June 26—27, 2005)

(Confucius was one of Master Djwhal Khul's past lives. 2011)

SECTION 12—LAST WORDS #3

CLOSING STATEMENT—Djwhal Khul

I AM Djwhal Khul. Good morning, dear one; I have come to end cycle with my energies in this third book. Readers, as you have read our words, there arose in you many questions at the same time, I imagine. That is one of the purposes of a book such as ours—to raise more questions than it answers. We purposely have made our mini-lectures *short and sweet*, as the saying goes. While the lectures were short, they carried a great deal of our energies that we had put into those pages. That is why it is important for people to keep returning to the books and finish reading the pages in order to reap that energy-harvest in those pages.

As your summer months dwindle and the seasons go into fall, you also experience the seasons in your physical body. Your energies react to the changes of the seasons. Some people become more energetic after the heat of summer has dissipated. Others become saddened for they are anticipating coming holidays and the changes in weather not to their liking. It depends upon your particular body. Some bodies like heat, others prefer the cold. Hence, so it is with Readers of a book. Some prefer reading the more personal experiences of the masters; other Readers just want the teachings. Some do not want information revisited or repeated. Others like hearing it again in a different way so that they can become more familiar with a concept that may be new for them. Others say that they knew all of that already and were wishing for new information. Therefore, you can see how these books can touch people in different ways.

However, for those of you who may have known most of the presented material, the gift for you in these books would then be the energies in the pages. Many times people read books over again just so they can feel the energies and again experience their strong influence. Dear Readers, we of the Spiritual Hierarchy know your thoughts on these books. We can feel your reactions, for we are monitoring how our words are affecting you. We are not judging you but are merely watching how our words may be affecting you, as well as humanity, as the books spread across the country.

You have been told that masters walk the Earth all the time. However, conditions are not such that we can come into your home and sit, sup, and chat with you. We hope someday this will be, but it is not at this period. However, one of these days we will be able to meet in person with you and converse with you about the various books you have read. We do hope you will have read **these three, which will appear as a Trilogy some day in the not-so-distant future**. These books will be published in book form, versus spiral-bound manuscript. There is timing involved, you see. When the time is correct for all concerned—the Author and the publishing house—then will these books be put in your shopping cart on the Internet. There will be more, several more books. We will all enjoy watching their creation and being a part of them in a way that you Readers may not be expecting.

We thank the Author for her time and dedication. We thank you, Readers, for your time you have devoted to reading our words.

I remain your friend, Djwhal Khul.

(*I had forgotten what Djwhal Khul had said about these three books being published as a Trilogy. Little did I realize that he was prophesying! 2011)*

CLOSING STATEMENT—Jesus

I AM Jesus. Dear Readers, the title of my closing remarks with you tells you that we are ending BOOK THREE. We have come to you many times throughout these pages—giving you bits and pieces of ourselves plus wisdom of the ages. We have enjoyed every moment of our time with you. We thank you, dear Readers, for choosing our books in order to read our varied points of view. Not everyone will agree with us. However, many more will embrace our words and find that a certain chapter speaks to them. If you feel a particular sensation while reading a segment, pause and reflect what it is that was touched. You have been informed that the words carry our energies. Therefore, whatever you were feeling was sparked by those energies in those words.

If you are reading this closing statement before you have finished the books, and we know that many of you do this, do go back, and pick up the lectures you may have skipped. Each one is not given lightly to you. Each one contains a message that could be just for you. You may find that the combined energies in the book facilitate a shift in consciousness for you. Those who are especially tuned to feeling energies will be able to feel that shift take place. Others will not fully recognize that a shift has occurred. I can assure you, anyone reading these three books is affected. We have woven the energies just for that purpose. Therefore, as this latest book ends, know you have just experienced and received our energies through these written words.

The Author has worked steadfastly to bring this book to fruition. It does not seem like a task to her, for she enjoys her service greatly. However, we want to acknowledge and thank her for her dedication and long, long hours of labor, not only in bringing our words through her telepathically, but also with all the typing on the computer afterwards. **She writes each word in long hand** before going to the computer in order to type and print out our messages. We recognize the tremendous amount of work involved. We thank her and bless her efforts mightily.

There will be another book—BOOK FOUR. It will take longer to birth, for it will be a book full of adventure, versus lectures. Sananda tells of this in his closing statement.

Therefore, dear Readers, we thank you for spending time with all of us Presenters. We will enjoy chatting with you in the coming book. However, it will be more in a *commentary* form versus small lectures of wisdom, as I have stated.

Until we meet again, Beloveds, I AM Jesus and bless you all.

CLOSING STATEMENT—Sananda

I AM Sananda. Dear Readers, it has been our privilege to come forth and spend time with you through the pages of this BOOK THREE. We are greatly honored to be able to be of service to each and every one of you in this way. I also wish to thank the Author for her dedication and perseverance in bringing forth this work.

Readers, many of you who read books such as ours, appreciate the hours the Author has given of herself in service in order to bring such a book to its successful conclusion. However, there may be new Readers who are not fully aware of the work entailed. Let us try an experiment. Go to your favorite chair or couch, still yourself, say some prayers and wait for us to speak telepathically. I forgot to say that you might put on some inspirational music on your CD player also, so that it can help create the mood. Now wait, still your mind the best you can. If your mind does wander, pull it back in order to think only about God and Heavenly Wonders. Wait some more. If your CD plays 45 minutes, wait for 45 minutes. You do not get up, stretch, sip water, or answer the phone during that time. Those Readers who are more proficient at meditation time will be in an altered state by now.

Wait some more. Have you felt goose bumps? Have you felt tearful, even sobbing, as you feel our presence? Have you heard our thoughts? Most likely, you have not. The point I am making, Beloveds, is that for a person to be able to accomplish what this Author has done is a huge undertaking—one in which she took on excitedly, as well as with some trepidation, for she had her inner struggles to overcome before she could proceed. Readers, some of you may already have been able to write a few phrases or even sentences. However, how many of you have had enough sentences to write a hundred plus pages for a book, let alone three of them? That is the point I am emphasizing. Please do not flip through these books and think even for one minute that this has been an easy journey for this Author, for it has not. However, with each book that she completed and distributed, there has been a tremendous expansion of her energies—most of which not even she is aware. This is enough on birthing books for now. However, I wanted to draw your awareness to the fact that this outstanding accomplishment is not just a little effort, but one of many horrendous efforts, which carry even finer energies.

I now wish to address BOOK FOUR, *Realities of the Crucifixion..* This book will not be written as quickly as the other three books were. This next coming book will have more of a personal touch. The Author will be given some extraordinary experiences that will propel her into different timelines and dimensions. She will revisit several of her past lives and will have total recall of those lives. I am not speaking of lives where she learned how to suffer through adversities being a street urchin in the Elizabethan period of yesteryears. I am speaking of walking the Appian Way as a Roman citizen. I am speaking of being the sister to the Lord Jesus—of their love and devotion for each other. (*I was Mariam, Jesus' adopted cousin-sister.2011)* I am speaking of her life in Egyptian times with Joseph. (*I was Ephraim, Joseph's second son.2011)*

These lives will be written in full detail, so that the Reader will feel as if he or she is walking with the Author through all her trials and tribulations. I am speaking of one of her lives as a Catholic nun ministering to the lepers. I am speaking of when the great Shekinah, the Holly Essence, comes upon her and the gifts that were bestowed. In fact, as I look at all the stories she will be telling, as she revisits back in time, there could be several books. Therefore, Readers, get set to relive some of your past through her. The Author has a slight sense of all of this, but it has yet to take place, so she does not have it in her consciousness at this time. She probably is as surprised as you are, although she has notations in her journal where we have told her seven times what her future holds, this being the eighth time. That is all I will say for now. I am giving you a peek into the future of the next books.

It has been our pleasure, Readers, to converse with you. We appreciate your eagerness to read our wisdom and Teachings. However, always keep in mind you also have greatness to tap into. You too carry magnificent past lives. Every one of you has been a well-known personage in at least one of your past lives. How could you not, if you were going to experience your royalty games. Ponder this!

I leave you now through these pages. I will come again in BOOK FOUR, for we will make many comments as well, throughout this next book.

I bless you. I AM Sananda.

CLOSING STATEMENT—God

I AM the Lord your God. Good afternoon, my precious daughter. I come to give you and your book My blessing. The book has come together exceedingly well and swiftly. I congratulate you on a service well done. Now I wish to convey to you a message I am giving not only to you, but also to many other great Beings who serve with their devotion.

In the months to come I will be descending somewhat so that America may benefit from My blessings. She has struggled recently through much criticism and adversity. Her choices were not always of the highest Light but she has been able to maintain most of her integrity. I say *most,* for there are dark forces that would like to see her fail. This is a critical time for America. I will give a special blessing to her to help sustain her.

The planet will be going through some difficult changes. Many people will be afraid. I am bringing more *love, peace, and Truth* to Earth in order to help transmute some of the fear. I will spread My blessings over the Earth in a mantle of golden Light. People may feel this energy when it occurs. It will be the Holy Spirit Essence of Me. People may find that they will fall to their knees, unable to stand, as My Energy touches them. I will touch every living creature—human or animal—on the planet. However, America will receive a double portion, for she will need to be especially strong during the tribulations that will come upon her.

I will bring this special blessing in the fall of this year 2005. Everyone will react uniquely, but all will be touched. It has been many centuries since I have done this in the world. Your Bible tells of My visits throughout history. Now this will be a blessing, not a curse, for America has suffered at the hands of cruel people, and yet she has persevered. There are many who cry out for Me on the battlefield. I will bring them *peace* for that short moment before man's free will again dominates his destiny.

Therefore, Readers of this latest book, know you have heard and read the Words of your Father. I bless you and permeate each word with My Energies. I bless the Author one hundred-fold, for she has stayed true to the mission I have given her.

I will end My comments and seal these words with Amen, Amen, Amen.

I AM Jehovah, your God, and Father.

THE END #3

As I sit in my *still time* this **Sunday, July 10, 2005**, I can hardly believe that BOOK THREE is finished. It came together faster than I had imagined. I am feeling a slight sense of grief—a loss. This takes me by surprise, as I feel the tears that are ready to surface. As I muse over what I am feeling, I realize the physical part of me must let go of the attachment to knowing the Masters will come every day in order to give me their transmissions. I loved having them make contact. Sometimes they would come just to make comments for my journal.

The Lord Jesus always came first in order to alert me that another Lord was coming to speak—Sanat Kumara, Metatron, Confucius and Kuthumi. I feel this to be protocol—a courtesy that the Masters practice. Jesus also introduces God before He speaks. For example, Jesus said to me, *dear one, I will speak for just a moment in order to prepare the way for your Father who wishes to give you and this book a Blessing.* You have just read His awesome Closing Statement.

Therefore, I must practice letting go—to release the book so that it can fulfill its purpose. The Masters will come again, for we have BOOK FOUR to write, but I do not know when or how it will manifest. I am in a state of formlessness, which is not always comfortable, for it carries no answers. It is the soul's domain and I must walk in *patience, trust, and faith* in Self.

I will close this BOOK THREE—my mission—with these words from the Bible that seem apropos: *Also I heard the voice of the Lord, saying, Whom shall I send, and who will go for us? Then said I, Here am I; send me (Isaiah 6:8). I will write these books, Lord* (CHAKO).

AFTER-THOUGHTS 2011

Readers, as I pause to gather my closing thoughts on this project—this Trilogy, as Djwhal Khul suggested—I am struck at how timeless these Teachings are. I read each page as if I were reading someone else's work. I marveled at the variety of subjects. I laughed at the masters' humor in naming their chapters. In fact, I took great delight in all three of the books. I think it has taken me all of these six years to appreciate fully what was given to me.

I was such a neophyte when it came to channeling, but now as I have re-read the material, I am allowing myself to acknowledge that I had done well indeed. And **that** is a huge shift in consciousness for me—another piece of my karmic tapestry falling into the place of self-worth!

I found that as I read the pages, the material would spark my memory banks and I would remember little tidbits that I thought you readers might enjoy knowing. On the other hand, I would add a snippet of history so that you would recall also what the masters were referring to.

I feel no grief with the closing of this project this time, only joy in what I have accomplished. I hope, Readers, you too are delighted finally in having my first three books as one for your perusal! Enjoy and do take time to bask in the Masters' Energies and contemplate what they have said.

In deep appreciation for your interest in our books, I AM Chako, with blessings.

ABOUT THE AUTHOR

Verling CHAKO Priest, PhD, was born in Juneau, Alaska, hence her name of Cheechako, shortened to just Chako by her mother, a medical doctor, and her father, an orthodontist. Chako was raised in Napa, CA. She attended the University of California at Berkeley, where she met her future husband. Upon their marriage and after his training as a Navy pilot, they settled into the military way of life. They lived twelve years outside of the United States mainland in various places, which included Hawaii, Viet Nam, Australia, and Greece. Little did she know that these exotic lands and peoples were preparing her for her spiritual awakening years hence!

After her husband's retirement from the Navy, they resettled in Napa, California. It was during this time that she returned to school at Berkeley, transferred to Sonoma University where she earned her first two degrees in Psychology. Chako then entered the doctoral program at the Institute of Transpersonal Psychology (ITP) at Menlo Park, CA, which is now located in Palo Alto, CA. She successfully completed that program which consisted of a Master, as well as the Doctorate in Transpersonal Psychology. Ten years and four degrees later she was able to pursue her passion for Metaphysical and New Age Thought—her introduction into the realm of the Spiritual Hierarchy and the Ascended Lords and Masters.

In 1988, Dr. Priest moved to Minnetonka, Minnesota. She co-authored a program for Methodist Hospital called *Second Time Around* for those with recurring cancer. She, as a volunteer, also facilitated a grief group for Pathways of Minneapolis and had a private practice.

She studied with a spiritual group in Minnetonka led by Donna Taylor and the Teacher, a group of highly-developed entities channeled by Donna. The group traveled extensively all over the world working with the energy grids of the planet and regaining parts of their energies that were still in sacred areas waiting to be reclaimed by them, the owners. They climbed in and out of the pyramids in Egypt, tromped through the Amazon forest in Venezuela, rode camels at Sinai, and climbed the Mountain. They hiked the paths at Qumran, trod the ancient roadways in Petra, Jordan, and walked where the Master Jesus walked in Israel.

The time came, November 1999, when the Teacher sent Chako on to her next phase of growth in Arizona. This is where she found her beloved Masters, who in reality had always been with her. They were **all** ready for her next phase, bringing into the physical three books—mind—provoking books—telepathically received by her, from these highly-evolved, beautiful, loving Beings. Each book stretched her capabilities, as well as a few of her belief systems. Nevertheless, it was a challenge she gladly embraced.